Parnell to Pearse

✦

CLASSICS OF IRISH HISTORY
General Editor: Tom Garvin

Some recent titles
Original publication dates of reprinted titles are given in brackets

Parnell to Pearse

Some Recollections and Reflections

✦

JOHN J. HORGAN

*with a biographical
introduction by
John Horgan*

UNIVERSITY COLLEGE DUBLIN PRESS
Preas Choláiste Ollscoile Bhaile Átha Cliath

First published in Dublin by Browne and Nolan Ltd. 1949
This edition published by University College Dublin Press, 2009
© Madoline O'Connell and John Horgan 2009
New Introduction and notes © John Horgan 2009

978-1-906359-29-4
1393-6883

University College Dublin Press
Newman House, 86 St Stephen's Green
Dublin 2, Ireland
www.ucdpress.ie

Cataloguing in Publication data available from the British Library

Typeset in Ireland in Ehrhardt by Elaine Burberry
Text design by Lyn Davies, Frome, Somerset, England
Printed in England on acid-free paper by
CPI Antony Rowe, Chippenham, Wilts.

CONTENTS

ILLUSTRATIONS

JOHN J. HORGAN
BIOGRAPHICAL INTRODUCTION

John Horgan

Although John J. Horgan's *Parnell to Pearse* concludes with the events of 1918, its author was publicly and journalistically active for almost a further half-century. Much remains untold. With the benefit of additional archival material illustrative of the period covered by this memoir, some of the narrative gaps in *Parnell to Pearse* can now be filled out, some of its emphases modified, and some significant changes of opinion identified. At the same time, sources available for the later years reinforce, if anything, the agenda of the memoir – an agenda he took little trouble to hide – and amplify the influence of elements of his personal history on the direction and strength of his engagement in public life.

Two of these elements, in particular, stand out in sharp relief. The first is his parentage. His pride in his nationally mixed ancestry is transparent. Although his grandfather was a Cork farmer and later a businessman, his solicitor father married an Englishwoman,[1] and he himself made a similar choice. He saw in his own family tree the combination of a sturdy English constitutional and civil liberties tradition with a nascent Irish nationalism, and believed – probably correctly – that this contributed a unique strand to Irish public life, often unacknowledged or minimised in the competition and conflict between the more visible Irish, English and Anglo-Irish traditions. In his case, this was manifested by a passionate and unrepentant commitment to the spirit and politics of John Redmond which lasted for years after Redmond's death, and in an openness to, and understanding of, Northern unionism which was rare, if not unique, amongst Irish nationalists of his and later generations.

Until quite late in his life, he was describing himself with precision as 'a nationalist of an older and more moderate school'.[2] His was a nationalism which was primarily constitutional, political and economic; and it was a nationalism from which the traditional underpinnings of ethnicity and culture were noticeably absent. At one juncture in the 1930s, he specifically rejected, in public debate with Mary MacSwiney, her contention that until Ireland was free from the domination by another nation, they would have no art, literature or modern music of their own. Citing Swift, Davis and Pearse, he riposted that 'all the time we find English blood coming in to break the conquest.'[3]

The second is his urge to communicate via the written word. The initial stirrings of this are evident in the memoir: the production of a family newspaper while still a schoolboy, his brief and inglorious debut as a playwright in 1905, his pamphleteering, his biographical writings, and his general readiness for verbal fisticuffs. 'Had fate so willed', he wrote, 'I might have become a journalist.'[4] But to a significant degree he actually became one, although this aspect of his career was masked by the anonymity which shrouded some of his most significant journalism in later years.

Not all of it, even when signed, is easily traceable, except by inference. His papers in the National Library include a riposte by the provost of Trinity College, Dublin, Professor Traill, to an article he had written about the National Board of Education in an unspecified periodical. 'You write', Traill told him, 'in absolute ignorance.'[5] He was an early admirer of D. P. Moran and *The Leader*, and within a few years had become an evidently valued contributor to that journal on political and constitutional matters.

Although his memoir goes into considerable detail about his political activity between the late 1890s and 1918, it does not overstate it, and omits some interesting aspects of his background and this period of his life. His father's papers and diaries, on which he based part of *Parnell to Pearse*, have not survived, but there is ample evidence elsewhere that his involvement was was bred in the bone. Not only was his father one of Parnell's lieutenants, but his uncle John, also a solicitor, was an energetic supporter of another Irish MP, Joseph Ronayne, before emigrating to Australia. There, he made a name for himself as a scourge of the landed gentry of Western Australia, winning a notable by-election victory in Perth in 1888 on a platform of opposition to the colonial governor and rich landowners.[6]

Michael Joseph Horgan, J. J. Horgan's father, was also the first in a line of Horgan coroners that seems to have been virtually hereditary, stretching for a period of well over a century. He was succeeded as coroner by his eldest son, as noted in *Parnell to Pearse*, in December 1914;[7] and his younger son Michael (who died in 1925) was also a deputy coroner for a time. John J. held the post until his resignation in 1967, shortly before his death, a period of more than half a century. After a brief lacuna, John J.'s son Ivor was appointed to the same post in 1973, and held it until 1979, shortly before his own death in 1980. Nor were their roles purely administrative. Michael Joseph Horgan was actively involved in the preparation of a Coroner's Bill which Tim Healy steered through the Westminster parliament in 1881; J. J. Horgan performed a similar function in relation to a Coroner's Bill in Dáil Éireann in 1925, and again as late as 1962.[8]

Coincidentally or not, all the three coroners for the Cork region appear to have been closely involved in the Irish Party politics of the era. John J. Horgan's papers in the National Library of Ireland include the acknowledgment from Tim Harrington MP of his membership subscription for the Central Branch of the United Irish League (UIL), dated October 1892.[9] His fellow coroners, McCabe and Murphy, were also members, and, until they joined him in simultaneously resigning from the UIL in 1919,[10] as will be noted later, were linchpins of the movement in the city and the county generally. Horgan's involvement in the League was far from nominal, and it is altogether probable that but for his personal and professional engagement in his native city, particularly in the second decade of the twentieth century, he would have played as great a role in the events of that period as many of his Dublin-based contemporaries. His father's lengthy illness between 1909 and his death in 1917, as this memoir attests, also tied him to his practice and the city.

This aspect of his engagement in public affairs underlines the relative obscurity in which non-metropolitan public figures have languished in Irish historiography down to the present day. It also suggests some reasons why he delayed writing this memoir for so many years, and why he ended the period covered by it in 1918, three decades prior to its year of publication, despite his considerable public activities in the intervening period. To have carried it further might have made it more difficult to conceal his authorship of the pungent commentaries in Irish affairs in *The Round Table*, for which he became the Irish correspondent in 1925, and to which he contributed without a break until a year before his death in 1967. However, it is also possible that he had a sense that history had passed him by, and that – had the events of 1918–22 turned out differently – he could have played a role on the national, and not just the provincial, stage. This could, in turn, have generated his increasing conviction – not at all evident in the earlier years – that the political clock had stopped for him at some point, and his regret that it was not possible to turn it back.

Although he was listed as a speaker for the initial meeting of the National Volunteers in Cork in 1913[11] he was not apparently present on that occasion. What is more interesting is that for some years during this period, but not referred to in his memoir, is that he was simultaneously involved with the Ancient Order of Hibernians (AOH) and the UIL, placing him firmly in opposition to William O'Brien. He is listed as a member of a special AOH 'Watch Committee' set up in June 1914, and he is referred to again in documents from August of that year, remaining active until his resignation is recorded on 16 October 1918,[12] just before the election, whereas he is also listed as National Director of the Cork leadership of the UIL in 1916.[13]

He was an early and constant advocate of proportional representation, and went to London in 1912 as part of a delegation of the Irish Proportional Representation Society in an attempt to persuade the British government to include PR in its Home Rule Bill. The delegation included such luminaries as the Rev. J. O. Hannay, better known as the writer George Birmingham, and Mr E. A. Aston, Secretary of the Irish Society.[14] Almost half a century later, he pleaded the same cause at a public debate in University College Cork in late 1959, during the first attempt by Fianna Fáil to replace PR with the so-called 'straight vote'.[15]

His home in Lacaduv, on the Lee Road, was more than just a house. It was also, particularly during a period when developments in Irish politics were attracting attention from *bien-pensants* in England and further afield, a sort of reference point or visual aid where visitors from abroad might take the temperature of the new Ireland that would, it was confidently expected, follow the introduction of Home Rule. The house was also a focal point, not only then but for at least half a century afterwards, of much of Cork's cultural life, a privately funded staging point for musicians, artists and writers at a time when public support for the arts was virtually non-existent. Although his interest in creative writing manifested itself only fitfully, and expired after the production of his play in Cork in 1905, he founded the Cork Drama League in 1925, was elected President of the City's Literary and Scientific Society in 1928, and was for many years Chairman of the Cork Opera House. In 1940, a journalist recorded that 'I have never had to lift my hat so often as that evening when I walked with him . . . to Lacaduv. I deducted that the few who did not spontaneously greet my companion . . . must have been strangers to his city.'[16] At home, he was host to many visiting luminaries. They included Mícheál Mac Líammóir and Hilton Edwards, and others such as the conductor Sir John Barbirolli and composer Arnold Bax – who had a heart attack in Lacaduv in 1953 just after Horgan had taken him on a scenic trip to Sheep's Head, and who died shortly afterwards at the Fleischmann's house in Cork, where he was staying. Horgan was an early patron of the sculptor Seamus Murphy, and the frequently impoverished painter Patrick Hennessy was a guest for considerable periods.

Lacaduv was, of course, also a home, which maintained until his death the kind of atmosphere described tellingly by Harold Begbie and quoted from Begbie's book in his memoir.[17] It was a warm and open house for children and, later, nephews, nieces and grandchildren: the huge attic was a treasure house of lovingly preserved toys, available to all. He would benignly shepherd an assorted clutch of descendants to the pantomime in the Cork Opera House every Christmas. The later generations, unaware of his turbulent past, could bask in the aura of his extraordinary popularity in his native city, as when he was conferred with an honorary LLD by University College Cork in 1953. Two years earlier, he had celebrated his seventieth birthday with his extended family in Edwardian splendour in Lacaduv. There was a huge assembly of guests, open fires in every room, and his sister-in-law, Rita, who had been a dancer with the Carl Rosa Opera Company, sang 'Danny Boy' to a harp accompaniment.

As yet, all this was in the future. A constant throughout this early period of his political engagement was his closeness to Northern affairs, evidenced not least by his relationship with Joseph Devlin in Belfast. Correspondence between him and Devlin in the period up to 1917 shows not only that they were politically close, but that Devlin regarded him as an important ally, and vice versa.[18] In March 1911, Devlin was asking him for details of Cork demographics to enable him to refute unionist allegations about sectarianism in the South;[19] in June 1916 Devlin was advising him that his attendance at a UIL directors meeting would be of vital importance;[20] and a month later the compliment was returned, Horgan telling Devlin 'how much we realise the sacrifice and statesmanship shown by the Northern Nationalists and particularly by yourself'.[21]

His election to the Cork Harbour Commissioners in 1912 underlined his growing local influence. In the same year, he was present in the gallery of the House of Commons in London as Redmond addressed the House on the Home Rule Bill,[22] and addressed meetings on the topic in Dublin and elsewhere. 'What Ireland wanted', he told one disappointingly small but appreciative assembly in Dublin, 'was freedom, and she would not be satisfied with gold.'[23]

More interestingly, his memoir downplays to a considerable extent the nature and degree of his participation in public controversy and other nationalist activities in the period between 1916 and the end of the Civil War. He joined Redmond in outspoken opposition to the 1916 executions: a letter signed by virtually all the UIL leadership in Cork protested that the shootings and arrests were 'having a most injurious effect on the feelings of the Irish people, and if persisted in may be extremely prejudicial to the peace and future harmony of Ireland, and seriously imperil the future friendly relations between Ireland and England'.[24] In private, he went even further, indicating the degree to which even moderate nationalists were being radicalised by the executions.

The reasons for the wretched rebellion are as clear as daylight. They are (1) the way which Carson and Co. were permitted to break the law with immunity. (2) The distrust of Ireland and the tinkering with Home Rule. On both these counts the English misgovernment of this country stands indicted before the world and the sooner they make up their minds to settle the Irish question in the only way it can be settled – namely full and immediate self-government – the better for England and Ireland.[25]

He was recorded by the Royal Irish Constabulary (RIC) Special Branch as having been selected as a city delegate to the 1917 National Volunteer Convention in September 1917,[26] but by 1918 the wind had left the Irish Party's sails, and the squabbles about abstentionism were probably only the symptoms of a deeper malaise. In a final flurry of activity, imaginative but unsuccessful moves were made by him[27] and others, including enrolling the Catholic bishop of Cork, Dr Cohalan in an unsuccessful attempt to try and engineer a pact with Sinn Féin to ensure joint representation at the post-war Peace Conference.

This initiative was rejected out of hand by John Dillon, and this rejection was largely responsible for his own resignation from the party in 1919.[28] His disillusion with the Irish Party, however, was not only related to Redmond's death and Dillon's obduracy, but was also to some degree now secondary to his antipathy to the Ulster Unionists, whom he described as being 'primarily responsible' for the sad state of Ireland.[29] His vocal opposition to conscription in 1918 and 1919 (he was secretary of Cork's anti-conscription campaign) earned him a chiding from one of his local political rivals, a Cork Harbour Board member named Haughton, who reminded him of pro-enlistment sentiments he had uttered, no doubt under the influence of his strong attachment to the Redmonds, in the headier days of 1914.[30]

As the Irish Party imploded, his political energies sought other outlets. Again he turned to journalism, this time to the Jesuit periodical *Studies*, to which he first contributed an article in memory of Redmond in 1917. He was represented in its pages almost every year between then and 1941, writing on subjects as varied as President Wilson and the Peace Conference, and Ireland's place in world affairs. Nor were his interests narrowly political. He visited the Ford plant in Dearborn, Michigan, in or around 1921 and was highly impressed by the scale and method of its operations, about which he also contributed an article. The company employed his firm as its legal agents when they set up business in Cork, and indeed its local manager bought Clanloughlin, the original Horgan family home on the Lee Road, at auction in 1927. It was bought back by his older brother James B. Horgan a number of years later. His articles also evinced a growing interest in the structures of national and local local government, and included observations on prohibition in the US (in both 1925 and 1931), on Switzerland (1938) and Sweden (1939).

As part of this agenda, he expressed, in the run-up to the passage of de Valera's new Constitution in 1937, a brief, well argued, and wholly unrealistic preference for the Swiss system of government, in which the executive would represent Parliament as a whole proportionately, and would serve for a fixed term. The silence that greeted this proposal was deafening.[31] There is a consistent, high-minded, and somewhat elitist tone and approach in all of these articles, expressed most cogently in a paper he read to the Scientific and Social Inquiry Society of Ireland in 1945.[32] Most public administration, in his view, was top-heavy, prone to corruption, institutional paralysis and inefficiency, and highly resistant to the reforms he advocated, many of which would – as did his work on local government reform in the 1920s and subsequently – curb the powers of elected representatives and transfer considerable autonomy and executive functions to permanent officials.

None of this seemed to interfere unduly with his legal and political activities after the collapse of the Irish Party. Although he had been for some time Crown Solicitor, an important source of income, there is also some evidence that he may have covertly helped the Republicans during the War of Independence, legally and with propaganda advice. Various memoranda written by him, including one entitled 'The Plundering of Ireland' were among documents seized by the RIC in a raid on Eamon de Valera's house in Greystones.[33] He defended one or two of the IRA prisoners who were sentenced to death, and appeared occasionally as a solicitor before the Dáil Courts, acting for plaintiffs and defendants alike.[34] He was a patron of the Tomas McCurtain Memorial Fund when it was established in March 1920,[35] although in this he was in conspicuously non-Republican company – both the Catholic and Church of Ireland bishops were also patrons.

The cathartic experience of 1918 had not only helped to detach him from the remnants of the Irish Party, but had moved him some distance towards Sinn Féin's position. Although this did not manifest itself in terms of overt political allegiance, his contemporary correspondence with Erskine Childers demonstrated a marked evolution in his strategic, if not necessarily his constitutional, thinking. Responding to a plea by Childers in late 1918 to support Sinn Féin, not least because the 'follies, betrayals and crimes of English policy have made Sinn Féin inevitable even if it had no innate strength', Horgan replied warmly:

> I quite agree with all you say. It is the absolute duty of men like myself who care more about Ireland than we do about party to give Sinn Fein full support in its demand for self-determination. I urged this publicly and privately on the party before the election without avail. Dillon was too busy labelling all Sinn Feiners as pro-German and Bolshevists to have time for constructive thought.[36]

The depth and strength of his relationship with Childers during this period is barely alluded to in his memoir. Indeed, in 1948 he went to some length to obscure it, merely noting, in relation to Childers's letter, that 'the opportunity for such a policy [i.e. support for Sinn Féin's claim for self-determination] had . . . passed',[37] and forgetting his own enthusiastic response to the Sinn Féin leader's plea. It was still a substantial friendship, however, as an incident during the occupation of Cork by the Republican forces during the Civil War attests. In the course of this occupation J. J. Horgan met Erskine Childers by chance in the Grand Parade in the city, a stone's throw from Horgan's office at 50, South Mall. The two, as already noted, had been correspondents since at least 1917. In October 1919 Childers sent the British MP Wedgewood Benn to Horgan in Cork so that the British politician could hear, from a source Childers evidently trusted, about 'the condition of the country under military law'.[38] In April 1921 Mary Childers was writing to him also, to sympathise with him on the death of his wife Mary.[39] The correspondence continued throughout 1921, with J. J. Horgan expressing occasional agreement with articles by Childers in the *Catholic Bulletin* and *Studies*, and suggesting a 'need to talk'.[40] After Childers's execution in November 1922, Horgan received a letter from his widow in which she revealed that before his death Childers had spoken warmly of him, and this prompted him to write in reply. He had, he said, not wanted to write earlier because he felt that it would have been an intrusion on her grief, but that he had seen her husband during the occupation of Cork 'haggard and tired and much in need of rest'. Accepting that the two men had not seen eye to eye recently, he added: 'No Republican has ever more stoutly upheld his honour and the sincerity of his motives than I have.'[41]

What he did not tell her, and could not have brought himself to tell her, was that on that occasion Childers, with the Republican forces staring defeat in the face, had asked his Cork friend to keep two things for him – some papers, and a revolver.[42] Horgan accepted the papers, hid them in a filing cabinet in his office, and in all probability later destroyed them. Taking responsibility for the revolver was, however, a bridge too far for him, even when asked by a man he liked and respected. This was quite possibly the weapon that had been given to Childers by Collins, and for the possession of which Childers was later executed.

Although we do not have his own word for it, it seems very likely that his patriotic fervour of the 1917–19 period was to a considerable extent attenuated by the outbreak of the Civil War. He was, interestingly and untypically, silent about the War of Independence and about the Treaty at the time that the latter was enacted and for some time afterwards, although his later writings returned to these events with a metronomic frequency. The inference is that he was, at the time, genuinely unsure about what the future might hold, and there is evidence, as will be seen, that he was not without political ambition in the new state.

The end of the Civil War was followed by his election as Chairman of the Harbour Board in 1924, and during his first term of office he organised adequate turning space for large vessels at the port, deepened the river channel, provided modern machinery for unloading grain, and created a new industrial site at Tivoli by pumping ashore dredged material. However, his political ambitions were also rekindled. His political connections with the Free State government may not have been formal, but he was plainly seen as a Redmondite available for co-option – an opinion which would have been buttressed by his already formidable reputation for independence and civic spirit. As it turned out, civic duty and political ambition failed to converge and may even have militated against each other. In February 1925 he was appointed as Chairman of the Intoxicating Liquor Commission by the Minister for Justice, Kevin O'Higgins.[43] This Commission reported in double-quick time, recommending that the ratio of public houses to population should be reduced from its then ratio of 1: 230 to about 1: 400 – a ratio equivalent to that obtaining in England, but lower than that in Scotland, which was 1: 695. This recommendation was no doubt deeply unwelcome to publicans who, then and for many years afterwards, exercised a pivotal role in Irish political life.

Perhaps encouraged by this indication that he was being considered for a national, as opposed to a purely regional role in public life, he put himself forward – probably with Cumann na nGael support, which was similarly afforded to a number of other ex-Nationalist candidates – for nomination by the Seanad as a candidate in the 1925 Seanad election. Unsuccessful here, he was put forward again for nomination by the Dáil, and this time he was selected a creditable eighth of the 38 candidates nominated by the Dáil, ahead of such luminaries as Henry Harrison (Parnell's former secretary), and Darrell Figgis.[44] His willingness to accept a nomination, implying as it did acceptance of the Treaty and the structures it created, suggests strongly that the trenchant views he was to express in later years, criticising this constitutional solution to the Anglo-Irish political log-jam, were at this stage far from settled.

It was a unique election, conducted on a country-wide basis with the electorate restricted to voters aged over 30.[45] In the event, he polled respectably, with more than 80 per cent of his votes coming from the Cork area, but even at that he polled slightly behind other, better-connected Cork candidates such as George Crosbie of the *Cork Examiner*, and was eliminated on the 23rd count.[46] During the election campaign, he briefly and in a qualified manner endorsed the anti-income tax campaign being waged by a number of businessmen, particularly in Cork,[47] but, if this was an election ploy, the odds elsewhere were stacked against him. In particular, the newspapers were replete with accounts of the proceedings of the Commission and of the hostile reaction of the Licensed Grocers' and Vintners' Protection Association, which was highly exercised about the threat it posed to their members. This Association, which was one of the best organised lobbies in this election, would not – to put it mildly – have been impressed by his candidacy, and succeeded in getting both its own candidates elected. Writing not long afterwards, he commented wryly on this campaign that 'while

Mr O'Higgins [Kevin O'Higgins, the Minister for Justice] was seeking cover on one side of the Border to escape the fusillade of the publicans, Lord Craigavon was fleeing on the other from the scalping knives of his temperance braves'.[48]

The method of election to the Seanad was subsequently changed to one in which senators were elected from a constituency comprised solely of their own members and members of the Dáil, and changed again under the 1937 Constitution. He was actually nominated again, by the Cork Chamber of Commerce, as a candidate on the Cultural and Educational Panel for the Senate under the new electoral structures in 1938 but was again unsuccessful. Although many of the candidates on this panel received no votes at all, and he received only two (the highest number of first preferences went to the horse breeder and trainer J. J. Parkinson), he was pipped at the post by Sean O hEochadh, the Fear Mór of Ring, Co. Waterford, who had acquired no votes at all on the first count but, under this arcane electoral system, achieved election on the basis of transfers. There was a hint of wounded *amour propre*, as well as righteous indignation, in his later, necessarily anonymous condemnation of the new system as one which 'afforded opportunities for bribery and corruption which it was widely believed were not entirely neglected' and his pointed reference to the fact that a breeder of horses (i.e. Parkinson) had topped the poll in the cultural and educational panel.[49] His final venture into national politics saw him feature as one of the vice-presidents of the 'National Movement for Harmony between North and South' which, despite a cautious welcome from Eamon de Valera, rapidly disappeared from view.[50]

The Round Table, from which the quotations about the Senate are taken, now afforded him considerable latitude for his often controversial political opinions. By then he had been well acquainted with the journal and its editors for some time. In May 1921 John Dove, who had just been appointed editor, went to Ireland to observe at first hand the outcome of the War of Independence with Lionel Curtis, who had played an important role in the Treaty negotiations and in the formulation of Dominion status. His 1921 article on Ireland was very significant of its kind.[51] Like many other political, intellectual and cultural tourists of the era, they stayed with Horgan at Lacaduv in Cork, and this included an episode

referred to over a decade later when Curtis, still a member of the Round
Table editorial board, sent a copy of one of Horgan's articles to Sir
Edward Harding, permanent secretary at the Dominions Office (which
dealt with Ireland), noting that 'Dove and I were once nearly murdered
in his company.'[52]

Curtis's admiration for Horgan was to be put under serious strain
later on, but it is safe to assume that when Horgan began his series of
articles for the journal in 1925 he was highly ranked by this exclusive
group of British intellectuals and Dominion advocates. His reputation
with them would have been enhanced by his long commercial connections with Northern Ireland. From 1924 until the late 1950s he was
a director – and, from 1928, chairman – of the drapery firm Robertson
Ledlie Ferguson, which owned the Bank Buildings in Belfast, Todds in
Limerick, and the Munster Arcade in Cork. He was centrally involved
in fighting a hostile takeover bid for the company by Isaac (later Sir
Isaac) Wolfson's Great Universal Stores,[53] an event which generated an
extraordinary offer from the former IRA man, General Tom Barry, at
that time an employee of the Harbour Commissioners. At the height of
the takeover battle, Barry – at the opposite end of any conceivable political spectrum from Horgan – went to see the chairman in his offices
on the South Mall, produced a large revolver, and indicated to the
astonished chairman that if any additional help was required to fend off
Mr Wolfson, it would be willingly provided. Needless to say, the offer
was refused.[54]

From the start, there is evidence of the absence of any party line in
his writing. He could describe some of W. T. Cosgrave's actions as
'fatuous';[55] and remarked of his fellow-Corkonian J. J. Walsh that 'his
ignorance of economics is reputed to be only equalled by his knowledge
of political organisation'.[56] But he warmly praised personalities as dis-
parate as Thomas Johnston and Ernest Blythe, even as he warned his
readers about the presence of de Valera in the wings. He expressed a
passionate belief in a federal solution to the problem posed by Ulster
Unionism, even as that possibility evaporated, and this theme was to
become, together with his equally early opposition to official policies in
relation to the Irish language, a *leitmotif* of his coverage of Irish affairs
over the next four decades.

His strong Catholicism did not prevent him from expressing serious doubts about the report of the Committee on Evil Literature in 1926, and more particularly about the vigilante activities, such as the burning of English newspapers, common at that time. 'It may be doubted', he wrote, 'if such methods of propaganda will improve either our morals or our manners, but that they should be employed with the active approval of ecclesiastical dignitaries displays a mental attitude that is difficult to understand and more difficult to justify.'[57] He was even harsher about what he regarded as the dilatory attitude taken by the bishops to the IRA. After they issued a pastoral letter in October 1931 condemning that organisation, he described it as 'a clear and accurate statement of Catholic doctrine', but added pointedly: 'it might have been written and promulgated with equal truth fifteen years ago, and that, if it had, there would have been no necessity to do it now.'[58] This was accompanied by continual criticism of the Cosgrave government's policy on Irish, which he believed 'has now virtually ceased to be a language and has become an industry'.[59]

The change of government in 1932 evoked warm praise for Cosgrave's stewardship during the first decade of the state's existence, and caution rather than alarm in relation to de Valera's accession to power. He praised the early editions of the *Irish Press*,[60] and, although he saw in Sean MacEntee's first Budget the work of a combination of 'a Glasgow Communist and a die-hard tariff reformer',[61] he found subsequent Fianna Fáil financial policy more to his liking.

He served as a member of the Town Tenancy Commission under Mr Justice Creed Meredith,[62] and as a Council member of the Incorporated Law Society in the late 1920s and early 1930s, but his public service activities were thereafter largely confined to his native city and county. They were none the less significant for all that, and centred largely on his membership of the Cork Harbour Commissioners, on which he served for more than half of the twentieth century. Elected for the first time in 1912, he was Chairman of the Board from 1923 to 1925, and was a major figure in the proceedings of the Tribunal on Ports and Harbours (1926–7). Simultaneously, the Cork Progressive Association asked him to draft a new system of municipal government for the city of Cork, which was enshrined in legislation in 1929 and was later used as a template for local government for the whole country, including Northern Ireland, where it reached in 1942.[63]

In the 16 years following 1932, Fianna Fáil's brand of nationalism, and in particular its irredentism and its passionate but also mechanistic approach to the revival of the Irish language, stirred the embers of controversy in this former member of the Gaelic League and long-time advocate of a gradualist approach to the vexed problem of Northern Ireland and its million unionists. By the mid-1930s his public opposition to the new government's language policy (and in particular to its over-simplified and eventually doomed attempt to ensure that instruction in all infant classes in primary schools would take place through the medium of the Irish language) was attracting the attention of foreign newspaper correspondents, who found him readily available for comment.[64] Denis Gwynn, a friend for many years, wrote many years later that 'his first attribute was his unflinching moral courage on any issue that seemed to him important even if it meant provoking opposition where none existed before.'[65] Paradoxically, the other side of this occasionally combative temperament was a rare skill in brokering peace deals in one or other of his capacities as a solicitor, a member of the Harbour Board, or of the Cork Chamber of Commerce. In 1934, the Federated Union of Employers and the Irish Transport and General Workers' Union agreed that all dock disputes should be referred to him as referee: 'the result was a virtual total absence of dock strikes in Cork for about 30 years.'[66]

By the beginning of the Second World War, he had achieved a prominence and a reputation for independence that prompted an unusual query from the American Minister in Dublin, David Gray, who asked him privately for his assessment of the condition of the Irish Defence Forces during the war. His report to Gray was brief but informative, praising the Irish army as a highly disciplined and efficient force which 'would resist any attack on the country from whatever direction'.[67] His final piece of advice evidently came from the heart. 'All this is of course qualified by the fact that if England is defeated we cannot hope to make any effective resistance to invasion and will have to accept a servitude such as we have never known. Let us pray this will never happen.' He was not, however, an unqualified admirer of Gray, describing some of the American diplomat's later allegations about the

Irish government as 'unjust and untrue'.[68] He supported de Valera's policy of neutrality during the war, even as he derided the censorship that accompanied it.

In 1943 he lost his seat on the Harbour Board. This was not due to anything he had said or done, but to a concerted lobbying campaign on behalf of another candidate which had disturbed the normal tranquillity of the electoral process for this body. There is some evidence that he experienced this keenly as a rejection, and indeed that he was to a degree depressed by it, at least until his re-election to the Board of the Harbour Commissioners in 1949. It also prompted a reaction that had one substantial long-term consequence. This was his memoir, *Parnell to Pearse*, which was composed at intervals between then and its publication in 1948.

His role in the management of Cork harbour after his re-election to the Board – he was to serve one of the longest terms as Chairman in the history of the Board, from 1949 to 1961 – was marked by substantial progress in the recovery of the port after the Second World War. Most of the quays were reconstructed, new dredging and pumping machinery provided, and modern tenders built to service the transatlantic liners. He presided at meetings with authority. He was not impatient, because he enjoyed the role, but he could be brusque if he felt that an undue attention to detail was impeding the flow of business. He also played a major role in the development of the Verolme Cork Dockyards, of which he was a director, which, along with the Whitegate oil refinery and the extension of the steel works, brought a much-needed fillip to the harbour area in the late 1950s and early 1960s. His retirement, when it came, was handled with dignity, as he was succeeded by Tom Doyle, then Chairman of the Chamber of Commerce. He remained a member, and sat as part of an unusual troika with his old acquaintance and political rival, Seamus Fitzgerald, and his younger *protégé*, Liam St John Devlin, who himself was to play a major role later, not only in the Harbour Commissioners (as the Board was to become) but in Irish public administration generally. Although he later turned down an invitation from Devlin to become a temporary vice-Chairman – it would in any case have been a retrograde step as he saw it – the Commissioners agreed unanimously to name a new wharf after him. It was a surer route to remembrance than another proposal made at the time – that one of the new liner tenders would be named after him. At a time when the days of the liner trade into Cobh were patently numbered, the former honour would have been singularly short lived.[69]

Although he could be scathing about Irish language policy and de Valera's policy on Northern Ireland, nothing appeared to engage his ire more than the declaration of the first inter-party government in 1949 that Ireland would no longer be a member of the Commmonwealth, and its associated decision to formally declare Ireland a Republic. He noted that the declaration of the Republic did not evoke comment from either Sir Basil Brooke or Mr de Valera,

> the former presumably refusing to recognise the Irish Republic because it claims that its territory includes Northern Ireland, and the latter because it does not in fact do so! . . . The final act of separation has been consummated, for tactical reasons, at the instance of a party pledged to 'unequivocal membership of the British Commonwealth.' This callous repudiation of public pledges must for long poison Irish politics.[70]

His fulminations about the Costello government's decision created alarm in some influential circles. The historian Nicholas Mansergh, later Smuts Professor of the History of the British Commonwealth at Cambridge University, wrote privately to his friend Dermot Morrah early in 1950 criticising the Irish correspondent of the *Round Table* for adopting the standpoint of 'an unrepentant Redmondite who believes that everything went wrong in 1916'.[71] This was more caricature than characterisation, in that it exaggerated or distorted Horgan's political antipathy to the Rising and its effects, and ignored much that was positive in his assessments of post-1922 Ireland. It also missed a central point. Virtually all of Horgan's critique of Southern politics was based, not on a rejection of irredentism, but on his despair at the widening gulf between Dublin and Belfast, and his belief that this was being deepened by Dublin's mistaken belief that Britain would solve the partition problem. With the benefit of hindsight, it is arguable that – his occasionally intemperate outbursts aside – he was more right than wrong on this issue

Mansergh suggested that although Horgan should not be dropped, additional articles should be commissioned from time to time from 'other points of view' (he instanced Terence de Vere White and Professor W. B. Stanford of Trinity College).[72] Lionel Curtis, the historian and another member of the *Round Table* editorial board, who only four years earlier had been expressing his confidence in Horgan to Ivison Macadam, now wrote to Morrah to express his 'entire agreement' with Mansergh's letter.[73] It is worth noting that Curtis's role in the Treaty negotiations and in the formulation of Dominion status had been very significant, and that he was, not least for these reasons, a strong admirer of W. T. Cosgrave. Mansergh's initiative was not successful.

In fact, the differences between Mansergh and Horgan on the question of partition may have been more of emphasis than of content. Mansergh's thesis was, broadly speaking, that partition was not a product of a British 'divide and rule' strategy, but of a political process fuelled by rival nationalisms in the context of imperial retreat.[74] There was also a sense in which Horgan's sense of betrayal by the Costello administration was at least partially at odds with his own analysis of the partition problem. If, as he argued repeatedly, the obstacles to a solution were incapable of solution by fancy political or constitutional footwork, it could equally be argued that political and constitutional flag-waving generated by a traditional Irish nationalism that ignored Unionist sensibilities merely replicated the status quo, and did not necessarily make the underlying situation very much worse.

Thus demolished by Costello, his potential confidence in any administration led by Fine Gael was difficult to rebuild. He mocked the same government's attitude to NATO: 'we do not want to fight even against Communism, believing that we should be fools to do so when someone else is prepared to fight for us'.[75] He maintained stoutly that Ireland should be prepared to support a nuclear alliance, accepting if necessary the possibility of nuclear war, and depicted Mr Costello as someone who 'regards Mr de Valera as a more immediate menace than Stalin.'[76]

His anti-Communism, on the other hand, while it was fairly typical of the Cold War era, did not make him an uncritical supporter of ecclesiastical power-plays. He admired Noel Browne's attempt to introduce major health care initiatives, argued in specifically theological terms against the bishops' condemnation of Browne's Mother and Child scheme, and pointed out mordantly that 'the real objection, never publicly discussed, was the undoubted fact that it would have seriously interfered with the income of the medical profession'.[77] He saluted the electorate for returning Browne and his colleague Dr Michael ffrench-O'Carroll at the subsequent general election. When Browne lost his seat in 1954, he observed that 'if the doctors rejoice at the disappearance of their *bête noire*, the public may well mourn his defeat.'[78] There is a certain evolution observable here, given that forty years earlier, as an ardent young Catholic apologist, he had personally presented a copy of his book *Great Catholic Laymen* to Pope Pius X, and had, in 1925, criticised Yeats's speech to the Senate on divorce as 'symptomatic of the old Ascendancy spirit'.[79] A dozen or so years later, his conservative views on divorce had presumably faded into the past, or were regarded as irrelevant, when he became a trustee of a committee that eventually provided a gravestone of Wicklow granite to mark Parnell's final resting place in Glasnevin.[80]

His piquant commentaries on Irish political, economic and social life during these years were further enlivened by thumbnail portraits of many of the protagonists and their institutions. Fianna Fáil, he observed at one point, was 'less a political party than an act of faith in Mr de Valera'.[81] He deprecated de Valera's 'ceremonial tomfoolery'[82] in paying a formal visit to the German legation on Hitler's death, and observed later:

> Mr de Valera's opponents are fond of suggesting that he is an apt student of Machiavelli, while his supporters cherish the view that he is a second Einstein. Both views are exaggerated. He is merely an extremely competent and very wily politician.[83]

De Valera's principal rival, John A. Costello, who had fallen from favour for his political sins against the Commonwealth, was 'a dogged character with small political experience and less judgment';[84] Costello's successor, James Dillon, despite Horgan's admiration for his views on Irish in the schools and on the importance of the Commonwealth connection, was neatly skewered. 'If he suffers from exaggeration and a tendency to repeat himself, these are sound political weapons which

nearly every Irish leader since O'Connell has used with effect.'[85] Oliver
Flanagan's 'speciality is monetary reform through the printing press';[86]
the Labour Party was 'a strange mixture of Victorian liberalism and
what may perhaps be described as Catholic Socialism imperfectly
understood and applied';[87] the Anti-Partition League was 'a body of
noisy cranks';[88] Conor Cruise O'Brien was 'an idealist intellectual
theorist ill equipped to deal with practical problems';[89] C. J. Haughey,
whose Succession Bill the Round Table correspondent, as a solicitor,
found particularly objectionable, 'has had no legal experience and has
clearly been influenced by his civil service advisers';[90] and Jack Lynch,
whose inexperience in dealing with his first Cabinet post in education he
had cannily noted in 1957, was saluted a decade later as 'a quiet, soft-
spoken Cork man of clear intelligence and integrity'.[91]

His observations on O'Brien were in relation to the Congo episode, but
he had earlier had dealings with him in relation to the controversial
publication of a book on partition by Michael Sheehy, *Divided We Stand:
A Study in Partition*,[92] to which he had contributed a characteristically
pugnacious foreword. The thesis of the foreword reflected that of the
book – that it was, in Sheehy's words, 'the most childish of evasions, the
most ignoble of pretences to place the responsibility for Partition on
England, and to ignore the many and fundamental differences which
more than adequately explain the political division of Ireland'.[93] In the
service of this argument, his earlier, highly critical opinion of Carson was
now dramatically – and probably unnecessarily – revised. The Northern
leader whose 'evil influence' in the 1913–18 period he had decried only a
decade earlier,[94] was now 'a Northern Parnell' driven by a belief that a
federal solution in which the province of Ulster was a natural unit offered
'the best chance of securing eventual Irish unity'.[95] Such a reversal must
have strained the loyalty of even some of his closest allies.

This book, as the Faber and Faber archives testify, had a long ges-
tation and an ill-starred birth. It was sent originally to the publishers in
1953 and, when the publishers asked Horgan to suggest someone who
would read the book for factual and historical detail 'with a scholarly and
sympathetic eye', he wrote confidently to Donal O'Sullivan, whose book
on the Irish Free State and its Senate had also been published by Fabers,
and who had married the widow of one of Horgan's older brothers. His

optimism was misplaced. O'Sullivan did as requested, but told Charles Monteith, the editor at Fabers who had accepted the book – and who was an Ulsterman – that he strongly disapproved of its thesis, and that its publication would reflect adversely on authors and publisher alike.

Although O'Sullivan's diagnosis was coloured by a deep antipathy to the unfashionable but well-argued political views of both men (which antipathy would of course have been widely shared by the political establishment of the time), his prognosis was accurate enough. Although it was reviewed favourably by the *Belfast Telegraph*, the *Sunday Press* published 'a page of hysterical nonsense' about it,[96] and even the *Cork Examiner*, over which Horgan might have been expected to exercise some influence, published a 'schizophrenic' review written by the company chairman, Tom Crosbie, who in Horgan's view was 'truly mad'![97] There were favourable academic reviews by Mansergh and R. Dudley Edwards, but the *Sunday Times* decided not to publish the positive review it received from Frank McDermot,[98] and most of the newspapers in the Republic 'refused to discuss Sheehy's thesis and devoted themselves to abuse and innuendo'. Nonetheless, Browne and Nolan's shop in Dublin sold out its allocation rapidly.[99]

As part of his efforts to publicise the book and its thesis, Horgan also contacted Conor Cruise O'Brien, then still attached to the department of External Affairs in Iveagh House (and who had been, as a civil servant, the first Director of the Irish News Agency, charged after 1949 with the task of disseminating Sean MacBride's views on partition to the world). O'Brien wrote to him to say that while he knew and respected his views on Ulster, he was 'sorry in some ways . . . that you lent the authority of your name to Sheehy's book which I think overstated some true things and painted rather too flattering a picture of the Ulster side'.[100] A decade later, the book and its attendant controversy had still not been forgotten. In the mid-1960s Professor Desmond Williams of University College Dublin entertained the present writer, then a young journalist, to dinner in the University Club in St Stephen's Green, in the course of which he passed on, without comment, a rumour that the publication of the book had been subvented by MI5 – a rumour for which the material in the Faber archives provides no evidence whatsoever.

Horgan hopefully, but unsuccessfully, suggested to Charles Monteith in Fabers that some of his own journalism, particularly his articles for the *Belfast Telegraph*, might form the basis for another book. Undaunted, he was an inveterate correspondent to the *Irish Times*, where he stirred up opposition and approval in almost equal proportions on a wide range of issues, contributed a controversial series of articles to the English Catholic periodical *The Tablet* in 1949, and was a frequent anonymous contributor to the *Belfast Telegraph* in the late 1950s and early 1960s during Jack Sayers's editorship, under the soubriquet of 'Our Correspondent in the Republic'.

The barometer of his attitude towards de Valera swung between initial exasperation and occasional approval. The exasperation was evoked primarily by de Valera's more irredentist utterances about the North, and by his policy on the Irish language. His approbation, on the other hand, was generated by de Valera's increasingly hard-line attitude towards the IRA, first of all during the Second Word War, particularly when de Valera went personally to a Fianna Fáil convention in Cavan in 1940 to defeat a motion calling for the release of 'political prisoners' (i.e. interned IRA men),[101] and later during the 1956–62 IRA campaign on the border. The more Lemass's industrial strategy veered away from protectionism, the more *The Round Table* favoured Fianna Fáil's economic policy, although he remained wary about the possible effects on domestic industry of too rapid an opening up of Ireland to international competition.

The issues which principally exercised him after Lemass assumed power in 1959 were the relationships between Ireland, England and Europe, and, of course, partition. He was quick to note Lemass's new policy towards Northern Ireland – although he criticised the occasional lapses into traditional Republic rhetoric with which the new taoiseach from time to time camouflaged it – and greeted Lemass's visit to Stormont in 1965 with the ringing declaration that 'after forty-three years of constant friction, the process of ending this irrational and unchristian quarrel between Dublin and Belfast has begun.'[102] He was less certain about Europe, believing that Ireland and England together formed a more natural economic unit, and saw Lemass's 1960s initiatives aimed at freeing up trade between the two islands in preparation for EEC membership as an altogether positive development primarily in the context of this conviction. His final verdict was down-beat. By opting for Europe, he suggested, the government 'must now accept without demur a derogation of our sovereignty far greater than any which was entailed by our merely nominal membership of the Commonwealth'.[103] With the benefit of hindsight, it can be seen that he underestimated the potential advantages of the EEC as much as he overestimated the potential commonality of economic and political interest between our two islands.

His continual opposition to what he saw as public hypocrisy about the Irish language led him to accept an invitation, in the mid-1960s, to become a patron of the Language Freedom Movement – a distinctly odd end-game for someone who had joined the Gaelic League in his youth. Some time later, and as he became aware of the very mixed motives of some of the founders of that campaign, he privately admitted that he had perhaps been unwise in this.[104] His own remedy for the state of the language had already been expressed a few years earlier, in terms that betrayed no real expectation that it would ever be adopted: 'I would end the humbug by making all nominees for Dáil and Seanad, as well as all higher civil servants and judges, pass a stiff qualifying examination in oral Gaelic.'[105] It is possible that the energy he devoted to these frequent forays into print and public controversy at this time led him to neglect his legal practice somewhat. He regarded with seeming equanimity the growing unwillingness of the present author – then an apprentice in his office – to accept his designated role as part of the dynastic succession, but entertained him frequently to lively discussions on Irish politics and history over lunch in the Cork County Club on the South Mall, and on Sundays at Lacaduv. After his death, his legal practice was in poor shape, and it was left to his son Ivor, and later his grandson Michael O'Connell, to build it up again.

Early and late, however, his most unalloyed journalistic praise was reserved for Sean Lemass. As early as 1932 he had characterised him as 'the coming man in the Fianna Fáil party' who was 'a clear speaker, and . . . reputed to be reasonable in his views'.[106] From the early 1940s on, Lemass is saluted as the ultimate realist, as disinterested, patriotic, as the possessor of 'the only inquiring mind in government',[107] and 'by far the ablest and most dynamic of de Valera's lieutenants'.[108] As taoiseach, he was a 'forthright and audacious'[109] leader who had earlier had the courage to reverse industrial policy and confront the 'parvenu industrial magnates of modern origin'[110] and who now was 'both ready and willing to bury de Valera's past policy [but] does not desire that it should be given a public funeral.'[111]

In effect, he welcomed Lemass's Northern Ireland policy as a tacit abandonment not only of Costello's ersatz Republicanism of 1939 (as he saw it) but also of the old Sinn Féin policy, which he had denounced for decades, particularly as enunciated by de Valera. 'Poor little Griffith', he told his Northern Ireland readers in December 1959, 'He and his friends unjustly and bitterly accused John Redmond of agreeing to the division of Ireland, but whilst Redmond had never agreed to a permanent division, they themselves, tricked in the end by Lloyd George, had perforce to do so.'[112] In other words, his powerful critique of traditional Irish anti-partitionism was itself profoundly irredentist, but enunciated in terms which were unfamiliar and unwelcome to the mainstream of Irish political discourse almost to the end of his life.

Two decades before his death, he had written, in what was almost an *apologia pro vita sua*, that partition was

> the result of deep religious, political and economic divisions which cannot be cured by oratory, exaggerations or appeals to outside influence. It can be ended only by a slow process of patient consideration and education in Ireland itself, and by the eventual realisation that the issues which still divide us are in fact already obsolete. The unity of Ireland is not dependent on the 19th century conception of Irish nationalism, fine, heroic and vital as that conception often was. Cooperation for the welfare of all its people, development of all its resources, free intercourse among all its inhabitants and the defence of common ideals constitute the real unity of a country ... The real solution of the problem is to place the two governments in a position of complete political equality and let them settle their differences and their difficulties in their own way.[113]

Intriguingly, one of his last trips to Dublin, in the early 1960s, was to pay a private visit to Eamon de Valera, his old adversary, now retired from active politics and President of Ireland, and whom he was to predecease.[114] No formal record remains of the meeting, but they must have had a great deal to talk about. He would have been unaware – and astonished if he had been aware – of a secret initiative taken by de Valera and Aiken early in 1958, as the ageing and virtually blind taoiseach felt the need to address urgently one of the two most substantial legacy issues still troubling him – partition – before leaving office.

The detail of this initiative – which in effect aligned the two men more closely in political terms than Horgan could ever have imagined, and which suggests a radically altered perspective on the events of 1949 – is contained in a confidential briefing note[115] prepared for a visit that Lord Hailsham made to Dublin in that year. It recorded that in March de Valera and Mr Aiken had seen the Commonwealth Secretary and had proposed that Northern Ireland should surrender its direct allegiance to the Queen in return for a United Republic of Ireland within the Commonwealth, which would recognise the Queen as its head. The British government – the Irish visitors suggested hopefully – should take the initiative towards such a solution of the problem. The Commonwealth Secretary replied, first, that the British government could not be expected to go to Northern Ireland and suggest that its people should be less loyal to the Queen than they wished to be; and secondly, that if they were to believe the Irish press, and took note of the teaching in the Irish schools, there could be no confidence that Southern Ireland would in fact accept the Queen as head of the Commonwealth.

Mr de Valera, according to the note, 'seemed unhappy but resigned to it; Mr Aiken said he would be back here in July and hoped we would have changed our minds'.

All that survives of the final meeting between Horgan and de Valera is the author's memory of his grandfather recalling one of the things de Valera said to him on that occasion, with a profound sense of loss and perhaps also of loneliness that must have been shared by the two men, born within a year of each other almost a century earlier. 'I'm going to the morgue too often' de Valera told him.[116] That said, John J. Horgan's ghost, the ghost of Eamonn de Valera, and perhaps also that of John Redmond, would have observed their country post-1998 with a rare sense of historical perspective. But they would have been intrigued rather than satisfied, and they would undoubtedly have had things to say about it.

Notes to Introduction

1 Her family originally came from Jersey.

2 *The Round Table*, 37 (146) Mar. 1947, p. 160.

3 *The Irish Times*, 21 Dec.1937.

4 *Parnell to Pearse*, p. 78.

5 Traill to Horgan, 21 July 1901, National Library of Ireland (NLI), MS16703

6 Charles Stannage, *The People of Perth: A Social History of Western Australia's Capital City* (Perth: Perth City Council, 1979).

7 J. J. Horgan had been his father's deputy for a number of years before this, owing to M. J. Horgan's ill health.

8 *The Irish Times*, 3 Apr. 1962.

9 NLI, MS16703.

10 *Cork Examiner*, 1 Feb. 1919.

11 WS 91 J J Walsh: Bureau of Military History statement, NAI. I am grateful to Dr John Borgonovo for this and a number of other references to J. J. Horgan's activities in Cork in the 1916–21 period.

12 AOH Second Degree Meeting Book. It was not publicly known until early the following year.

13 Guys Directory Cork, 1916.

14 *Journal of the Proportional Representation Society* (July 1912), p. 40, quoted in the Seanad by Senator Owen Sheehy Skeffington, Seanad Debates, 11 Mar. 1959. Birmingham's novel, *The Red Hand of Ulster* (1911), is a colourful tapestry of the various shades of Unionist opinion in that period.

15 As a student in University College Cork at that time, I attended the debate.

16 'Spectator', *Irish Independent*, 30 Oct. 1940.

17 *Parnell to Pearse*, pp. 163–4.

18 NLI, MS 18,271. I am indebted to Dr John Borgonovo for this NLI reference.

19 NLI, MS 18,271, Devlin to Horgan, 2 Mar. 1911.

20 NLI, MS 18,271, Devlin to Horgan, 30 June 1916.

21 NLI, MS 18,271, Horgan to Devlin, 1 July 1916.

22 This is as stated in an interview in the *Irish Times* in 1962 (cf. infra). His memoir, however, says that the debate was about Irish education. His memory, generally extremely accurate, may have failed him in this detail.

23 *The Irish Times*, 15 Feb. 1912.

24 *Cork Examiner*, Letter to the Editor, 11 May 1916.

25 J. J. Horgan to Col. Maurice Moore, 31 May 1916, NLI MS 18,273 (Colonel Maurice Moore Papers).

26 RIC Special Branch report from Cork, 29 Aug. 1917. University College Cork, 'British in Ireland' microfilm series.

27 J. J. Horgan, 'Precepts and practice in Ireland, 1914–1919', *Studies* (1919), pp. 210–26.

28   *Cork Examiner*, 1 Feb. 1919, reports a UIL meeting at which he and a number of other UIL leaders all resigned their positions.

29   *Cork Examiner*, 21 Feb. 1919.

30   *Cork Constitution*, 18 Apr. 1918.

31   *The Irish Times*, 25 Sept. 1936.

32   J. J. Horgan, 'The development of local government in Ireland', *Journal of the Social and Statistical Inquiry Society of Ireland* 27 (1946), pp. 423–37.

33   The National Archives (TNA), Kew, CO 904/23, RIC Epitome of de Valera's documents seized from de Valera's home in May 1921.

34   Reference courtesy of Dr John Borgonovo.

35   *Cork Constitution*, 31 Mar. 1920.

36   Horgan to Erskine Childers, 30 Dec. 1918, Trinity College Dublin (TCD) MSS 7848 (Childers MSS) Childers to Horgan 516–47. I am indebted to Dr Brian Murphy OSB of Glenstal Abbey for this and other references to the Childers papers.

37   *Parnell to Pearse*, p. 353.

38   Childers to Horgan, 1 Oct. 1919, TCD MSS 7848 (Childers MSS) Childers to Horgan 516–47.

39   The children of John and Mary Horgan (*née* Windle) (1888–1920) were Ivor (1909–80), Michael Joseph (1910–69) and Madoline (b. 1915), matriarch of the family for more than three decades. John J. Horgan remarried, in 1923, Mary Brind (1895–1972), with whom he had two children: David (1924–99), and Joan (1926–62)

40   Horgan to Erskine Childers, 24 Aug. 1921, TCD MSS 7848 (Childers MSS) Childers to Horgan, 516–47.

41   Horgan to Mary Childers, 29 Dec. 1922, TCD MSS 7848 (Childers MSS) Childers to Horgan, 516–47.

42   Horgan revealed this many years later to his *protégé* and long-time associate, Liam St John Devlin, in private conversation. Liam St John Devlin interview (29 Dec. 2008).

43   Dáil Debates, vol. 10, 10 Feb. 1925.

44   Dáil Debates, vol. 12, 8 July 1925.

45   See John Coakley, 'Ireland's unique electoral experiment: the Senate election of 1925', *Irish Political Studies* 20: 3 (Sept. 2005), pp. 231–69.

46   He omitted both this candidacy, and a later one in 1937, from an interview he gave in 1962, when he averred that he had ceased to be a politician in 1918 (*The Irish Times*, 7 July 1962). This can perhaps be best understood if 'politician' is understood as 'party politician'.

47   *The Irish Times*, 7 Mar. 1925.

48   *The Round Table*, 17: 67 (May 1927), p. 585.

49   *The Round Table*, 33: 130 (Dec. 1943), p. 67.

50   *The Irish Times*, 23 Dec. 1938. Other vice-presidents included Major-General Sir Hubert Gough, Major-General Sir G. Franks, and Frank McDermot, TD.

51 *The Round Table*, 11: 43 (June 1921), pp. 473–529.

52 Curtis to Harding, 26 July 1932, Curtis papers, Bodleian Library, Oxford, MSS Curtis 90.f.63. I am indebted to Dr Deirdre McMahon for this and other references to the Curtis/*Round Table* papers.

53 For a typical episode in this saga, see *The Irish Times*, 6 Apr. 1955.

54 J. J. Horgan told this anecdote to the present author in 1960.

55 *The Round Table*, 16: 62 (Mar. 1926), p. 587.

56 Ibid., p. 588.

57 *The Round Table*, 17: 6 (May 1927), p. 593. It is probable that Fr R. S. Devane, SJ, was the dignitary he had in mind.

58 *The Round Table*, 31: 85 (Nov. 1931), p. 145.

59 Ibid., p. 154.

60 Ibid., p. 149.

61 *The Round Table*, 31: 88 (June 1932), p. 762.

62 Dáil Debates, vol. 18, 25 Jan. 1927.

63 Mary Leland (2001), *That Endless Adventure: A History of the Cork Harbour Commissioners* (Cork: The Port of Cork Company, 2001). Some of the other details about his work with the Commissioners are also taken from this valuable overview.

64 He is quoted on this topic as 'an influential Cork businessman' in a United Press newsagency reported published widely on 10 February 1936, for instance.

65 Obituary notice of J. J. Horgan by Denis Gwynn, *The Clongownian* (1968), p. 101.

66 Leland, *That Endless Adventure*, p. 172.

67 Horgan to David Gray, 10 Sept. 1940, National Archives and Records Administration (NARA), Maryland, 8410.20/27

68 *The Round Table*, 48: 189 (Dec. 1957), p. 74.

69 Personal interview, Liam St John Devlin, Baltimore, 29 Dec. 2008.

70 *The Round Table*, 30: 155 (June 1949), pp. 219–20.

71 Mansergh to Morrah, 23 Jan. 1950, MSS Curtis 98 ff.217a,b.

72 Ibid.

73 Curtis to Macadam, 4 Sept. 1946, MSS Curtis 90 f.110.

74 See for example Antoine Mioche (2007), 'India or North America? Reflections on Nicholas Mansergh's partition paradigm', *Eire-Ireland* 42: 1 and 2 (Spring/Summer 2007), pp. 290–310.

75 *The Round Table*, 39: 155 (June 1949), p. 216.

76 Ibid.

77 *The Round Table*, 41: 164 (Sept. 1951), p. 362.

78 *The Round Table*, 44: 176 (Sept. 1954), p. 397.

79 *The Round Table*, 15: 60 (Sept. 1925), p. 757.

80 *The Irish Times*, 30 Mar. 1938.

81 *The Round Table*, 35: 140 (Sept. 1945), p. 313.

82 Ibid., p. 330.

83 *The Round Table*, 37: 147 (Jan. 1947), p. 282.

84 *The Round Table*, 50: 198 (Mar. 1960), p. 185.

85 *The Round Table*, 37: 147 (June 1947), p. 280.

86 *The Round Table*, 38: 150 (Mar. 1948), p. 198

87 *The Round Table*, 44: 175 (June 1954), p. 276.

88 *The Round Table*, 44: 174 (Mar. 1954), p. 185.

89 *The Round Table*, 52: 206 (Mar. 1949), p. 188.

90 *The Round Table*, 55: 217 (Dec. 1964), p. 97.

91 *The Round Table*, 57: 122 (Jan. 1967), p. 122.

92 Michael Sheehy, *Divided We Stand: A Study in Partition* (London: Faber and Faber, 1955).

93 Ibid., p. 102.

94 *Parnell to Pearse*, p. 337

95 Foreword to Sheehy, *Divided We Stand*, p.11.

96 Horgan to Monteith, 5 May 1955, Faber Archive CM 17/35.

97 Ibid.

98 Horgan to Monteith, 5 Jan. 1956, Faber Archive CM 17/35.

99 Horgan to Monteith, 23 May 1955. Faber Archive CM 17/35.

100 Conor Cruise O'Brien to Horgan, 11 July 1955, NAI DFA 316/27/747.

101 *The Round Table*, 30: 119 (May 1940), p. 637.

102 *The Round Table*, 55: 219 (June 1965), p. 295.

103 *The Irish Times*, 7 July 1962.

104 In a conversation with the author, *c.*1965.

105 *The Irish Times*, 7 July 1962.

106 *The Round Table*, 31: 87 (May 1932), p. 501. It was a view he held without substantial modification until the end of his life.

107 *The Round Table*, 44: 175 (June 1954), p. 280.

108 *The Round Table*, 76: 172 (Mar. 1956), p. 280

109 *The Round Table*, 52: 209 (Dec. 1962), p. 68.

110 *The Round Table*, 51: 202 (Mar. 1961), p. 177.

111 *The Round Table*, 53: 209 (Dec. 1962), p. 69.

112 *Belfast Telegraph*, 28 Dec.1959; signed review of Padraic Colum's 'Life of Griffith'.

113 *The Round Table*, 37 (147), June 1947, p. 283.

114 John J. Horgan died in Cork on 21 July 1967. His estate, which included Lacaduv, was probated at £27,264, or just over €500,000 in 2009 terms.

115 TNA, Kew, DO 35/7891.

116 Personal recollection of the author, conversation with J. J. Horgan, early 1960s.

John J. Horgan
By Marshall C. Hutson. *Royal Academy, 1938*

Parnell to Pearse

Some Recollections and Reflections

✦

JOHN J. HORGAN

Some said, John, print it; others said, Not so:
Some said, It might do good; others said, No.
Now I was in a strait, and did not see
Which was the best thing to be done by me:
At last I thought, since you are thus divided,
I print it will, and so the case decided.

— JOHN BUNYAN

Love's art is this, to conquer and retain
A soul so rich that rising in her train
One climbs to wider vision, light unknown;
So poor, that in her need she shares her own.
                    – From the French of PAUL GÉRALDY.

FOREWORD TO THE ORIGINAL EDITION

History should not, and indeed cannot, be written without prejudice. A point of view is not only inevitable, but even necessary. Our conception of persons, places or periods is for instance usually coloured by our environment. Hitler in 1940 seemed a criminal to the people of England, a hero to the people of Germany; my native city viewed on a sunny autumn evening from the heights of Montenotte, its spires rising like silver lances from the mist of the valley, hardly looks the same place as when approached on a wet winter's night through the ugly industrial district of Blackpool; a child now being educated in Cork has a quite different idea of Irish history from one being educated in Belfast. I felt, therefore, that the title of this book, arrived at after several alternatives had been discarded, would best indicate the character of a volume which is not only an autobiography but also a record of Irish affairs as they have presented themselves to an Irishman, who, born at Cork in the year 1881, has witnessed the birth of modern Ireland, and who knew both Parnell and Pearse.

Separated by a quarter of a century the careers of these two men were yet strangely alike. Both were partly English by ancestry. Both 'loved not wisely but too well', Parnell an ignoble woman, Pearse a noble ideal; in the one case Katherine O'Shea, in the other Kathleen ni Houlihan. The life of the former ended in national disaster, and so ended also, as I and those who think with me believe, the life of the latter. The legend of each still persists.

My story ends with the collapse of the Constitutional movement in 1918 when there began a new and bloodstained era of which Pearse was the forerunner. But the bitter harvest since reaped was sown in the preceding quarter of a century. That period of germination – one of the most critical in our history – with which my book deals, provides the key to all that has happened, and, indeed, is yet to happen, in Ireland.

It is, however, a personal record. I make no claim to give the whole picture. I write as a son of one of Parnell's few personal friends and an unrepentant believer in the principles which inspired his successor, John Redmond. The tragic result of Redmond's failure to attain his ends only emphasises their validity. As Burke wrote in a letter to a Bristol constituent: 'I wish to have as close a union of interest and affection with Ireland as I can have; and that I am sure is a far better thing than any nominal union of Government.' Politicians on both sides of the Irish Sea might well ponder his words, for they are still true.

Like Lord John Hervey 'I very freely declare my part in this drama was only that of the Chorus in the ancient tragedies who, being constantly on the stage, saw everything that was done and made their own comments upon the scene without mixing in the action or making any considerable figure in the performance.' But I was not, as we say in Ireland, merely 'a hurler on the ditch'. During many years I played an active if minor part on the Irish political stage and was acquainted with many of the principal characters. History is like a coral reef. Its substance is drawn from innumerable and often apparently insignificant sources. So I make my small contribution.

In dealing with the background of the Parnell period I have derived both information and enlightenment from that great book *Gladstone and the Irish Nation*, by J. L. Hammond. I have also made free use of my father's papers and diaries as well as his contributions to Barry O'Brien's *Life of Parnell*. Quotations relating to other periods are duly acknowledged in the footnotes. I am under a deep debt of gratitude to my friends Donal O'Sullivan and Professor William H. Porter who have patiently read and revised my manuscript at all stages; to my friends Mr Justice Eric Hallinan, Professor Denis Gwynn and Captain Henry Harrison for valuable criticism and advice; and finally to my wife for much wise counsel and constant encouragement.

THE Chinese, in their wisdom, honour the ancestors of their
famous men rather than their descendants, for they regard
the former as the source of their greatness. Moreover, they
argue quite sensibly, that ancestors, being dead, cannot
abuse such honours, as descendants are unfortunately sometimes prone to do. Our ancestors are indeed the road by
which we approach, and eventually arrive in, this world,
paternal and maternal lines converging to form a main
thoroughfare from different, and perhaps even as in my
case opposite directions, inevitably influence and sometimes
determine the direction of our journey. It is in fact impossible
to think of a person without taking into consideration the
family into which he was born and the inherited past with
which he starts, for in a very real sense, as the Church has
always taught, the individual human person and society
are one. "We are members one of another." So before I
go forward I must look back along the way whence I
came.

On the map of the Four Masters, reputed to be one of
the oldest maps of Ireland, the name O'Horgan (in Irish
Ua hArgáin) appears in two places, both within the
boundaries of the modern county of Cork—the district
of Carbery near the present town of Skibbereen and
West Muskerry near the present town of Macroom. It is
from the latter branch of the Horgans that my father's
family derive. The surname Horgan, of which there are
several English variants, is apparently derived from the
Irish name O'hAnradáin, which means the descendant of
the little warrior. In O'Hart's *Irish Pedigrees* the O'Horgans
are cited in the list of Irish families existing from the eleventh
to the sixteenth century. As no records were kept of
Catholic births and deaths during the Penal Days it is not
easy to trace the descent of my father's family. I do know,
however, that my grandfather, my great-great-grandfather,
and my great-great-great-grandfather, and an uncle, were
all John Horgans, and so my son and grandson are certainly

the sixth and seventh members of the family respectively to bear that name.

The dower list of the Countess Clancarty, compiled about 1700, gives the name of Daniel Horgan as making a payment out of the lands of Lacaduff or Mount Hedges, and he was almost certainly one of my ancestors, for it was on these lands, which seem to have extended from the western end of Macroom Castle demesne along the hill to a point south of Raleigh on the way to Carrigaphooka, that my great-great-great-grandfather, John Horgan, lived. He was well known throughout Muskerry as a man of fine physique, a good rider and a " strong " farmer. My great-grandfather, another Daniel Horgan (1750–1847) resided at Canovee to the south east of Macroom. He was the son of John Horgan by his wife Ellen Nunan, who came from Lismore, County Waterford. He married Mary Dunlea of Mahalaugh, County Cork. It was in his time that the family came to be known as the " Slasher " Horgans, and in this wise. One day as my great-grandfather was walking through the Square at Macroom, an officer of the yeomanry, who then policed the country and terrorised the people, approached, and hit him with the flat of his sword calling him a " Papist dog." My great-grandfather, a big, powerful man, wrenched the sword out of the ruffian's grasp and there and then publicly chastised him with it till his clothes were slashed to ribbons. For this defiance of tyranny he was brought before a bench of Protestant magistrates who, be it said to their credit, respected a brave man and refused to convict him. His bravery had lost him nothing, but it gained for us a nickname of which I at all events am not ashamed.

Irish conditions at that time may be illustrated by the tragic fate of Arthur O'Leary. This brave man, who belonged to one of the leading Catholic families in Muskerry, and who, whilst in exile, had fought as an officer in the Austrian army, was outlawed because he refused to sell his valuable mare to a Protestant for £5 as the Penal Laws required him do to. Besieged by the military in his home at Raleigh, Macroom, not far from my great-grandfather's home, he beat off the attackers, but he was eventually betrayed and shot by the soldiers at Carriganima on 4th May, 1773. The *caoine*, or lament, composed by his wife, Eileen Dhuv, over his dead body is one of the finest poems in modern Irish and indeed need not fear comparison with the greatest tragic poems of all time.

A better-known member of the family was Father Matthew Horgan, parish priest of Blarney and Whitechurch, who died in 1849. A Gaelic scholar, antiquary and poet, he discovered the key to the Ogham alphabet, a primitive form of writing found on early-Irish stone monuments, and explored every aspect of Irish archaeology. He was a member of the Royal Irish Academy and a contemporary and friend of such famous Corkmen as Crofton Croker, Maginn, Windele, and the Rev. Francis Mahony, better known as " Father Prout." Mahony indeed, in order to give a touch of verisimilitude to his work, introduced him into his famous book *Father Prout's Reliques* as one of the executors of that fictitious and amazing clergyman. Strange to say in the same volume Mahony also mentions Dr. Bowring, a literary member of my mother's family, of whom more anon. Father Mat wrote two poems in Irish, one the *Legend of Cahir Conri*, and the other *Gortroe*, a *caoine* or lament for nine men who were killed by the British military forces near Rathcormac, County Cork, during a tithe collection on 18th December, 1834. This tragic dirge, together with a full report of the inquest on the victims, was published anonymously in Cork in 1835. It throws a considerable light on the stubborn resistance of the people to the oppressive levy of tithes for the support of an alien church. It is the memory of such incidents that has unfortunately helped to poison relations between Great Britain and Ireland. Father Mat also translated some of Horace and of Moore's poetry into Irish. He was an excellent draughtsman and architect and both designed and built several churches. At Waterloo church, near Blarney, and at Whitechurch, he erected round towers to prove the Christian origin of these much-discussed edifices. The Cork wits, however, rather unkindly said that, whilst the ancients erected round towers to puzzle posterity, Father Mat erected them to

puzzle himself. One of these quaint monuments to his antiquarian zeal, not properly completed owing to lack of funds,
may still be seen from the train as one approaches Cork by
the main line from Dublin. Someone has wittily called it
an architectural churn. I have his portrait done in crayon
by Samuel Skillin, the well-known Cork artist of that time.
It shows him dressed, as priests were then, in the high linen
collar and dark cravat of the layman, with a heavy frieze
coat. He has the gentle, dreamy face of a poet and writer.
Brash the well-known antiquarian said that Father Mat was
" one of the best Irish scholars of his day." He was a priest
of the old school, zealous, hard working, earnest, simple,
proud of his country, its language, its history, proud also
of his flock, and anxious for their welfare, loving them and
being loved in return. When he died only a few shillings
were found in the house. It was all he had. Such men
kept the Faith alive in dark and evil days.

My grandfather, John Horgan (1780–1874), who was the
eldest son of Daniel Horgan of Canovee, forsook the country
for the town and became a shopkeeper in Macroom, but
he had some land and I suspect was as much farmer as
merchant. The dividing line between these two occupations
in a small Irish town was then, and indeed still is, very thin.
Macroom, a typical West Cork town, is situated some twenty-
four miles from Cork near the head of the Lee Valley where
the fertile lands of County Cork begin to merge into the
rugged Kerry landscape with its small fields and stone fences.
Its main street, terminating in a square, castle, and church
overlooking the river, is unique only in a certain cold, tough,
quality, which its inhabitants share. They are a border
people, very much on their guard, and in those days they
were even more remote from the great world than now.
The place was sacked during the Cromwellian wars.
William Penn's father lived in its castle for some years.

My grandfather married Elizabeth Murphy (1806-1880)
who was also of Macroom farming stock. The name Murphy
means the descendant of a sea warrior. This suggests that
they belonged to one of the numerous races that invaded
Ireland in prehistoric times. Be that as it may, the Murphys

have long since deserted the sea for the land and are now firmly rooted in the soil. They are a numerous and prolific clan, so numerous indeed that the various sections of the family have different nicknames to distinguish them. My grandmother belonged to the Murphy Stuaics, an old Muskerry branch of the family. My grandparents were blessed with fifteen children of whom my father, Michael Joseph Horgan, was the fourteenth. Of these five died in early youth, four entered religion, and of the rest only my father and his brother John, who went to Australia, had issue, so that of this large family my father's children are the only surviving descendants in Ireland. My grandfather was a personal friend of Daniel O'Connell the Liberator, who emancipated the Irish Catholics both legally and spiritually. O'Connell sometimes stayed with him when he was posting through Macroom en route for his Kerry home at Derrynane. I have an old woodcut of O'Connell refusing to take the objectionable oath in the House of Commons, which he gave to my grandfather, and which has his clear decisive signature across the back. This oath compelled a Catholic to abjure the fundamental tenets of his faith.

Let us now explore the English road by which my mother came. The Bowring family, to which she belonged, came originally from Saxony to England about 1184 in the reign of Henry II. In 1190 they took an estate and manor farm in the north-west of Devon which still goes by the name of Bowrings-Leigh. They were at first largely engaged in the woollen trade. In 1400 the branch of the family from which my mother derived moved to Cerne, a small village near Dorchester, in the county of Dorset. Here they lived for many years at Cerne Manor Farm, the property of Lord Rivers, and held leasehold livings under the name of "Bowrings livings." In the year 1635 John Bowring (1614–1710), the eldest son of the family, being then twenty-one years of age, left Cerne and took from Lord Pomfret the Manor Farm of Urless, in the parish of Corscombe, about ten miles away. His son Robert Bowring (1647–1734) succeeded him. Robert's son, another John Bowring (1704–1786) (the name John was apparently as popular in the

Bowring as the Horgan family), also lived at Urless and
married one Margery Smith of that parish. In 1815, the
year of Waterloo, their son, my maternal great-grandfather,
George Bowring (1774–1830), migrated to Jersey where he
married a Jersey woman, Elizabeth Aubin, on 11th June,
1822. She was a Catholic. Through her we link up with
the Norman-French and their predecessors the Norsemen.
Their son, my grandfather, George Philip Bowring (1826–
1864), was born at St. Helier, Jersey, and married on 18th
July, 1854, his second cousin Mary Pope Genge, who was
also of an old Dorset stock. The wedding took place from
Waterson House, Dorset, where her uncle lived—better
known to readers of fiction as Weatherbury Farm, the home
of Bathsheba Everdene, in Thomas Hardy's famous novel
Far from the Madding Crowd. To Hardy, in the novel, it
" presented itself as a hoary building of the Jacobean stage
of the Classic Renaissance." " Fluted pilasters, worked
from the solid stone, decorated its front, and above the roof
pairs of chimney were here and there linked by an arch,
some gables and other unmanageable features still retaining
traces of their Gothic extraction. Soft brown mosses, like
faded velveteen, formed cushions upon the stone tiling, and
tufts of the houseleek or sengreen sprouted from the eaves
of the low surrounding buildings." Such small manor
houses, formerly the homes of the lesser gentry, in the
eighteenth century, gave the country districts of England a
solidarity and an atmosphere now unfortunately almost
extinct. Of my grandfather's marriage there were four
children, two boys and two girls, of whom my mother,
Mary Bowring, was the youngest. She was born at St.
Helier on 20th April, 1857. Seven years afterwards my
grandfather died of meningitis at the early age of thirty-
eight, and the family returned to England.

The only member of the Bowring family who seems to
have attained fame was Sir John Bowring, F.R.S. (1792–
1872), a cousin of my grandfather. A scholar, linguist,
political economist and traveller, he was reputed to have
spoken fifteen languages fluently and to have known forty
critically. He was an intimate friend and adviser of Jeremy

Bentham, the great English Law reformer and utilitarian philosopher, whose collected works he edited and whose life he wrote. He received the degree of Doctor of Laws from the University of Groningen and is the Dr. Bowring referred to in Father Prout's *Reliques*. Mahony, its author, probably met him during his wanderings abroad. Bowring was an authority on public accounts, and his investigations and reports concerning those of other countries led to a complete change in the form of the English exchequer returns and to many subsequent alterations. In 1856, whilst Governor of Hong Kong and plenipotentiary to China, he achieved international notoriety by the measures which he took to punish Chinese insults to the British flag, measures which led to war with China and a general election in England. The following year an attempt was made at Hong Kong to poison him and his wife, with eventually fatal results so far as she was concerned. In parliament as member for the Clyde Burghs, and subsequently for Bolton, he advocated parliamentary government for the Isle of Man and Malta, and was a strong free-trader. A poet of some distinction, he wrote at least one famous hymn and collected materials for a history of popular poetry in all countries—a work which unfortunately he never completed. He was also the first editor of the *Westminster Review*.

Bowring at one period collaborated with that strange genius George Borrow, who was also a considerable linguist, in translating some Scandinavian poetry. But this partnership ended, as such associations often do, in a literary feud, as the penniless Borrow resented the fact that Bowring did not, as he thought, exert himself sufficiently on his behalf. Borrow subsequently devoted the last chapter in the appendix to *The Romany Rye* to a thinly veiled attack on Bowring whom he describes as the old Radical. From this diatribe the following acid portrait of Bowring may be quoted :

The writer had just entered into his eighteenth year, when he met at the table of a certain Anglo-Germanist an individual, apparently somewhat under thirty, of middle stature, a thin

and weaselly figure, a sallow complexion, a certain obliquity of
vision, and a large pair of spectacles. This person who had
lately come from abroad, and had published a volume of translations, had attracted some slight notice in the literary world,
and was looked upon as a kind of lion in a small provincial
capital. After dinner he argued a great deal, spoke vehemently
against the Church, and uttered the most desperate Radicalism
that was perhaps ever heard, saying he hoped that in a short
time there would not be a king or queen in Europe, and inveigh-
ing bitterly against the English aristocracy, and against the Duke
of Wellington in particular, whom he said, if he himself was
ever president of an English-speaking republic—an event which
he seemed to think was by no means improbable—he would
hang for certain infamous acts of profligacy and bloodshed which
he had perpetrated in Spain.

It is ironic to reflect that Bowring, whose thirty-six
miscellaneous volumes are now unread and indeed forgotten,
may well have attained immortality through Borrow's
pen.

These, then, are the roads by which I came—one purely
Irish, the other Anglo-Saxon with a Norman-French tribu-
tary, but all alike leading from that peasant stock which
in the long run is the true strength and master force of every
community. I am in fact of Irish-English descent, a very
different thing from Anglo-Irish in the ordinary meaning
of the term. The Anglo-Irish are colonists, English settlers
and planters long established in Ireland, the Irish-English
are the result of modern intermarriage between two races.
The influence of English blood in Ireland is a subject that
would well repay detailed investigation. The Anglo-Irish
furnished most of the leaders in the struggle for Irish colonial
and constitutional freedom, such men as Grattan, Flood,
and Burke during the struggle for colonial liberty, Parnell
and Redmond in more recent times. Irish nationalism, in
the modern sense, was in fact an English idea, quite beyond
the conception of the old Irish aristocracy or their peasant
successors. The Native Irish were always more concerned
with such fundamental objectives as the recovery of the land,
Catholic Emancipation, and the restoration of the old Irish
way of life with all this implies—in short the abolition of

the ascendancy imposed upon them after the Treaty of
Limerick in 1691. But the Irish-English have been an even
more disturbing factor ; they were the spearhead of the
final revolt against English rule. Wolfe Tone, Emmet,
Davis and Mitchel, the forerunners of modern Irish Republicanism, were all men of Irish-English blood. In more
recent times Patrick Pearse, Terence MacSwiney, and
Erskine Childers, to name three of the most prominent
leaders of the modern revolt against England, were all
children of Irish and English parents. The sturdy and
inherent love of liberty, so characteristic of the English,
seems to germinate with remarkable speed and strength in
Irish soil. So, by a strange paradox, the Irish-English have
been a major factor in destroying English rule in Ireland.
Their English blood, without hesitation, denied and challenged the validity of the English conquest. But, like most
cross-bred peoples, the Irish-English, as I have personally
experienced, suffer from the results of different inherited
racial characteristics and the demands of a divided allegiance
which, whilst they add to the interest of life, do not always
conduce to peace of mind. As a northern poet, Richard
Rowley, has well written :

> The words I speak, my written line,
> These are not uniquely mine,
> For in my heart, and in my will
> Old ancestors are warring still.

Such an origin does, however, enable one to bring a charitable and comprehending mind to the consideration of Anglo-
Irish differences and problems. To see the view-point of
both sides enables one to understand and to pardon much
that might otherwise be incomprehensible and unpardon-
able. The difference between my English and Irish relatives
is perhaps best illustrated by the following true story. A
brother of my father's, who was also a Catholic priest,
happened on one occasion to be spending a holiday in
England, and during his travels visited the Dorset farm-house
home of my mother's great aunt, Mrs. Sarah Bartlett. The

day passed off pleasantly and, after he had departed, old Aunt Sarah delivered herself of this judgment on her guest : " Father Horgan may be an Irish Catholic, and he may be a priest, but all I can say is that he is a very nice man." Upon which rather startling revelation of the gap between my Irish and English ancestors I may well close this record of their doings. *Requiescant in pace !*

My father was born on 3rd October, 1845. It was the eve of the " Great Famine," that terrible and momentous event which vitally affected not only the course of Irish history but that of the world. The population of Ireland was then about eight millions : before my father died it had fallen to four. To understand the attitude of his generation and mine towards England the story of this appalling calamity must be briefly told. In 1845 three-quarters of the Irish people were miserably poor and dependent on the potato for food, as the export of their wheat and other crops provided the money to pay their rent. The flourishing trade and industry of the country had, since the Union, suffered from the competition of freely imported English goods, manufactured under greater advantages, as well as from strikes and local disorders. Neither had the country the necessary raw materials to feed a manufacturing industry. Early marriages and sub-letting combined had caused a too rapid and uneconomic increase in the population, and emigration was discouraged by the leaders of public opinion. In 1841 Ireland was, next to England and Wales, the most densely populated country in Europe. This situation was pregnant with disaster and it was not long delayed. In the autumn of 1845 the potato, always a precarious crop, was attacked by a new enemy, the blight, which had first appeared in North America the previous year. It swept over Northern Europe, and Ireland soon felt its worst effects, scarcely a district escaping its ravages. The country was full of food and there can be no doubt that a native government would have stopped its export when famine became imminent. But even if this had been done the problem would not have been solved. The great majority of the people could not afford to buy corn, much less meat. If they did not sell their produce they could not pay their rents. The British govern-ment could therefore intervene to prevent famine only by a general interference with the rights of property. They might indeed have safeguarded those rights by compensating the landlords, but this could not have been done without violating what were then regarded as the sacrosanct laws of political economy, that policy of *laissez faire* which forbade the state to interfere with the free play of economic forces. The workhouse thus became the only remedy for famine. It is, however, fair to point out that, whilst the Government foresaw the prospect of famine and had been warned of its results, it did not anticipate its magnitude or continuance. The failure of the potato crop continued in fact for five years. During that time the population was reduced by two and a half millions. Typhus fever, dysentery and other diseases followed in the path of famine and killed more people than actual starvation. One of my father's earliest memories was of seeing the people dying in the streets of his native town. Large funds were raised in England and America to succour the stricken country, but the main part of the task fell naturally upon the British government, whose administrative machinery was not adapted to cope with such a catastrophe. In 1846 the duties on imported corn were lowered but the export of corn was not prohibited. Under the Navigation Laws it could be imported only in British ships, and these were not available. Public works were established to relieve poverty but they were not reproductive and the whole charge fell upon the country. In a country where there were large areas of bogland to be reclaimed and whole districts without a railway the people were employed making roads leading to nowhere. It seemed clear that the British Government did not really wish to retain the Irish people in Ireland.

A great exodus then began which has profoundly affected the course of world affairs even to this day. It is comparable to the dispersion of the Jews. In the six years following 1845 over a million people left Ireland, principally for the United States of America. They carried with them in their hearts a bitter hatred of England and landlordism which was to mark the beginning of Ireland's influence as a force in world politics, an influence directed always against

the British Empire. In that flight, which continued inter-
mittently for seventy years, many of my father's family
took part. All five of his mother's brothers went to America.
One of them, Timothy Murphy, was the founder of a great
hospital in San Francisco. One of his father's brothers, an
engineer, also found refuge there. Two Horgans fought in
Meagher's Irish Brigade during the American Civil War
of 1863. My cousin, Dr. John Dwyer of New York, served
as surgeon to the famous " fighting 69th " Irish regiment
of New York Volunteers in the same conflict. Fifty-seven
years afterwards, when ninety-two years of age, he stood
with me on Brooklyn Bridge and told me the story of its
construction and of the growth of the great city around us.
He had seen the rout of the Northern Army at the first
Battle of the Bull Run, tended the wounded at the shambles
of Gettysburg, and served with Grant in the Wilderness.
The son of a County Cork farmer, his memory went even
further back, for, during his youth in Ireland, O'Connell's
agitation for the Repeal of the Union was in full swing, and
he well remembered and described one of O'Connell's
famous " monster " meetings held at Blarney, a few miles
from Cork, in 1843. He witnessed also as a lad of sixteen
many of the harrowing scenes of the Great Famine. In
after years he knew and worked with John O'Mahony and
other leaders of the Fenian movement in America, and later
saw his old regiment depart for the Spanish-American and
first World wars. On this latter occasion his pride was
saddened by the thought of their going to fight side by side
with the English to save the British Empire. Such men
as he were the embodiment and the inevitable result of
Irish history.

Even the Irish landlords did not escape the common
disaster of the Famine years. Many impoverished themselves to help the people, others squandered their substance
in riotous living abroad. When their rents failed their
incomes ceased and insolvency followed. Evictions became
a commonplace as new and harsher landlords replaced the
old. It was a ghastly period which left its mark on both
country and people.

Against this background my father grew to manhood.
Educated first at a small school in Macroom, he came
to Cork when nineteen years of age in January, 1864.
In May, 1865, he passed the Benchers' Examination
in Dublin and was admitted as a solicitor's apprentice
to his elder brother John, who practised as a solicitor
in Cork. As the youngest of fourteen children his lot was
not exactly enviable. The deprivations and misfortunes
of the Famine years had reduced the family fortunes,
and after rearing a large family his parents had little help
to offer him. For many years he was dependent on such
precarious and uncertain assistance as his brothers could
give him and often during his student days in Dublin he
went hungry to bed. But he struggled on, educating himself,
and doing his best to make ends meet—a shy, proud, and
rather sensitive boy. His diaries record his reading. In
addition to his legal studies he found time to digest Burke,
Macaulay, Hallam, and the Jesuit philosopher Balmes—
a good foundation for a professional career. What he calls
" the all absorbing topic of the Fenians " is frequently
referred to. This famous organisation was beginning to
exert that influence both secret and open which was to raise
Ireland from its condition of torpor and demoralisation,
and eventually frighten the British Government into making
concessions which it had unfortunately refused to more
peaceful methods of agitation. In December, 1867, he
witnessed a striking manifestation of this new portent—
the procession of a vast crowd through the streets of Dublin
to mourn the execution of the Manchester Martyrs. These
three Cork men had been executed in England, after a trial
in which resentment obscured justice, for complicity in
a Fenian raid on a prison van containing two of their
organisation, during which a police officer was shot accidentally. Amongst those profoundly influenced by this event
was a young Wicklow squire whom my father was later
to meet and follow in dramatic circumstances. A Protestant
barrister, Isaac Butt, a man of moderate views and considerable ability, was then the leader of the constitutional
movement in Ireland. In November, 1868, my father

records attending a great meeting in Dublin to demand
the release of the Fenian prisoners, at which he heard
Butt speak. The two Irish movements, moderate and
extreme, were even then beginning to converge towards
that unity which Parnell afterwards achieved.

In May, 1870, my father passed his Final examination
with distinction and was admitted a solicitor. Two years
later, in December, 1872, he began to take an active interest
in politics. He supported Joseph Ronayne, a veteran
Nationalist who was in some ways Parnell's forerunner, in
the election campaign which resulted in Ronayne's return
as member for Cork. In the following year my father was
unanimously elected as Coroner for the Cork district of
Cork County. This was in many ways the turning point
of his career. The election to this ancient office was in
those days by the vote of the parliamentary electors but my
father was fortunately spared the trouble and expense of
such a contest, for, daunted by the support he had
obtained, the two rival candidates retired at the last
moment and left him in sole occupation of the field.
From now on he had a small but assured income and
a position from which to advance. He was soon to take
part in more dramatic events on a wider stage.

In 1875 a new leader appeared in the Irish political
firmament who, for sixteen years, until he plunged meteor-
like into the darkness, was to be the guiding star of the
Irish race. This great man, Charles Stewart Parnell, a
young Protestant landlord from County Wicklow, son of
an Anglo-Irish father and an Irish-American mother,[1]
became in a few years, in Tim Healy's famous phrase, " the
uncrowned king of Ireland." Intellectually cold and
reserved, politically immature, he quickly became by sheer
force of character and resolve the master of the British parliament. Although certainly no orator in the popular sense
he could express in a few powerful and penetrating words
profound and decisive political ideas that both embodied
and directed the aims of the Irish people. In his efforts for

[1] Her father, the famous Rear-Admiral Charles Stewart of the United
States Navy, was the son of Irish-born parents.

Ireland he was supported and advised, at least in the initial stages, by two remarkable men, Michael Davitt and Joseph Biggar. Davitt, the son of an evicted tenant, a man of the people, had in early life, whilst working in England, been an active member of the Fenian organisation, and when Parnell first met him had just emerged from seven years penal servitude imposed as punishment for his political activities. In spite of this terrible ordeal he was singularly free from bitterness. The nobility of his nature and the selflessness of his aims impressed Parnell.

The contrast between Parnell and Davitt is one of the most extraordinary in Irish history : Parnell, aristocrat, statesman, egotistic realist ; Davitt, peasant, demagogue, unselfish idealist : Parnell imbued with a deep relentless racial distrust of the English people ; Davitt hating the injustice of the English government but not the English people themselves. Davitt held that the struggle for the land was in some ways more fundamental than for political liberty, but although Parnell had studied the land question before they met and had already considered land purchase as the solution he hesitated before committing the national issue to an anti-landlord campaign. It was inevitable that two such men could only act together for a temporary purpose and a limited time. In an Irish parliament they would have been diametrically opposed. Parnell was undoubtedly the greater statesman but Davitt the nobler man.

Biggar, an uncouth little Ulster tradesman, who was also a Fenian, instructed Parnell in these obstructive tactics which under his intelligent direction were soon to turn the proceedings of the House of Commons into a farce and focus attention on Ireland's claims. Biggar himself had learnt their efficacy from Joseph Ronayne, M.P. for Cork, who had seen them practised in the 'fifties by George Henry Moore, the father of the famous novelist, a previous champion of the Irish tenants. Parnell in turn convinced both Davitt and Biggar that by constitutional methods, fighting the British Government on its own chosen ground, they could accomplish more than by secret warfare. Moreover he saw that, whilst the nobility and gentry, who still dominated England, owned most of the land in Ireland, it was impossible for the British Government to concede Irish self government. The establishment of peasant proprietorship was, he finally realised, the key to Irish freedom.

In October, 1879, Parnell and Davitt founded the Land League for the development of their new policy. The country was once more threatened with famine and the situation was desperate. " Show the landlords," said Parnell to the farmers at Westport, "that you intend to hold a firm grip on your homesteads and lands. You must not allow yourselves to be dispossessed as you were dispossessed in 1847." These words were to become the slogan of the Irish agrarian revolution.

In December, 1879, Parnell, accompanied by John Dillon, a son of John Blake Dillon, the Young Ireland leader, set out for America to collect money for food and clothing to relieve the national distress. They had a difficult task. The Irish in America were strong supporters of extreme courses and their organisation, the Clan-na-Gael, was committed to a policy of violent action against the British Government. Parnell had to reconcile them to methods of constitutional agitation, to persuade them to support a lawful movement for self government. His methods were characteristic. At New York in January, 1880, he told them frankly : " Not one cent of the money contributed and handed to us will go towards organising an armed rebellion in Ireland," but at Cincinnati a few days later he gave them the equally positive assurance that " None of us, whether we be in America or Ireland or wherever we may be, will be satisfied until we have destroyed the last link which keeps Ireland bound to England." The Clan-na-Gael, without changing their aims, decided that the new movement and the new leader should have their chance. The visit was a triumphant success. In three months the Irish envoys travelled from one end of America to the other and collected £40,000 from the Irish exiles. Parnell was accorded the honour, previously granted only to Lafayette, Kossuth and Father Mathew, of addressing

the House of Representatives.   They returned to Ireland on
21st March, 1880, and that night my father heard Parnell
speak at a dinner given in his honour by the Cork Farmers'
Club.

The country was in the throes of a General Election.
Ten days afterwards, on 31st March, my father nominated
Parnell for Cork city.   The story of how this happened is
both peculiar and sensational.   Three candidates had already
been selected representing respectively the Tory, Whig, and
moderate Nationalist parties.   Up to the day fixed for the
nomination of candidates the advanced Nationalists had
taken no interest in the election, but that morning a
local politician of supposed Nationalist leanings came to
my father's office.   He handed him a nomination paper
nominating Parnell as a candidate which had already been
signed by two Catholic priests and other electors.   He asked
my father to sign it as nominator and hand it to the sheriff.
My father inquired if he had obtained Parnell's sanction to
this course.   He replied in the affirmative and produced
£250 in bank-notes which he stated he had received from
Parnell.   Of these he gave my father £50 towards initial
expenses.   My father, convinced of his *bona fides*, signed
the nomination paper and was only just in time to lodge it
with the sheriff.   The crowds waiting in the street burst
into loud cheers when they heard the startling news.   That
night my father had a telegram from Parnell thanking him
for nominating him and stating that he would arrive in
Cork by the night mail on 2nd April.   His first question on
arrival was to inquire how he came to be nominated, and
on being told he replied that he had not authorised the
nomination and did not even know the local politician
who had approached my father.   Next morning a council
of war was held, the local politician concerned was sent for,
and Parnell immediately asked him where he had procured
the £250.   He shuffled for a while and finally confessed that
the money had been supplied by the Tory party to run an
extreme Nationalist candidate who would take Nationalist
votes from the Whigs.   Parnell then demanded the balance
of the £250 and threatened that if it was not forthcoming

he would at once expose the whole affair to the electors.
It was immediately produced and handed over to Tim
Healy, Parnell's secretary. Someone suggested that it
should be paid back to the Tories. " Nonsense," said Healy,
" We'll fight the election with it. It will be all the sweeter
to win the seat with Tory money." And so indeed they did.
Parnell swept from one end of the constituency to the other
in a triumphant progress, the people taking the horses from
his car and dragging it through the streets. On the night
before the poll he spoke from the window of the Victoria
Hotel in Patrick Street, his slow measured opening words
acting, as my father said, " like an electric shock on the
excited people." " Citizens of Cork. This is the night
before the battle. To your guns then." He had stood for
three constituencies, Meath, Mayo and Cork. He was
elected for all three and decided to sit for Cork. He remained
its member till the end. A few weeks later he was elected
leader of the Irish parliamentary party—now about to enter
on its greatest hour. After the election the Tory election
agent threatened proceedings for the recovery of the £250,
which had indeed produced unexpected results. My father
replied that he would have great pleasure in accepting
service of a writ on Parnell's behalf but, needless to state,
it was never issued.

The relationship which thus began between Parnell and
my father endured until Parnell's tragic death, and deeply
influenced my father's life. In every subsequent election
he nominated Parnell and acted as his agent. He was with
him, as I shall later recount, during the last grim fight.
The year 1880 was also marked indelibly for my father by
a more personal and romantic event, in which chance again
played a part. He had escaped the snares of various anxious
matchmakers, and like most young men of his age, had
suffered from "the pangs of despised love." He was now to
meet his fate. In May of that year professional business
took him to London for the first time. He stayed with some
Irish friends at Clapham and at their house he met my
mother. It was a case of love at first sight. He thought at
first, as he naively records in his diary, that " she was one

of those English damsels I would not care a rush for," but
" after a few minutes I was charmed." He saw her home
and asked when they might meet again, to which she
demurely and properly replied that she hoped they would
meet in heaven. Three days afterwards they met again.
He proposed and was accepted. My mother had been
baptised a Catholic, her father's faith, but after his death
her mother, who was a Protestant, had brought the children
up in her own religion. Shortly before she met my father
my mother's favourite brother, a subaltern in the 54th
Regiment, had been given up for lost on a journey to India.
She wished to pray for his soul but found that her religion
made no provision for such prayers. This started her
inquiring into its validity and ended in her being received
into the Catholic Church.

My parents were married at the Redemptorist Church,
Clapham, on 7th August, 1880. Soon after their engagement my father had taken his betrothed to the House of
Commons and introduced her to Parnell who, in my
father's words, " talked away pleasantly, took her over the
House, said smilingly ' he was glad Horgan was going
to have someone to take care of him ', and was altogether
perfectly charming."

A few days later Parnell received another visit at the House
of Commons which eventually had tragic consequences.
Mrs. Katherine O'Shea, the clever and attractive English
wife of one of his parliamentary colleagues, Captain William
O'Shea, piqued by his refusal of her invitations, drove down
with her sister to Palace Yard and sent in her card to the
member for Cork. She told long afterwards how he came
out, " a tall, gaunt figure, thin and deadly pale, and how
he looked straight at me smiling with his curiously burning
eyes looking into mine with an intentness that threw into
my brain the sudden thought ' This man is wonderful and
different.' " It was another case of love at first sight. He
promised her to come to dinner at the earliest opportunity. While saying good-bye she dropped the rose she
was wearing in her bodice. He picked it up, lifted it to
his lips and put it in his buttonhole. When he died it was

found treasured carefully amongst his most private papers. This dramatic meeting not only sealed his fate but altered the course of Irish history.

Parnell came to my father's wedding and acted as best man. The rumour had got around that he was coming and the church and street were crowded with people anxious to see him. When he called to fetch my father he noticed that the latter was nervous and insisted on his drinking some champagne before they set out for the church. After the ceremony, in which he acted as a witness, he came to the wedding breakfast at the Grosvenor Hotel—which was as the menu attests, a truly gargantuan repast—responded for the bridesmaids and entered into the spirit of the whole celebration. The bride used to recount how she sprayed his fair beard with scent. He did not leave until the happy pair had departed for their honeymoon. This incident shows that, in spite of his habitual reserve, which was in fact the natural armour of a proud, shy and sensitive man, Parnell had a kindly heart. My father, who was himself a man of great reserve, touched this genial and hidden side of Parnell's nature as few others did. Parnell was no ordinary man. He was indeed one of the most remarkable personalities of the nineteenth century. At my father's wedding he unbent as he had not done before and was seldom to do again. It was a high honour which my father never forgot and which laid the foundation of a lifelong regard and devotion. A few weeks later my parents modestly started their domestic career in a little house by the banks of the Lee and there on 26th April, 1881, I was born. " Saw the youth," chronicles my father, with paternal pride, " apparently a fine fellow." A cautious verdict but neither original nor peculiar in the circumstances.

III

MY first excursion into the outside world was also nearly my last. When I was three months old, my mother, no doubt anxious to show her first born to her family, took me to London. There I at once contracted scarlatina, with which I infected my mother and subsequently my father, who had hastened to the scene. Given up by two doctors, who at first wrongly diagnosed my complaint as diphtheria, I was finally saved by the assiduous nursing of my mother's step-father, an engaging if somewhat unscrupulous Irishman, who refused to give up hope whilst life remained and who is therefore largely responsible for the existence of this book. Finally, in September, 1881, my somewhat shaken parents returned to Ireland with the innocent cause of all the trouble.

One's earliest recollections are seldom clear and precise and mine share this defect. I do remember, however, that my first language was not English. My mother and her aunt who resided with us, both Jerseywomen, spoke French fluently and as they at first addressed me in no other tongue I replied accordingly. Even after other influences began to operate I remained bi-lingual for many years and the sound of the French language still revives nostalgic memories of my childhood.

But my earliest and most vivid recollection is concerned with a dappled grey horse. This magnificent animal, who was made of wood and plaster of Paris, duly harnessed and equipped, supported an outside jaunting car amidst a collection of vehicles exhibited by a local carriage-builder at the Cork Exhibition of 1883, one of the earliest industrial exhibitions to be held in Ireland. This life-size effigy had originally belonged to a veterinary college in France and every detail was perfect. The Exhibition itself is a dim memory, for the horse overshadowed it completely in my infantile mind. I contemplated him in silent wonder and delight and had to be taken regularly to visit him. After the Exhibition closed I tracked him to his permanent abiding place, the carriage-builder's show-room on the South Mall, Cork, where I was often taken to pay him the silent tribute of my admiration. Whether this early fixation had any terrible implications the psycho-analysts must determine. I am personally not conscious of any. This noble steed until quite recent years survived, to remind me of my child-hood, as a sign over a posting establishment which had taken over the business of the carriage-builder. Finally a touring theatrical company, presenting that hoary romantic melodrama *The Royal Divorce*, borrowed him as a charger for Napoleon in the great battle tableau, and he was never returned. It was at least a dramatic and imperial exit !

Even happier memories are however associated with long drives behind real horses when my father went to hold inquests in remote country places. These excursions I generally made perched on the precarious seat of an out-side car, well tucked up in rugs if the day were fine, and when it rained, as it too frequently did, in the comfortable depths of an inside car, that strange vehicle resembling a box on two wheels, which owed its origin to the steep hills of my native city. In this way I soon became familiar with Cork topography and learnt the pleasure of driving through a countryside rich in beautiful scenes and historic memories. In the winter the sunlit mist was often rising from the valley as we set out, the winding river burnished by the sunset as we returned. These jaunts were also made memorable by my father's tales of

> Old, unhappy, far off things,
> And battles long ago.

Later on, visits to friends and relatives in the country enlarged my knowledge of nature in all its mysterious and wonderful ways.

As the years went by five brothers joined me in the nursery. We had moved to another house on the Mardyke Walk, that beautiful old tree lined avenue which extends from the western approach to the centre of Cork city and was then more beautiful than it is now when hoardings and the activities of enterprising builders have obliterated the charming vista of meadow, river, and villa-covered hill. It was of this vista that Thackeray wrote in his *Irish Sketch Book* a hundred years ago, " On one side the river shines away towards the city with its towers and purple steeples : on the other it is broken by little waterfalls and bound in by blue hills, an old castle towering in the distance, and innumerable parks and villas lying along the pleasant wooded banks. How beautiful the scene is, how rich and how happy. Yonder in the old Mardyke avenue you hear the voice of a score of children, and along the bright green meadows, where the cows are feeding, the gentle shadows of the clouds go playing over the grass. Who can look at such a charming scene but with a thankful swelling heart ? " This vivid, if somewhat romantic, description gives a true picture of the scene amidst which my childhood was spent.

But these were difficult years for my parents. My father was a junior member of his profession, with his spurs to win, and he was not well off. In the summer of 1885 an unlucky speculation and the failure of a local bank swept away all his savings. But for the help of a noble and generous friend, spontaneously given, he might well have met with disaster. Moreover he was connected with the unprofitable side in politics, for though Parnell had captured the popular imagination his movement was looked on askance by the well-to-do merchants and landholders, to whom it naturally seemed well nigh revolutionary. To be a Nationalist at that time meant sacrificing much for one's convictions and my father sacrificed a great deal. In addition from 1880 to 1893 he conducted, in the Nationalist interest, all the legal work in connection with the elections in Cork city and county without charging one penny for his services. He also defended the tenants on the Ponsonby estate during one of the most bitter struggles in the long history of Irish agrarian agitation.

The first ten years of my childhood coincided with the opening stages of a social and political revolution which culminated forty years afterwards in the Anglo-Irish Treaty of 1921. In that rebirth of a nation my father played his full part and so I was cradled and brought up in a political atmosphere. They were trying days for my mother, coming direct, and without preparation, from a quiet English home. Often she had to sit up late into the night waiting for my father's return from some distant court or meeting, wondering whether he would return safe and sound. Fortunately she was adaptable to circumstances, and, united by a deep affection to her husband, in time she grew to understand it all. When political crises arose, or Parnell made one of his brief visits to his constituents, our house was more like the field headquarters of some general than a private residence. Members of Parliament, local politicians, messengers and telegraph boys followed each other in unending procession until something like chaos reigned and domestic problems became almost insoluble. At my father's table the leaders of the new Irish party were often to be found. William O'Brien, Tim Healy and his brother Maurice, D. B. Sullivan and others were familiar guests. One of my earliest amusements was a game invented by myself in which Tim Healy, playing the part of an angry bear, crawled about the floor emitting ferocious growls whilst I simulated an innocent sheep about to be devoured. Few would have recognised the vitriolic politician and future Governor-General of the Irish Free State in this genial personality trying to amuse a child. The general public knew little of this emotional side of Healy's character, which could not be ignored with impunity as Parnell afterwards discovered.

Already the political stage was set for momentous scenes in which a great and noble Scotchman was to play the leading part. Many Irish people still believe that it was Parnell who forced Gladstone to take up the cause of Ireland and bring it to an issue. This is untrue. Seventeen years before, on 1st December, 1868, when Parnell was still unheard of, Gladstone had received a summons to form his first Government whilst engaged in his favourite exercise of tree felling at Hawarden. An onlooker afterwards described how after a few minutes "the blows ceased

3—1818

and Mr. Gladstone, resting on the handle of his axe looked up, and with deep earnestness in his voice and great intensity in his face, exclaimed 'My mission is to pacify Ireland.'" This was not the unctuous remark of a hypocrite, but the deeply felt resolution of a Christian statesman who in fact consecrated the remainder of his life to the achievement of this great moral purpose, the reconciliation of England and Ireland. Without such a purpose he rightly felt that political life was a vain and empty pursuit. From that moment in 1868 there began a new chapter in the relations of the two countries. Gladstone understood also, what so few English statesmen have grasped, that a discontented Ireland was not only a blot on England's escutcheon but a menace to her safety. As far back as 1869 he had taken the first step on this perilous journey by disestablishing the Church of Ireland, which did not represent the great majority of the Irish people and had no right to state support. In the following year he courageously began the solution of the Irish land question by passing an Act which gave the tenant an interest in his holding, security so long as he paid his rent, and the right to sell his interest on quitting possession. It did not, however, give fixity of tenure or enable the tenant to secure the fixing of a fair rent. Gladstone apparently believed that these measures had practically settled the Irish question. They were in fact only a prelude to his final labours in that dangerous field. Ten years later, during his second administration, he found himself faced with the demands of Parnell's new party and he decided on the one hand to concede the Irish tenants' claim to the three F's, Fair Rent, Fixity of Tenure, and Free Sale, and, on the other hand, to deal firmly with the campaign of agrarian outrage which had broken out in Ireland. So on 25th April, 1881, the eve of my birth, the second reading debate opened of the Land Bill of 1881, an historic and revolutionary measure which not only granted the three F's, but also reduced rents in general by twenty per cent. and provided for a further reduction after fifteen years. Parnell, however, was not to be appeased by what he regarded as a half-measure. He soon made it clear that his demands went far beyond land reform and that he would be satisfied only by the concession of full political freedom. Speaking at Cork in September, 1881, he prophetically reminded the British Government that " those who want to preserve the golden link of the Crown must see to it that it shall be the only link connecting England and Ireland." He also refused to slow down the agrarian agitation and used the new Land Act as a lever to obtain further concessions.

In October Gladstone struck back. Parnell and his principal lieutenants were arrested and confined in Kilmainham Gaol, without trial, under special coercive powers. Agrarian outrages rapidly increased. As Parnell had prophesied, " Captain Moonlight " took his place. Moreover, his extreme supporters insisted on the publication of a manifesto calling on the tenants to pay no rent until the Government had restored the constitutional rights of the people. Finally an informal agreement was arrived at between Gladstone and Parnell, Justin McCarthy and later Captain O'Shea acting as go-betweens. This pact, or rather understanding, somewhat inaccurately described as the Kilmainham Treaty, provided in effect that if Parnell and his followers were released and the Government passed an Act cancelling the tenants' arrears of rent, Parnell would withdraw the " No Rent " manifesto, advise the tenants to settle with the landlords, and generally slow down the agitation. So on 2nd May, 1882, Parnell and his fellow prisoners were released. Four days later Lord Frederick Cavendish, the new Irish Chief Secretary, and the Irish Under Secretary, Mr. Burke, were stabbed to death by a gang of assassins as they were quietly strolling home through the Phœnix Park, Dublin. Everything was at once thrown back into the melting pot of hatred and despair. Parnell became overnight the most hated and feared man in England, while in Ireland the reaction, in a different way, was equally violent. My father, as his diary records, was plunged into despair. He writes of " the horrible news which will do fearful damage to this unfortunate country." In Cork the shops were closed in mourning and all decent people stood aghast. Once more, as so often before and since in Irish history, criminals had in a few moments undone the patient work of statesmen.

But Ireland climbed slowly back out of the pit of degradation. Parnell, who in the first moments of horror had offered his resignation to Gladstone and seems to have contemplated retiring from public life, took up again the fight for Irish liberty. In January 1885, he came to Cork on a visit to his constituents and stayed with my father. When he arrived at the station the people, wild with enthusiasm, took the horses from his carriage and drew it to my father's house. From the nursery windows, high up at the top of the house, I watched the dramatic scene. First the bands—which I am afraid interested me more than Parnell—then his carriage drawn by cheering people; one could almost have walked on their heads they were packed so tight along the Mardyke avenue below. It was with some difficulty that Parnell, with my father's assistance, finally reached the house. Then he went to the window, threw it up and in a few pithy words thanked the people and sent them away delighted. It was indeed a memorable scene. That night he spoke at the Cork Opera House. It was the eve of a General Election, the first to be fought since the extension of household suffrage to Ireland in the previous year. It was thus a testing time for the new movement in Ireland. For two years Parnell had been virtually silent, flashing only occasionally like a searchlight across the darkened political sky. Now both British parties once more hung on his words and he sounded the tocsin of war in a speech which made history. " We cannot," he said, " ask for less than the restitution of Grattan's Parliament with its important privileges and wide far-reaching constitution. We cannot, under the British Constitution, ask for more than the restitution of Grattan's Parliament. But no man has the right to fix the boundary of the march of a nation. No man has the right to say " Thus far shalt thou go and no further ; and we have never attempted to fix the *ne plus ultra* to the progress of Ireland's nationhood and we never shall." This final sentence now stands in letters of bronze on his monument in O'Connell Street, Dublin, as the epitome of his political faith. Like many great political aphorisms it has often been misinterpreted and misapplied by smaller men. I can still recollect him as I saw him for a few moments the following day—the tall slender figure, the handsome aquiline features, the slightly unkempt beard and piercing eyes. His clear voice had a distinctly English accent. Outwardly unemotional and reserved, he probably took little interest in children and I am sure he was as much relieved as I was when I was removed.

That night he had promised to lecture to the Young Ireland Society on Irish history. He candidly confessed to my father that he knew nothing about the subject and asked for some books to read. The lecture was to begin at eight o'clock. A quarter of an hour beforehand he retired to his room with writing materials and the books. An hour later my father anxiously inquired if he wanted further information. Parnell looked up smiling and said he was ready. He had made some notes in big handwriting on a few sheets of paper. " I think I shall be able to say something now," he said. They arrived at the lecture hall an hour and a quarter late, but nevertheless he received a magnificent reception. He dominated the scene and proceeded to deliver his lecture, which was punctuated by continual applause and eventually became a political speech. Coming home he was as proud as a child of the whole performance, " I think " he said " that I got through very well." My father, knowing how the lecture had been prepared, was so nervous that he could hardly listen properly to its delivery. Parnell was not, however, in the least perturbed. " He did not," said my father long afterwards to Barry O'Brien, Parnell's biographer, " seem to have the faintest notion that people looked up to him, not only as the greatest man in Ireland, but one of the most remarkable men in Europe. He spoke like a young man making his début at a debating society. I can see him now walking upstairs to bed with the candle in his hand, stepping quietly and lightly so as to disturb no one. He was like a young

fellow who had come home late and was afraid to wake
' the governor.' Yet with all his self-depreciation, modesty
and gentleness you always felt that you were in the presence
of a master."

Another historic incident which took place that year also
remains in my memory. In April the Prince and Princess
of Wales visited Ireland. Political feeling ran high. Parnell
advised that the royal visitors should be treated with polite
indifference. In Dublin his advice was followed. Thereupon *The Times* boasted that the royal party was received
everywhere with enthusiasm, that Parnellism was a sham
and that Ireland was loyal. The South determined to give
Ireland's answer. At Mallow station William O'Brien, at
the head of a deputation, tried to read an address to the
Prince setting out Ireland's demands. He and his friends
were promptly batoned off the platform by the police, band
instruments being smashed and heads broken outside the
royal carriage. In Cork worse followed. Black flags were
waved in the visitors' faces, rotten eggs and cabbages were
thrown at the procession. Cavalry charged and people
were injured. The Riot Act was read. From a platform at
the end of our garden overlooking the road I saw the Prince
and Princess—surrounded by an escort of hussars—drive
quickly past alternately boohed and cheered, the Princess
as pale as a sheet, the Prince trying to look unconcerned.
Ireland, he must have reflected, was far from loyal, Parnellism not altogether a sham. It was an exciting and interesting
day—the 15th April, 1885.

As the General Election approached it became clear that
the Irish question dominated the field. Lord Carnarvon,
the Conservative Viceroy of Ireland, probably with Lord
Salisbury's acquiescence, sought an interview with Parnell
in an empty London house in order to ascertain his views.
Gladstone, in the famous Hawarden manifesto, whilst still
adhering to vague generalities, pleaded for a reconciliation
between England and Ireland, insisting that "every grant
to portions of the country of enlarged powers for the management of their own affairs is in my view not a source of
danger but a means of averting it, and is in the nature of a

new guarantee for increased cohesion, happiness and
strength " : adding " I believe history and posterity will
consign to disgrace the memory of every man, be he who
he may, on whichever side of the Channel he may dwell,
that, having the power to aid in all equitable arrangements
between Ireland and Great Britain, shall use the power, not
to aid, but to prevent or retard it." But Parnell—anxious
to secure the balance of power—directed the Irish voters
in Great Britain to vote solidly for the Conservatives. In
the light of subsequent events this decision may seem to
have been wrong ; but it should be remembered that
Parnell had to preserve the balance upon which his parliamentary power depended, that Gladstone had not yet
committed himself to Home Rule and that Chamberlain,
his principal lieutenant, was seeking to dictate unsatisfactory
terms to Ireland. Had Gladstone secured the support of
the Irish vote his Government would probably have been
strong enough to survive the defection of Chamberlain and
his followers which eventually led to the defeat of the Home
Rule Bill and the fall of his administration. The result of
the election gave the Liberals a majority of 82 over the
Conservatives. The 86 votes of Parnell's party thus held
the balance. Only one Irish county, Antrim, had voted
solid against Home Rule.

My father had been pressed by Parnell to stand with him
for Cork, which returned two members, but my mother
intervened and prevented him from doing so. She was
undoubtedly right, for he had neither the aptitude nor the
temperament for parliamentary life. Finally, another young
solicitor, Maurice Healy, brother of the more famous, but
certainly not more able, Tim, was selected and elected. He
was a wise and prudent counsellor and subsequently gave
valuable service to Cork and Ireland during a long political
career. After the election Parnell wrote the following letter,
which, as it records his estimate of my father's services, may
properly be given here :

Irish Parliamentary Offices,
Palace Chambers,
9 Bridge Street,
London, S.W.
December 17, 1885.

My Dear Mr. Horgan,

I have to thank you very much for your letter also for the kind enquiries contained therein. I have been staying at the seaside recuperating after the hard and anxious work of preparing for the conventions, and the more recent fatigue of the election contests themselves, which combined had thrown my physical strength somewhat back. This absence prevented my earlier attention to your letter. Kindly accept my sincere gratitude for the able manner in which you conducted the Cork election and attended to my interests in my absence. It will always be to me a matter of regret that you could not see your way to take your place in the ranks of that body of gentlemen who I am convinced are destined in the near future to win the legislative independence of our country.

Yours very truly,

CHAS. S. PARNELL.

Parnell's hopes seemed not unjustified. Before the end of January, 1886, the Conservative Government had been defeated by the united Liberal and Nationalist vote and the stage was set for the introduction of the first Home Rule Bill.

IV

IT has always seemed to me that the chief contribution of British political genius to the modern world, has been the creation of the union of free peoples known as the British Commonwealth. The lack of generosity and wisdom shown by the younger Pitt in his Irish policy struck a potent, and perhaps, a deadly blow, at the hope of bringing Ireland freely and fully into that magic circle. Coleridge, the poet and philosopher, wrote prophetically in 1831 : " Mr. Pitt has received great credit for effecting the Union, but I believe it will sooner or later be discovered that the manner in which, and the terms upon which he effected it, made it the most fatal blow that was ever levelled against the peace and prosperity of England."

It was this tragic blunder which Gladstone now sought to undo. To other English statesmen Ireland had represented only a series of difficult and irritating problems such as land reform, the suppression of agrarian crime or the healing of religious discord. Gladstone was unique in realising that there was one supreme problem which transcended all the others, namely to find the best method of enabling the Irish people to settle their own problems themselves. From first to last he thought of the Irish not as farmers or Catholics but as a people. Above all, in his dealings with Ireland, he displayed at its best the great English virtue of magnanimity. Again and again he refused to be deflected from the course which he believed to be right by Irish hostility or ingratitude. His aim was to give Ireland self-respect and England security. Everything else became secondary to that great dual purpose. His efforts to establish good relations between the two countries by the disestablishment of the Protestant Church and agrarian reform had not succeeded, but he now saw at once the possibilities for good of the new movement in Ireland. He had studied Irish history to some purpose and he was convinced that a great

33

wrong had been done to the Irish people by his country. He believed he could persuade his fellow countrymen to right that wrong and he knew that its continuation could not be justified to the outside world. To that end he dedicated his declining years. How great and far-seeing were his plans is only now fully apparent.

His action immediately after the election of 1885 was characteristic. He rightly believed that the proper approach to a settlement was by the joint action of the two great English parties and that it would be a public calamity " if this great subject should fall into the lines of party conflict." With this object in view he offered the Conservative Government of Lord Salisbury his disinterested support in seeking a solution. There can be little doubt that this was one of the most fateful moments in Anglo-Irish history and that, had his offer been accepted, the entire future of the two countries, and perhaps even of Europe itself, might have taken a happier and more natural course. But it was not to be. Lord Salisbury's Government refused to consider the proposal. As in the case of Pitt's commercial resolutions of 1785, another of the rare and irrevocable opportunities of really uniting the two countries in purpose and spirit was lost.

Gladstone had waited a whole month, refusing to embark on negotiations with Parnell (although in touch with him through Mrs. O'Shea) and patiently hoping against hope for an agreed solution. Now that his offer was refused he had no alternative but to act. On 26th January, 1886, the Conservative Government was defeated and Gladstone formed an administration whose main purpose was to give Ireland self-government. The issue was soon knit. Bismarck, the Prussian Chancellor, had just embarked on that policy of repression and expropriation in Poland which sowed the seed for the bloody harvest of 1939. *The Times*—then and afterwards the deadly enemy of Parnell—in a leading article of 11th February, 1886, commended Bismarck's policy as suitable for application to Ireland. A few months later, whilst the Home Rule Bill was under discussion, Lord Salisbury, in a speech worthy of Hitler

himself, having by inference compared the Irish to Hotten-
tots, put forward the view that only people of Teutonic race
were fit for self-government. His hardly original solution
for the Irish problem was twenty years of resolute government. Such was the alignment of ideas in this grave debate.

The Home Rule Bill of 1886, viewed in the light of modern
developments, may perhaps seem a small and grudging
measure ; but in fact at that time it was both wide and
generous. Had it been passed into law it would undoubtedly
have provided a clear and direct road to full self-government
for Ireland and to friendly relations between the two
countries, a road now partially closed by the political
division of the smaller island. The freedom which Ireland
has since won from England by force would then have grown
naturally from free development and experience. The tragic
division which has arisen between English and Irish political
thought would have been bridged or avoided, and Irish
national life might have developed in a spirit of broad yet
critical enthusiasm instead of becoming, as it has, self-
centred, suspicious, and remote. Björnson, the great
Norwegian writer, said with truth that the Home Rule Bill
of 1886 was the greatest example of the politics of the heart
in the world—for it showed a great nation acting justly
from choice and not from necessity.

There were in fact three courses now open to an English
government, namely—to leave things as they were with
Ireland in a state of dormant revolt, to embark on a scheme
of limited federal devolution with local parliaments or
councils throughout the United Kingdom, or to grant
Ireland alone a form of self-government which might
develop into the fuller freedom of an equal state. It was this
last course, which would have fitted into the future Commonwealth, that Gladstone took. The Bill provided for the
establishment of a separate Irish parliament of two chambers,
with a separate government dependent upon it, both being
competent only in Irish—as opposed to Imperial—affairs,
and subject to the over-riding jurisdiction of the British
Crown and Parliament. Irish representation at Westminster was to cease. There would be no separate fiscal

system, post office, coinage or army. Provision was made for the special protection of minorities. The police were to come under the control of the Irish executive only after a period of probation. Parnell accepted these proposals as a settlement. He abandoned his claim for a restitution of Grattan's parliament, if, indeed, he had ever seriously set it up or understood its implications. The prophetic trend of his mind was indicated by his remark to Morley, " Once we have a parliament all the rest follows."

But now the personal element, so often more potent than principle in political life, intervened with disastrous results. Gladstone and Parnell had unfortunately both overlooked, and then underestimated, the peculiar purpose and power of another prominent politician—Joseph Chamberlain. Looking back now one can see that the subsequent clash of personalities was almost inevitable. Gladstone, then in his seventy-eighth year, found himself trying to steer a course between Scylla and Charybdis : on the one hand Chamberlain the clever, intriguing, unscrupulous and ambitious manufacturer from Birmingham, a true product of the industrial revolution, who had no real sympathy with the Irish claim for full self-government, and whose aim was to kill the Home Rule Bill : on the other hand, Parnell, the cool, yet passionate, reserved, suspicious Anglo-Irish squire imbued with all the arrogance of his caste, yet a man of honour and a disinterested patriot, inheriting from his mother, who was of Irish-American revolutionary stock, a deep hatred of English dominion, but himself, ironically enough, in all essential attributes, an Englishman. Gladstone, descended from a family of Liverpool East India merchants of Scottish origin, educated at Eton and Oxford, a scholar whose chief recreation was the study of Homer and Dante, a statesman who sought to apply the principles of Christianity to political problems, had little in common with these two ruthless and relatively uncultured personalities. His remote, sensitive, and rather subtle mind had no real contact with theirs. Even during the preparation of the Bill he had only one interview with Parnell, the negotiations being conducted by John Morley. Chamberlain, during the previous year, had, through the sinister channel of Captain O'Shea, engaged in negotiations with Parnell and had contemplated a visit to Ireland in the company of his colleague Dilke. But the negotiations had broken down, largely owing to O'Shea's mismanagement, and the visit to Ireland had fallen through because of the injudicious attacks made on Chamberlain and Dilke by *United Ireland*, the Nationalist paper. Gladstone, moreover, had hurt Chamberlain's pride by refusing his request for the post of Colonial Secretary, and by appointing Morley, his junior in years and experience, as Irish Secretary.

As soon as the details of the Home Rule Bill came to be discussed, it became clear that Gladstone and Chamberlain could not agree, and Gladstone took little trouble to avoid the breach. The ostensible difference arose over the question whether the Irish members should remain at Westminster or not, a point on which Chamberlain insisted. But, in the light of subsequent developments, it may be doubted whether concession even on this vital point would have placated him or saved the Bill. Finally Chamberlain resigned, the Liberal party was disrupted and, on 7th June, 1886, the Bill was defeated at the end of the second reading debate. At the subsequent General Election the Conservative Party was triumphant. A Land Purchase Bill, which Gladstone had introduced as a necessary corollary to Home Rule, had been previously withdrawn owing to Chamberlain's opposition. The Irish landlords were never again offered such a generous settlement.

A few days before the Home Rule Bill met its doom I had arrived in London with my great aunt on my second visit to England. I was just five years old. We travelled by one of the Cork Steam Packet boats to Bristol, but the tide was out when we reached the mouth of the Avon and as the steamer could not proceed up the river we had to land from a boat at the little village of Portishead. From the windows of a four-wheeler cab, in which we drove from Paddington station to Clapham, where my grandmother lived, I gazed enraptured on the busy streets, and watched the cabs and buses passing in a steady stream. It did not seem possible that so many people, carriages, and horses could exist. I was in due course taken to see the various sights and astonished my relatives by recognising the Houses of Parliament and Westminster Abbey, having seen them already in the *Illustrated London News*, which was our favourite nursery periodical. But the two places which pleased me most were the Crystal Palace, that glass relic of the Victorian heyday, and the Zoo. At the Zoo I discovered that the wild beasts in the picture-books were after all not fictitious and that, although I was beginning to be sceptical about the existence of Father Christmas, the lion and the bear were as real as myself. I am afraid they interested me more than the decisions then being made at Westminster concerning the future of my country. In spite of these excitements, however, I soon became homesick and at the end of a fortnight returned to Ireland with such elation that I could hardly bid good-bye to my English relatives.

It was an Ireland in which politics had again become dynamic. In the late autumn of that year Parnell's lieutenants launched a new movement against landlordism which became known as the Plan of Campaign. They proposed in effect that, where a landlord refused a reasonable reduction of rent, the tenants should withhold payment and pay the equivalent of a fair rent into a common fund controlled by a committee which would then be in a position to fight or negotiate on a collective basis. This plan spread like wildfire through the South and West. The new Government had rejected a Land Bill, introduced by Parnell, which was designed to relieve the poorer tenants by wiping out arrears of rent. He warned them that its rejection would lead to renewed agitation and, although he did not approve of the Plan of Campaign, his warning was now proved right. The Government was soon forced to abandon all hope of governing by the ordinary law and a permanent Coercion Act was added to the statute book. The ensuing struggle lasted from 1887 to 1889. Public meetings were suppressed, whole districts placed under semi-martial law, members of parliament arrested, and juries either selected from the anti-Nationalist minority or, more frequently, suppressed completely. Evictions increased and the constant clashes between police and people revived the dormant feeling of hatred and distrust. The police acted on the most trivial pretexts. If a Land Leaguer looked hard at a constable he was brought before the magistrates. If he looked away from him significantly he was brought before them likewise. If a person laughed while passing a member of the Royal Irish Constabulary he was prosecuted. If he whistled in a policeman's presence he was prosecuted. If he did not move away fast enough when ordered he was prosecuted. If he moved away too fast he was prosecuted. This on the face of it sounds like an amusing exaggeration. It is in fact an exact description of Irish coercive measures in the eighties.

The Government, late in 1887, sought to calm the storm by passing a Land Act which granted most of the concessions that Parnell had demanded the year before. He had taken no part in the agitation in Ireland and was in fact very ill during most of this period. In the meantime a close alliance had been formed between the Irish Nationalist members and the Liberal party. Irish members spoke on Liberal platforms throughout England, and Liberal members visited Ireland to see things for themselves, very often it must be confessed through rose-coloured and romantic glasses. Bernard Shaw's " Tom Broadbent " must have been born about this time. In Ireland Gladstone's name was honoured and his picture became a familiar sight in the homes of the people ; but Parnell remained distrustful and suspicious. On one occasion my father, noticing his silence about Gladstone, asked him what he thought of the old statesman. " I think," he answered coldly, " of Mr. Gladstone and the English people what I have always thought of them. They will do what we can make them do." This answer revealed the gulf which still yawned, and was indeed never bridged, between the English statesman and the Irish leader. It was this atmosphere which helped to make possible the disaster of 1890. Parnell, in fact, stood apart from his party in these years. He disliked going on English platforms, he shunned English society. He sought no advice and relied on his own strength and judgment. Bad health and his relations with Mrs. O'Shea, which were now notorious in political circles, helped to accentuate these tendencies. It seems clear that they were further aggravated by his fear of Gladstone's political ability and experience, which gave him a feeling of inferiority.

Meanwhile the struggle in Ireland went on and my father was in the thick of it all, attending meetings, and defending the interests of the tenants on the Ponsonby and other estates where the Plan of Campaign was now in force. One relatively trivial incident which took place in 1887, impressed itself on my childish memory and was typical of the times. It was the year of Queen Victoria's Jubilee and my brother George and I had been presented by my father's tailor, an old and charming gentleman of loyalist sympathies, with medals commemorating that historic event. With much delight we pinned them on our coats. Immediately afterwards our innocent mother took us into an adjacent hotel to visit William O'Brien, who had recently been elected member for Mallow. O'Brien, a brilliant journalist and fiery Nationalist demagogue, was one of those people to whom everything was either black or white. He lived in a world of romantic extremes. Tim Healy once said of him in my presence that if there was a mouse-hole in the room and O'Brien saw it, it instantly became the cave of Ali Baba and the Forty Thieves. On this occasion his reaction to our Jubilee medals was immediate and extreme. No sooner did he see them than he wrenched them from our coats with an expression of horror and flung them into the fire. We were led away in tears, for we naturally did not comprehend the enormity of our unpatriotic conduct.

In the April of the following year O'Brien and Gilhooly, another Nationalist M.P., were imprisoned in the Cork City Gaol, not far from my father's house, for political offences. The local brass bands desired to serenade the prisoners, but the police prevented them from doing so. My father came to the rescue by permitting the bands to perform in his garden and so our Sunday afternoons were enlivened for some time by these patriotic musicians playing national airs or selections from such popular operas as *Maritana* and the

Bohemian Girl, then, as now, beloved by the Cork people. These performances were, of course, a never-ending source of interest and excitement to us, and five small heads peered from the nursery windows at the crowds below. Another sensation was provided by a great meeting in the Cork Park where William O'Brien boldly defied the Papal Rescript which had been promulgated against the Plan of Campaign. Three years earlier the Pope, at the instigation of the British envoy to the Vatican, had condemned the Parnell Tribute, a fund raised to relieve Parnell's financial anxieties on the suggestion of Dr. Croke, the patriotic Catholic Archbishop of Cashel. The only result had been that three times the amount required was subscribed by an indignant people. Now the condemnation of the Plan yielded a like result. The Irish people were not prepared to accept political dictation from Rome.

All through these years, 1888–90, the political tempo in Ireland gradually quickened. Things were moving towards a climax. The coercive measures were intensified. During a political meeting at Mitchelstown, County Cork, at which my father was present, three men were shot dead by the police. " Remember Mitchelstown " became a slogan of the supporters of Home Rule both in Ireland and England. But calumny was now added to coercion in an attempt to ruin Parnell. In 1887 *The Times* published a series of articles, under the general heading of " Parnellism and Crime," the purpose of which was to prove that Parnell and his party had been the instigators and abettors of assassination and outrage. In support of this charge it published letters purporting to be written by Parnell which, if true, would have established his complicity in crime. After some delay the Government, on Chamberlain's initiative and pressure, set up a Judicial Commission of three judges, all opponents of Home Rule, to inquire into these grave charges, but they placed at the disposal of *The Times* the whole machinery of Dublin Castle to smash Parnell. For months a dreary procession of spies, informers and police filed through the witness box of the Commission in London. Meanwhile the Irish were not idle. 'Led by Sir Charles Russell, an indomitable

Northern Irishman who had terminated his retainer
from *The Times* in order to defend his countrymen, a team
of brilliant advocates appeared for Parnell and his colleagues.
Amongst them was a young Liberal member of Parliament,
Herbert Henry Asquith, who was eventually as Prime
Minister to introduce the last ill-fated Home Rule Bill.
Michael Davitt, Tim Healy and some other members of the
Irish Party conducted their own defence.   Behind these
front line forces many unknown soldiers, amongst whom
was my father, prepared material for cross-examination
and for the Irish answer to what was virtually the indictment
of a nation.   Finally, in February, 1889, the vital issue was
reached.   Richard Pigott, the fraudulent Dublin journalist,
who had brought the letters to *The Times* agents, was at
last called to give evidence.   Broken by the brilliant cross-
examination of Sir Charles Russell the wretched forger, for
he was the criminal as the Irish knew, fled to Madrid and
committed suicide.   When the Commission subsequently
refused to investigate the activities of the Loyal and
Patriotic Union which had financed Pigott, the Irish Party's
lawyers quite properly refused to take any further part in
the proceedings, but not before Sir Charles Russell had
delivered a speech which was both the vindication of a
people and a masterpiece of eloquence.   The subsequent
proceedings of the Commission dragged their weary length
along but the decisive battle had been fought and won—
Parnell had been vindicated.   In February, 1890, the Commissioners brought in their report, which had already been
anticipated by public opinion and which completely
acquitted Parnell and his party of complicity in crime.
During the same month *The Times* paid him a sum of £5,000
as damages for libel.   The great city of Edinburgh presented him with its freedom.   England was at his feet.
The triumph of the Home Rule cause, which Gladstone
was once more preparing to champion at the polls, seemed
inevitable.   " There is only one way," said Parnell, to an
enthusiastic audience of that famous Liberal organisation,
the Eighty Club, " in which you can govern Ireland within
the Constitution, and that is by allowing her to govern

herself in all those matters which cannot interfere with the greatness and well being of the Empire of which she forms a part."

But, at this moment when his triumph seemed complete, his political enemies struck again. In December, 1889, Captain O'Shea instituted proceedings for divorce against his wife, citing Parnell as co-respondent. The trial took place in November, 1890. There was no defence. "I would rather appear to be dishonourable than be dishonourable," Parnell said to his colleagues a few weeks later during the historic meetings in Committee Room 15. The meaning of these apparently enigmatic words has now at last been made clear. O'Shea was in truth a dispossessed but not a deceived husband. This fact, though it made no moral difference, at any rate acquitted Parnell of treachery or deceit. In two powerful and illuminating books my friend Captain Henry Harrison, who was intimately associated with Parnell during that last tragic year, has vindicated his memory and cleared his name of dishonour. He proves that O'Shea was fully aware, during the whole period of its existence, of his wife's liaison with Parnell, that he derived both pecuniary and political advantage from its continuation, and that he deliberately perjured himself in denying his connivance when giving evidence in the Divorce Court. It follows that the divorce proceedings must have been instituted with an ulterior motive, since they could not possibly have succeeded if seriously opposed. Parnell refused to plead the obvious and conclusive defence of O'Shea's collusion for the good reason that it would have been successful, and so have prevented him from marrying Mrs. O'Shea. O'Shea must have been sure that this would happen when he launched the proceedings. There can be little doubt now that he was the chosen tool of others; and all the available indications suggest that his friend, that malicious, ambitious and unscrupulous politician, Joseph Chamberlain, hungry for power and office, was foremost in the initiation and planning of the blow.

The first public reactions to this revelation of Parnell's apparent duplicity were inconclusive and misleading. The

National League Council, representing the Irish Nationalist organisations, pledged itself to his support in spite of the divorce proceedings. A great meeting at the Leinster Hall, Dublin, at which Tim Healy declared amidst tumultuous cheers that " Parnell was less a man than an institution," affirmed enthusiastically the people's confidence in his leadership. On 25th November, 1890, the Irish Party, meeting in the House of Commons, unanimously re-elected him as chairman. Yet all was not well. The very support thus given to Parnell only fostered his belief in his strength and led to his eventual undoing. Two members of the Irish party, however, at once spoke out honestly on purely moral grounds and refused to follow Parnell. They were Michael Davitt and T. D. Sullivan. Viewed against the purely expedient manoeuvres of many other members of that body, their honesty of purpose and action shines " like a good deed in a naughty world."

Parnell's enemies, however, were exultant. *The Times* proclaimed that no statesman could survive the blow of having such a charge proved against him in open court. Chamberlain attacked the Liberal leaders for their delay in denouncing Parnell's adultery. Gladstone at first remained silent. He watched events develop as a politician and not as a censor of morals. A man who had been a colleague of Palmerston and Hartington could not suggest that adultery was a bar to public office. But it soon became clear that the Nonconformists, who were in effect the backbone of the Liberal Party, thought otherwise. Cardinal Manning, also, was urging both Gladstone and the Irish Catholic Hierarchy to take action. Gladstone finally made up his mind to act. He made ineffective attempts to get into touch with Parnell. The lack of any intimate personal contact between the two leaders was now to prove disastrous. Failing a personal interview with Parnell, he wrote a letter to Morley, in which, only at the last minute request of his colleagues, he inserted the all important sentence that the continuance of Parnell's leadership of the Irish Party would render his own retention of the Liberal leadership, based, as it had been mainly upon the prosecution of the Irish cause, almost a nullity. The hasty publication of this letter was the first blunder in a tragedy of errors. The Irish Party, who had been quite ignorant of Gladstone's view when they re-elected Parnell, were now forced to decide the issue. Parnell replied to Gladstone in a fierce, and indeed unfair, manifesto in which he disclosed the purport of his confidential talks with Gladstone and Morley and charged the Liberal leaders with an attempt to cheat the Irish people out of a full measure of Home Rule—although he had in fact, shortly after these interviews, publicly expressed his confidence in Gladstone. This, he told the Irish, was the measure of the loss with which they were threatened unless they consented to throw him to the English wolves now howling for his destruction. These were terrible and decisive words which made any compromise impossible. The Irish Catholic Hierarchy, three weeks after the divorce court verdict, now added their condemnation of his conduct to Gladstone's ultimatum. This was in many ways the final blow. At fierce meetings in Committee Room 15 the Irish Party fought the matter out whilst the Irish people, breathless with anxiety, waited without. Parnell sought vainly to ride the whirlwind. His genius for strategy was never more apparent. Like Napoleon after Dresden he seemed for a moment to have snatched victory from the jaws of defeat when he persuaded his party to seek assurances from Gladstone, Harcourt and Morley as to the powers to be granted an Irish Parliament in the next Home Rule Bill. The Liberal leaders now made a further error. Resenting Parnell's conduct and language and the proposal that the Irish delegates should meet the three leaders instead of Gladstone alone, they refused, on the treacherous instigation of Healy and the other anti-Parnellite leaders, to discuss the matter further until the Irish had decided the question of their leadership. This refusal brought matters to a head and, on 6th December, 1890, the Irish Party, that fine weapon of tempered steel which Parnell had forged and used with such matchless skill, broke in two, forty-five members declaring themselves against Parnell, twenty-two supporting him.

Looking back through the veil of time, which has softened bitterness and eliminated hatred, one can realise that there were serious faults and mistakes made on both sides. The truth is that the Irish members, without any choice on their part, were faced with one of the most heart-rending problems ever presented to a body of patriotic politicians. These, for the most part, humble, self-educated men, nearly all Catholics, confronted by the immoral and apparently disgraceful conduct of their cherished leader, were challenged at the same time by Gladstone's ultimatum and the condemnation of their Church. The alternatives before them were hard and bitter, whichever road they chose. It is small wonder they broke under the strain and that bitter confusion fell upon them. Those who thought that Parnell's leadership could not be preserved without ruining the Irish cause were undoubtedly in their own way as honest, if not perhaps as consistent, as those who believed he was indispensable. Their gravest error was their initial and uncritical support of Parnell's leadership which made his subsequent withdrawal almost impossible. Yet Gladstone himself had hesitated to intervene or condemn until it was too late. To both sides in that epic struggle we Irish of this generation, who have experienced a similar tragic division, enacted without a Parnell but with rifles and machine-guns, must extend our understanding and sympathy. Nor must we think too hardly of Gladstone. For to this old man of eighty-one, who had dedicated the end of his life to the emancipation of Ireland, the blow, as he wrote to his friend Acton, was the heaviest he had ever received. His mistakes in handling this grave matter were errors of judgment, not the calculated schemes of a Macchiavelli. His sole and consistent aim was the preservation of the integrity of his party on which the success of his Irish policy rested. And even afterwards he went on with the fight for Ireland to the end. Irishmen should, therefore, not misjudge him nor allow the memory of these tragic events to obscure his unselfish service to their country.

These tremendous happenings had their repercussions in our Cork home. All Ireland was at once split into two fiercely hostile camps. My father, without a moment's doubt or hesitation, stood by Parnell. Almost at once a parliamentary vacancy occurred at Kilkenny, and Parnell determined to run a candidate against Sir John Pope Hennessy, who was the nominee of the Anti-Parnellites, as those opposing Parnell were now called. He chose Mr. Vincent Scully, a Catholic landlord from Tipperary, and wrote to my father asking him to conduct the election on his behalf. On 11th December Parnell came south to Cork. He was received by the people with all the old affection and enthusiasm. Cork, at least, had not wavered in its allegiance. He stayed at my father's house that night and I shall never forget his appearance as I saw him standing before the fire in the dining-room just after he arrived. He looked like a hunted fugitive, his hair dishevelled, his beard unkempt, his eyes wild and restless. My father made some vehement remark about those who had deserted him, and the hatred in Parnell's face was terrible to look upon. My mother received him in her kindly, gentle way as if nothing had happened. She had some supper ready but he would take nothing but some raw eggs. Next morning he asked my father to try to arrange an interview for him with Sir John Arnott, a rich Cork merchant of liberal views, in order to induce him to buy the Ponsonby estate and reinstate the evicted tenants. Finding a private interview would under the circumstances be impossible, he dropped the project. That day he and my father travelled to Kilkenny together.

The election lasted ten days. During that time Parnell showed wonderful vigour for a man in failing health. He went from end to end of the constituency, speaking, working, directing, returning each night much fatigued, retiring early to rest, and coming down again next morning full of fight and energy. " While I have my life," he said two days before the polling, " I will go from one constituency to another, from one city to another, from one town and village and parish to another, to put what I know is the truth before the people." At Castlecomer, where the rival parties clashed and where lime was thrown in his eyes, Davitt sent a message proposing that they should speak from the same

platform and answer each other's speeches. " Tell him,"
said Parnell with a grim smile, " that I have come to fight,
not to treat." My father conducted the campaign. For a
whole week he did not get to bed and had to content himself with snatches of sleep on a sofa in a committee-room.
The result was, however, a foregone conclusion, for the priests
had thrown all their influence against Parnell. Scully was
defeated by more than a thousand votes and Parnell left
Kilkenny a beaten man. He had no delusions as to the
struggle before him but he was determined to fight to the
end. My father kept in close touch with him through the
bitter months which followed. On St. Patrick's Day, 1891,
he stayed with us for the last time. He had come to Cork
to attend a meeting and banquet in celebration of the
national festival. My father and he stayed talking together
late into the night about the past and the future. He told
my father that night that he foresaw the failure of Gladstone's
Irish policy and, in that event, he said, the only course for
the Irish representatives to follow would be to return to
Ireland and, by organising a policy of civil disobedience,
make the government of the country impossible. Military
opposition to England he considered impracticable and
hopeless. A quarter of a century later the Sinn Féin party
followed virtually this policy.

Another dramatic event occurred in Cork in a few days
later and remains in my memory. On Good Friday, 27th
March, 1891, whilst Judge Monroe was trying five
Nationalist politicians at the Cork Court House for complicity in the Tipperary riots of 1890, the building took
fire and was burnt down. It was the first time a court had
sat there on that sacred day. As the Union Jack, which
flew over the portico, fluttered down into the flames, the
crowd in the street below cheered wildly. That cheer had
literary results for it was this incident which inspired
Rudyard Kipling, a young and then almost unknown poet,
to write his ballad *The Flag of England* which contains his
best known line—perhaps the best known line in modern
English poetry—" What should they know of England who
only England know?"

For me, now ten years old, the summer which followed was made memorable by my first visit to France. There I began to learn French history, as it can best be learned, in the streets of Paris. Conducted by my Jersey great-aunt I revived my knowledge of French, dined in the little restaurants of the Palais Royal, visited the churches, the picture galleries and the great white votive church of the Sacré Coeur, then just completed; went shopping in the Bon Marché, the mother of all department stores, and drove through the Bois de Boulogne to Versailles. At Gouville, a little country place near Coutances in the Manche, I learnt something of that peasant life and economy which is the basis of both the strength and weakness of France. From the roof of Coutances Cathedral, the most Norman of all French churches, I looked down over the hills and woods, the farms and fields of Normandy whence one line of my ancestors had come and whose warriors had been the real conquerors of Ireland. Amid these hedgerows and orchards was to be fought fifty-three years latter the decisive battle for the liberation of Europe. From Granville we crossed by coasting steamer to Jersey where, in my uncle's house at St. Helier, I met new cousins with whom I roamed through the wooded lanes and along the rocky shores of that then fortunate isle.

In Ireland things were now moving rapidly towards their appointed end. Appealing to the extreme elements, whom he had previously held in check, Parnell had been beaten in two more by-elections. Deserted even by some of his friends, rushing backwards and forwards between Dublin and Brighton, his frail physical strength finally gave way. He took seriously ill with rheumatic fever and died at Brighton on 6th October, 1891. The political assassins who had persuaded O'Shea to strike had succeeded beyond their wildest hopes. They had wrecked Gladstone's plans, disrupted the Irish people and killed Parnell.

All Ireland stood aghast at the tragic news. The life of the country seemed to have ceased with his. In Cork, business was paralysed, shops closed, strong men cried in the streets. Even his political enemies stood dismayed at this frightful climax to their campaign against him. He had died, as he had promised, fighting to the end. My father came home that night utterly broken down. I had never seen him cry before and it was terrible to see. He had with him *United Ireland*, Parnell's paper, but he could not read it. He asked me to read out the dramatic leading article on " the dead chief." Even I, who could not fully realise the issues involved, felt the loss Ireland had sustained. I read the article, full of impassioned denunciation of the men who had hounded Parnell to his death. It made a bitter and lasting impression on my childish memory—as indeed I expect my father intended it should.

On Sunday morning, 11th October, 1891, the mail steamer brought all that was mortal of Charles Stewart Parnell back to Ireland. A small band of faithful friends, amongst whom was my father, stood on the pier at Kingstown in the grey morning light to greet him for the last time. In the forenoon his body lay in state in the Dublin City Hall. " Dublin is true " he had said, and Dublin was true to the end. Rich and poor, merchant and artisan, passed in endless procession before the bier. That afternoon, followed by a vast concourse gathered from all parts of the country, they bore his remains to Glasnevin and laid him to rest. For fifty years his grave remained without a monument. But in 1940, on the initiative of Mr. Henry Boland, a committee, representing the few survivors of his party and their descendants, of which I was proud to be one, collected a fund and remedied this national disgrace. Had we waited much longer it would have been too late, for those who remembered him with pride and love were fast dwindling away. Over the green plot amidst the trees, where he lies with his indomitable mother, we raised a great unhewn stone of Wicklow granite on which is inscribed the one word " Parnell." No ornate or ordinary monument would, we felt, have commemorated the greatness of this man. For us he was " the Chief," and as a chieftain we honoured him.

V

The " Parnell Split " unfortunately did not end with the death of Parnell. It continued for ten unhappy years. During that period, in which I grew to manhood, families were divided, friendships were broken, and even religion was degraded by this political upheaval and its aftermath. " I would prefer," wrote my father in his diary on the day of Parnell's funeral " to be poor Parnell in his coffin than Tim Healy." These bitter words reflected the thoughts and feelings of many Irishmen at this time. Healy had been my father's intimate friend and colleague, yet for ten years they never spoke to each other, until in 1902 they met by chance at the Cork Exhibition and a reconciliation was effected. Some years earlier a common friend had urged Healy, when on a visit to Cork, to call at my father's office and make friends, but Tim had wisely refused, saying " the nail's rusty yet."

During the stormy debates in Committee Room No. 15 Healy's emotional and somewhat unstable nature had led him to use language towards Parnell that was both offensive and unjustifiable. Strange as it may appear, it was, I think, more than a personal issue, for these two men respectively personified the proud Anglo-Irish ascendancy which had governed Ireland for two hundred years and the repressed Catholic peasantry now at last demanding their rights. In the subsequent struggle Healy's courage and daring mind made him the natural leader of those who opposed Parnell. Thirty-one years afterwards, when he became the first Governor-General of the Irish Free State in December, 1922, there were still people in Ireland who would not accept the new régime because of that fact. Yet when I sent him a sincere word of congratulation old memories were stirred and he replied " I know that you represent your late dear father in the kindly good wishes sped to me."

In spite of his bitter tongue he was in many ways a
lovable and brilliant personality. One of his colleagues
at the Bar, who was devoid of political animosity, once
described him to me with some exaggeration, as being like
a beautiful clock in which there was a wheel missing so that
when the hour struck nothing but a discordant noise was
heard. It would perhaps, be more accurate to say that
like many other clever Irishmen he too often relied on his
intuition to make good other deficiencies. His brother
Maurice, who had none of Tim's brilliance and never
engaged in intellectual fireworks, was a much abler
lawyer. Together they formed a formidable combination.
For many years they corresponded in shorthand nearly
every day and their letters were an almost complete
record of Irish political history from the inside. Tim
published many of his own in his book, *Letters and Leaders
of My Day*, but during the " Black and Tan " War of
1920–21 he unfortunately in a moment of panic destroyed
those of Maurice.

Tim's brilliant intellect was too often swayed by the
emotion of the moment. On one occasion I had an interesting experience of this idiosyncrasy. In 1917, the year after
my father's death, my brother George and I gave evidence
in the High Court in support of the testamentary capacity
of a farmer whose will was disputed on the grounds of
mental incapacity. Healy was one of the counsel for the
other side, and, after diligently cross-examining us and
other witnesses for the will, he proceeded to address the
jury. Having fiercely criticised the evidence of the other
witnesses he proceeded in these words : " Gentlemen of
the Jury, you have heard the evidence of Mr. John Horgan,
solicitor, and his brother. I knew their father. He was my
dear friend. No more respected and honourable member
of the legal profession was to be found in this country.
Gentlemen, his sons have followed in their father's foot-
steps." With that he passed on to other matters leaving
our evidence uncriticised. The Judge who was trying the
case, Mr. Justice Kenny, was a rather unemotional person
who had suffered from Tim's tongue when a Member of

Parliament. When in due course he came to sum up he said drily to the jury : " Gentlemen, the principal evidence in this case, which must decide your verdict, was given by the two legal gentlemen, who, at various times, took instructions from the deceased and eventually made his will. If you believe their evidence the deceased was in full possession of all his faculties and of full testamentary capacity. I do not personally know either of these gentlemen, but Mr. Healy, the counsel for the defendant, has told you that they are persons of the highest professional repute and he has not attempted to challenge their veracity. You will not doubt realise the importance of this fact." Needless to state the jury, after a few moments deliberation, found for the will without leaving the box.

But Healy's brilliant, and often irrelevant, advocacy could, sometimes, snatch victory from the jaws of defeat. On another occasion he was defending, on my instructions, a priest who had, on suspicion, foolishly accused a neighbouring farmer of robbing his house, and had consequently been sued for slander. The action was heard in 1920 when the country was much disturbed and the words complained of had been spoken to the police. The leading counsel on the other side was Tim's relative, Serjeant A. M. Sullivan, K.C., who, shortly before, had pointed out in a letter to the press that it was the duty of the public to support the civil authority and report all crime to the police. When Healy came to address the jury he began : " Gentlemen of the Jury, we have been recently told on high authority "— with a pointed look at the unfortunate Serjeant—" that when Mary steals your silver or Tim robs your garden it is your duty to inform the police. But, Gentlemen, what will happen if you do ? The learned Serjeant will slap a writ at you." And so on in like vein until the Serjeant, looking very angry fled the Court. The jury, delighted with Tim's extravagant and quite irrelevant onslaught, promptly disagreed.

This gift of finding and exposing his adversary's weak spot by unorthodox methods was coupled with a tremendous power of invective. Few who heard it will forget his fierce

denunciation of the *Irish Times* at the Cork Assizes during
March, 1904, in the action for libel brought against that
journal by a poor country priest whom it had wrongfully
accused of demanding excessive dues from his parishoners.
Healy knew there was no real defence to the action and so
in his opening address to the jury he let himself go. Alluding
to the attempts made to destroy the bonds uniting priests
and people he vehemently asked " What the rack of
Elizabeth and the sword of Cromwell could not accomplish
did this anonymous scribbler think he could achieve ? "
As he stood there in court his large pallid face and tufted
grey beard turned full towards the jury, his sombre eyes
blinking through the thick pince-nez glasses under the high
bald forehead, his wig pushed back, his low vibrant voice
dropping occasionally almost to a whisper as he passed in
a moment from vitriolic contempt to humorous derision,
one felt that this was not only the plea of an advocate but
the cry of an outraged people ! When he sat down the
Court adjourned and before it re-assembled the defendants
had agreed to apologise and pay a substantial sum by way
of damages. When I met him later on the same day and
congratulated him on his eloquence the *enfant terrible*
emerged and he murmured : " Yes they fortunately libelled
the *wrong* man."

Of Healy's ready and devastating wit many stories have
been told. Two which I can personally recollect may be
unfamiliar. Once I was sitting next to him in the Assize
Court at Cork while the judge, a benevolent person of
rather clerical appeaiance and unctuous address, was
delivering the usual charge to the Grand Jury concerning
the state of the county. During this discourse he sententi-
ously remarked : " On one occasion an old friend of mine,
a parish priest in the County Clare, said to me "—Quick
as a flash Tim, with a wicked gleam in his eye, turned to
me and said : " His fa-ather." On another occasion in
Dublin I was present in Court when he was appearing for
the defendant in an action for breach of promise of marriage.
A few weeks before, William O'Brien and himself, who at
that time were on opposite sides in politics, had met on a

wagonette or brake in Dundalk and indulged in a public
bout of personal invective. When Healy proceeded rather
ruthlessly, but quite properly, to cross-examine the plaintiff
concerning her amorous adventures, the leading counsel
on the other side, a gentleman notorious for his convivial
outbursts, interposed with the remark : " Please remember,
Mr. Healy, that you are not on a brake at Dundalk." " I
would rather," quickly and justly retorted Tim, " be on a
brake in Dundalk than on a bend in Rathmines." At this
stage the trial judge interposed and restored peace.

But to return to 1891. James Joyce in that dramatic
scene at the Christmas dinner table of Mr. Dedalus which
is described in his novel, *A Portrait of the Artist as a Young
Man*, recaptures the tense atmosphere of those days. The
dialogue between Mrs. Riordan, Mr. Dedalus and Mr.
Casey, there recorded, with its bitter language reproduces
only too well the scenes which then occurred in many
Irish homes. The religious acrimony which that passage
illustrates was the worst feature of the controversy. The
clergy embarked upon a vehement campaign against Parnell
and his followers. They were denounced from the altar,
and many became, for a time at least, estranged from the
Church. In Cork the people were counselled by one
preacher, whose zeal exceeded his Christianity, to let the
grass grow on the doorsteps of the Parnellites. My father,
in common with many others suffered for his political
beliefs. He lost several clerical friends and some clients.
It speaks well for his faith that, in spite of much provocation, he never ceased to be a firm practising Catholic.

On Parnell's death John Redmond became the leader of
those who still stood for maintaining a party of independent
Nationalists. This really great man, of whom I shall have
much to say as this narrative proceeds, was of Norman-
Celtic descent. One of his remote ancestors—Raymond
Fitzwilliam de Carew, called le Gros—had crossed with
Strongbow from Pembrokeshire to Ireland after the Norman
invasion, and Redmond himself with his hawk-like face,
strong Norman nose and short thick set figure might well
have stepped out of the Bayeux tapestry. Like Parnell he

belonged to the landowning class but, unlike Parnell, he was a Catholic and his ancestors had suffered for their faith. When it became possible for Catholics to sit again in parliament they resumed their place as public representatives. John Redmond's father, as member for Wexford, was a typical representative of the landowners who formed the majority of Butt's Home Rule party. Redmond himself was educated at Clongowes Wood College, the Jesuit public school in County Kildare, at a time when Irish education had not yet succumbed to the contagion of the Intermediate examination system. There he learned to love great literature and acquired that dignity, eloquence and integrity of character which subsequently established his position in the House of Commons as an orator and a statesman. " I was taught there," he once said of Clongowes, " by precept and example the lessons of truth, of chivalry and manliness. . . . to accept success without arrogance and defeat without repining." There too he learned how to serve his country without any thought of personal reward or even of gratitude, an ideal which remained with him untarnished and undiminished to the end. Leaving Clongowes he studied Law at Trinity College, Dublin, and afterwards became a clerk in the House of Commons where he learned at first hand lessons in parliamentary procedure and debate which subsequently stood him in good stead.

When his father, who had become a member of Parnell's growing party, died in 1880, Redmond, at Parnell's request, withdrew his candidature for Wexford in favour of Tim Healy, then a political prisoner. Three months later, at the age of twenty-three, he was returned unopposed for New Ross. He took his seat in the midst of Parnell's campaign of parliamentary obstruction. The next day he was suspended with the rest of the Irish Party. Shortly afterwards, with his brother William, who had joined him in parliament, he made a tour of Australia and America raising large sums of money for the Irish cause. This experience brought home to him the true meaning of the British Empire. At Melbourne, in July, 1883, he stated with strength and clarity the political belief which was to inspire his whole career and which indeed foretold the basis of the future British Commonwealth. Speaking of the relations between England and Ireland he said : " Let us join for any Imperial purpose, and defend the Empire which is the heritage of both of us, but let us give up, once and for all, the attempt to rule the domestic affairs of each other. Let us have national freedom and Imperial unity and strength." Forty-eight years were to pass before Redmond's policy was embodied in the Statute of Westminster. During his travels he had seen the part which Irish emigrants and their descendants were playing in the British colonies and the United States. Henceforward his conception of the Irish people, to whose interests he had decided to devote his life, reached far beyond the boundaries of Ireland. He, almost alone amongst Irish politicians, realised that the Irish were in fact one of the parent nations of the British Empire.

This was the man who in 1891 became leader of the Parnellite minority, and who eventually, ten years later, succeeded to Parnell's place as Chairman of the Irish Party. It was the long debate in Committee Room No. 15, which became in the end largely a personal conflict between himself and Tim Healy, that revealed Redmond as the ablest of Parnell's supporters.

Mrs. Maev Sullivan, Tim Healy's daughter, in her book *No Man's Man*, which is a defence of her father's conduct during the Parnell Split, accuses Redmond of dishonourable conduct, because, during the debate in Committee Room No 15, he stated that he would resign if the Irish Party came to a decision contrary to his view, and subsequently did not do so. Unfortunately she does not quote him accurately and leaves out the vital words which acquit him of any such charge. What he said, according to the official report, was : " If this party, *acting in a regular way*, comes to a decision hostile to my view, then, before taking any steps to support Mr. Parnell if he chooses to go further, I will deem it my duty to resign my seat."[1] Mrs. Sullivan,

[1] See *Historical and Political Addresses*, 1883–1897, by John E. Redmond M.P., pp. 292–293.

however, omits the words in italics, which alters the whole context. In fact the Party did not act *in a regular way*. Those who disagreed with Parnell left the room before a vote was taken on the question of his leadership and formed a new party which elected Mr. Justin McCarthy as Chairman. Such methods of controversy are most unfair.

Redmond made a passionate appeal to the Party to resist the " intemperate and hysterical methods " which Healy had introduced into the discussion. " I want if I can," he said, " to bring you back from the heated atmosphere of vituperation and malice to that of reason and patient investigation of truth." He felt and said that if the Irish Party deposed Parnell at Gladstone's bidding its independence and usefulness as a political force would be gone. To preserve that independence he now decided, on Parnell's death, to continue the struggle. He resigned his safe Wexford seat and with fine courage contested the election at Cork caused by his leader's death. In that contest my father acted as his election agent. Redmond was opposed by Martin Flavin, an amiable butter merchant, and by Captain Sarsfield, a member of the historic Sarsfield family, who, strange to say, represented the Unionist and landlord party. Youth and the crowd were largely on Redmond's side, but the stolid bourgeois majority led by the Church was invincible and he was defeated by over 1,500 votes; the gallant Captain coming a bad third. Redmond had his reward, a few weeks later, when he was elected for Waterford city after a furious contest with Michael Davitt, and he remained member for that constituency until his death in 1918. His son succeeded him, and his son's widow still represents Waterford in the Dáil, a remarkable example of political fidelity.

Although the moral issue had clearly disappeared with Parnell's death the Church continued to maintain its attitude of bitter hostility to his former supporters. Dr. Nulty, Bishop of Meath, who was one of the most extreme opponents of the Parnellites, declared in a pastoral letter, that Parnellism struck at the very foundation of Catholic faith and sprang from sensualism and sin. " No man," he

wrote, " can remain a Catholic so long as he elects to cling
to Parnellism." A priest in his diocese went one better
when he told a man that he would turn him into a goat if
he voted for the Parnellite candidate. As a result of these
pronouncements, which were of course contrary to Catholic
teaching, Michael Davitt, who had himself protested against
such violent and ridiculous statements, was unseated after
an election petition. In another diocese it was declared to
be a mortal sin to buy, sell or read a paper edited and owned
by one of Redmond's supporters, and his business was
reduced to the verge of ruin. Nevertheless Redmond never
gave way to rancour, nor did he waver in his personal faith.

At the General Election of 1892 his party was reduced
from 22 to 9, but the Liberal Party, had, with the combined
Irish Nationalist vote, a majority of 45 in the new Parliament.
The division in the Irish ranks and the Irish reforms initiated
by the Unionist Party had alike contributed to this unsatisfactory result. Yet Gladstone, then eighty-four years of
age, at once went forward to his last battle for Ireland.
" It has now become," he said in his great speech on the
second reading of the second Home Rule Bill, " a question
in the strictest sense between a nation and a nation, and
not only between a nation and a nation, but between a great
nation and a small nation, between a strong nation and a
weak nation, between a wealthy nation and a poor nation."
After referring to the degrading spectacle of national
oppression he went on : " But on the other hand, there
can be no nobler spectacle than that which we think is
now dawning upon us, the spectacle of a nation deliberately
set on the removal of injustice, deliberately determined to
break—not through terror and not in haste, but under the
sole influence of duty and honour—with whatever remains
still existing of an evil tradition, and determined in that
way at once to pay a debt of justice and to consult by a bold,
wise and good act its own interest and its cwn honour."
In respect of powers the Bill followed the lines of the previous
measure. The vexed question of Irish representation at
Westminster was solved by the retention of 80 Irish members
for all purposes. Provision was also made for a revision

of the financial arrangements between the two countries after a period of six years, and a special commission, of which John Redmond was a member, examined the question in the meantime. Opposed by some of the ablest parliamentarians of the day and knowing that the House of Lords would reject the measure, the old statesman never wavered or lost heart and carried the Bill successfully through the House of Commons. It was the most remarkable achievement of his career. On 8th September, 1893, the Bill was rejected by the House of Lords. Gladstone resigned in the following March. He had failed in his great aim of ending the secular dispute between England and Ireland. The spirit of imperialism had prevailed over the spirit of justice. The results of that barren victory are still with us to prove that he was right.

Disheartened by the death of Parnell and its sequel, my father gradually ceased to take an active interest in politics. When asked by William Redmond, John's brother, to act as his agent in the election of 1892 he regretfully declined. I think his decision to drop out of political life was accelerated by the death of my brother Dick, after a protracted illness, in January, 1892. My father was a man of strong family attachments, and this loss for a time deeply affected him. It was the first time that I had come close to death.

A few years before—in September, 1888—we had begun our education proper at the Presentation Brothers' College, Cork, then under the control and management of the Rev. Brother E. J. Connolly. His educational maxim was *suaviter in modo fortiter in re.* He never forgot, as some modern schoolmasters seem to do, that the primary aim of education is the formation of character rather than the acquisition of miscellaneous information. His weekly talks to the assembled school combined moral instruction with practical advice and were not wanting in touches of humour, sometimes perhaps unconscious. I recall for instance what he said of a past pupil who was fond of " lifting the elbow "— " I got a telegram from him and I smelt drink from it." At the " Pres," as we affectionately called it, I received a sound foundation in " the three R's," and some small knowledge of Latin and French grammar. My years there were happy ones. Among my school-fellows were many who are still my friends. Amongst them were the late James Dwyer, long an outstanding figure in Irish commercial life, William Carey, who until recently filled the responsible position of Chairman of the Irish Revenue Commissioners, Monsignor Joseph Scannell, Dean of Cork, who was twice decorated when acting as chaplain to the Guard's Brigade in the first World War, and the late Vincent Hart, who became one of the leading public works engineers in India. Old Presentation boys have then and since made their marks in many callings and all continents.

In the autumn of 1893, when I was twelve years old, I was sent with my brother George to Clongowes Wood College. Our English grandmother, naturally enough, was anxious that we should be sent to an English public school, but my father thought that an English education would unfit us for life in Ireland. He felt also that at an Irish school we should be more likely to make friends who would be useful to us in after life. In both these conclusions I am satisfied from experience that he was right. The differences in the life of the two peoples are fundamental, though concealed by superficial resemblances due to identity of language and to some extent, of law and social habits.

Clongowes is the oldest public school in Ireland, having been established by the Society of Jesus about the year 1813. From its fine playing fields there is an uninterrupted view across the flat central plain to the Wicklow mountains. The school, an impressive line of grey castellated buildings, comprised the old castle of Clongowes Wood, used by the community as a residence, the study hall and refectory, the "Third Line" quarters and the infirmary, and behind these buildings the chapel, class-rooms and dormitories. The country around is rich in historic associations, for this was the " debatable land " of Ireland where the struggle between the Irish and the invaders was waged fiercely throughout the Middle Ages. Quite near the school building runs the old rampart of the Norman Pale which long marked the effective limits of the invaders' rule. Not

far away in Bodenstown Churchyard is the grave of Wolfe
Tone, himself a native of Kildare. That " most extraordinary man," as Wellington called him, brought from
France not only an army but, what proved far more disturbing, the idea of an Irish republic which has since
obsessed the minds of some Irish idealists. The old castle
of Clongowes itself, which had formerly belonged to the
Wogans, also had its legends. One told how in 1757 one
of that family, then serving as a marshal in the Austrian
army, had appeared one night to his old servants, wrapped
in his white cloak, mounting the staircase from the hall,
his face pale and strange, his hand pressed to his side.
Months later came the news that on that day he had fallen
mortally wounded on the battlefield of Prague.

   Another story concerned Hamilton Rowan, one of Tone's
friends and a member of the United Irishmen, the ruins
of whose house at Rathcoffey are not far away. It was
said that, pursued by the British soldiery, he had jumped
from a window of his house and ridden straight to Clongowes,
then a private dwelling. His pursuers reached the hall-
door just in time to see him pass into the " round room "
at the top of the staircase and immediately fired at him.
But he had closed the door and the bullets struck the
panels where their mark can still be seen. He rushed into
the library and seeing that one of the windows was open,
with great presence of mind, he flung out his hat and hid
in an adjoining room. His pursuers, seeing the open window
and the hat lying on the grass outside, concluded that he
had again risked his neck and sprang out in hot pursuit,
whilst Rowan lay low and eventually escaped by another
way.

   Like all big schools Clongowes had its peculiar divisions
and games. The boys, then about three hundred in
number, were divided into three " Lines," namely, the
Higher, the Lower and the Third. Each Line had its own
playroom, playgrounds, library and dormitory, and lived
a distinct social life under the control of its Line prefect—
one of the Jesuit community—who was responsible for the
conduct of the boys out of class hours. The classes were

divided in accordance with the Intermediate education system, into one Senior, one Middle, four Junior and three Preparatory. In addition there were two classes of Poetry and Rhetoric, relics of a nobler past, which prepared boys for the university examinations. Over the entire educational system hovered, the Prefect of Studies, the Rev. James Daly, S.J., better known to many generations of Clongownians as " Jimmy," a small, bald and rather irascible man, whose unexpected descents upon a class boded ill for idlers. One of his duties was to test the qualifications of new arrivals and I was duly examined by him for this purpose. On this occasion, as I fear on many others in after life, I succeeded, unconsciously no doubt, in persuading my interrogator that I possessed a great deal more knowledge than was actually the case. The delusion did not eventually operate to my advantage, for, having questioned me about my knowledge of English and French, the two subjects about which I knew something, he proceeded without more ado to assign me to the class of First Preparatory, for which in every other respect I was quite unfit. There I remained for a year vainly trying to follow instruction intended for cleverer boys, and losing time which should have been devoted to learning the rudiments of Latin and Mathematics.

But this miscasting of my part on the scholastic stage was not altogether without advantage. The class itself was a brilliant one, and its master, Father Tom Nolan, was one of those rare men who can inspire and direct boys without apparent effort. Nothing could be more eloquent of our respect for his personality than the fact that he had no nickname. A tall, dark, handsome man and a fine cricketer, his character was as straight as the bat he wielded. He was a friend as well as a master to his class. As one of his most brilliant pupils, my old friend, John M. Fitzgerald, K.C., wrote of him after his death : " In all the fullness and variety of his manifold talents there were surely none greater than he as a teacher of boys in those formative years of youth, before the real taste for learning and scholarship had been developed, when success depended on the personal influence and inspiration of the teacher. He had every gift and grace that could attract and hold the affection, as well as the attention of his pupils. His splendid figure, easy dignity and manly lucidity of thought and expression made the task of learning seem almost easy and pleasant. He knew the secret of learning without labour, teaching without tears." Punishment received from such a man was certainly well deserved. At Clongowes this was administered not by the master who imposed it but by the delinquent's prefect to whom he was sent with a note indicating the appropriate chastisement. This took the form of slaps on the palm of the hand administered with a leather strap called a pandy-bat, the maximum number of slaps, or " pandies " as they were called, being " twice nine," never described as eighteen.

If I was happy in my teacher I was not, however, happy in my line prefect, who was unfortunately a petty tyrant, the sort of man who drives homesick boys to run away from school and afterwards flogs them with unctuous rectitude. On one occasion my father wrote to him about some complaint I had made in a letter home, and he promptly gave me " twice nine " with the warning that he would flog me if I made any more complaints to my parents.

In my second year at Clongowes I fortunately passed out of his control. I had by this time been relegated to a more suitable class, having failed in the Intermediate Preparatory examination, a performance which I repeated in the Junior Grade the following year. Education at Clongowes in those days meant success in the Intermediate, and the boy who could not obtain an exhibition or prize in this educational obstacle race was not smiled on. Boys who so distinguished themselves sat at special tables in the refectory and received extra food and other privileges. This was hardly conducive to making us regard learning as an end in itself. In fact this educational materialism created a special class within the school whose subsequent achievements did not always justify their early pre-eminence.

But those Clongowes days had also their pleasurable and memorable hours. Amongst these were warm summer afternoons punctuated by the click of bat and ball from the cricket pitches, long walks on winter playdays through the flat, wooded countryside to places of historic interest, followed by a plunge into the warm, turf-coloured water of the swimming bath, and evening play hours spent in the well-stocked library or round the billiard table. In my time the Intermediate system had practically destroyed such cultural activities as the debating society and the performance of Shakespeare's plays, which in John Redmond's day had constituted a valuable feature of Clongowes life. My proficiency at games was even less than at studies, although I eventually became captain of one of the cricket clubs. Amongst its members was Arthur Clery, afterwards to find his own peculiar and honourable place in Irish legal history, that gentlest and most lovable of persons, who usually disappeared with a book into the long grass at the back of the cricket field. Other Clongownians of my time were T. M. Kettle, brilliant writer, speaker and politician, whose death in the First World War was a grievous loss to his country; Oliver Gogarty, wit, poet and surgeon; the late John M. Fitzgerald, K.C., afterwards for many years one of the leaders of the Irish Bar and one of its most eloquent advocates; and the late Hugo Flinn, who after being an electrical engineer eventually found his real vocation as a politician, and became Parliamentary Secretary to the Minister for Finance in Mr. de Valera's government. Flinn even then displayed those Puckish qualities which distinguished him in the political arena. On one occasion I remember he filled with ink the holy waterfont in the Chapel with results which can perhaps be better imagined than described. On the other side in the new Irish Parliament, Clongowes of my time was represented by James Fitzgerald Kenny, K.C., the courageous Minister for Justice in Mr. Cosgrave's administration, and Professor J. M. O'Sullivan, Minister for Education in the same Government. In the ranks of the higher civil service who have helped to build the new Irish state are John Houlihan and Pierce Kent. In the Jesuit Society itself Father Stephen Brown has done splendid work for Catholic literature and libraries.   On the whole it may be claimed that the Clongowes vintage of 1894-7 was not a bad one.

In January, 1896, our school life was enlivened by a week's skating, thanks to the hard frost of that winter. The College lake, lit at night by tar-barrels, was the scene of this delightful exercise, our labours being fortified by coffee and buns served *al fresco*. The three days before Lent were known as Carnival, following the Continental custom, and were devoted to holidays and various entertainments. Clongowes also had its peculiar game, gravel football, played on gravel courts with a very hard ball and goal posts without a cross stick—any ball going between the posts scoring a goal.   The gravel football season ended on St. Patrick's Day with a "colour" match between sides representing red and green respectively, so picked that the green side was virtually sure of victory.

My last year at Clongowes, 1896-7, was much the happiest.   I had now decided to enter my father's profession and was preparing for the Solicitor's Preliminary Examination.   But I was happy for another reason also.   I was now in the Higher Line, the prefect of which was that remarkable man, Father Henry Fegan.   His influence on me and many other boys was I think partly the result of personal magnetism and partly due to the sincere interest he took in all our affairs.   On the football field and cricket ground he was just as much a boy as we were.   Small and ugly to look at, with a voice devoid of charm, he yet dominated his surroundings by the force of his personality.   I remember that on one occasion he preached a sermon against the pernicious habit of reading "penny dreadfuls," and asked us to destroy them.   That night the long gallery was littered with their remains.   Every evening he would sit in a corner of the big Higher Line playroom and talk for the benefit of an admiring circle—touching on every subject under the sun and conveying to his hearers many a lesson for use in after life.

The Captain and Secretary of the school during my last year at Clongowes were two other Cork boys—Dominic O'Connor and Barry Egan—both still my good friends—

the former now an architect of distinction and the latter a well-known connoisseur who has done much to revive the arts of the jeweller and the silversmith in Ireland, particularly in the domain of religious art. Both have retained that charm of manner and integrity of spirit which even then secured the recognition of their school-fellows. In May, 1897, when I was just sixteen I passed my examination and a few weeks later, was apprenticed to my father. My schooldays were over. What Clongowes had forged was now to be tested in the fire of life.

VI

ADOLESCENCE is a difficult and often an unhappy time. I experienced some of the difficulties but very little unhappiness. I fell in love and felt myself a very Romeo because the lady's family and mine were not on good terms. But as she had more sense than I and regarded my precocious advances with somewhat cynical amusement, the tragedy of the Montagues and Capulets was not re-enacted. I had spiritual doubts and difficulties, I felt myself misunderstood, I began to write poetry. In short I went through the usual adjustments of mind and body which normally take place in that wide estuary where the river of youthful idealism meets the flood tide of reality from the sea of life. But taken by and large those student days were full of happiness. This was largely due to the home in which we lived and the affectionate care by which we were surrounded.

My memory of those days is largely of Clanloughlin—the new home which my father had purchased in November, 1894, and in which we took up our abode the following spring. Standing four square on a wooded hillside overlooking the river Lee, this substantial early Victorian house, with its massive walls and well-shuttered windows, fits into the landscape and repels the onslaughts of our damp southern climate in a manner modern jerry-builders and architects might profitably study. Behind its solid structure are out-offices, greenhouses, gardens and fields leading up to a hillside crowned by a furze-brake from which on a clear day one can survey the gentle pastoral beauties of the Lee valley and discern in the far distance the dim outline of the West Cork Hills, blue grey on the horizon. On Midsummer Eve we gathered on this height to light the traditional bonfire, now dedicated to St. John but probably of pagan origin. As the great pyramid of cut furze blazed we watched the answering fires burst into life in the velvet dusk among the surrounding hills. At the western end of the grounds a field path along the river bank, under the beautiful Mount Desert woods, now unhappily and unnecessarily destroyed, led one by many a quiet pool and murmuring rapid to where the gaunt Elizabethan structure of Carrig-rohane castle towers on its rock over the dark river. It was a boy's paradise. In summer we disported ourselves on the river in canoes or swam in its deep pools. Later on a boat was added to our fleet. In the stables a Connemara pony and a donkey provided mounts on which we learned to ride. Cows and hens wandered through the fields and about the yard. In the autumn we helped to cut the hay in the meadows and to gather in the fruit. It was in fact agriculture without aches. As time went by a tennis-court and billiard-room were added for our delight. These I think were also my father's happiest years. He took a legitimate pride in this house and land which were the fruit of his labours ; he had attained an honoured place in his profession, the financial worries of earlier years were over, and he rejoiced to give us advantages and amenities which he had never known in his own youth.

But we were happy also in our wider surroundings. Cork is situated amidst one of the most beautiful districts in Ireland. On Sundays in summer the black and white " river steamers "—as those old paddle-boats were called—took one down the Lee under the wooded, villa-dotted heights of Montenotte, across the broad expanse of Lough Mahon and through the Passage gorge, past the quays and terraced hillside of Queenstown, to the Lower Harbour. The wide and sheltered waters of this great anchorage were then a port of call for ships, both sail and steam, of every nationality, for the wireless had not yet made such visits unnecessary. Occasionally the vessels of the Channel fleet, engaged on manoeuvres or their annual cruise, would add excitement and diversity to the scene. Sometimes we were permitted to board and inspect one of the great warships. From their Passage terminus the railway company ran a rival line of green and white paddle-boats known as the " railway steamers " or " green boats."

These latter served the districts of the Lower Harbour and eventually survived their opponents. The captains were well-known local personalities, and we worshipped them from afar, as they paced, resplendent in blue uniform and gold braid, on the narrow bridges of their clanking craft.

It was in the Lower Harbour that I soon learnt to handle and steer a yacht and to identify every type of vessel from yawl to liner. In the south-western corner of the harbour at the seaside resort of Crosshaven many of our summer holidays were spent in swimming, rowing, and sailing, to our heart's content. In the spring we could mount our bicycles, take our fishing-rods and choose any of half a dozen streams on which to cast a fly. Less than a day's journey away to the West, amidst the mountains, lakes and fiords of Cork and Kerry, is some of the finest scenery in these islands. There also we spent several holidays on our bicycles, riding along the Lee valley to " lone Gougane Barra," where the river rises in a small mountain lake, through the narrow pass of Keimaneigh to the mountain-locked harbour of Glengarriff, hidden in its woods, and then on over that wonderful hill road, with its far-flung vistas of mountain, lake and sea, which leads through Kenmare to Killarney. In recent years the motor car has made it possible to compass all this beauty in a few hours, but remembering those pleasant pilgrimages of long ago I still think it is best savoured on foot or bicycle. And if one preferred a sea trip one could take the small coasting steamer which plied between Cork and Dingle, as I did once with Jack Fitzgerald, and spend a pleasant week cruising along our south-western coast, riding the big Atlantic rollers by day under the high grey cliffs, and anchoring for the night in little land-locked harbours where the luxuriant woods, bright with arbutus and fuchsia, swept down to the water's edge, whilst behind them the green tiny fielded land dotted with white farmhouses climbed up to the barren purple hills.

After passing my Solicitor's Preliminary Examination I did not at once begin my legal studies. As I wished to attend law lectures at the Queen's College, Cork, it became necessary for me to pass the Matriculation examination of the Royal University, in preparation for which I returned to the Presentation College. Here, in a small students' debating society, I had my first lessons in public speaking. Long experience has convinced me that much mental agony, to both the public and the exponents of that dangerous art, could be saved if boys were taught, as we were, that its essentials are to have something to say, to think about how you are going to say it, to say it clearly and briefly, and then to sit down. The " eloquent Dempseys " who abound in Irish public life have, unfortunately, learnt none of these things. The rising generation, which owing to our present system of education is often illiterate in two languages, has, as a rule, not even learnt how to enunciate properly in common speech. Even some of our leading politicians, bemused by the microphone, are content to mumble incoherently from prepared typescript, knowing that a copy has been handed to the press in advance. Some advice about public speaking which Father Fegan gave me about that time in a letter helped me perhaps more than anything else to become a proficient speaker. " Do your best," he wrote, " not to talk for the sake of killing time and don't deal in green flag oratory. Get up the facts—then arrange them, a good one first—the weak ones in the the middle and tied together to make a strong bundle—the one or two strongest at the end. If you anticipate an opponent's objection let it be a downright objection. I mean a real difficulty. Don't set up mere poppy heads to knock them over with your walking-cane—aim at rigid accuracy in your facts. Write your *sensible* peroration word for word and deliver it clearly, distinctly, boldly. You will be helped enormously by the practical experience of life. How often, in the pulpit for instance, do we not hear men speak as if those they addressed had none of life's realities to face—as if going to heaven were as simple and easy as the preacher's vapid sentences. Nothing gives life and reality to a man's talk like life itself, and especially of course the life experience of those you talk to. No use sledging outside the anvil."

My first speech, which I am afraid lacked conviction,

was a defence of war as the best method of settling international disputes. Shortly afterwards I delivered a lecture
to the same debating society on the Franco-Prussian war
of 1870–1, in which I had long been interested, probably
owing to my visits to France where the conflict was still
fresh in people's memories. Out of my small pocket-money
I had purchased, as it appeared, Cassel's history of that
dramatic conflict in green covered weekly parts, one of the
first, I think, of many such serial publications. Although
then, in the spring of 1898, that struggle seemed a
tremendous and terrible occurrence, it was in fact, as
we now unhappily know, only a curtain-raiser to the
coming world tragedy in which so many of my generation were engulfed and of which the end is not yet
apparent. In eighteen foolscap pages I described its
origin, history and result, winding up with a passionate
plea for peace in which I pointed out, with some
reason, that modern science was at hand to heap the
battlefields of the future with yet more devilish suffering
than the past. My sympathies in that struggle, like those
of most Irish people, were on the side of France. So much
so that even that tragic, weak, and rather ineffectual person,
Napoleon III, became for me a romantic figure in defeat.
In those halcyon days of the late nineties when the warlike
activities of such persons as Arabi Pasha, Cetewayo, and
the Mahdi had recently engaged the might of the British
Empire, and had assumed, in the popular eye, the proportions of major wars, the Franco-Prussian war seemed a
truly world shaking catastrophe, as indeed in one sense it
was. For then one could still travel across Europe without
a passport, and customs officials were interested only in
cigars and perfume, the possession of which seemed to
constitute, in their eyes, the highwater mark of male and
female depravity.

Another paper, written shortly afterwards for the same
society, was entitled " The Realism of Shakespeare." This
more ambitious effort, which was an attempt to appraise
the vast humanity of Shakespeare's plays, owed much to a
diligent study of Hazlitt, but more to Frank Benson and his

gifted company of players. All through my boyhood our
Christmas holidays were enriched by their presentation of
Shakespeare comedies and tragedies, until by the time I was
twenty there was hardly an acted play of the great poet
which I had not seen. The names of Benson's company,
afterwards to become known on a wider stage, were
"familiar in our mouths as household words." Shakespeare's plays can be best known and loved when seen
and heard on the stage, and their presentation by such
actors as Benson himself, Henry Ainley, O. B. Clarence,
Lyal Swete, Oscar Ashe, and that greatest of modern
Shakesperian clowns, George Weir, was something to be
remembered with delight. I can still recollect the first
occasion on which I saw them, a cold snowy night in
December, 1894, when my father took me to the Cork
Opera House to see *Othello*, and I was transported from
the bitter night outside to a new and glowing world of tragic
beauty. Benson was not himself a really great actor,
although in a few parts, such as Richard II, Henry V, and
Mark Antony, he touched greatness ; but he was, what was
far more important, a great enthusiast, and his enthusiasm
was infectious. I once heard him say humorously to a
Cork audience, during a stage speech, that he translated
our civic motto, *Statio bene fida carinis*, to mean "A safe refuge
for Benson and his wandering caravan." I am glad to
think that by our attention and applause we may have been
able, to some extent, to repay the debt we owed him.
Many years later when he came as Sir Frank Benson, one
of the oldest and most honoured members of his profession,
on a farewell visit to Cork, I was proud to join in arranging
an entertainment in his honour at which many of us who
were his life-long debtors were able to thank him in person
for his noble service to dramatic art. Although he had
suffered more than most "the slings and arrows of outrageous fortune " he was still the noble enthusiast we had
always known.

In the summer of 1898 my great-aunt Elizabeth Bowring
again took me to London and Paris. On the top of the
new Tower Bridge I watched the river traffic flow into

the Pool of London, and from the Great Wheel in the popular Earl's Court Exhibiton looked out on the spires and domes of the vast city, itself wrapped in summer mist. In Westminster Abbey I saw the plain, freshly laid slab in the North transept which bore the inscription " W. E. Gladstone, 1898." Many of the passers-by walked over it heedlessly, others looked with curious stare. None, I reflected, stopped to pray. He had already passed into history.

The paddle-steamer took us from Newhaven to Dieppe and I can still recall the wonder of that landfall at 3.30 a.m. in the half-light of a summer dawn, a three-master inside us pitching heavily like some gigantic spectre whilst the red and green beacon light flashed mysteriously from the pier head. Once on French soil my dawn dreams were dispelled by cranky, grimy customs officials and gendarmes who seemed to resent our interference with their repose. At Rouen, which was our first stopping place, we stood in the heart of Normandy and in its great Cathedral saw the full fruit of its genius. Statues and pictures alike reminded us that in the market place Joan of Arc had faced her martyrdom by fire. In Paris I witnessed the celebration of the National Fête day—14th July. An article which I wrote on my return for the *Cork Examiner* marked my first appearance in print. It was entitled " Paris en fête " and, as it resurrects some aspects of the Third Republic in its heyday, it may perhaps be worth quoting here.

" Paris heralded the dawn of the National Fête day with salvoes of artillery and the metallic crash of military music. We were roused from our slumbers by the booming guns of distant Mont Valérien and the nearer strains of the *Marseillaise*. Outside it was warm with bright sunshine, yet not too hot, for there was just enough breeze to refresh the blue-coated, red-trousered soldiers as they marched at a swinging quick step down to Longchamps. Quiet reigned till noon, for the Parisian allows nothing, not even the national holiday, to interfere with the sacred institution of *déjeuner;* then as everyone seemed bound for the Place de la Concorde I followed in their wake. Round the

Strasburg statue, wreathed in crape, a huge crowd had gathered to pay silent homage to 'the lost provinces.' The white costumes of a gymnastic society from Alsace, laying wreaths of immortelles on the statue, stood out sharply against the black drapery as they reverently placed their tokens of loyalty to France on the monument. From the crowd there was no sound, but the look on the set faces showed how well they remembered Gambetta's dictum concerning 1870—'Never talk about it, but think about it always.' The crowd dispersed, as it had come, silently, and I walked on down the Rue de Rivoli into the heart of the city. The streets were gorgeous in red, white and blue, the horizontal stripes of the Russian flag alternating with the vertical ones of the French. Near the Opera House one saw occasionally the Union Jack and the Stars and Stripes. Variety of colour was given by the flags of exotic South American republics and Eastern potentates, flying from the windows of the great hotels. On the Grands Boulevards the cafés were full, the side-walk tables crowded. Here and there the strains of music were heard and strong men and clowns performed their antics on the street. Now and then everything had to give way whilst a dusty regiment marched past amidst shouts of *Vive l'Armée*. In the gardens of the Palais Royal people danced to the strains of ' Ta-ra-ra-boom-de-ay ' played by a brass band very much out of tune.

"In the afternoon the main tide of people was setting towards the Bois de Boulogne ; the attraction being a military review by the President on Longchamps race-course. Under the trees in the Champs Elysées his body-guard were watering their horses ; fine strapping cuirassiers with steel breastplates and helmets. Up to the Arc de Triomphe and down beyond into the Avenue de la Grande Armée stretched the long line of carriages bound for the review. Crowds poured out into the Bois, crowds on foot, crowds on bicycles, and—sign of the times—one might almost say crowds in motor cars. At the entrance to the Bois are more cavalry under the trees and more excited *agents* trying to direct the traffic, till one sighs for the burly form and competent handling of a Dublin policeman. Near the racecourse were hundreds of people picnicking under the trees or down by the side of the lake. On every side are soldiers; now a battery of artillery goes by, the caissons lurching from side to side as they swing over the grass, then a mounted orderly rides past, dusty from head to foot, whilst in amongst the trees in the distance gleam the bayonets of infantry. At three o'clock mounted gendarmes clear the main entrance to the review ground and the dancing pennons of the lancers are seen, as column after column gallop past escorting carriages containing the Ministers of the Republic. After them, also escorted, the Ambassadors, the Russian receiving an enthusiastic reception More carriages follow with officials of various kinds and in their wake several daring cyclists who rush past the official barrier to the amusement of the crowd and the obvious annoyance of the mounted gendarmes who try to intercept them. Then we wait expectantly, for the next arrival is to be the President. The crowd does not appear to be excited, they chaff each other, they chaff the waiting soldiers, but there is no pushing or scrambling, all are good-tempered and polite. Then an officer rides down the avenue brandishing his sword, the crowd becomes silent, expectant, and the cuirassiers go thundering by, in their midst an open carriage where a broad-shouldered, white-haired man, with clear cut, massive features, bows acknowledgments on all sides. There were a few shouts of *Vive Faure*, nothing more, and yet Frenchmen will tell you that this one time journeyman tanner who consummated the Franco-Russian Alliance is the most popular President the Third Republic has yet known. His carriage draws up before the State box and then a fanfare of trumpets announces the commencement of the review. Far away from under the trees the dark masses of infantry are deploying and they come on at a swinging pace in line formation. First, the marine infantry in dark blue with yellow facings, then the infantry of the line in the familiar blue coat, red trousers and white gaiters. They defile past line after line, till one's eye is wearied of soldiers.

Frenchmen have evidently grasped the fact that, though black guns may blaze at each other and glittering squadrons crash together, it is volley firing at five hundred yards that beggars treasuries and alters maps. Still more regiments, some tanned and swarthy from Algeria or Madagascar, others raw youths with pink and white complexions, who carry their knapsacks as if there were nothing more delightful than soldiering. The dust is rising now from the tramp of their myriad feet and the heat is becoming more intense as the crowded ambulance tents testify. At last the infantry have passed and the ground shakes to the tread of cavalry as they go by at a trot, fine men on fine horses who would strike home, boot to boot and sword in air. Dragoons blue, red, and flashing steel; lancers in red and yellow as befits the lighter arm; chasseurs d'Afrique in sky-blue and scarlet ; all pass in seemingly endless array. Now there is a clank of steel and rumble of wheels as the artillery approach. They are proud of their guns, these little men in blue, as one can see by the careful way they drive them over the turf. It is late now, and the cavalry charge past as a grand finale. The sun glinting on helm and breast-plate makes a brilliant spectacle and one feels their forefathers must have looked like that as they charged up the slope at Waterloo on that never to be forgotten day in June, 1815. The President drives off in a cloud of dust. The generals and their brilliant staffs on horseback follow him and the crowd greets them with enthusiasm. But it is perhaps only a temporary popularity ; one can never speak with certainty of to-morrow in France. It is all over at last. The tired troops march back along the hot roads with the usual escort of admiring gamins. The people toil back too, panting and sweating under the fierce July sun, but happy as only a Parisian crowd can be, and quite ready for an evening of fun and frolic. In the evening the boulevards are crowded. At many street corners dancing goes on, the music rising on the still evening air. Here and there also voices rise in chorus but there are no brawlers or drunken men. Far into the night the fête continues and the grey dawn of another day will see many still awake.

That night I dreamt of endless soldiers marching through crowded streets to the triumphant strains of the *Marseillaise*."

Re-reading this description of festive Paris as it presented itself to my seventeen year old vision I feel that, had fate so willed, I might have become a journalist.

Two years later my interest in journalism led me to start a family newspaper which bore the grandiose title of the *Clanloughlin Mail*. This amusing production contained, amongst other features, a leading article, literary critiques, poetry, short stories, travel sketches, and even a page of humorous advertisements. Its contributors included my brothers, Jack Fitzgerald (who wrote a serial story which was never finished) and one or two other intimate friends. But if the truth be told, I myself, under various *noms de plume*, was the chief contributor. Like all such undertakings, it began as a weekly, degenerated into a monthly and, after surviving for six months, quickly died as a quarterly. The editorial purpose was explained in the following lines which appeared as a prologue to the first number—

> To swing the balance even is our aim,
> Not to win glory or to ape at fame ;
> To tell most truly all we know or see
> And work for Ireland in the great to be.

Grandiloquent if you like, yet full of the honesty and idealism of youth. It was an interesting and not altogether valueless experiment. Looking through the faded numbers now revives the atmosphere and hopes of those days.

Immediately on my return from France I entered my father's office to begin my legal training and in the autumn of that year, 1898, I became a law student at the Queen's College, Cork. The position of the College in relation to the community was peculiar. Standing on a wooded bluff over the Lee, its beautiful buildings had all the amenities of a university and were competently staffed. Yet it had failed to fulfil its purpose. It had been placed under ecclesiastical ban, on its inception some fifty years before, because it did not conform to the religious requirements of the Catholic hierarchy, and extreme pressure had been

brought to bear upon students not to attend its Arts classes.
But the objections raised to attendance at the medical and
engineering schools, where alone in Munster these bread
studies could be pursued, had not been nearly so effective.
Hence these departments flourished while the Arts faculty
was almost deserted. By this educational quarrel between
Church and State many generations of southern students
were deprived of the instruction and advantages to which
they had every claim. Yet those who studied at Queen's
College, Cork, and they must still number many doctors
and engineers in remote parts of the world, are not likely
to forget the ability and *esprit de corps* which distinguished
its graduates or the results which the College achieved
against heavy odds. It was at least true to its motto :
" Where Finnbar taught let Munster learn."

The Law faculty, which I now joined, was the Cinderella
of the professional schools, largely because Irish legal studies
were centred in Dublin. Brereton Barry, the Professor of
Law, a bluff, hearty, Limerick barrister, was in high favour
amongst us because his exposition of the dry technicalities
of real property, and the more human mysteries of contract
and torts, was illustrated with stories based on his personal
experience at the Bar. Stokes, the Professor of Jurisprudence,
was, on the other hand, as dry as his subject. He required
us to copy verbatim his interminable recitations from a
large black notebook beginning with the memorable statement that " Jurisprudence is the science of positive law "
which we could not dispute and did not, I fear, understand.
As we were subsequently examined on these notes we
developed a technique of asking him as many questions as
possible so that the area of our studies might be thereby
reduced. None the less I succeeded, in that and subsequent
years, in winning several scholarships.

In October, 1899, I set out for Dublin to attend the
lectures prescribed by the Incorporated Law Society for the
instruction of prospective solicitors. It was my first solitary
expedition into the outside world. My destination in Dublin
was a boarding-house in one of the old Georgian streets
abutting Rutland (now Parnell) Square above O'Connell

Street. It was in every way true to type. Its proprietors—three formidable old maids—were both forbidding and resolute ; its inhabitants diverse and peculiar. There was a retired bank clerk who relieved the monotony of life by heavy drinking bouts during which he disappeared from public ken, a bachelor member of parliament who was said never to have missed a division or made an intelligent speech, a Scottish accountant who took a poor view of our casual Irish ways, a civil servant whose allegiance hovered between Kipling and Kathleen ni Houlihan, a Presbyterian divine of Northern origin and rather gloomy views, a lady of uncertain age who talked loud and long of her aristocratic connections, a rather skittish hospital nurse with a sense of humour, a university professor with a terrible stammer. In addition to this more or less permanent population there was constant coming and going of law students, dispensary doctors, solicitors, and others whose business brought them for a few days or weeks to Dublin. The house itself had been built in the spacious pre-Union days when Dublin was still the home of an aristocracy and the capital of a nation. Its large rooms contained fine mantelpieces and ceilings strangely out of keeping with the boarding-house furniture and atmosphere. It was on the whole an interesting spot to study human nature and I did not neglect the opportunity. Nearly every political and religious opinion was represented at its table and discussion often became lively. My arrival synchronised with the beginning of the Boer War, and I created both indignation and amusement by remarking, during an after-dinner debate, soon after my arrival, that the conflict was certain to last for a couple of years. But in fact the war was still proceeding when I left, two years afterwards.

Like most Irishmen I was vehemently pro-Boer, a feeling I see no reason to regret, and my prophecy was, I fear, inspired by emotion rather than knowledge. Then, and for long after, I was fascinated by Kipling's strong, lilting verse and repelled by his Imperialist sentiments. I wrote what I hoped and believed were savage parodies of the original. Thus *The Old Issue* became *The Old, Old Issue*, a warning to the Boers :

> Step by step, and word by word, who is ruled may read,
> Suffer not the Saxon, for we know the breed.

In other poems I gave an Irishman's answer to the Imperial bard's question concerning the flag of England and his famous *Recessional* with its refrain " Lest we forget." Some of these effusions got into print. They harmed no one and relieved my feelings.

My life in Dublin followed a fairly constant pattern. The morning was spent in the office of my father's Dublin agent or at the Four Courts, where I attended to routine business or listened to the *cause célébre* of the moment. The Four Courts, a fine classical building designed by James Gandon, the famous Dublin architect in the eighteenth century, is the centre of Irish legal life. It was burnt down, together with the Public Record Office and its precious contents, during the wanton activities of armed irresponsibles which started the Civil War of 1922–3, but it has since been rebuilt on more modern lines without destroying its original dignity or appearance. Under its lofty and elegant dome is a great hall from which radiate the principal courts where judges of the High Court sit to deal with the civil business of the law. In the adjoining wings are the various offices of the courts, and behind these the Law Library of the Bar and offices of the Incorporated Law Society. Twice a week my afternoons were devoted to the lectures for which I came to Dublin. They took place in a typical lecture room with benches in tiers facing the lecturer. This worthy, a junior barrister, discharged his duties by reading us copious extracts from the text books set for the examinations, while we read a newspaper or novel by stealth or conversed in whispers. It was, we thought, waste of time to listen to recitations from books which we must, in any event, subsequently study carefully. My desk companion combined a taste for alcohol with poetic activities, and spent much of the lecture time composing verse about the lecturer, his fellow students, or the momentary object of his affections. These were passed to me for revision or criticism. In the evening I worked, visited friends, or went to the theatre. Around the corner in Rutland Square was the home of Dr. J. E. Kenny, M.P., Parnell's personal physician and friend, a kindly general practitioner of the old school, who made me welcome for my father's sake. There also lived Mrs. Gogarty, Oliver's mother. It was at her house I first met, about this time, W. B. Yeats, then becoming recognised as a poet. One memorable evening he talked to us of fairies—" the little people "— as he called them, with a gravity that was fascinating if not convincing. Sitting in the firelight we listened to his strange tales, intoned rather than spoken. He was then the young Yeats with clear cut features, mysterious eyes and dark disordered hair that Sargent has immortalised. It was of some such evening that Oliver Gogarty was to write later in his elegy on his dead friend :

> O happy were your days on earth
> When we sat by the household hearth
> And as the Autumn glow went out,
> Bandied the whole wide world about,
> Making reality betray
> The edges of sincerer day.

Oliver himself was then a medical student at Trinity College. He had about this time come under the influence of Edward Dowden, the Professor of English Literature, and already showed those literary tendencies which have since borne fruit in several entertaining books and fine poetry. At Trinity also was my friend, Jack Fitzgerald, and in his rooms, situated in the Botany Bay Square, we spent many pleasant hours discussing literary, legal and human problems. His fine taste and keen intelligence, burnished by wide reading and a brilliant scholastic career, helped to sharpen my more pedestrian mind. New movements were already taking shape in literature and politics and our minds shared in the ferment without.

On Sundays, with Jack or other friends, I often took train to Bray and walked through the beautiful Glen of the Downs to Greystones or climbed the Wicklow hills. On the other side of the Bay Howth provided us with a pleasant rambling centre. From its hilltop one could enjoy a spacious panorama of sea, mountain and distant city. In the long summer days we sometimes got as far as Glendalough and lost ourselves in the silence and solitude of the mountains. One trip to Poulaphouca on a glorious May morning produced this sonnet :

> Pool of the fairies, shadowed neath the trees
> Dark, deep and cool thou liest at our feet.
> The hills beyond are draped in drowsy heat
> And loud, the brawling river, like a breeze
> That jangles tunes in many different keys
> Comes leaping through the gorge in glittering foam
> As if it sought with thee a final home
> Nor wandered forth to tread again the leas.
>
> So in the stream of life we search in vain
> For some deep pool of quietness and peace
> Where we may dream secure from strife and pain,
> And when we find it for a little piece
> The fairies soothe us, till we hear again
> The rushing stream, and then our musings cease.

But it was at the Solicitors' Apprentices' Debating Society that some of my most enjoyable evenings were spent. There I learnt, in the clash of argument and opinion, to state my views with conviction and effect. At the first meeting which I attended the motion for discussion was " That England's policy as regards the Transvaal is deserving of our approval." I spoke of course on the negative, which was naturally the popular side, and I remember that so strong was the pro-Boer feeling amongst the members that speakers had to be specially assigned to support the resolution. The scope of our debates and the nature of the problems which interested us are indicated by some of the subjects we discussed. In addition to legal problems we debated such matters as the trial of Dreyfus, American Imperialism, the endowment of a Catholic University in Ireland, the revival of the Irish language, the establishment of peasant proprietorship, the

" open door " in China, the soundness of municipal trading,
and the necessity for conscription to preserve the integrity
of the British Empire.   In the last mentioned discussion
I quoted the tribute of " a young but experienced British
journalist and soldier " called W. S. Churchill to the Boer
commandos, and declared, not unprophetically, that what
England wanted to defend her Empire were men such as he

>   . . . certain of sword and pen
>   Who are neither children nor Gods but men in a world of
>   men.

The climax of these debating activities was reached in
May, 1900, when we held an inter-debate with the Literary
and Historical Society of University College, Dublin, on
the subject of the Intermediate education system, in which
we were assigned the attractive role of affirming that it
had been injurious to the country.   I was chosen as one of
the six speakers to represent our Society,   It was the first
big meeting I had ever addressed and I felt horribly nervous.
I wrote out everything I intended to say and committed it
to memory with the result that I forgot some of my best
points and wandered off into fierce attacks on previous
opposition speakers.   But the audience, if large, was fortunately not critical.   Our opponents were a brilliant team
who subsequently left their mark on the history of our times.
Arthur Clery, their leader, with his gentle voice and gracious
manner, quiet and yet convincing, was destined to become
Professor of Law in the new National University and to
maintain a standard of political integrity which was both
an example and an honour to his profession.   One would
hardly have recognised in Hugh Kennedy, the slender
and rather insignificant stripling, with a boy's voice and
appearance, the massive person who later became the first
Chief Justice of the new Irish State.   It was said, not without malice, that when the Committee charged with selecting
the garb of the new Irish judiciary met, one rash member
suggested that the High Court Judges should wear a
tricolour sash of the national colours, green, white and
yellow, but that one glance at the figure of the Chief Justice,

who presided over the meeting, ended the discussion.
Other opponents of ours that night were Louis Walsh, who
combined the callings of country attorney, and afterwards
of district justice, with those of dramatist and novelist ;
John Houlihan, a distinguished civil servant ; Tom Kettle,
even then an outstanding personality, that master of paradox,
epigram and wit, who died, one of the " lost leaders " of my
generation, in the battle of the Somme,

> . . . Not for a flag, nor King, nor Emperor
> But for a dream, born in a herdsman's shed
> And for the secret Scripture of the poor.

Most of them had been my schoolmates at Clongowes.
Nearly all were my personal friends. Our leader was John
J. McDonald, afterwards solicitor to the Great Southern
Railway. On both sides in that debate the reaper has
taken a heavy toll. At the conclusion Father William
Delaney, S.J., the distinguished Jesuit educationalist, who
presided, admitted that he preferred the old system of
education, although he also claimed, somewhat inconsist-
ently, that the Intermediate had done more good than
harm. It was a memorable night and I am proud to recall
that we by no means got the worst of the discussion. By
the end of my time in Dublin I had won all the prizes of
the Society including its Gold Medals for Oratory and
Composition, and felt that in this field, so important in my
future career, I could at least hold my own.

What were we thinking in those days ? Some at
least of our aspirations are indicated in a speech which
I made about that time on the future of Ireland. As it is in
every sense a period piece I venture to quote some of it here.
" Our soil," I said, " would be divided amongst many
occupiers who would be encouraged in their affection for it,
instructed in its cultivation and protected against foreign competition. Manufactures and commerce would be fostered
by the hand of the State. Our cities would be surrounded
by trees and crossed by long white streets. The military
spirit of our people would have its natural national outlet in
a national army. Their natural eloquence would find vent in

an atmosphere of enthusiasm, their wit in one of fancy, their pathos in one of sensibility. Their religious aspiration would be gratified by noble churches, solemn music, majestic ceremonies, great processions and pilgrimages. Their artistic faculty would be developed with a southern grace and warmed with a southern glow. Their national language would be the universal medium of intercourse. Their national intellect would show a deductive genius, a power of analysis, a love of combining the items of knowledge and shaping them into a symmetrical whole. Trade and agriculture would be pursued with energy, in a spirit of thrift rather than of enterprise. You will say that this description of a free Ireland is that of a visionary, that the reality would be immensely different. Let us give it a fair trial and see. The demand of Ireland," I concluded, " is a temperate one. It may not always be so." Sixteen years later, indeed, the Irish demand ceased to be temperate. The dam of patient moderation, sapped by constant disappointments and broken promises, burst, releasing a spate of violence that swept away nearly all that we had worked for, destroyed more than English rule, and left behind a legacy of " envy, malice, hatred and ill-will," that is not yet exhausted. Yet I cannot regret that in those far off days, we " hitched our waggon to a star."

VII

ALREADY in 1900 the waters of Irish nationalism were
beginning to rise. Two years before, Ireland had celebrated
the centenary of the rebellion of 1798, an event which
revived the romantic and revolutionary memories of the
people. The outbreak of the Boer War in the following
year was, as already noted, the occasion for a further
recrudescence of anti-British feeling. A small number of
Irishmen actually joined the Boer commandos in the field ;
but for every Irishman in the Boer ranks there were thousands
fighting with valour and endurance in the historic Irish
regiments on the British side. In April, 1900, Queen
Victoria, then eighty-one years of age, as a mark of her
appreciation of her Irish soldiers, abandoned her annual
visit to the South of France and came to Dublin instead.
She stayed for three weeks and was on the whole well
received, driving unescorted through the streets. It was
one of the few occasions during her long reign that she
had deigned to recognise the existence of her Irish realm.
Some people, with a mixture of credulity and malice not
uncommon amongst us, went so far as to allege that the old
lady did not actually realise where she was and believed
herself to be in France. I saw her one afternoon, during
her visit, outside the Mater Misericordiae Hospital, Dublin,
while she listened to an address of welcome, her heavy
Hanoverian face rising large and somnolent over the side
of the carriage. When I look at the large, and I fear, satiric,
statue of her by Hughes which until quite recently squatted
on Leinster Lawn, Dublin, outside the Irish parliament
house, I am always reminded of that scene. Although Cork
was not included in the royal progress we have reason to
remember the event, for our Mayor having called on the
old lady at the Viceregal Lodge emerged not only with a
Knighthood but also a Charter which entitled him to be
called Lord Mayor. The Cork Corporation, however,

being both frugal and patriotic, refused to accept the Charter or to pay the customary fees therefor. Lord Mayor Hegarty's successors have nevertheless enjoyed the honour.

In fact the British Empire of my boyhood did not long survive the Queen. The process of disintegration had begun even in Ireland. In 1898 the Conservative Government introduced, and carried into law, the most far-reaching Irish reform yet proposed—namely the establishment of a complete system of local government by elected bodies in place of the Grand Jury system under which the country's local affairs had been hitherto managed by a small, and often corrupt, oligarchy of the landlord class. It was the first step. From that moment it became inevitable that England should grant full legislative freedom to Ireland. But the Government did not apparently realise the full implication of this measure. They regarded it rather as the first step in a policy of "killing Home Rule with kindness." A Land Act was passed to facilitate and encourage the sale of estates to the tenants and, largely through the ceaseless and devoted labours of Horace Plunkett, an Irish Unionist of progressive views, a Department of Agriculture was set up to promote economic prosperity.

The attitude of the respective Irish leaders in parliament to these proposals disclosed a complete divergence of view. John Dillon, who had now become the leader of the majority party, distrusted measures which he believed to be an insidious attempt to destroy the national movement. He "feared the Greeks even when they brought gifts." Redmond, on the contrary, held that every concession made by the English Government only increased the strength of the national demand and prepared the people for freedom. He therefore, with true statesmanship, welcomed and supported this new policy. Eventually in February, 1900, moved by their common sympathy with the Boer republics and forced by public opinion in Ireland, which had long been tired of the senseless quarrel, the two sections of the Irish Party re-united and elected John Redmond as their leader. The larger section had long been rent by animosities in which the highly temperamental personalities of Tim Healy and William O'Brien were predominant. O'Brien and Davitt had started in 1898 a new organisation called the United Irish League, which originated in the West of Ireland, with the object of dividing the large grazing farms but which eventually became a national organisation with wider aims. Healy played a characteristic part in the negotiations for unity. " I had to conceal from the Dillon party," he wrote, " my friendly relations with Redmond and pretend to be hostile to the projects of re-union. I therefore treated them in a grudging spirit while at the same time I was caucusing with Redmond and his friends." [1] Redmond's strength largely arose from the fact that he had never indulged in these personal intrigues.

That summer I paid my first visit to the House of Commons and listened to an Irish debate. My journal records—" Up a narrow staircase, through a turnstile where you sign your name, and then in the distance you hear a feeble 'hear, hear.' It is one's first impression of the House of Commons. Then you enter and look down. Below you lies the greatest legislative assembly in the world —at first sight you would also call it the most undignified. Question time was just over when we entered and some preliminary business was being disposed of. The members sprawled over the green benches, some apparently asleep. From the table comes the droning voice of the Clerk as he reads out an order. Then the Speaker rises and goes out, the Clerk announces ' the House will now go into Committee on the Irish Education Estimates.' A tremor of activity passes over the assembly—it wakes to life and almost in a body drifts out into the lobbies leaving behind the Irish members, some stray onlookers and the Minister responsible. Mr. O'Malley, an Irish member, rises. He asks for a measure of bilingual education in Ireland, presenting the facts clearly and moderately. Presently most of the few remaining English members leave the chamber. We are not allowed to govern ourselves and those who do so will not trouble to discover our point of view. Then John Redmond

[1] *Letters and Leaders of My Day.* Vo. ii., p. 435.

7—1818

speaks. Dignified, incisive and eloquent, he is an orator who would command attention in any parliament and a few English members troop back to hear him. He argues trenchantly for teaching Irish-speaking children through their own language and his fine peroration wakes the sleepy house to a burst of 'hear, hears.' After him comes a member of mature years whose accent betrays the fact that he hails from the North of Ireland. He promptly raises the ire of the Nationalist members, who interrupt him with angry cries. Mr. Balfour rises to reply. Thin, gaunt and angular, he stretches his long arms across the table, and whilst at first seeming to favour the teaching of Irish philosophically evades the main issue and shows that he has no intention of granting the Irish request. Mr. Chamberlain, just behind him, in a grey frock coat with a scarlet orchid in his button-hole sits regarding space through his eye-glass, his mind clearly remote from Ireland. As we left the House Mr. Balfour's thin voice was still rising from beneath. Outside, the terrace by the river was gay with bright parasols, smart frocks and pretty faces. The members were holding little tea parties. Ireland and her language were far from their thoughts. Drinking tea is undoubtedly a pleasanter occupation than trying to rule another country —especially when there is a little flirting thrown in."

This debate on bilingual education was symptomatic of a new and vital trend in Irish life. My generation, thoroughly disillusioned by the Parnell Split and its aftermath, had turned aside with disgust from politics which were fouled with personal hatreds and paralysed by a sense of frustration and despair. We began to ask ourselves if the realisation of a distinct national existence was dependent solely on the success of a political campaign, and to realise that the foreign domination was intellectual as well as political. In the very year of Parnell's death two young men, Father Eugene O'Growney, a professor at the ecclesiastical college of Maynooth, and Eóin Mac Neill, a civil servant from the Glens of Antrim, became acquainted through their mutual interest in the study of the Irish language. They had seen a great leader bring the Irish people within sight of the Promised Land and then dissension had swept every fair hope away. " The whole thing is enough to drive a man mad," wrote Father O'Growney to another friend in January, 1891. Yet in those days of sadness and despair the meeting of this delicate young priest and quiet thinking student was the precursor of a new movement, at first spiritual rather than political, for the regeneration of Ireland—a movement which had for its principal object the seemingly hopeless aim of reviving the Irish Language. In the following year, 1892, they were joined by a young Protestant graduate of Trinity College, Dr. Douglas Hyde, who was eventually to become the leader of this new movement, and equally well known to his fellow countrymen under his Gaelic pseudonym of *An Craoibhin Aoibhinn* (" The delightful little branch "). Hyde was descended from an old County Cork family of Norman origin. Receiving his early education from his father, a parson in the County Roscommon, he had learnt Irish from the peasantry and became a fluent speaker and writer of the language. He was endowed also with a sane patriotism, great enthusiasm, charm of manner and untiring energy which made him an ideal leader for a popular movement. Mac Neill and O'Growney had for some time been forced to the conclusion that unless the language was brought to the homes of the people as a living language its extinction was inevitable. Almost dead, save in some scattered seaboard districts, it was fast disappearing as spoken tongue and was little more than a subject of study for curious linguists and antiquarians. In Dr. Hyde, Mac Neill and O'Growney found a fitting companion-in-arms for the forlorn hope upon which they were about to enter. As a result of their efforts the Gaelic League was founded in July, 1893, with the primary object of preserving and spreading the Irish language as a means of oral intercourse and of creating a modern literature in Irish. Hyde was elected President, Father O'Growney, Vice-President, and Mac Neill Honorary Secretary. Father O'Growney had already written a popular Irish grammar, which became the chief text book of the new organisation ; but he never took an active part in its work, as owing to ill-health he had to go to Calfornia, where he died in 1899.

It is interesting to recall the objects and aims which inspired these men. Addressing the National Literary Society in 1892, Hyde said : " When we speak of the necessity for de-Anglicising the Irish people we mean it, not as a protest against imitating what is best in the English people, for that would be absurd, but rather to show the folly of neglecting what is Irish and hastening to adopt pell-mell and indiscriminately everything that is English simply because it is English," and in his *Literary History of Ireland*, published in 1899, he wrote : " Will it be believed that the Board of National Education insists upon the Irish-speaking child starting out from the first moment to read a language it does not speak ? " Yet it is exactly this procedure which is now being applied to English-speaking children throughout Ireland by our own Department of Education with results equally disastrous to their education and the Irish language. Father O'Growney also made it clear that his aim was not to banish the English language from Ireland, for that, he wrote, would be impossible and also absurd, but to establish a system of bilingual education under which every child would speak both English and his native language.[1] They rightly ascribed the loss of culture in modern Ireland to the fact that we had ceased to be Irish without becoming English.

By 1900 the Gaelic League had become a powerful organisation and, before the Commission set up in that year to inquire into the system of Intermediate Education, Dr. Hyde joined issue with Professors Atkinson and Mahaffy of Trinity College who decried Irish as a peasant *patois* in which it was "impossible to find a text which was not either religious, silly or indecent." Fortified by the opinion of leading European linguists and his own knowledge, he made short work of his opponents and, as a result of his advocacy, Irish was recognised as a necessary subject in the secondary education of Irish children. It was the first decisive victory for the new movement.

[1] *Irish Ecclesiastical Record*, November, 1890.

Irish cultural life had also begun to develop in other directions. In the previous year, 1899, W. B. Yeats, Lady Gregory and Edward Martyn had started the Irish Literary Theatre and Dublin had echoed with the controversy over Yeats' play, *The Countess Cathleen*. In October, 1900, I was present in the Gaiety Theatre, Dublin, at the first performance of *Casadh an tSúgáin* (" The Twisting of the Rope "), a one-act comedy in Irish by Dr. Hyde in which he himself played the principal part of O'Hanrahan, a wandering poet. It was a memorable night—the first occasion on which an Irish play was played in Irish in an Irish theatre. During the intervals we in the gallery sang old Irish songs and the more fashionable seats below applauded our efforts. After a long night we seemed to be emerging into the brightness of the dawn and to be witnessing a visible and material sign of an Irish intellectual revival. The performance, which followed, of a curious and unsuccessful play in English by Yeats and George Moore dealing with the heroic love story of Diarmuid and Grania, acted by Benson and his company, was somewhat of an anti-climax.

But the new movement had also its political side. This found dramatic expression the following years in a one-act play by W. B. Yeats. This powerful allegory, *Cathleen ni Houlihan*, did more than hundreds of political speeches to influence the rising generation. It was first played in a small hall in a Dublin back street to crowded houses, the title part being taken by Miss Maud Gonne, a tall handsome young woman who was already a prominent figure in revolutionary circles. She was the daughter of an officer in the British army. Simple in plot, yet deeply moving and poetic, this play depicted the scene in a peasant's house at Killala during the French invasion of 1798. We see the eldest son leave his prospective bride to join the French invaders at the bidding of a poor old vagrant woman who is no other than Cathleen ni Houlihan—the spirit of Ireland. Few who saw the original performance, as I did, will forget the great climax of the play when Michael goes out to follow the strange old woman, and his father asks the younger son if he saw an old woman going down the path. " I did not," replies the boy, " but I saw a young girl and she had the walk of a queen." No more potent lines were ever spoken on an Irish stage. All our hopes were in that answer. It had an echo in every heart. It symbolised and rekindled that flame of romantic revolutionary nationalism which was to consume so many of its devotees and which has not even yet been quenched by the healing waters of freedom and experience. Poets have much to answer for !

The vision of a new Ireland was now to find more practical political expression through the pen of Arthur Griffith. In January, 1899, this young Dublin journalist, who had just returned to his native city after a sojourn in South Africa, helped to found a small weekly paper called the *United Irishman*. His journal quickly became the mouth-piece of a new political movement. Griffith's sincere and powerful articles soon attracted attention. He preached the doctrine that Irish self-government could never be won through parliamentary action at Westminster, where Irish national policy had to be subordinated to the necessities of English party politics, and where, inevitably, Irish members became remote from, and indifferent to, Irish influence. I can remember, one day during those student years, calling on Griffith to obtain information concerning some aspect of the industrial revival, which he also strongly advocated. To find him I had to climb the narrow stairs of an old house in a street running down to the Liffey. There in a dusty back office surrounded by piles of MSS., files, and the other odds and ends of a small newspaper office, he sat at a little table, a small, stocky, man, his short-sighted eyes peering from behind thick glasses, his mouth hidden under a heavy moustache. Here, I felt, was a man of dogged determination but little sense of humour ; a man with a mission, not a politician.

His policy was finally crystallised and expounded in a series of articles which appeared in his paper during the first six months of 1904, under the title of " The Resurrection of Hungary ; A Parallel for Ireland." Subsequently repub-lished in pamphlet form, these articles had a wide circulation and a considerable influence. Hungary, he claimed, had

become a nation because she turned her back on Vienna
and realised that the political centre of the nation must be
within the nation, remembering the words of Kossuth that
" only on the soil of a nation can a nation's salvation be
worked out." Ireland, which sixty years before had been
Hungary's exemplar, had failed, he asserted, because she
had chosen the path of compromise and expediency and sent
her representatives to London. In the history of the struggle
for Hungarian freedom he found the same ingredients that
had been familiar in Irish history, namely religious discord,
absentee landlords aping the civilisation of the conqueror,
and the decline of the native language and culture. He
told how Szechenyi taught the Hungarians the necessity
for the revival of their language, the education of the people,
and the building up of agriculture and industry. He
described how two young men, Francis Déak, the barrister,
and Louis Kossuth, the journalist, arose in Hungary, and
saw that no prosperity, no intellectual life, could endure
in a country unless they were sustained by free political
institutions. Déak's programme, Griffith pointed out, was
embodied in the declaration that Hungary was a free
country, independent in its whole system of legislation and
administration and subordinate to no other country. Déak
took his stand on the Pragmatic Sanction, which was,
wrote Griffith, as if we in Ireland took our stand on the
Renunciation Act passed by the English Parliament in
1783, which declared that Ireland in future could only be
bound by the laws enacted by the Parliament of Ireland.
Kossuth, on the other hand, was prepared to take up arms
for the independence of Hungary.

The story of Kossuth's struggle, the establishment of the
Hungarian Republic, the catastrophe of Vilagos, the
oppression and tyranny which followed, Déak's refusal, in
spite of cajolement and flattery, to recognise the right of
the Austrian Parliament to legislate for Hungary, and his
final triumph over all opponents, were brilliantly described
in Griffith's pages. Nor did he fail to draw the moral.
He claimed that if there had been in Ireland in 1867, after
the failure of the Fenian insurrection, one strong, able,

honest man—like Déak—who undeistood the significance
of the coronation of the Emperor Francis Joseph at Buda,
he could have rallied and led Ireland to victory. But we did
not produce such a man. On the contrary, asserted Griffith,
there appeared Isaac Butt, the apostle of compromise, who,
himself and his successors. had led the country to the
brink of destruction. In John Mitchel, the revolutionary
leader cf 1848, Ireland, he claimed, had a rough equivalent
of Kossuth, but she never had a Déak.   Griffith did not
propose an Irish Republic, on the contrary he recognised
the King as King of Ireland. The Act of Union with Great
Britain was, he claimed, never valid, because the members
of the Irish parliament had no legal powers to terminate
its existence, and therefore no authority existed under the
Constitution to legislate for Ireland except the King, Lords
and Commons of Ireland. We were, he said, in regard to
the settlement of 1782 (embodied in the Renunciation Act
of the following year) precisely in the same position as
Hungary in regard to the Constitution of 1848. He therefore advocated that the Irish people should retrace their
steps and take their stand on the Compact of 1782 and the
Renunciation Act of 1783, as Déak had taken his on the
Pragmatic Sanction and the laws of 1848.

Fifteen months afterwards, in November, 1905, at a
meeting in the Rotunda, Dublin, Griffith elaborated his
adaptation of Hungarian methods to Irish conditions in
what he called the Sinn Féin policy. The Irish words
Sinn Féin, meaning simply "ourselves," were chosen as
expressing the attitude of himself and his follcwers to the
accepted policy of the majority of Irish Nationalists led
by John Redmond, who relied on the policy of persuading
the English electorate, or on the inter-play of English party
politics, to assure self-government for Ireland. His new
organisation thus became know as the Sinn Féin party. He
advocated a policy of high protection for Irish Industry on
the lines of the Zollverein of Friedrich List, and the setting
up, in Dublin, of a National Council of three hundred
members representing the local government councils of
the country, and constituting themselves a *de facto* Irish

Parliament. His policy was, he said, in a word, to teach the Irish people to rely upon themselves and to establish in Dublin a national legislature endowed with the moral authority of the Irish nation.

This new policy made a definite appeal to many in my generation. Here, we felt, was a new approach to the old problem which was both sincere and realistic. But in fact the time was not yet ripe for such a development. After the General Election of 1906, a Mr. Dolan, who had been elected as an Irish Party candidate for North Leitrim, resigned his seat and stood as a Sinn Féin candidate but was badly defeated. The return to power of the Liberal Party in England had completely altered the situation and Irish hopes revived. The Irish Party claimed and received the support of the people in a policy which eventually succeeded in securing from the British Parliament the introduction of a Home Rule Bill and other ameliorative measures. The centre of political gravity had shifted from Dublin to London and thirteen years elapsed before Griffith's Hungarian seed germinated and yielded a strange harvest. He was not then, and never became, a great popular leader. A journalist and not an orator, bourgeois in mentality and background, he had no interest in, and little sympathy with, labour demands or problems of social reform. He was essentially a city man and had little knowledge of rural Ireland. His policy had consequently not much support outside Dublin. Even there it declined after 1910 and at the time of the rising of 1916 there was actually only one branch of the organisation in existence. Its subsequent revival in another form is perhaps therefore all the more remarkable and proved the stubborn pertinacity of the man.

In July, 1900, my brother George and I were reminded of this new Irish movement when on our way to Paris to visit the Exhibition of that year. A fellow traveller on the cross-channel journey to Dieppe was Miss Maude Gonne, attended by various members of her party. She was in fact on her way to Paris to make arrangements for French passports for Irishmen going to South Africa to join the

Irish Brigade fighting for the Boers, one of whom, Major
MacBride, she shortly afterwards married. On arrival at
Dieppe she was met by a deputation of French officials.
One small fat man, girt with a tricolour sash, who was obviously the Mayor or Prefect, presented her with a bouquet
and made a speech of welcome. There was no *entente
cordiale* in those days. A few days later we found on President
Kruger's statue in the Transvaal Pavilion at the Exhibition,
an Irish wreath on which was pinned a manifesto composed
by Father Kavanagh—a humble but fiery Franciscan priest
—denouncing " England's Robber War." We realised that
Miss Gonne and her friends had been there before us.

Paris was like a furnace that summer. Beating from
above and burning from below the sun struck at us fiercely
and there was no relief till the cool evening hours. Nevertheless we conscientiously explored the Exhibition with all the
ardour and curiosity of youth. Like many international
exhibitions, before and since, it consisted of a Street of
Nations along the banks of the Seine where each country
had its own building—England an Elizabethan Manor,
Norway a timber house, and so on. Great palaces of glass
in the adjacent thoroughfares were dedicated to the arts
and crafts of man, and being French, of woman. Above
all the Eiffel Tower, still an engineering curiosity, rose
supreme. At night the buildings glittered with lights in
the clear air. All was instinct with that grace and charm
which France can command. But it was also very overwhelming and we were often very tired. All the world had
come to see this record of progress and the guests at our
small hotel in a quiet side street were truly cosmopolitan.
Amongst them were a South African from Kimberley who
had a supreme contempt for all foreigners ; a Scotch doctor
with a broad accent and a canny face who took his flaxen-
haired daughter to *Les Ambassedeurs* where they laughed at
Yvette Guilbert whom they fortunately did not understand ;
a few naïve Americans ; an English engineer and his wife ;
some French provincials, a whole giggling family of them ;
and a jovial Irishman who was certainly an Alderman in
his native town. The ostensible manager was a little nervous

man with long moustaches and hair that seemed to stand on end with excitement, but the real manager was the stout *concierge* who spoke broken English impulsively when the fit took her. She it was who harangued the postman about our letters, fought with our cabmen about fares, cajoled waiters, and magically solved all difficulties.

When we had satiated ourselves with the Exhibition we went further afield. We spent a long day in a tourist char-a-banc exploring the glories of Versailles, worshipped in Notre Dame and the Madeleine, and looked down in the cool light under the dome of the Invalides at the great granite tomb of Napoleon. It was all very exciting and I felt somewhat superior as I piloted my brother through these, to me, already familiar scenes. The Third Republic had just been shaken by the Dreyfus case, and, though it was still intact and even, as it seemed, leading the march of civilisation, all was far from well. Frenchmen, one felt, did not want to rule, they wanted to live. For them the pursuit of life, of charming sensations, of laughter, of intelligent apprehension, of individual development seemed more important than the desire to govern, to make laws, to fight. Yet I reflected that both history and common sense taught that if a nation neglects politics it will sooner or later become the victim of aggression. Could France survive another Sedan and remain a great nation ? The answer to that question remains the central problem of European civilisation. At Dieppe as we travelled homewards we saw the humble Norman country folk, the hardy peasants in their blue blouses, the women's sunburnt faces. Here, I thought, rather than in Paris, was the real France—a people courteous and kindly, frugal and brave, who earn their living, love their kin and do what the priest tells them. Paris ignored them and the world outside hardly knew of them but they were the backbone of France.

In January, 1902, I returned to Dublin to grind for my Final examination and took up my abode in lodgings on the South Circular Road. There in a small sitting-room and bedroom I lived remote and solitary for six months. The loneliness, at first somewhat appalling, soon gave way to a feeling of selfish misanthropy which did not improve my

manners. I worked often from 6 a.m. till the small hours
of the next morning and the only break in this monotonous
toil was when I went out to attend a special grinding class
or read a novel for half an hour after meals. My landlady,
an elderly but obliging person who boasted of her descent
from Daniel O'Connell, was my principal source of contact
with the outside world. The other inhabitants of the house,
two chronic medical students and a shop girl, seldom crossed
my path. On one occasion, however, the medical students
presented a touch of light comedy. One night the oil in
my lamp having run out I went out to buy some at an
adjacent shop, my landlady having provided me with a
bottle which had originally contained Three Star Brandy.
As I was returning home I met the two medicals in a slightly
inebriated condition. When I regained my room I found
that the bottle had mysteriously vanished from my pocket.
The medicos believing it to be brandy had removed it for
refreshment purposes. Although they subsequently " saw
stars " they were certainly not of the kind they expected.

In June, 1902, I duly passed my Final examination and
was admitted a solicitor. Jaded by six months' hard work
I decided to return to Cork by sea. Never have I had a more
satisfied feeling than when I stood at the stern of the Clyde
boat *Eddystone* that evening and watched dusk settle down
over Dublin Bay. Howth stood out sharp and clear like a
knife edge against the Northern sky and the long sweep of
the Wicklow mountains glided past like a dream in the
gathering dusk. As darkness fell the lighthouse beacons along
the coast flared up one after another out of the shadows.
Presently the whole sky was studded with stars and nothing
broke the stillness of the night but the throbbing of the screw
and the click of the log. It was past midnight when I
finished my pipe and went below. Before I sank into the
dreamless sleep of youth I remembered that I was just
twenty-one and felt that life was about to begin in earnest.

VIII

AND life did begin, for Cork was *en fête* that summer. On the wide stretch of meadow land, bordering the Lee under the villa covered heights of Sunday's Well, its enterprising citizens were holding an International Exhibiton. Where cattle had grazed peacefully a few months before there now rose, amidst the trees of the Mardyke, domes, towers and minarets, adding a new note of red and white to the familiar landscape. In the large Industrial Hall Irish products had a prominent place. It was the forerunner of our modern industrial revival. Irish tweed, Irish lace and Irish soap defiantly proclaimed their virtues ; Irish matches attended on somewhat powerful Irish cigars ; Irish threshing machines made their *début*. In one avenue the Department of Agriculture and Technical Instruction had brought together, from many lands, expert workmen who carried on before our eyes such crafts as silk-weaving, wood-carving, pottery-making, hat making, and boot making. It was a practical and useful lesson which had fruitful results. In the Agricultural section examples of modern methods used elsewhere were also displayed ; Danish farm buildings standing side by side with the latest American machinery. An Art Gallery, containing a representative collection of pictures, educated our eyes. On the adjacent river a water chute and a fleet of Thames skiffs provided open air entertainment. In the large Concert Hall and the band-stand outside famous choirs and orchestras gave concerts for our delight. Amongst the memorable musical visitors that summer were the Berlin Philharmonic Orchestra. For the first time I heard great music nobly played. Sitting under the trees by the river during the long summer evenings we listened to those gifted German musicians performing the classical masterpieces of Beethoven, Bach, Brahms, Schumann, Wagner and Tschaikovsky. I can still recollect their performance of the

last named composer's " 1812 " overture, the descriptive
nature of which appealed to my immature musical taste.
Listening to them I heard also, for the first time, the majestic,
minatory music of Beethoven's Fifth Symphony.   The
children of those musicians had reason to remember the
sombre warning notes of both those famous compositions.

The Exhibition, like most such enterprises, was primarily
due to the energy of one man—Alderman Edward Fitz-
Gerald, the Lord Mayor.   It was his conception, and his
was the driving force that carried it to a successful conclusion.
" Fitzy," as he was affectionately called by his fellow-
citizens, was a remarkable personality.   Coming to Cork as
an artisan from the country whilst a young man, he became
a prosperous building contractor and a prominent local
politician.   He always reminded me of those rather savage
lines of Kipling, about the Irish in America :

There came to the beach a poor exile of Erin
The dew on his night robe was heavy and chill,
Ere the steamer that brought him had passed out of hearing.
He was Alderman Mike introducing a Bill.

What he lacked, however, in education and polish he
made up for by a native wit and shrewd intelligence that
stood him in good stead amidst the intrigues of municipal
affairs.   He was what the English call a " card," and the
stories and legends about his doings and sayings were manifold.   In August, 1903, he persuaded King Edward VII to
visit the Exhibition, which had been kept open for a second
year.   The King received a tumultuous welcome as he
drove from his yacht to the Exhibition through the crowded
streets. It was probably the best reception ever given to a
British monarch in Ireland.   His sporting proclivities had
already made him popular and Fitzy's manoeuvres did the
rest. I saw him as he drove with the Queen at walking pace
through the city, his small portly person resplendent in
Field Marshal's uniform and cocked hat, his carriage
flanked by detectives thinly camouflaged in tall hats and
frock coats.   As he beamed upon the cheering crowds he
must have reflected, somewhat cynically, on the difference

between this and his previous reception eighteen years before. So delighted was the King by this unexpected triumph and by the bluff congenial character of his host that he there and then made him a baronet. Not long afterwards Fitzy was travelling to Dublin with some cronies who persisted in addressing him as " Sir Edward." At last, annoyed by this unaccustomed homage he burst out " Be quiet boys, remember we're travelling *infra dig*." An instance of his wit and resource appears in another story. On one occasion, while Lord Mayor, he was approached in the street by a deputation collecting for a walking race. " Ah," said Fitzy, " the young men nowadays don't know how to walk, I'll show you." Whereupon he strode down the street and round a corner leaving the unfortunate deputation to its fate. At a later date he stood as an Independent candidate during a parliamentary election. His rivals had organised large election committees and made elaborate arrangements for the contest. Fitzy addressing the electors reminded them that his election committee was located under his hat ! Unfortunately he was not elected for he would probably have enlivened the proceedings of parliament. In fact the success of the Cork Exhibition of 1902–3 was his greatest triumph and its site, now a public park by the river, appropriately bears his name.

I was soon immersed in the practice of my profession. Like most young professional men I discovered the fact, mercifully hidden from the general public, that it is only after qualification that one really begins to learn one's business. It might indeed be said with truth that a professional man, if he is wise, is always learning, and I am not ashamed to confess that, after some forty years of practice, I still find fresh fields to explore and improved methods to follow. The practice of the law in an Irish provincial city is seldom exciting but never monotonous, for specialisation, which often atrophies both mind and soul, is impossible. At one moment one may be defending a client on a criminal charge, or for a breach of some of the multifarious regulations which combine the functions of reducing personal liberty and increasing a lawyer's income, at the next one may be drawing a marriage settlement for a farmer's daughter or drafting complicated articles of association for a limited company. A solicitor in Ireland may appear as an advocate in both the district and circuit courts, which roughly correspond to the petty sessions court and county court in England, although we have long since, I am glad to say, abolished unpaid magistrates. Even in the High Court a solicitor may sometimes, in the absence of counsel, be called on to conduct his client's case, and I have myself done so before the High Court on Assizes.

My first important case had its origin in a tragic occurrence. On 15th January, 1903, the SS. *Upupa*, a small cross-channel cargo steamer belonging to the City of Cork Steam Packet Company, was lost with all hands. She had left Cardiff the previous day with a general cargo bound for Cork. That evening she was seen labouring in a heavy sea off the Smalls by another vessel of the same company. In the night a fierce gale sprang up. She was never seen again. At the Board of Trade inquiry which ensued I represented the relatives of the lost crew. During the proceedings it transpired that in November, 1901, whilst she was on voyage to England, in somewhat similar weather conditions, her bilge pumps had refused to work and she had been forced to seek refuge at Falmouth with a list of thirty degrees to port and her stokehold full of water. The Board of Trade had then intervened and compelled the company to overhaul her. In cross-examination I elicited from the Secretary of the Company the damaging fact that shortly after this occurrence the captain of the ship, a brave and experienced sailor, had written to the company complaining that the engines were defective and untrustworthy, and that the Directors had replied in a cruel letter suggesting that he was losing his nerve and should take a holiday, or in other words, retire. These dramatic disclosures created a considerable sensation. The tragedy was accentuated by the fact that several farewell messages in bottles, which purported to come from members of the crew, but were probably spurious, were washed ashore. Although I was able to show that the loss of the ship could not have been due to bad seamanship or the nature of the cargo, the Court refused to draw the obvious conclusion that she was unseaworthy and begged the question by finding that she " was in good and seaworthy condition as regards hull and equipment, always assuming that the serious defects recorded in November, 1901, had been effectively repaired." But public opinion had already given a different verdict and it was the one I asked for.

My interests were, however, by no means entirely professional. I believed then, and still believe that an existence confined within the boundaries of one's calling in life is incomplete and unsatisfying. To attain such happiness as is possible one's interests must be varied and one's dutie⸱ to the community fully realised and discharged. I therefore from the first took a lively interest in local and national affairs.

The work of the Gaelic League appealed particularly to my youthful idealism and I threw myself into it with ardour and conviction. In the Cork Branch, of which I eventually became Vice-President, I found ample scope for my activities. A Gaelic League branch was in those days a vital and inspiring place, a social as well as an intellectual centre. Its principal objective was to teach the Irish language, but this by no means exhausted its work. In the hundreds of branches throughout the country its members also studied Irish history and learnt Irish dancing and music. In small halls in back lanes, and in remote country schoolhouses and barns, they gathered night after night to nourish themselves at the roots of Gaelic culture. My friend Alice Milligan has captured some of the spirit of those days in her poem " The Man on the Wheel " which describes the progress of a Gaelic League teacher across the snow clad hills to the little hall where his class waits :

A man goes by on a wheel with the rain on his face
Against the way of the wind and he not caring :
Goes on through the winter night towards a distant lonesome, place,
For his heart is hot with the glow of the ancient hero-daring.

8—1818

For the most part they were humble folk, for it was a people's movement, but it attracted all ages and classes. In its ranks farmer and labourer, shop-boy and shop-keeper, professional man and clerk, met on terms of perfect equality, united by patriotism. It was a great movement and might have had a great future. Here the seeds of a new Ireland germinated but never flowered. Had it continued to develop on those lines it might have given us that solid moral and social foundation which Bishop Grundtvig's High Schools gave to Denmark. Unfortunately this splendid beginning was futile. The means were mistaken for the end and what was then a crusade eventually became a ramp. I learnt the language with enthusiasm and pleasure ; my grandchildren's generation learn it because they must. In fact the Irish language has now ceased to be a language and has become a profitable but uneconomic industry.

Culture is the normal result of what is called a liberal education. It implies largeness of view, balance of judgment, a sense of proportion, the appreciation of the beautiful in art and nature, that sense of fineness in conduct which is sometimes called honour and sometimes courtesy. The cultural history of our people began from the sixth to the ninth century with a period of brilliant development. Intellectual and spiritual giants like Columbanus and Scotus Eriugena held aloft the lamp of learning and philosophy to a darkened Europe. Unfortunately this old Gaelic order, shattered by the successive invasions of the Danes and Normans and denied all the amenties which contribute to cultural development, finally collapsed in complete con-fusion. Its distinguishing mark had been charity, urbanity, refinement and wide learning. Like all true culture it was tolerant, liberal and universal. The Gaelic League made the mistake of believing that by the revival of the Irish language alone Irish culture could be revived and, that if the language died, the Irish nation would also cease to exist. It failed to see, or it forgot, that to restore Gaelic culture something more was needed, namely to raise the general cultural standard of the people ; and that the language was only one element, and not necessarily a vital one, in that culture. All people speak some language but not all are cultured. In truth if language were a vital ingredient of nationality the Irish nation would no longer exist, a proposition with which few people, least of all the Irish, are likely to agree. The Gaelic League also forgot that the extreme form of nationalism, which it eventually propagated, is destructive of all culture for it *ipso facto* refuses to learn from other lands and other times. In effect it closed the door on the common heritage of civilised man and became narrowminded, intolerant and insular. The simple, unsophisticated, and often boorish, native speaker was elevated to the scholar's throne. His standards of speech, manners and literature became the criteria of the new movement. Finally it was captured by the politicians for their own purposes and with the coming of the new Irish state ceased to count. Yet, if it had followed the path set by its founders and realised that true culture is tolerant and universal, that we were denationalised, not by England but by English vulgarity, and that the restoration of the language was only a means to an end—namely the restoration of a true native culture through the general education of the Irish people—great things might have been achieved. Unfortunately it was not to be, and the enterprise, which we began so hopefully in those days, ended in frustration and defeat. It is no doubt true that the language lingers on, kept alive by spasmodic injections of lip service and state aid, but our traditional culture, with all it signified, is dead. A few years ago, whilst sleeping in a Dublin hotel, I was awakened in the small hours of the morning by two drunken men quarrelling under my windows in Irish. Here, I felt, was reality. I remembered the quay porters at Holyhead talking Welsh as they loaded the mail boat and I wondered if there might be some hope for the Irish language after all. But even two swallows do not unfortunately make a summer and the experience has never been repeated.

In the domain of native art we made a similar mistake. Mere imitation of early Irish art was mistaken for inspiration. The practice of making endless copies of copies debased the ancient models until all sense of line, proportion and purpose perished. Ornament which was once full of life became, when wrongly applied, mechanical and meaningless. We did not realise that copies of interlaced Celtic patterns were not necessarily Irish Art. This trade in Irish ornament reached its absurd apotheosis when the beautiful Ardagh chalice, that masterpiece of early Christian art, was reproduced as a racing cup, complete even to the names of the apostles ! ·Ornament is like a language. Until we master the vocabulary of forms—so that words come to us without effort—we cannot say anything ; we cannot design in a particular style until we have made the form language of that style our own. Happily the present generation of Irish artists and craftsmen have begun to realise this basic truth. But in music the worshippers of folk tradition still refuse to realise or admit that art music is as much a national necessity and part of any normal cutltural development as folk song, and that its development can only take place through the study of the masters who speak in the universal language of art.

Yet in the early nineteen hundreds all this was not so obvious as it is now. The enemy was Anglicisation ; our aim the creation of an Irish Ireland. We had yet to experience the more deadly peril of Los Angelisation ! My feelings at that time were clearly expressed in the peroration of an address which I gave on National Self-Reliance and which I see no reason to regret or recant. " The voice of a new Ireland," I said, " is speaking clearly if we will but hear. It is urging us to look back upon the past, not to revive bitter memories of English persecution and oppression, ' still less to feed the lazy reveries of seanachies or poets upon legends of a golden age hid in the mists of antiquity, but rather to rear a generation whose life will be strengthened and ennobled by the knowledge that there have been great men of their race and great actions done on the soil they tread ' ; a generation whose resolution and fidelity will be fortified by knowing that their ancestors have left their mark for ever on some of the most memorable eras of European history, that they are heirs to a culture and a language unsurpassed for its power and value, and to a

line of scholars, soldiers and ecclesiastics no more question-
able than the marshals of Napoleon or the poets of Weimar.
An Ireland mean-spirited, imitating alien manners and
customs is an Ireland poor and despised, but an Ireland
self reliant, confiding in her own energy and cultivating
her own culture and characteristics within the larger frame
of Western civilisation, is Ireland a nation."

My contribution to this movement consisted of teaching
history to the local branch of the Gaelic League. For many
years I dedicated several evenings each month to this work
and studied in the language classes as well. I soon learned
that imagination is no substitute for learning though it is
often its debtor. Each history lecture had to be carefully
prepared, sources examined and references checked, for my
pupils were both adult and critical, often with views or
theories of their own. I found that maps and illustrations
were an indispensable part of my instruction, and these had
to be prepared or procured. Altogether it was a valuable
and interesting experience which incidentally helped me in
my professional work, for it impressed upon me the importance of authority and accuracy.

I began also to take part in public affairs. For this
development, David P. Moran, the editor of the *Leader*, was
primarily responsible. This remarkable man, " the philosopher of Irish Ireland," whom I afterwards came to know
intimately, played a leading part in the history of that
period. A native of Waterford, he had served his apprenticeship in the excellent school of English Liberal journalism.
In 1898 he visited Ireland and his keen critical intellect
began to examine Irish life in all its phases. He had
surveyed Irish affairs for some time from a distance and now
he was able to see things at close quarters and to measure
what he saw by his experience of English life and methods.
The result was an article entitled " Is the Irish nation dying?"
which appeared in the *New Ireland Review* for December,
1898. " If one were asked," he wrote, " to sum up the
present condition of the country in one epigram one might
say that our activities spring from a foreign inspiration and
that we only preserve a national colour about the manner

in which we don't do things." The new Ireland struggling for expression under the banner of the Gaelic League seized his interest and sympathy. Other articles followed in which he developed and expounded his views on the existing stagnation and future possibilities of Ireland. He did not at first obtain a hearing. The people were dominated by old shibboleths and catch cries and had little use for independent thought. But Moran was not a man to be daunted by difficulties or apathy, no matter how great. In 1900 he returned to Ireland to practise and propagate what he had preached, and the *Leader*, a new weekly review of literature, politics, industry and art, came into existence under his editorship. It soon made history. Moran's style was vigorous, always clear, often aggressive. He realised that desperate conditions needed desperate remedies and acted accordingly. His description of a certain type of bigoted Protestant as a " sourface " and his reference to the drink trade as " Bungs " were hardly tactful or polite but nevertheless effective. Nor did he spare the Catholic Church, for he poured scorn and ridicule on the bad German stained glass and synthetic pictures which then disfigured, and in many cases still disfigure, our country churches. In a poor country like ours, he pointed out, the Church was the principal patron of the arts and one had a right to expect that it would show good taste and encourage native craftsmen. The contrary was, however, the case. The metropolitan press, irked by his criticism, maintained an ostrich-like policy of ignoring the existence of the new journal. But the *Leader* pursued its course, gathering adherents, as it went, and the policy of silence, adopted towards it by its elder brothers, was perhaps its best advertisement. Moran's policy was indeed one of " taking the bull by the horns." He tackled at once several of the biggest vested interests in the country. The drink trade, the railway companies, the Protestant ascendancy, the decadent music hall stage, were all trenchantly exposed by his mordant pen. Some of them ran away, others stood their ground, fought, and were beaten. O'Connell had achieved the political emancipation of the Irish Catholics at the commencement of the

nineteenth century but even in 1900 we were still, at least
to some extent, socially unemancipated. In commerce and
official life the Protestant ascendancy still preserved its
prestige, power and position. Moran believed the time
had come to complete the work O'Connell had begun.
He himself was not unlike The Liberator, well set up, broad
shouldered with a leonine head, keen humorous eyes and
the strong determined chin of a fighter. Yet he was
insistent that the new Ireland must be founded on love not
hate, and he quoted with approval Grattan's words concerning our relations with England—" As her equal we shall
be her sincerest friend ; as anything less than her equal we
shall be her bitterest enemy." In some ways he was a
greater power in public affairs than Arthur Griffith, whose
influence was purely political. There was no love lost
between them for each thought that " the other lion had
a louder roar," and Moran's description of Griffith's Sinn
Féin organisation as the " tin pikers " added fuel to the fire.
But Moran is now almost forgotten and Griffith, because
of his associations with the Sinn Féin policy and the
foundation of the Irish state, is assured of fame. Of the two
Moran was certainly a more human and I think, in some
ways, a bigger personality. His judgments on men and
things were always apt and penetrating. I remember on
one occasion discussing with him the political vagaries of a
certain unstable but lovable Cork personality. " The worst
of it is," I said, " that he is such a decent fellow one can't
quarrel with him." " Unfortunately," he promptly retorted,
" the decent fellows are the curse of Ireland."

I first met him in 1902 after the *Leader* had exposed the
way in which the clerical staff of the Great Southern Railway
(nicknamed by Moran the Great Sourface Railway) which
was the principal line in the country, was closed to Catholics
in spite of the fact that the large majority of its shareholders
belonged to that faith. As a result of Moran's exposure
of this state of affairs a committee of Catholic shareholders, of
which I acted as secretary, was formed to demand redress.
The directors at first refused to give us any information,
alleging that they did not inquire as to their employees'

religion although the Chairman had publicly stated at the previous meeting of the Company that the allegations were untrue, which he could not know if he had not inquired. It was in fact notorious that the staff were selected almost entirely from a Protestant orphanage with which a prominent official of the company was officially connected, a not unnatural but definitely unfair proceeding. Finally at the next general meeting of the Company, in February, 1903, the directors acknowledged the justice of our allegations by conceding our demand that the Company's clerical staff should, in future, be recruited entirely by competitive examination. The other railway companies, where similar conditions prevailed, were rapidly forced to follow suit. This event marked a definite step forward in the emancipation of Irish Catholics, a process which was eventually completed when we obtained control of the national government.

My association with this committee also brought me into touch with another remarkable man—Edward Martyn. He was in many ways the complete antithesis of Moran although their aims were very similar. Of Anglo-Norman stock, he was directly descended from Geoffrey Martyn, one of Strongbow's officers. So influential and popular was his family in the West of Ireland that Oliver Martyn, M.P. for Galway, another of his ancestors, was specially exempted by statute, in the reign of Queen Anne, from the penalties inflicted on Roman Catholics. Educated at the English Jesuit school, Beaumont, and at Christ Church, Oxford, where he took his degree, he travelled widely and acquired considerable knowledge of Church music and religious art. His youth was that of a typical Irish landlord, managing local affairs as a member of the Grand Jury and following the famous Galway Blazers in the hunting field. In 1899, however, he read Lecky's *History of Ireland in the 18th Century*, and for the first time a true conception of Irish history flashed upon him. He became almost at once a Nationalist. Shortly afterwards a local concert was held at Tulira Castle, his country house, and, without his consent, an attempt was made to terminate the proceedings with the British National

Anthem. This he immediately prevented. He was promptly
called on by Lord Clonbrock, the Lord Lieutenant of the
County, to explain his conduct, and replied in a dignified
letter, boldly stating his reasons and resigning his positions
as Justice of the Peace and Deputy Lieutenant. The
correspondence between them appeared in the Press and
caused no small sensation. But he was soon destined to
travel even further on the rough road of Irish nationalism.
In 1903 an attempt was made to present King Edward, on
the occasion of his visit to Ireland, with an address of
welcome from the Dublin Corporation. Martyn, Arthur
Griffith, and others who agreed with them that such action
would amount to a moral recognition of the Union, formed
a National Council, and by their spirited protest at a
political meeting in the Rotunda, Dublin, secured the defeat
of the project. His subsequent activities as President of the
Sinn Féin organisation, in its earlier stages, led to one of
the most interesting of modern lawsuits. He was a member
of the Kildare Street Club, the social forum of the most
ultra loyal and conservative type of Irish landlord, and after
he had made a speech against recruiting for the British
Army, its outraged members expelled him from the club.
Unfortunately for them their indignation was greater than
their knowledge of the rules. Martyn, acting on the advice
of legal friends, myself amongst others, refused to admit the
legality of their proceedings and immediately brought an
action against the Club committee in which he was successful.
He remained a member of the Club till his death and often
recounted with glee the reactions of his brother members
when he said his rosary in the smoking room or brought
Franciscan fathers in their brown habits to lunch.

Although he was thirty years my senior Martyn and I
became close friends and remained so in spite of some
differences of opinion, until his death in 1923. When I
first met him he had already by pen and purse contributed
a great deal to the initiation of the Irish Literary Theatre,
his play *The Heather Field* being one of their first productions
in 1899. This play, his most important dramatic work,
which may be briefly described as the tragedy of an idealist

married to a prosaic, unimaginative woman, was strongly influenced by the work of Ibsen. It was a drama of mental conflict rather than of action. Although he subsequently wrote several other plays, none of them attained, or indeed deserved, success. Martyn, once, alluding to the human failing which causes so many people to fancy themselves in their least successful roles, described to me Douglas Hyde's pride in his prowess as a sportsman, saying " I think he is prouder of shooting a sparrow in his garden than of having compiled *The Love Songs of Connaught.*" This was also true of Martyn himself, for, although he fancied himself as a dramatist and a politician, he had no real aptitude for either calling and was at his best, as Arthur Symons said of him, " a talented amateur." As a politician his guileless nature, lack of oratorical ability or experience, and his tenacity of principle were fatal defects, and he soon deserted a field of activity which he should never have entered. " What we in Ireland have to do," he once wrote to me, " is to keep honestly to our principles and never relax them no matter what rumours we hear of the Government being prepared to do this or that, if we will only consent to do something against our principles. Principles are no use unless they are held to in a great crisis." The writings of Swift and the career of Parnell, whose policy he had opposed as a young landlord, were his principal inspiration. When he visited us he never tired of discussing Parnell's work and personality with my father.

His real talent, however, lay in his cultured taste and leadership. Hyde once described him to me as " the best citizen in Ireland," and that I think was true for he was ready to support with voice and purse any movement for the advancement of the people. His most notable achievement was the foundation in 1899 of the Palestrina Choir for the sorely needed reform of Catholic liturgical music in Ireland, a step which proved to be an intelligent anticipation of the decree of the Holy Father himself. This Choir, subsequently, with his approval, merged into the Dublin pro-Cathedral Choir, has done solid and enduring work for the improvement of Church music in Ireland, only equalled by that of the Cork Cathedral Choir under the direction of my friend Aloys Fleischmann, which another friend of mine, Sir Arnold Bax, the distinguished composer, once publicly praised as amongst the finest in Europe.

Martyn was also deeply interested in the work of the Gaelic League and was for many years a member of its Coiste Gnótha or executive committee. There his efforts were largely directed to the revival of our rich national music, and he was the first critic to call attention to the beauty and value of traditional singing amongst the peasants. It was while listening to such music at a country *féis* or musical festival that he first heard John McCormack sing. Delighted with the quality and beauty of his voice he helped to launch him on his subsequent meteoric career. In 1901 he initiated a movement for the reform of Church art and was largely instrumental in starting a studio for the manufacture of Irish stained-glass. It was this movement which eventually produced such artists as Harry Clarke and Michael Healy, whose work can challenge comparison with the best elsewhere.

Martyn has been immortalised in the famous trilogy *Salvo, Ave, Vale*, written by his cousin George Moore. But, while Moore has made Martyn a figure of fun and a scapegoat for his own personal antipathies, depicting only the ludicrous side of his personality, he is still, even in Moore's pages, a person whom one regards with affection. In fact it is Moore himself who eventually appears as a posturing humbug and Martyn as a man of strong humanity, character and charm. " Dear Edward," as Moore called him, was clever enough to deprive George of the pleasure of knowing what his victim thought of this offensive caricature, for he steadily refused to read the Trilogy saying " George is a pleasant fellow to meet and if I read the book I might not be able to meet him again," a remark which did credit to both his astuteness and his charity. He once described to me how, after the book appeared, Moore approached him with trepidation and made vain attempts to draw him on the subject, to which he replied " My dear George I never read anything about myself but people tell me it's very clever." I have an amusing and characteristic letter written by Moore to Martyn on the eve of the famous trip to Bayreuth, which the latter gave me and which runs as follows :

92 Victoria Street,

July 14, 1897.

My dear Edward,

Could you be here before the 22nd ? That will not leave us much time to get to Bayreuth, only four days. I have got the rooms and am assured that they will be clean. I have read with great interest your play ([1]) ; it seems to me very good indeed. I strongly advise you to publish it ; you will have a better chance of getting it acted when it is published. It will act very well ; but of course it will not attract popular audiences any more than Ibsen. But we'll talk about it when we meet. I have been writing very well. I have written Evelyn's scruples of conscience and her confession ([2]). It is all quite convincing and I believe I have at last run a dead heat with my illustrious competitors. I am sure that nothing could be better than the confession. It is much better than the confession in *En Route*, that is to say, it is more human and more generally sympathetic.

As ever,

GEORGE MOORE.

Martyn was at his best in his country home, Tulira, County Galway, where his genius for hospitality and kindness had full scope. He lived himself, not in the fine modern Gothic building which his mother had induced him to erect, but in an old twelfth century tower attached thereto where his Norman ancestors had no doubt often withstood " the slings and arrows of outrageous " Ireland. There, in a cold, bare, whitewashed room, whose only ornament was a crucifix on the wall, he slept in monastic solitude and discomfort, and, at a hard bench in the adjoining equally bare and uncomfortable study, worked during the day at his books. Downstairs in the large hall was an organ on which, in the evenings after dinner, he sometimes played the austere, sombre, music of the polyphonic masters. In

[1] *The Heather Field.*
[2] A reference to his book *Evelyn Innes.*

the living rooms of the modern building valuable pictures of the French Impressionistic School and Sargent's drawing of Yeats bore witness to his fine artistic tastes. Of many happy evenings spent under his roof I remember best an amusing dinner at which the *dramatis personae* were, in addition to our host, Lady Gregory, Yeats, Musek, the chief comedian of the Bohemian National Theatre, and myself. Musek was a small man with beady eyes and funny features, a typical comedian. His knowledge of English was slight and he had a large notebook in which he took laborious notes of Yeats's *obiter dicta* with a reverential air. Martyn objected to oil lamps and Yeats, in the rather dim mellow candle light, after dinner, sat wrapped in clouds of tobacco smoke from Martyn's long churchwarden pipe, descanting like a prophet, in that delicate and fastidious language of which he was a master, on the eternal verities in art and beauty. From time to time Martyn would burst in with some matter of fact, and sometimes slightly malicious comment, which brought the proceedings down to earth. At one stage he tried to elicit from Musek whether there was a Sinn Féin movement in Bohemia, a question which the latter found it difficult to understand or answer. Not far away from Tulira was Lady Gregory's historic home, Coole, which we visited on several occasions. Yeats found it a perfect refuge for his literary work and he was assiduously sheltered from all profane disturbance. " The old ladies worship him," commented Martyn, " but the young ones are frightened." Martyn himself was that *rara avis*, a natural celibate. I often thought he might have made a great bishop and helped to reform Irish church music and art. " I find it impossible," he wrote to me in October, 1912, " to convince the Bishops that Fra Angelicos are not to be picked off every gooseberry bush and that the most we can really expect is to get some work that won't look ridiculous. This a competent artist can give them. However they still hanker after the idea that the monumental tradesman, the stained-glass ditto, and the parish plasterer, can supply the necessary religious spirit. So monstrous is this reasoning that were it applied to other matters generally understood by people I fear its proposers would be set aside as incompetent for any business."

At Coole one felt that only Yeats and his work mattered, as he sat remote and sheltered in his room or paced, a solitary figure, in dark cloak and hat by the romantic lonely lake beyond the hazel woods. But it was a house instinct with the great traditions of Irish hospitality and culture and its hostess—Lady Gregory—was one of the most charming and distinguished Irishwomen of our time. I can remember one dinner there where the talk ran freely on such diverse subjects as the then comparatively recent tragedy of Wilde and the language of the Kiltartan peasantry which Lady Gregory's book and plays had made famous. It was a delightful evening. Her work for the Irish theatre is one of the few things in that time of re-birth which has remained as a permanent contribution to our cultural life. The Abbey Theatre, which she helped to found, is now endowed and recognised by the Irish Government. The memory of that house, at that time a gracious centre of artistic life, is something to cherish. It is sad to reflect that it was eventually demolished by an Irish government department. So Yeats' prophecy was fulfilled, for now

> . . . nettles wave upon a shapeless mound
> And saplings root among the broken stone.

Her kinsman, Captain Shawe Taylor, a young Galway squire, had, about the time I first met Edward Martyn, helped to write a new and hopeful chapter of Irish history. In December, 1902, a conference composed of leading Nationalists and landlords, called on his suggestion, with the approval and support of George Wyndham, then Unionist Chief Secretary for Ireland, had agreed unanimously to a scheme for voluntary land purchase, subsequently embodied in the Land Act of 1903. It was, as John Redmond said, " the most substantial victory gained for centuries by the Irish race for re-conquest of the soil of Ireland by the people." Shortly afterwards Wyndham whose descent from Lord Edward Fitzgerald, the '98 leader, had doubtless influenced his attitude to Ireland, appointed

Sir Antony MacDonnell, the son of a Mayo landowner who had risen to be an Indian Governor-General, as Under Secretary for Ireland on the understanding that a more liberal policy was to be followed. It seemed indeed as if at last an agreed step forward was about to be taken in the larger field of national self-government, but, when, with the approval of the Lord Lieutenant, Lord Dudley, MacDonnell sponsored a scheme for the devolution of certain domestic affairs to an Irish Council, the stupidity and prejudice of the English ruling classes re-asserted themselves and Wyndham, placed in an impossible position, had to resign. Once more Irish hopes were disappointed and another opportunity lost of lifting the long standing Irish quarrel above the bitterness of party warfare.

SIDE by side with the language and political revivals, represented by the Gaelic League and Sinn Féin respectively, and in some respects complementary thereto, there now began a third movement which aimed at the encouragement and development of Irish manufacturing industry. In this Cork played a prominent and notable part. In February, 1903, the Cork Literary Society (which was in fact more revolutionary than literary in its aim) largely on the initiative of my friend Mr. William Roche (now perhaps better known by the Irish version of his Norman name—Liam de Roiste) called a meeting of various public organisations for the purpose of forming a society to encourage the development of Irish industry. As a result the Cork Industrial Development Association was established at a public meeting in the Chamber of Commerce on 7th May, 1903. The *raison d'etre* of this development was perhaps best expressed by Arthur Griffith, the founder of Sinn Féin, in a speech made two years later, in November, 1905, at the first National Convention of that organisation, when he said that an agricultural nation is like a man with one arm who has to make use of an arm belonging to another person, whilst an agricultural-manufacturing nation is like a man who has two arms of his own. Free Trade, he maintained, was the enemy which the Union with Great Britain had admitted within the gates; it could be defeated only by national freedom and the power it would give to protect Irish industry. Meanwhile we should, he urged, do what we could by voluntary effort to protect and foster native industry.

We now know that this was a simplified, and not entirely accurate, diagnosis of our condition. It is quite true that the second quarter of the nineteenth century had witnessed the decline of many industries fostered by the former Irish parliament. It is not altogether true to say that they were the victims of British competition and policy. These were no doubt contributory causes, but others equally important arose from neglect on the part of our industrialists to adopt modern mechanised methods and from interminable, disastrous, labour disputes. Deprived of protection against their larger and more efficient English rivals these small, and often inefficient, concerns finally collapsed.

But if Free Trade was the final undoing of such established industries it was also the parent of others which owed their prosperity to the free imports and free competition which had proved fatal to their predecessors. Even in the Famine years there arose the linen and ship-building industries whilst during the second half of the nineteenth century the brewing, provision and distilling trades developed. These great industries commanded a world market and, so far as some of them were concerned, drew their raw materials from the native soil. Belfast linen and rope became world famous, her ships sailed the seven seas ; Dublin stout, if not yet proclaimed a universal tonic, enjoyed a world reputation; Cork whiskey made celebrated the name of a humble commercial traveller, " Paddy Flaherty ", and her bacon and butter went far afield.

Our economic position at the commencement of the twentieth century was not then as dark as Griffith and his supporters painted it. During three generations of Free Trade we had built up a flourishing export market in both agriculture and industry. It is therefore both false and misleading to suggest, as is still sometimes done, that Ireland in 1900 was a poor, impoverished, agricultural country entirely devoid of industrial enterprise. Agriculture no doubt was, as it still is and must remain, the trunk of the Irish economic structure, industry only a powerful but productive arm. Griffith's simile was therefore misleading. No doubt the industry fostered by Free Trade was of a specialised and highly skilled type, no doubt also it had resulted in the growth of large concerns catering for foreign markets and in the extinction of small industries based on the home market, but that it occupied an important place in our economic life cannot be disputed.

That great Irishman, John Mitchel, writing nearly one hundred years ago, clearly stated the fundamental truth concerning our economy when he wrote that " the land is the fund whence we all ultimately draw ; and if the terms on which the land is cultivated be unfair—if the agricultural system of a country be unsound, then the entire structure is rotten and will inevitably come down. Let us never forget that mere appeals to the public to encourage native industry in other departments must be utterly futile so long as the great and paramount industry of the farmer is neglected." These words, afterwards cited by Michael Davitt in the famous Land League Manifesto of 1879,[1] should be written in letters of bronze over the door of the Irish parliament.

Apathy and lack of confidence in Irish manufactured goods were, however, widespread. Our young Cork organi-tion, with which I was associated from the start as an elected member of its council, therefore found itself faced with many difficulties. The prophets of evil, never silent on such occasions, assured us that we should be lucky if it survived six months. Many business men and shopkeepers treated it as a joke or regarded it as a combination designed to destroy their trade. My friend, Mr. E. J. Riordan, the first secretary of the Association, to whom much of its subsequent success was due, and who as an officer of the Department of Industry and Commerce has since done good work for Irish industry, used to tell of an incident which was a fair example of the kind of prejudice we had to fight against at that time. He was informed by the manager of a large public institution that he could not get their laundress to use a certain Irish-made starch as she found it was not equal to that made abroad. She was, he said, a woman of great experience and he felt sure that prejudice had nothing to do with her refusal. Mr. Riordan then asked him what brand they were using, and, on being informed, pointed out that the only difference between the starch she could not use and that which she said was excellent

[1]See *Irish Historical Documents*. Edited by E. Curtis & R. B. McDowell, p. 258.

was that the former was put up in a box bearing an Irish brand with the Irish maker's name on it, whilst the latter, taken from the same bulk of material was put up by the same Irish firm in a box with a fancy brand which did not bear their name. Another example of this curious attitude was afforded by the experience of a firm of Irish millers who, in order to satisfy the Irish farmers' preference for American flour, sold some of their product in bags branded with the Stars and Stripes, but without their name. The result was that for every bag sold bearing their own brand and name, six bags bearing the American emblems were disposed of.

But in spite of this latent dislike and disparagement oɩ Irish goods the new association was not long in making its presence felt. Offices were taken, tests made of Irish manufactured goods, exhibitions held, and shop-keepers induced to display Irish articles. By degrees branches were established throughout the country, a handbook was published giving a list of Irish manufactured goods and public boards were induced to give a preference to them. Finally at a National Industrial Conference, held in Cork in November, 1905, which was attended by leaders of public opinion from all over the country, the movement, under the title of the Irish Industrial Development Association, was placed on a national basis and the modern Irish industrial revival, since encouraged and fostered by a native government, was launched on its career. The most important fruit of that conference was the institution of an Irish National Trade Mark. This move was made possible under the Trade Marks Act of 1905 which gave the Board of Trade power to permit an association such as ours to register a trade mark in respect of goods which we certified to be manufactured in accordance with certain specified conditions. In the following year, 1906, with the assistance of John Boland, M.P., I carried through the registration of the Irish National Trade Mark, which proved to be of great help and protection to Irish manufacturers whose goods were often counterfeited by dishonest foreign firms · it is still widely used. As it was issued only in cases where the quality and origin of the goods were clearly established it also protected the public against fraud and misrepresentation. Its circular emblem of Celtic design with the words "Déanta i nÉirinn"[1] inscribed thereon, has become the hall-mark of Irish manufacture. The design itself was a replica of an early Irish torque, or collar, which was alleged to contract if the judge who wore it gave an unjust decision. We believed, not without reason, that it would have the same effect on fraudulent foreign firms who tried to counterfeit Irish products.

Much of the success of this movement was due to the late George Crosbie, the first chairman of the Association. His genial and kindly personality, his tolerance of contrary opinion and his simplicity and humility, joined with a rare tenacity of purpose and principle, constituted a combination both rare and charming yet very characteristic of our native city. His personality was reflected in his political views and in the policy of his paper, the *Cork Examiner*. An Irish Nationalist of uncompromising sincerity, he believed that Ireland was more important than political forms or doctrinaire theories and that, in the last analysis, the welfare of the people was what really mattered. His keen interest in the industrial development of the South, shared with his father, was reflected in the columns of his paper which was a tower of strength to our movement. To this object he devoted a considerable amount of time and money. He took a prominent part in the negotiations which, in 1918, led to the establishment of the Ford Factory at Cork, and also helped in inducing Furness Withy to purchase and develop Rushbrooke Docks in Cork Harbour, a valuable adjunct to the port. It was my good fortune, as will later appear, to be closely associated with him during the final stages of the Home Rule struggle. On the whole it may be said of George Crosbie—and he would wish for no better epitaph —that he was a typical Corkman, intensely proud of his city, sometimes perhaps inclined to exaggerate its importance but always anxious to promote its prosperity. Above all he was a sincere and upright Irishman who placed the interests of his country and its people first, and who fully

[1] " Made in Ireland."

realised that those interests could never be advanced by
any policy which ignored the dictates of common sense and
derived its inspiration from a barren hatred.

My interest in the industrial movement moved me to
write a play, *The Nation Builders*, which was performed by
the Cork National Theatre Society, in March, 1905. This
drama, which was of course pure propaganda of a rather
crude kind, dealt with the struggle of an Irish manufacturer
to surmount the twin obstacles of native apathy and English
competition. Naturally the hero was a young Irish-
speaking doctor who not only foiled the plots of the
manufacturer's opponents but successfully wooed his
daughter. The second act was concerned with a meeting
of the manufacturer's creditors, and, being based on a
personal experience of such gatherings, was the best part
of this rather precocious production. Edward Martyn's
very merciful criticism of my effort was, " I think it is
remarkably good for a first dramatic work by a man so
young as you are. The good points of it are that you tell
a story directly and coherently and bring all to a natural
conclusion. The characters are also well defined. However, you have not had sufficient practice in writing
dialogue. Your dialogue is not like conversation and has
more the effect of people speaking essays to each other. This
spoils the dramatic movement ; but it was inevitable since
your mind was filled with propaganda you wanted to make,
and you had not sufficient practice in dialogue to keep it
subservient." It only remains to add that my complete
ignorance of the theatre was revealed by the fact that the
play consisted of only two relatively short acts. After this
experience I wisely decided that my literary talent, if any,
was not dramatic.

I had moreover by this time found a more fruitful use
for my pen in another direction ; that of biography. My
first essay in this field was a lecture delivered in 1903, on
Montalembert, the French statesman, orator and historian.
He was a contemporary of O'Connell and had found in
Ireland inspiration for both his political and literary work.
With Lammenais and Lacordaire he had demanded that

the Catholic Church should throw itself into the rising
torrent of democracy, not to stop it (for its current was
irresistible), but to regulate it, to direct it, and to lead it to
its aims without disorder and in accordance with Christian
principles.   In this work they, in fact, anticipated the
message that Leo XIII, then a young and unknown theological student, was soon to proclaim to the world.   But
they came before their time and suffered the fate of many
pioneers.   Their labours for the freedom of religious
education and of the press were, however, successful.
Gladstone, then a young politician, met Montalembert and
was much influenced by his work and personality.   His
great historical work, *The Monks of the West*, to which he
devoted the closing years of his life, but which was never
finished, dealt in part with the work of the Irish monks who
had carried the light of Christianity throughout Europe.
This lecture brought me into touch with two distinguished
priests, Canon Sheehan of Doneraile and Monsignor
O'Riordan of Limerick, both of whom exercised a profound
influence on my mental and spiritual development.   Each
in his own way, one as a writer and a novelist, the other as
a controversalist, made a major contribution to the intellectual life of Catholic Ireland.   They were also close
personal friends.   My lecture on Montalembert interested
Canon Sheehan, who was a friend of my father, and he
wrote to Monsignor O'Riordan, at that time a priest in
Limerick, suggesting that I should also deliver the lecture
to the Catholic Literary Institute in that city of which the
Monsignor was President, which I subsequently did.   They
both insisted that I should continue the work thus begun
and so I came to write a series of biographical sketches of
leading Catholic laymen, published in Dublin and New
York in 1905, under the title *Great Catholic Laymen*, with an
introduction by Canon Sheehan.   I felt that many people
who would never think of reading the life of a saint or
theologian would willingly, and with profit, read the life
of a great layman who had carried into everyday life the
practice and precepts of his religion.   Yet in English at
least biographies of this kind were almost non-existent.   My

book was an attempt to supply this want and as such had a considerable success.   It was not only a book about Catholic laymen, but also one of the first books on a religious subject by a Catholic layman to come out of Ireland, and it was hailed as indicating a revival of intellectual activity amongst the Irish laity.

As patriots and statesmen it dealt with Andreas Hofer, "the man of Tyrol"; Garcia Moreno, President of Eucador; Windthorst, the champion of the German Catholics against Bismarck; and our own O'Connell; as journalist with Frederick Lucas, the founder of the *Tablet*; as philanthropist with Frederic Ozanam, the founder of the great Society of St. Vincent de Paul; and as scientist with Louis Pasteur.   It was a comprehensive list taken from different nations and periods and sought, as Canon Sheehan wrote in the foreword, to show that the Catholic Church cast its own illumination around every step and effort of the modern world "all the brighter because, when the lesser lights of human knowledge are extinguished, it alone is destined to continue for ever."   In writing of O'Connell I dealt, not with his public career, already well known, but with his private life which all the records proved to have been sincerely charitable and deeply religious.   I challenged specifically the tradition, never proved, that he had been a libertine in his younger days, and was able to show that, not only was there no trustworthy evidence whatever for such a suggestion, but that his strict habits of temperance and his family relations as a devoted husband and father alike belied the charge.   The book was dedicated to Monsignor O'Riordan and the members of the Catholic Literary Institute, Limerick, " as a small recompense for the inspiration and sympathy " responsible for its creation.

The friendship thus formed with these two remarkable men was a fruitful and inspiring relationship and is now a happy memory.   Alike in their love of learning and in their spiritual approach to the problems of life they were nevertheless very different in temperament.   Canon Sheehan was essentially a scholar and a writer, very reserved and

shy yet full of fire within ; Monsignor O'Riordan, although
also shy and reserved in manner, was a man of action, and
when once aroused a deadly opponent. Canon Sheehan
shunned the limelight, yet he would like to see things
written and done which he would not do himself; and it
was he in fact who made Monsignor O'Riordan write his
famous reply to Dr. Starkie's criticism of the Catholic school
managers and his even more famous answer to Sir Horace
Plunkett's book.

Their careers and personalities were both remarkable.
Patrick Augustine Sheehan was a Mallow man, having been
born in the little town by the Blackwater on St. Patrick's
Day, 1852. He did not play a noisy part amongst the
juvenile " rakes of Mallow," but grew up a reserved,
solitary boy. Left an orphan at an early age, he had little
experience of domestic life, as his books sometimes showed.
My uncle, Father Patrick Horgan, who was then a curate
at Mallow, often told me how he gave Canon Sheehan his
first musical lesson in the church choir. Readers of *My New
Curate* will remember the village choir over which Father
Letheby presided, and how he " brought clear to the
front the sweet tenors of the schoolboys, on which he said
all his hopes depended." It was a picture of his own
schoolboy triumphs in the Mallow choir and my uncle
always liked to believe that he had some part in the creation
of the hero of that famous book.

But he was a delicate lad and, even during his ecclesiastical studies, had to rest for long periods. As with many
other writers this enforced leisure enabled him to develop
his literary tastes, and he was attracted by the work of
Carlyle and Tennyson,. From the former, he learned the
gospel of work which had a marked influence on all his
after-life. He was fascinated by Tennyson's dreaminess and
mysticism, and by the music of his verse, and always maintained, with good reason, that he was not now sufficiently
appreciated. You will find apt quotations from Tennyson in
all his works and in most of his addresses. Later on, however,
he was repelled by Caryle's hatred of the Church and by his
unchristian doctrine of brute force, and Tennyson yielded

first place in his affections to the more robust thought of Dante and Browning.

On ordination in 1875, his own diocese of Cloyne, Co. Cork, being fully supplied with priests, he was lent to the less fortunate English diocese of Plymouth. His experience on the English mission led him of necessity to master methods of theological controversy and provided that deep fund of pastoral experience on which he afterwards drew so freely in his books. On his return to Ireland his health again broke down, this time from overwork, and again leisure turned his thoughts to literature. He began to write, at first tentatively and with diffidence, for periodicals like the *Irish Monthly*, then edited by his friend, that saintly Jesuit priest, Father Matthew Russell, a brother of the great Irish lawyer, Lord Russell of Killowen.

In 1895 he was appointed parish priest of Doneraile. Here the aid of two curates left him sufficient leisure to achieve the literary work which has placed the Catholic world under a debt of gratitude. *Geoffrey Austin*, his first novel, a study of school life, was followed in 1899 by *The Triumph of Failure*, in which some of the same characters appear. This was his favourite work. It did not meet with much favour, but his next book, *My New Curate*, raised him at once to a prominent position in the world of letters. This study of Irish clerical life, both human and humorous, appeared first in the *American Ecclesiastical Review*, and had an instant success. In it he revealed himself as a master of a singularly pure, lucid and cultured style, and as one of the little band of great writers who have truly and sympathetically portrayed Irish life. There followed from his pen a series of novels, essays and poems, many of which enhanced his fame. Of these *Glenanaar*, with its dramatic description of O'Connell's defence of the Doneraile conspirators, has always seemed to me the best. I remember a visit I made to him at Doneraile in May, 1906, about the time he was writing this book. It was a glorious spring day. Overhead soft white clouds drifted in a sky of vivid blue. As we drove along the high road from Mallow, suddenly, at a turn in the way, a beautiful panorama of wood, valley and hills burst into view. There was Doneraile below us, as he himself once described it— " nestling in a deep well, sheltered by the impenetrable umbrage of woods and forests," whilst behind lay the brown and green solitudes of the Ballyhoura hills and to the right the towering Galtees, still topped with their winter nightcaps of snow. Across the hills the cloud shadows chased each other in the sun, while below us in the fields a busy farmer guided his plough over the fresh green turf. All was peaceful, quiet, remote. And then we came down into the valley, along the winding road well shaded with interlacing trees, past the comfortable labourers' cottages where Canon Sheehan's name was a household word, and there at the end was the Mecca of my pilgrimage, the little two-storied, unpretentious house where he lived. A few yards away Spenser's " gentle Mulla " flowed on its even way through reeds and shallows. Across the road towered the great trees of Lord Castletown's demesne. All around was the quiet, leisured flow of life in this typical little Irish town.

These were the surroundings amidst which he carried on, not only his literary work, but what he placed first, his work as priest and guardian of his people. I had come for a week-end, one of the many I had the honour and privilege of spending under his roof. In the afternoon we drove to visit the ruins of Kilcolman where Spenser lived and where he wrote the *Faerie Queene*. It is an old, grey, frontier castle perched above a brown bog. From the summit on a fine day one can see five counties. Standing amongst the ruins we recalled that it was there Spenser welcomed the adventurous freebooter, Raleigh, just home from his voyage round the world, bringing with him those two common-place necessities of modern life—potatoes and tobacco ; of how there, too, he wrote the *Epithalamion*, that magnificent lyric of love triumphant, in honour of his Irish bride ; and how there finally, in revenge for his ruthless policy, the " wilde Irishe " as he called them, burnt his castle to the ground. It is a place rich in historic memories.

Back in Doneraile again we spent some hours walking in

the garden he loved so well—a *hortus conclusus et dissàeptus* surrounded by high trees and shrubs with which his readers are so familiar. We paced up and down the narrow sheltered path amidst the crocuses, those gay heralds of spring. There, much of his work was thought out. There, too, was the little wooden summer house where in summer he often wrote. Until his last illness prevented him, he often worked in the garden himself, directing or helping the gardener. It was his place of peace and meditation. Secure from all interruption or observation it was there, I think, he spent the happiest hours of his life. When the evening came we strolled out along the quiet country roads in the dusk and talked of books and men. He was at his best under such conditions for he never shone in a crowd. His natural shyness and reserve, which he so often admitted and deplored, seemed in a larger gathering to dry up that easy flow of genial, speculative conversation to which those who knew him loved to listen. But with a friend on a country walk or by his own fireside few people were more interesting or entertaining—interesting not only because he talked well himself, but because like all good talkers, he drew from his companion the best he could give. Many Americans, and other strangers eager to meet the famous Catholic writer travelled to Doneraile to see him but I fear that most went away without ever meeting the real Canon Sheehan that his friends knew so well. His house reflected his tastes. Books everywhere ; on the drawing-room table, in broad compact bookcases around the dining-room, in marshalled ranks lining the little study upstairs where he read and wrote ; and all methodically neat. As he wrote somewhere himself, he was a precisian, and this neatness and order was reflected in his writings and his life. But there was no luxury, no ostentation, no display. Most of the profits from his books went to diocesan charities. On the following day, Sunday, I had the privilege of attending his Mass and listening to his simple, sincere sermon in the old parish church which he had done so much to repair and beautify. In the afternoon we went up together to the playing fields beyond the river, where every Sunday young athletes from the surrounding districts contended for supremacy. There was a hurling match in progress, a fine exciting match well played. It was delightful to see him there amongst his people, quiet and unpretentious, the gentle parish priest beloved by all, sharing the pleasures and sports of the crowd with all the enthusiasm and interest of a boy. Those who wish to read one of the best descriptions of a hurling match ever written should turn to the first chapter of his novel, *Glenanaar*, and they will find there, a description of such a scene as we watched that afternoon. I like to think of him as I saw him that Sunday, with a genial smile lighting up his thoughtful face as he pointed out to me the best players and the points of the game ; one prefers to remember a dear friend at his best, and he was at his best then.

His political outlook, in its wide, constructive, and con-ciliatory vision, was very similar to that of his celebrated fellow-townsman, Thomas Davis. He abhorred the plausible equivocation and party rancour which so often masquerades as statesmanship in Ireland. I may perhaps cite one personal experience of his attitude. In 1911, during the Home Rule campaign when party feeling ran high in Cork, I had occasion to say a few kindly words, during the sitting of the Court for the revision of the voters' lists, to my professional opponent, Maurice Healy, the solicitor who represented the All-for-Ireland or O'Brienite party, with whom, in spite of political differences, I had always maintained pleasant personal relations. A few days afterwards I got the following letter from Canon Sheehan :

> Doneraile,
> Co. Cork.
> Sept. 29, 1911.

My dear John,

Very many thanks for your book on Home Rule which has just reached me. I am familiar with some of the chapters already ; but I shall give them a more leisured perusal. I perceive that you have got together a lot of hard telling facts.

Better however than anything you have written (no matter how excellent) were the few words you spoke at the Revision

Court the other day. They were honourable, manly words ;
and the little interchange of compliments from Maurice Healy
gave me hope that the political question was now about to be
raised to a higher plane than any it has yet occupied. The
fact is we expect men of liberal education to rise above the
asperities of the hustings and polling booths, and to give the
lead to the public by discussing the questions that are before
them in a broad and philosophic spirit. That little incident has
given me more pleasure then anything that has occurred for a
long time ; and it has added very much in the eyes of thinking
men to your reputation.

Ever sincerely,

P. A. SHEEHAN.

It was a tribute of which I was and am proud.

Monsignor O'Riordan, as I have already indicated, was
distinguished in quite a different way from Canon Sheehan.
Although he wrote well and forcibly his interest in literature
was rather as a weapon than as a means of expression.
Canon Sheehan once suggested to him that he should
write a novel and he replied that it would take him twenty
years to write it and twenty more to revise what he had
written. Like Canon Sheehan, he had served a hard
apprenticeship on the English mission in a large London
parish, but he was educated and ordained at the Irish
College in Rome of which he afterwards became Rector.
When I first met him he was a curate in St. Michael's
parish, Limerick, living, at the top of a stately old eighteenth
century house which served as a presbytery, in a large
untidy room, very characteristic of the man. His active
mind and indifference to personal comfort made him quite
regardless of appearances and sometimes even of his
surroundings. A fellow-curate used to tell how Monsignor
O'Riordan would come into his room to consult a book,
say " Good evening," take down the required volume,
note what he wanted, mechanically replace the book, again
say " Good evening " and depart without another word.
His mind was for the moment elsewhere unravelling some
abstruse problem. Unless one knew him well this idyosyn-
crasy might easily be mistaken for rudeness, although he

was really one of the most kindly and courteous of men.

At St. Michael's he laboured for ten years unostentatiously amongst the poorest of the poor. I remember how he once showed me his personal census of the entire parish in which the details of his flock were carefully set down for reference as occasion required. He was soon, however, to become known to a wider public. Early in 1902, Dr. Starkie, then Resident Commissioner of National Education in Ireland, and so in charge of the primary education of the country, delivered an address to the British Association, then meeting in Belfast, in which he asserted that the Inspectors of the Board of Education reported that the majority of the school managers, who were principally Catholic priests, were quite indifferent to education, and that in many places the schools were wellnigh derelict. Both the place and the audience were alike unsuited for the launching of such a charge, even had it been true. Monsignor O'Riordan at once took up the challenge and, in a series of brilliant articles, which appeared in the *Leader* over his now famous initials M.O'R., and were afterwards published in pamphlet form, he was able to show that Dr. Starkie had not only garbled and misrepresented the reports of his own inspectors, but had censured the managers for not doing what was not their duty. In short, Dr. Starkie had made a sweeping charge which was falsified by the facts. Moreover, he carried the war into Dr. Starkie's own camp by showing that the Commissioners of Education themselves, as managers of the so-called " model schools " had been guilty of mismanagement and incompetence. Dr. Starkie had in fact been throwing stones from a glass house. Monsignor O'Riordan's answer was complete and final.

Three years later, in 1905, he crossed swords with an opponent of a different calibre—Sir Horace Plunkett—a man who had done and was doing, through his work for the co-operative movement and the improvement of agriculture and technical education, a great deal for the prosperity of Ireland. In his book, *Ireland in the New Century*,

which in other respects was a valuable survey of Irish
political and economic conditions, Sir Horace saw fit to
make accusations against the Catholic Church. His leading
contention may be given in his own words as follows :
" Roman Catholicism strikes an outsider as being in some
of its tendencies non-economic, if not actually anti-
economic." Upon this statement he erected a purely
materialistic conception of religion and its functions in the
state and proceeded to indicate, as the fruit of Catholicism,
" excessive and extravagant church building," " costly and
elaborate monastic and conventual institutions," want of
character and morale amongst Irish Catholics, inadequate
support of temperance reform, and the " excessive inculca-
tion of chastity." These were large and highly controversial questions to dispose of in a chapter, and Plunkett's
treatment of them, apart from other defects, was sketchy
and ill-digested. Hence, when Monsignor O'Riordan
decided to reply, his task became quite as much one of
amplification as of elucidation. He had to explain as well
as to comment, to delve in the pages of history as well as
of statistics. This was his initial difficulty, but not his
least. Sir Horace had delivered his criticism from the
standpoint of a candid friend and was therefore more
difficult to answer than an open foe. Monsignor O'Riordan's
answer, contained in his great book, *Catholicity and Progress
in Ireland*, was far more than a reply to Sir Horace Plunkett.
Like a powerful searchlight it illuminated the historical
antecedents and inner life of the Irish people, revealing the
glib and inaccurate conclusions of Sir Horace in their true
perspective. It discussed not only the meaning of human
progress as revealed by Catholic teaching, but examined
the application of that teaching to other Catholic nations
and the application of other teachings in other countries.
After a detailed examination of the charges made by Sir
Horace he proceeded to a complete survey of Catholic
progress and policy in Ireland and then, boldly assuming
the offensive, showed how little the Protestant Ascendancy
in Ireland had done with their power, position and opportunities. Sir Horace had of course made the common

Protestant mistake of identifying character with the industrial spirit and holding the Church responsible for the industrial progress, as well as the moral welfare of the people because he could not discriminate between the two. He made no attempt to answer Monsignor O'Riordan's book, for the latter had, in his own words, proved to conclusion " that material progress is only part of human progress and the least important ; and when it is allowed to assimilate the other elements by which it should be checked and controlled it draws its votaries back to barbarism." His book must always remain, not only a supreme vindication of his country and his religion, but of the highest human and spiritual values. The truth of his thesis is now only too well established by the ruin of material civilisation which we see around us. It should be emphasised, too, that he was not only crushing but courteous, for never did he descend to personal abuse, that last resource of incoherent incompetence, or depart from those high standards of writing and criticism which are essential in great public controversy. He once wrote to me, " One of my greatest worries in argument consists in seeking to avoid giving offence or hurting people's feelings and at the same time to do justice to my case and close in upon my opponent. If I hurt anyone's feelings it costs me the keenest pain—makes me almost ill." These works, written mostly in the small hours of the morning after an arduous day's parochial work, will remain as a monument to the nobility of his character and the quality of his mind. Re-reading them now one reflects that while in him the Church gained a great priest, Ireland perhaps lost a statesman who might have ranked with O'Connell.

It was my privilege to be in close touch with him during those years and when, in 1905, he was appointed Rector of the Irish College in Rome, we continued to correspond until his death in 1917. During those closing years he had little time for writing, but two notable contributions from his pen deserve to be remembered, one, his sermon on *The Merit of Martyrdom*, an eloquent tribute to Irish Catholicism and the virtue of Faith, preached in St.

Patrick's Church, Rome, on St. Patrick's Day, 1916, and the other, a pamphlet, *La Recente Insurrezione in Irlanda*, a clear explanation of the causes and consequences of the Insurrection of 1916, based on British official documents and reports, and written in Italian. This pamphlet, published in September, 1916, whilst not seeking to justify the Insurrection, exposed the duplicity of British statesmen and showed that they had treated as a " scrap of paper " their solemn agreements with Ireland. It was his last service to his country.

Memory also recalls another great priest—Canon Peter O'Leary—perhaps better known as An tAthair Peadar (Father Peter)—with whom my Gaelic League activities brought me into contact at that time. What Canon Sheehan did for modern Catholic literature in English, this other parish priest of the diocese of Cloyne, did for it in Irish. His early years as a priest were devoted to the education and uplifting of the people but he used to say that it was not until the start of the Gaelic League gave him the chance of exercising his fine intellect and his fluent knowledge of Irish, that he really began to live in a full and worthy sense.

This little, white-haired man who became the Vice-President of the Gaelic League after Father O'Growney's premature death, seemed to sum up and embody our Gaelic civilisation. He had a horror of red tape, taking no interest in committees, agenda or discussions but holding that the people alone could save the language and make a literature. His work for the simplification of Irish spelling and his ambition to see the native speaker of Irish develop into a writer, were characteristic of his direct approach to such problems. As a priest, his work for the language was naturally directed to its religious aspect and his translation of *The Imitation of Christ* and *The New Testament*, in which his knowledge of the classics was of great help, are models of their kind. As a writer, he was prolific and his clear, precise style reflected the simple directness of his personality. Plays, newspaper articles and translations of classic tales flowed from his pen but his *magnum opus* was

Séadna which may justly be described as the first modern novel in Irish. The story of *Séadna* was built on an entirely different foundation from the ordinary English or continental novel in which the passion of love is enthroned as the master motive in all human actions. It is founded rather on the fact that a person may be placed in a position where a sense of duty may require that he should subdue in his own heart the passion of love, no matter how noble, how true, how disinterested it may be. This is a truth which is part of the very nature of the Irish mind in its own thought world. The other principle, so common in English fiction, is foreign to and, indeed, utterly antagonistic to Irish thought. But *Séadna* was not only a great novel ; it was also a great masterpiece of style. There are few greater passages in modern Irish than the description of the fairy music and the horse fair. Canon O'Leary was, however, more than a great writer, he was a great personality, cheery, bright and humorous. At his little house in Castlelyons there was always an open door and a hearty welcome for a student of Irish, whoever he might be. As a speaker he was ready, witty and convincing, but he never prepared a speech in the ordinary sense. I once asked him how he managed to be so fluent and he replied in Irish " I call on the talk and it comes." His speeches had just that homely, simple quality of spoken thought. His writing was equally effortless. The words seem to flow from his pen. And he was as effective in his English propagandist articles, which were gems of clear thought, terse, and full of practical good sense. Had he wished, he might have been as distinguished an English writer as Canon Sheehan. As a writer of Irish he has, unfortunately, no successor.

The Church has every reason to be proud of these three men : Canon Sheehan, fine writer and unerring guide to literature ; Monsignor O'Riordan, logical thinker and writer, firm in his grasp of great principles; Canon O'Leary, scholar, enthusiast and natural genius. Yet they are almost forgotten now, even in their own land, and you will not find their names in the *Dictionary of National Biography*, although many lesser Irishmen are chronicled there. I was fortunate to have known them in those formative years. They taught me to winnow the grain from the chaff, to realise that public controversy should be conducted not only with truth and courage but with courtesy and dignity, and to understand and apply those eternal values which are the final criteria of life.

X

CHANCE—or is it destiny ?—plays a large part in human affairs. It now intervened decisively in mine. Early in 1904 a Ratepayers' Association was started in Cork with the purpose of improving our municipal life. This body of representative merchants and ratepayers in order to attain its ends decided to run candidates for the city council and, as a first step, retained me to act on its behalf at the annual revision of the voters' lists which took place in September. This professional engagement prevented me from taking my holidays at the usual time and I was only able to leave, for a short visit to London, on 7th October. On that day I was detained in Court till late and just managed to catch the mail train to Dublin. As I entered a crowded smoking carriage a gentleman in one corner courteously moved his despatch case to make room for me. Shortly after, seeing me reading *An Claidheamh Soluis*, the Gaelic League journal, he asked me if I knew Irish. After discussing various aspects of the language movement and the general position of education in Ireland, he began to question me about Queen's College, Cork, and the attitude of the Church to its activities. He was particularly anxious to obtain information concerning the ban placed on Catholics attending the College. I was able to tell him that this was more apparent than real and that, at least so far as " bread and butter " studies were concerned, there was no difficulty in obtaining permission from one's confessor to enter the College. We discussed in much detail this question, with which as a recent student of that institution I was naturally familiar, and the prospects of the various local candidates for the position of its President. This office was then vacant owing to the recent retirement of Sir Rowland Blennerhasset, a Kerry baronet, who had been mixed up in the rather unsavoury intrigues which culminated in the publication of the forged Pigott letters by *The Times*. His appointment as President of Queen's college

Cork, was no doubt a reward for this and other services to the Unionist Party, for he had few other qualifications for the post. His discharge of the duties of President was in fact, as I had reason to know, of a perfunctory kind, with disastrous results for the College.

My travelling companion, a fair-haired, clean shaven man of middle age, whose character was indicated by his firm mouth and the alert, piercing, blue eyes behind his gold-rimmed spectacles, was much interested in all I had to tell and I decided that he was an Englishman studying Irish educational affairs. The fact that he was reading, for the purpose of review, a recently published book on *The Origin and Influence of the Thoroughbred Horse*, by Sir William Ridgeway, a former professor of Greek at Queen's College, suggested to me that he was a scientist of some sort. When we reached Dublin, after a long and friendly conversation, he expressed the hope that we might meet again and handed me his card which disclosed that he was Professor Bertram C. A. Windle, M.D., F.R.S., Dean of the Medical Faculty at Birmingham University. The reason for his interest in Irish education in general and the Queen's College, Cork, in particular, became clear a few weeks later when I read in the Irish papers of his appointment as its new President.

In reply to my letter of congratulation he wrote—

The University,
Birmingham,
Oct. 25, 1904.

Dear Mr. Horgan,

I am delighted to get your letter and to hear that you are back again in Cork, where I shall hope to see you next week.

It was nothing short of providential that I should have sat by you in the train on my way back from Cork where I had been to look at the College. I could not mention my errand to you then, for I was asked—seeing that the whole matter was in an unsettled state—not to mention who I was or what I was in Cork for. After a great deal of consideration and after having once refused to consider the appointment I was led by representations as to the possible use that I might be to the cause of Higher Education in my own country to accept the appointment.

I do not for a moment suppose that it will be a bed of roses at first but I have lain on thorns before and managed to turn them into down and I will try what I can do in Cork. I hope I may not be too badly received there but I am happy to think that there is one person who knows that I am of Irish heart as well as of Irish race.

I suspend any further remarks until we meet, which I hope will be before long, but this I will say that I hope to take as active a part in the work of the Gaelic League as is permitted to me. With thanks for your letter.

I am,

Yours very sincerely,

BERTRAM C. A. WINDLE.

My future father-in-law, for such he later became, sub-sequently told me that the information as to the real Catholic attitude to the College which I gave him during that railway journey encouraged him to decide in favour of accepting the Cork appointment. It was therefore a momentous conversation for us both.

When he arrived in Cork a fortnight later I met him and his wife at the station in order to introduce them to the large crowd of enthusiastic students who escorted them in triumph to their new home. Thus began a relationship which was to have decisive effect on my life. Windle was in fact, in spite of his English voice and manner, an Irishman. As he reminded the cheering students during his speech in the College quadrangle that day, he had left Ireland twenty years before as a young medical man, and, during the interval, had never forgotten the country to which he belonged. He promised them that he would identify himself not only with the College but the city, a promise which he certainly kept.

Windle, was born in England at Mayfield vicarage, Staffordshire, on 8th May, 1858, where his father, the Rev. Samuel Allen Windle, whose family came from Shropshire, was then Church of England vicar. His mother, Sydney Katherine Coghill, daughter of Admiral Sir Josiah Coghill by his second wife, Anna Maria Bushe, was of Anglo-Irish descent. The founder of her family was, however, a German soldier of fortune, one Colonel Tobias Cramer, who served James the First in Ireland; one of her ancestors was Ambrose Cramer, Mayor of Cork in the year 1724. On her mother's side she was a grand-daughter of Charles Kendal Bushe, a member of the Irish House of Commons, afterwards Lord Chief Justice of Ireland. Bushe voted consistently against the Union, and, although he was a relatively poor man, there appears after his name, in Sir Jonah Barrington's famous " Red List," the word " incorruptible." Only one other member of the House was thus described. There is no doubt that he received the most dazzling offers for the withdrawal of his opposition to that measure but steadfastly refused them and risked his career for his principles. Fortunately his legal ability could not be ignored and he did not suffer in the end. His speech against the Union was generally considered to be the best made in that historic debate. It is one of the great masterpieces of eloquent indignation.

Windle's family had other connections with the County Cork, as the Coghill and Somerville families of Castle Townsend are descended from the brother and sister of his mother ; her uncle, the Rev. Charles Bushe, who married a daughter of Sir Josiah Coghill by his first wife, was rector of Castlehaven. His son, Seymour Bushe, K.C., carried on the family tradition, for during my youth he was one of the most brilliant and eloquent members of the Munster Circuit. Only an unfortunate scandal, in which he was, indeed, " more sinned against than sinning," prevented him from rising to the same judicial eminence as his great ancestor. Windle's Somerville relatives included several distinguished soldiers and sailors, and Miss Edith Oenone Somerville, the well-known Irish writer, whose book *Some Experiences of an Irish R.M.* is a classic of its kind. When Windle came to Cork as President of the Queen's College, he was therefore, in one sense at all events, returning to the home of his ancestors, a fact which, as will latter appear, undoubtedly affected his attitude to many things.

His early education was received at Repton, a school chosen no doubt because of its evangelical atmosphere, where he made a somewhat reluctant acquaintance with the classics. In November, 1875, he entered Trinity College, Dublin, and there his natural talent for English literature and science quickly developed. His early years, under the control of his father, who belonged to the narrow Calvinistic party in the Church of England, left an impress on his mentality never wholly erased. " How I loathe Calvinism " he was to write long afterwards " and with good reason, for it did me an injury from which I shall never quite recover in this world—namely making me think of God as a policeman instead of a tender Father." And it undoubtedly was responsible also for that tyranny of scrupulosity which he once described as his bane after he entered the Church. At Trinity his extreme Protestant upbringing led him to join the Orange Order. A natural revulsion, however, soon took place and before he left the University, he had become a complete agnostic. He had by this decided to follow the profession of medicine, and a brilliant academic career ended in 1882 when he took first place in his M.B. examination. After qualifying he was appointed demonstrator in anatomy and histology at the Irish College of Surgeons, and in September of 1882, pathologist at the General Hospital in Birmingham.

In this great city Windle was destined to spend twenty years of his active career. He soon became Professor of Anatomy in its Medical School, at that time affiliated to Queen's College, Birmingham, an Anglican theological seminary. Windle never tolerated or endured unsatisfactory educational conditions for long and he soon started a movement which resulted in the transfer of the Medical School to the undenominational Mason College, where he became Dean of the Medical Faculty. Here again, greatly helped by the commanding influence and civic spirit of Joseph Chamberlain, whose support he had enlisted, Windle's talent for agitation and organisation was the real driving power in transforming that College into the University of Birmingham. Chamberlain had in full measure the faculty, common to great advocates and politicians, of making up a difficult subject at a moment's notice. An instance of this capacity was often cited by Windle. During the negotiations for the establishment of the University Chamberlain had to introduce a deputation of Birmingham citizens to the responsible Minister at Whitehall, and though he himself had never had a university education, after half an hour's coaching from Windle, he made a speech which in the grasp it displayed of the subject would have done credit to an educational expert.

Already, in the year 1883, soon after his arrival in Birmingham, Windle's mind had been once more providentially turned towards religion, and after much investigation and no little personal sacrifice, he was received into the Catholic Church, of which he was eventually to become one of the leading and most effective apologists. The initial impulse for what, in view of his antecedents and upbringing, may well be described as an extraordinary change, was quite fortuitous. Being the only agnostic house doctor in the Birmingham Hospital he had invariably to spend his Sunday mornings on duty while his colleagues were attending to their religious duties. Finally, desiring to escape from this predicament, but determined not to renew his acquaintance with any form of Protestantism, he decided to attend a Catholic service, and so found himself, for this very mundane reason, hearing Mass in St. Chad's Cathedral, where the Gregorian music and the preaching alike interested him. A sermon on the subject of the Immaculate Conception led him to inquire more closely into the truths of Catholicism. A critical examination of its claims was followed by his complete acceptance of the Faith. Three years later he married Madoline, daughter of William and Emma Hudson of Birmingham, who was also shortly afterwards received into the Church.

During this period Windle began to write, and published a number of books on medical and topographical subjects. Amongst them may be mentioned : *The Proportions of the Human Body* (1892); *Life in Early Britain* (1897); *Shakespeare's Country* (1899); *The Malvern Country* (1900) ; *The Wessex of Thomas Hardy* (1901) ; *Chester* (1903); *The Prehistoric Age* (1904) ; *A School History of Warwickshire* (1906). These

were the fruits of his medical teaching and of his literary
and historical studies.   His book on Hardy's country,
written with the great novelist's approval and advice,
remains the best guide to its literary topography and a
lasting memorial of Windle's rambles during many summers
in Dorset.   His interest in this delightful district, I may add,
furnished another link between Windle and myself; for
Dorsetshire was the home of one branch of my mother's
family, her uncle, William Pope Genge, having being Mayor
of Dorchester, Hardy's ' Casterbridge.'   In a copy of this
book which he gave me, he wrote the famous lines of
Barnes, the Dorset poet :

> Vor Do'set dear,
> Then gi'e woone cheer
> D'ye hear ?   Woone cheer.

His closing years in Birmingham were darkened by the
death of his wife and two infant sons.   Two daughters,
Mary and Nora, the former of whom was to become my
wife, were born during those years.   Before coming to Cork
he had married secondly, Edith Mary Nazer, a relative
of his first wife, who still happily survives and who
remained his devoted companion to the end.

Windle's associations with the Catholic life of Birmingham,
in which he played an active part, naturally brought him
into touch with the Irish in that city, and he joined their
organisations.   He soon became a popular speaker on
Liberal platforms in support of the Irish demand for self-
government, and his knowledge of his country's history,
combined with his gift of presenting clearly and concisely
the issues at stake, was used to good purpose.   He had
also during those years begun to concern himself actively
with the wider aspects of education, having, in the Catholic
interest, served on the Birmingham School Board and also
as a member of the Consultative Committee of the Board of
Education.   These activities naturally placed him in a
foremost position amongst English Catholic educationalists.
It was therefore natural that when George Wyndham, as

Chief Secretary for Ireland, having successfully tackled the Irish land question, turned his mind to the equally thorny subject of university education, he should have selected Windle to advise and assist him. It was, indeed, on the understanding that drastic reforms in Irish university education were about to be made that he accepted the presidency of Queen's College, Cork.

Windle's characteristic thoroughness appears in his private visit to Cork in order to investigate the situation before accepting Wyndham's offer. As his letter to me discloses he fully realised the difficulty of the task before him. Queen's College, Cork, was then, as I have already indicated, little more than an excellent medical school, which manufactured doctors, principally for export. It had little or no connection with the life of the community in which it was situated, and it was tolerated rather than approved by the Church, which had effectively paralysed its Arts faculty. Outside the football field its students had hardly any opportunity for social intercourse. In addition to all this it was poorly endowed by the State, and had been somewhat casually treated by its previous Presidents with the notable exception of the late William K. Sullivan. It is a tribute less to the merits of the institution itself than to the loyalty of its graduates that they still remember it with pride and affection.

Such a situation offered to Windle a field for difficult but congenial work, which he did not hesitate to tackle boldly. From the very first professors and students realised that conditions had changed. Queen's College had at last an effective head—one who, unlike most of his predecessors, was both seen and heard. No detail of the College life was too small to escape his notice, no student too humble to be received and listened to in the presidential study. A new social life began in the President's house, a life in which professors, citizens and students participated. For the first time " town and gown " were brought into normal and friendly intercourse. The appearance and voice of the new President became familiar at Cork civic gatherings and on many public platforms throughout the country. His well-informed mind and critical intelligence were freely placed at the service of every deserving cause.

Very soon projects for the development of the College were successfully launched. With the warm support and strong financial assistance of old graduates from all over the world, a Students' Club, which had long been a necessity, was inaugurated; new lecturers were appointed, and money for additional buildings extracted from the reluctant Treasury. In 1908, after much anxious negotiation, in which Windle took part as one of the chief advisers alike of the recently elected Liberal Government, the Irish Nationalist leaders and the Catholic hierarchy, the University Act was passed; whereupon the religious ban was removed and the Cork College, in its new guise as a constituent college of the National University, took its place in the intellectual life of the community. As one of the special commission, appointed to draft the statutes of the new university, Windle, with the great experience he had already acquired in Birmingham, played a decisive part.

But his activities during those years were by no means confined to Cork. As a member of the General Council of Medical Education, Senator of the National University, and President of the Irish Technical Education Association, his active interest in general education and its problems was of great use to the country. As President, at various times, of such bodies as the Cork Literary and Scientific Society, and the Irish Industrial Conference of 1905—already mentioned—his practical experience was invaluable. It was he in fact who first suggested the desirability of having a distinguishing mark for articles of Irish manufacture, the establishment of which was one of the chief results of that conference. All this public work necessitated much travelling and frequent absence from Cork but the development and interests of the College remained always his first and constant preoccupation. A new chemical and physical laboratory, a new biological laboratory, a new engineering school, a re-conditioned and re-organised medical school, and large playing fields, remain as a permanent monument to his labours. Private benefaction was also secured in support of projects for which Government assistance could not be obtained. Prominent amongst these gifts were the Honan Hostel, the Honan scholarships, and the Honan Chapel. This last building—a unique Celtic Romanesque Church, inspired by Cormac's Chapel at Cashel—with its beautiful stained glass (including some of the best work of that great Irish artist Harry Clarke) is a reminder of his good taste and his desire to bring the life of the College into intimate and permanent relationship with religious observance.

Before his arrival in Cork his services to Science had been recognised by his appointment as a Fellow of the Royal Society, the blue ribbon of English scientific life. In 1909 his services to the Church and education were honoured by His Holiness the Pope, when he was made a Knight of St. Gregory the Great. Three years afterwards he received the honour of knighthood from His Majesty the King.

The acquaintanceship between Windle and myself, which had begun in such an accidental manner, quickly ripened into intimacy. During his first years in Cork he had much need of advice and information concerning local conditions and this I was able and glad to give, for our interests and aims were identical. In return his wide knowledge and great experience enlarged and enriched my intellectual life. There was another reason also, dominating all others, which eventually brought us into a closer relationship. Shortly after his arrival in Cork, on 24th January, 1905, at a dinner party in his house, I met, for the first time, his eldest daughter Mary. She was nearly eighteen and I was only twenty-three, yet at that first meeting we both knew that we were clearly destined for each other. I can still remember, as if it were yesterday, every detail of that evening—the President's drawing-room with its Gothic windows, Mary standing there as I came in, fresh, young and graceful in her simple evening frock before the great fireplace. We entered at once that enchanted land where youth and love conspire to create the most perfect happiness possible in an imperfect world. For us both mean streets became noble, little things great, all things wonderful. Thus began a true union of minds and hearts which surmounted all obstacles and survived all tests, constant and faithful to the end.

Across the background of those happy years many famous figures passed and re-passed. Chief among them was Douglas Hyde, who had been a contemporary of Windle's at Trinity College and remained his close personal friend. When Windle was appointed to Cork the Irish press, inspired no doubt by disappointed local candidates, had been far from sympathetic, and Hyde had come forward to pay tribute to Windle's loyalty to Ireland. I, also, through my interest in the Gaelic League and its work, became a friend of Hyde's. In February, 1905, he came to lecture in Cork and I met him at Windle's house. The chair of English Literature had just become vacant, and Windle at first thought of Hyde as a candidate, but eventually, at Hyde's own suggestion, recommended William F. P. Stockley, another Trinity man, whose point of view resembled Hyde's and who had been a colleague of his at an American College. The choice was a happy one for Cork as Stockley had a real love for great literature and the ability to communicate his ardour and knowledge to his students.

Hyde had great personal charm, and Mary and I were both inspired by his enthusiasm. I remember a garden party at the College on a lovely June day in 1905 when the assembled guests were startled, and some perhaps even shocked, by the arrival of a kilted pipers' band. Such native revivals were then hardly considered good form. It was on that occasion that Hyde and I fled with Mary and another charming young lady to a secluded portion of the grounds where we spent the afternoon in pleasant converse whilst emissaries were vainly seeking for him to do the honours elsewhere.

In the winter of that year he passed through Cork again on his way to America. It was my privilege, as a prominent official of the Gaelic League, to meet him at the railway station and conduct him to the City Hall where a public meeting was held. As he drove through the cheering crowds, amidst torches, tar-barrels and the music of many bands, corner boys kept jumping on the carriage step demanding " Tuppence for a pint, sir." Hyde in astonishment remarked to me that he had never in his travels through Ireland had such an experience before and inquired the reason for this local habit. I replied in two words " William O'Brien," for it was indeed the largesse of that famous Cork demagogue which had created this mercenary thirst.

In the following year, 1906, Hyde stayed at my father's house when he came to receive the Freedom of the City— an honour conferred on him in recognition of his services to the language movement and the success of his American mission. It was just after that visit that Edward Martyn wrote to me, " I saw Hyde last night who was greatly impressed by your wisdom for your years."

Hyde was spending himself in the service of the Gaelic League, constantly travelling from one end of the country to the other and working late and early. None of its members had a wider vision and no one did more to forward its aims.

Another friend of those days, whom I met for the first time at the College, was John Boland, M.P., afterwards a member of the University Commission, one of the few members of the Irish Party who was really interested in the new movements. Slim and fair with an Oxford accent he was more like an English professor than an Irish politician.

During the Industrial Conference of November, 1905, I met other notable Irish figures at the Conference functions and at Windle's table. Amongst them were Lord Dunraven, then flirting with a scheme for devolution of self-government to Ireland ; Shawe Taylor, a rather self-confident young man flushed with his success in promoting the Land Conference ; T. W. Russell, M.P., that stalwart Presbyterian who was chiefly interested in the maintenance of temperance ; William Field, M.P., who had been one of Parnell's sup- porters, a venerable figure with a wide-brimmed hat and picturesque appearance reminiscent of Buffalo Bill ; that redoubtable Belfast Orangeman, Tom Sloan, M.P.; the

Rev. James Hannay, then Rector of Westport, County Mayo, and now better known as " George A. Birmingham," surveying Irish life with a novelist's critical eye ; T. P. Gill, Horace Plunkett's right-hand man at the Department of Agriculture, whose famous beard George Moore has immortalised in his memoirs ; Charles Gatty, delightful dilletante and art critic, whose speech was the one humorous interlude during the Conference proceedings ; Edward Martyn who stayed with us ; and finally the romantic figure of William O'Brien, M.P., for Cork city, who, seconding a proposition of T. W. Russell's, reminded us that they had not always been able to fraternise so cordially.

About this time I also met two other famous Irishmen, T. P. O'Connor, M.P., and Lieutenant-General Sir William Butler, who, although they differed widely in character and background, shared the same aims and gifts. At Easter, 1907, business took me to London and my father's cousin, Dr. Thomas Neville, asked me to spend the holiday week-end at his country house near Deal. Dr. Neville was himself an interesting personality combining the shrewdness of a West Cork peasant with all the urbanity and *savoir faire* of a leading London doctor. His career had been varied and adventurous for in his youth he had served as a surgeon in the Turkish army during the Russo-Turkish war and taken part in the historic siege of Plevna. His description of the horrors of that campaign and of the surgical methods then in vogue was terrifying. His practice, as one of the leading Irish doctors in London, had brought him into touch with the leaders of the Irish Party, many of whom were his friends and patients. Amongst these was T. P. O'Connor whom I was therefore not surprised to meet as a fellow-guest in the doctor's house.

The son of a shopkeeper in Athlone, " T.P.," as he was affectionately called, after a distinguished career at Queen's College, Galway, had become by sheer ability one of the leading figures in the world of journalism and politics. His genial smile and easy manner were both disarming and captivating. One could easily understand how he had

My parents, August 1880

Lacaduv

Charles Stewart Parnell

Left: **Sir Bertram C. A. Windle, FRS**
(Photo: Elliot and Fry)
Below: **Mary Windle, 1906**

William O'Brien, MP, from the drawing by Sir William Orpen, Cork School of Art.

John E. Redmond, MP,
Dublin, April 1912
(Photo: *Sphere*)

Mr and Mrs Winston Churchill with Lord Mayor O'Shea, Cork Show, July
1912 (Photo: *Cork Examiner*)

W. H. K. Redmond, MP, J. E. Redmond, MP and W. A. Redmond, MP.
Clongowes centenary, June 1914. (Photo: Chancellor)

WILFUL MURDER
The Kaiser, 'To the Day . . .' Death, ' . . . of Reckoning' *Punch*, 19 May 1915
(Reproduced with the permission of Punch Ltd.)

At the Oireachtas, Killarney, 26 July 1914 (*left to right* self,
Edward Martyn, Mary, Dr D. Hyde) (Photo: *Cork Examiner*)

Self, Erskine Childers and Stephen Gwynn, MP. Irish Convention,
Cork, September 1917. (Photo: *Cork Examiner*)

become the confidant of statesmen and one of the most popular figures in the House of Commons, where he represented the Scotland Division of Liverpool, as an Irish Nationalist, the only representative of that party in Great Britain. Like many others of the younger generation in Ireland I was suspicious of the Irish Party and its policy, but I fell a victim at once to his charm. Yet I soon realised that, in spite of his apparent success, he was an unhappy man. Of a Bohemian and careless temperament, he had already made and lost several fortunes in his journalistic ventures, and now, close on seventy years of age, was in straitened circumstances and bad health. His domestic life, too, was unhappy, for his wife, an American lady, was just as romantic and extravagant as himself, and they had separated some time before I met him. Dr. Neville used to describe a reception given by T.P. at which, while the host and hostess were receiving the guests in the drawing-room, the baliffs were discreetly removing the piano by the back-door.

Although a Catholic by birth and upbringing, and the accepted leader of the Irish in Great Britain, he was careless about his religion, and it was only with great difficulty that Mrs. Neville, a sister of Reginald McKenna, the well-known statesman and banker, herself a devout convert, succeeded in persuading him to attend Mass on Easter Sunday. This he finally agreed to do only on condition that he was supplied with a copy of the Authorised Version to read during the ceremony as he insisted that the literary style of the Douai, or Catholic Bible, was not good. At this particular time he was engaged, as John Redmond's confidential adviser and representative, in the long and tortuous negotiations with the new Liberal Government which culminated a few months later in the introduction of the ill-fated Irish Councils Bill. He regaled us with stories of Augustine Birrell's reaction to the atmosphere of Dublin Castle where he had recently been installed as Chief Secretary. One felt that T.P., in spite of his Irish blood and sentiment, was quite indifferent to, and indeed ignorant of, the new Ireland represented by Sinn Féin and the Gaelic

League and that his real interests were, naturally enough, centred in Fleet Street and Westminster.

Sir William Butler was a quite different kind of person. Descended from an old Tipperary Catholic family, after a distinguished career as a writer and a soldier, he had come back to Ireland to end his days with his own people. Ten years before, as Commander in Chief and High Commissioner in South Africa, he had resigned the latter office, and quietly endured public contumely and secret vilification rather than be a party to the intrigues of Chamberlain and Rhodes which eventually ended in the Boer War. The long series of despatches which he sent home would, if they had been heeded, have averted the disasters which subsequently befell the British Army. He knew the facts, urged them persistently upon the Government, and as a reward was recalled, snubbed, ignored and calumniated. " What South Africa needs," he wrote, " is peace and not a surgical operation." As chairman of the South African War Stores Commission he subsequently had the satisfaction of sitting in fearless judgment on those who ignored his advice, and was largely responsible for the exposure of corruption contained in its memorable report. He was, indeed, as much at home with the pen as with the sword. " Heaven knows," said John Ruskin to him on one occasion, " you could have written all my books if you hadn't been at harder work." That this is no exaggeration anyone who has read *The Great Lone Land* or his biography of Gordon will readily agree.

I met him first in March, 1908, when he came to Cork to address the Catholic Young Men's Society. His championship of the freedom of the Boer Republic and his well-known sympathy with Irish national aspirations had made him a deservedly popular figure and the Opera House, where he spoke, was crammed from floor to ceiling with an enthusiastic audience. As his stalwart figure appeared a great burst of cheering swept the house. Not since Parnell spoke in the same place, many years before, had such a scene been witnessed. The lecture was a great success for he spoke as well as he wrote. Its mysterious title " The Clan and the Boat's Crew " referred, as we soon found out, to the respective units of the Celtic and Saxon peoples. It proved to be a vivid summary of their distinguishing characteristics, ending with an appeal to us young Irishmen to be worthy of our historic past and to give unselfish service to our country. I seconded the vote of thanks which was not a difficult task, and afterwards was introduced to him. A few months earlier I had written an article for the *Clongownian* on the careers of Butler himself and Thomas Francis Meagher, in which I reflected that it was tragic that Ireland should have lost the services of two such men. " I read your article," he said, " and you see I have taken your hint. If I am now too old to do much for Ireland myself I can yet try to keep the coming generation at home." We met a few times afterwards, and I had several kind letters from him on matters affecting the new National University of which he had been appointed a Senator.

The address he gave us that night is to be found in his last book, *The Light of the West*, which also contains a fine tribute to Parnell. " But remember," he said to us in his concluding words, a message which should not be forgotten to-day, " in order to guide you must be guided; in order to teach you will have to learn; in order to lead you will first have to follow." He was already beginning to play a big part in Irish life when he died in June, 1910. He had ruined his military career by the action he took in South Africa but he could not, as he said himself, countenance what he knew to be wrong. Such men are unfortunately few, but their " name liveth for evermore."

During these years I enlarged my experience and know-ledge by further travel. In June, 1905, with three older friends, I visited Southern Germany and Austria. At Nuremberg I saw for the first time an unspoilt mediaeval city. In Munich we tasted the delights of German beer and German opera. From there we moved on to Salzburg still unspoilt by cosmopolitan patronage, and to Berchtesgaden not yet polluted by Hitler. From Ischl, where the old Emperor Franz Josef could still be seen setting out for the mountains from his shooting-box, we turned South to Innsbruck. There I was able to examine the mountain

terrain in which Hofer had for so long successfully resisted
Napoleon's armies. We returned by Lake Constance, the
Black Forest, and Heidelberg to the Rhine. Carrying no
passports we passed from one country to another almost
without knowing it. Amongst the Tyrolese mountains, in
the woods of the Black Forest and on the vine-covered hills
along the Rhine, the peasants in the summer sunshine
worked their land, tended their cattle, gathered in their crops.
Yet the flash of arms and the tramp of marching men were
always present in the background. Unknown to us, the
overture to Europe's long agony was about to begin. On
the way home I made a detour to visit Louvain where one
of my old Jesuit masters, Rev. T. Corcoran, afterwards
Professor of Education in the National University, was
completing his scholastic studies. He was a good guide to
that old town with its historic Irish Capuchin Church of
St. Pierre, its Catholic University, and its connection with
Father Damien, the leper's friend.

In July, 1905, I made another foreign excursion, this
time with three of my brothers, to Norway, that nursery of
many nations, in the cruising liner, *Ophir*. Cruising is,
I think, a pastime the merits of which are exaggerated
save as a holiday for old or lazy people. It is no doubt a
pleasant way of getting round for those who like to take an
English hotel about with them and do not really want to
meet the people of the lands they visit. Norway, however,
is one of the few places where cruising is justified ; great
fiords can best be seen from the deck of a steamer and the
hotels were few and far between. We were a merry ship's
company and the fortnight we spent on board passed quickly
enough. Delightful weather conditions, which are essential
to such an excursion, added to our pleasure. From the
old Hanseatic town of Bergen, with its picturesque old
wooden houses and its modern villas dotting the steep hills
above, we went North to Molde. Steaming through great
fiords with sides often rising five thousand feet sheer from
the water, we found ourselves each morning anchored in
some deep inlet. On shore little hamlets of red-roofed
wooden houses could be seen clustering round a white-

painted church. And soon, as we went North, there was
no more night, only a long unbroken twilight in which sleep
seemed unnecessary. The people, in their simple bright
costumes, were as picturesque as the land, industrious,
polite and hospitable, often speaking English with fluency.
I recollect a tram conductor at Bergen, whom I complimented on his mastery of the language ; " Oh," he replied,
" I have only a smattering of it." It was a country in which
there were no rich and few poor. One felt also the presence
of a strong, cultured, healthy patriotism. Only a month
before our visit the Union with Sweden had been dissolved
by the almost unanimous vote of the national parliament,
and Norway had become once more an independent
sovereign state. Sweden, as befitted another democracy,
had peacefully accepted the verdict, a striking example, as
I pointed out to some of our English travelling companions,
of international good manners and good sense.

The life in our large luxurious liner with its cosmopolitan
atmosphere of over-eating, amusement and idleness seemed
strangely remote from this frugal, patriotic land. Cupid
was also at large on board and one at least of my brothers
was temporarily disabled by his darts. I was already
mortally wounded before we set out. In *L'Envoi*, a
poem which was a parody of Kipling, and duly appeared
in the ship's journal, I endeavoured to depict the feelings
of the unfortunate officers, condemned to a repetition
of this experience for an entire summer—The first verse
ran :

When the last of the launches is lifted, and the tenders are off
    on the tide,
When the silliest question is answered, and the sorriest joke has
    been tried,
We shall rest, and faith we shall need it—lie down for a minute
    or two
Till the toot of the out-bound tender shall call us to work anew.

Back in Cork I found Windle greatly interested in *Great
Catholic Laymen*, which I was then writing, and particularly
in my biography of Pasteur. This he was good enough to
read and revise. " I find it most interesting and admirably

carried out," he wrote, " and congratulate you on the way in which you have done your work. I have devoted a good deal of thought to it because I think it is a thing that wanted doing and doing well from the Catholic point of view and that it will be valuable when done. Hence if I have criticised minutely you will understand that it was because I am anxious to see the thing as good as it can be. I have added the definitions you require which you can modify or not as you please. . . . I will make one general criticism. I think it is a mistake to write down all scientific men who do not accept Christianity as second-rate, and if I were you I would very much modify the parts of your paper in which that idea is conveyed. If you convey that idea to a reader and he then finds out that Darwin, for example, who certainly was a first class-mind, was not a believer, you are apt to do harm rather than good. Darwin was not a crass materialist like Huxley, but he was not a believer. Huxley again, though I am not a blind admirer of his and quite believe he owed more to force of character and an admirable English style than to real scientific ability, was certainly a man of genius. It is abundantly true that lots of small fry, e.g. the miserable Grant Allen and the egregious Clodd, have won notoriety by attacking Christianity. There is only one way in this world by which it can be easier attained and that is by a Catholic who chooses to gain it by attacking his own Church. This recipe is quite infallible. But you must guard yourself against the inevitable and accurate retort when pointing out how many scientific men of the atheistic sort are second rate. What I should do myself if I were working on this line would be something of this kind :—1. To point out that many of the greatest men of science were also *croyant* and that it is obvious that there is, therefore, no incompatability between religion and science of the most advanced and far-reaching character. This is incontrovertible and a great gain when established. 2. Then I would frankly admit that other men of science did not accept Christianity and I would divide them into (a) sciolists, like Grant Allen,—no rational person would call him a man of science—who need not be considered,

(b) the genuine men of science of whom there are those of the Huxley type, arrogant and cock-sure, who can never become as little children and can therefore never enter into the Kingdom of Heaven nor—*mea sententia*—into the real kingdom of science, for no man can do that who is not a metaphysician, and a *humble* metaphysician as well as a physicist." These criticisms, expressed in Windle's usual clear and forthright way, were most helpful and were gladly accepted. The only condition he made was the characteristic one that in the book I was to make no reference to the assistance he had given me.

Like most self-centred men of action, Windle was oblivious of domestic affairs that did not directly cross his path, and he remained entirely blind to the now obvious relationship which existed between his daughter and myself. It was not, indeed, till a year had passed, and then only when his attention was drawn to it, that he recognised the situation and began to take what, in naval parlance, is called " avoiding action." In June, 1906, he wrote to his old friend, John Humphreys of Birmingham, " Strictly *entre nous* I have been having a bit of bother about Mary, who had attracted an estimable young man. . . . She is much too young and immature for anything of the kind, so I stamped on it and sent her off for a couple of months rambling. It did not come to a declaration, thank goodness." [1] While he was quite right in describing Mary as young she was far from immature and had, indeed, already made up her mind. The stamping did not put out the fire in our hearts, quite the contrary. When she returned to Cork, in September, 1906, I immediately proposed and, while, in deference to her father's views, she refused to pledge herself, she left me in no doubt of her real feelings which indeed, I had long known. Windle, as he was quite entitled to do, refused his consent to her marrying anyone until she came of age, but he also clearly intimated that even then he would continue, for reasons which seemed good to him but which naturally did not appeal to his daughter or myself, to oppose her marriage to me. There followed two

[1] *Sir Bertram Windle.* A Memoir, by Monica Taylor, p. 181.

years of separation which fully tested our affection and forged it into tempered steel. Sent first as a governess to a French family at the little watering place of St. Jean de Luz, near the Pyrenees, she later returned to England as secretary and companion to a friend of her late mother, Mrs. Ellen Pinsent, whose advice and sympathy never failed us in a time of great delicacy and difficulty. This lady, wife of a distinguished Birmingham solicitor and sister of that great judge and scientist, Lord Parker of Waddington, distinguished alike for her public service and literary ability, made us welcome at her home, Lordswood, Harborne near Birmingham, and there on 18th March, 1908, Mary's twenty-first birthday, we became formally engaged. In June she returned to Cork and we were married on 16th September with her father's reluctant assent. She had submitted dutifully to the test imposed on her but never wavered in her attachment to me. Windle entered in his diary that he had that year lost a daughter and gained a University settlement.[1] Yet had he been as clear-sighted about the former as the latter he might have gained both. My parents, on the contrary, felt that they had not so much lost a son as gained a daughter—a gift all the more valuable as they had none of their own. Windle's attitude continued unsympathetic and our friendship remained in abeyance for six years, as much I think to his loss as to ours. " It is very nice theoretically to be at the head of a college," he wrote in his diary on 30th September, 1909, " but when it, and its university, are going through the melting-pot, it is a very anxious and responsible position, and I often feel the need of what I haven't got, that is some wise, confidential friend to talk to."[2] Perhaps I might, in part, have filled that blank. But he suffered another loss that could never be repaired. Twelve years afterwards, in November, 1920, when Mary died, he wrote to me from Canada, " It is just a year since I left Cork and bid good-bye to Mary. Till that moment I did not really know that she was so fond of me as was the case and now I shall never see her again in this world."

[1] *Sir Bertram Windle.* A Memoir, by Monica Taylor, p. 198.
[2] *Sir Bertram Windle.* A Memoir, by Monica Taylor, p. 208.

XI

THESE future events were mercifully hidden from us as we sat in the dining car of the Rosslare express that morning in September, 1908, looking out on the rain-swept Blackwater valley and enjoying our modest wedding breakfast of bacon and eggs. That night two very self-conscious young people were swallowed up in the whirlpool of London. From there after a few days we went South, as we had planned, through Switzerland to Italy. As our train swept down the long twisting incline from Airolo to the Lombard plain we entered a new land which summer had not yet deserted. Under the strong sun vineyards nestled on the foothills against a darker background of walnut and chestnut trees, while each mile of our journey revealed fresh glimpses of snow-topped mountain, dark-blue lake and little red-roofed towns.

That first day in Italy had its appropriate end in our midnight arrival at Venice as we passed suddenly from the dim-lit station down the wide steps to the gondola waiting at the water's edge below. The sense of easy motion after the rocking train, the clean coolness of the night after the hot dusty day, the long, narrow, silent canals and the musical cries of the gondoliers as they gave warning of our approach, all combined to weave a magic spell. We had passed, it seemed, into another age, and when we came at last to the Grand Canal and the brightness of our hotel we woke as from a dream.

There followed days of wonder and delight as we went from Venice to Florence and so on to Rome. We were both young, filled with great happiness, and ready to absorb the beauty and culture which surrounded us. In the great churches and picture galleries of Florence—that unique city—we wandered entranced. One evening we watched from Fiesole the sun setting over the valley below. The Arno ran like a band of silver into the dim distance, while beneath us lay the city—the great dome and campanile of the cathedral, Giotto's masterpiece, rising amidst the gathering dusk and dominating all. As we watched, the sun sank slowly—a great gold ball fading into crimson, and filling all the western sky with a dark red afterglow. Soon the outline of the cypresses in the foreground alone remained —all else had faded into the night.

In Rome, through the influence of Monsignor O'Riordan, who was now Rector of the Irish College, we were granted the great privilege of a private audience with His Holiness Pius X. Dressed in the appropriate ceremonial garb we reached the Vatican at the appointed time, and were ushered up numerous staircases by the Swiss Guard in their medieval dress to the ante-room of the Papal apartments. From there we were conducted by a Papal Chamberlain in court dress to a small throne room just outside the Pope's private rooms. In a few moments the Holy Father came in, accompanied by Monsignor Bisletti whom we had already met. In spite of his white soutane and scarlet cloak the Pope looked, as indeed he was, a kind and gentle parish priest bearing the burthen of the earthly father of Christendom. The child of Venetian peasants, he was a living proof that the Church is essentially democratic, that every parish priest is a potential Pope. But there was something in his face, not only of gentle dignity and peace, but of resignation and humility. He walked with a slight stoop as if the cares of his great position weighed heavily upon him. We both knelt and he walked straight over to us, giving us his ring, a great emerald surrounded by diamonds, to kiss. Speaking in French I asked him for his blessing on ourselves and our families and presented him with a specially bound copy of my book. He blessed us both, and then speaking in Italian which Monsignor Bisletti translated, he expressed his appreciation of my effort, saying that a more useful and meritorious work could hardly be attempted than that of bringing home to the Catholic public that their co-religionists were and are as forward in the march of civilisation as those of any other religion. He spoke also with evident affection of Ireland. Monsignor Bisletti then handed us two medals, struck to commemorate that year of Jubilee, which he said the Holy Father wished us to keep as a reminder of our visit and a token of his affection. He added that His Holiness was going at once to receive a pilgrimage from Pisa, and perhaps we should like to follow in his train. Pleased at this unexpected prolongation of our visit we followed the Papal procession, now augmented by several Chamberlains and an escort of Swiss Guards, into the Sala Regia, outside the Sistine Chapel, where the pilgrims were assembled. After the Cardinal Archbishop of Pisa had read an address the Holy Father replied, speaking for nearly half an hour in a clear distinct voice with simple, homely eloquence which even we could partly understand. His main, and consistently repeated theme was his desire to " restore all things in Christ "—*Instaurare omnia in Christo*—the motto of his Pontificate. As he left the room the pilgrims, who were mostly peasants, burst into loud vivas as they pressed round him to kiss his hand. It was a memorable and impressive sight. One Cardinal, in speaking of his election, had said " The finger of God is here. No one can see Pius X without admiring his humility, simplicity and goodness." Those words best described our feelings as we left the Vatican.

Home once more we started housekeeping in a little house on a terrace looking out over Cork from the heights of St. Luke's. In the following spring we moved into Lacaduv, the home my father had generously built for us near Clanloughlin, on a bluff overhanging the river Lee. There on 5th September, 1909, our first child, John Ivor, was born. A few years later, in 1912, Harold Begbie, one of the many English journalists who came to Ireland during the Home Rule campaign of those years, and who was for a few days our guest, thus described our home :—

" I met," he wrote, " at the house where I was staying just outside the town—a house on a wooded hill whose windows and balconies look towards the sunset across a curving river, and a wide stretch of meadow land glimmering far away to fold upon fold of distant hills—a most amiable and cheerful company of Catholics and Protestants. The whole atmosphere of that house with its babies and flowers, its pets and toys, its music and literature, its hospitality and its cheerful domesticity, was quite charming and convincing ; one could not mix with the family and its guests, could not share in that kind and hospitable life, believing for a moment the wicked calumny of Catholic intolerance. It would have been like suspecting an English hostess of stealing from one's dressing-case, or an English host of cheating at cards. To know the Irish people one must stay in their homes and share their domestic life. One must not merely discuss political opinions, but must pay visits to the nursery, perambulate the garden, go shopping with one's hostess, take pleasure in the pictures and the furniture, if possible make toffee or toast barm brack at the schoolroom fire." [1]

Begbie was an amiable person who had written two or three second-rate novels and a book about the Salvation Army. Later he wrote *A Gentleman with a Duster*, which appeared anonymously and created some stir, as it dealt with the seamy side of English politics. His book on Ireland was good of its kind but its kind is not usually good. He came to me with a letter from my friend, Stephen Gwynn, who then introduced such visitors to Ireland on behalf of the Irish Party. By that time I had entered the maze of political life from which I did not emerge for a decade. It was an interesting and valuable experience.

To understand the position as it then existed it is necessary to go back a few years. After the death of Parnell " one man power," as William O'Brien pointed out, " was replaced by eighty men powerlessness ".[2] When re-union of the two Irish parties took place in 1900 the majority could not agree on any one of their leaders, John Dillon, William O'Brien or Tim Healy, as Chairman. As a compromise John Redmond, the leader of the Parnellite minority, was chosen. Those who proposed him said at the time that he could easily be removed later, but he so bore himself that every year strengthened his position. He never sought dictatorial power. All his efforts were for reconciliation among all

---

[1] *The Lady Next Door*, by Harold Begbie, p. 143.
[2] *An Olive Branch in Ireland*, by William O'Brien, M.P., p. 67.

Irishmen and he never attributed mean or corrupt motives
to others. That was the essential character of his leadership.
But his task was a difficult and thankless one. Hardly had
he been elected chairman when the personal dissensions
already latent in the majority party disclosed themselves.
O'Brien and Dillon almost immediately insisted that Tim
Healy, who hovered like a gadfly in the background, should
be either fought or ostracised. In spite of Redmond's
efforts to preserve the peace, O'Brien, at the ensuing general
election, insisted on opposing Maurice Healy, Tim's brother,
in the Cork constituency. The issue was not in doubt.
Tim wrote to his father after the election on 19th November,
1900, " Money is all powerful and O'Brien spent it, while
Maurice hadn't it. If he could have hired a mob he would
have won." [1] O'Brien was a great mob orator and drew
the crowd, but in addition to his oratorical powers he did
not hesitate to spend money lavishly ; so Maurice Healy
was defeated by an overwhelming majority. Tim himself
held North Louth, but disgraceful scenes were enacted in
that constituency when he and O'Brien abused each other
one Sunday for five consecutive hours from the same
wagonette.

Unfortunately the elimination of the Healys from the
Irish Party did not ensure peace within its ranks. New
dissensions soon broke out. These centred around the
dispute between William O'Brien and John Dillon concerning the Land Conference of 1903 and its results. Until
then they had been close friends and political allies, the
" great twin brethren" of many a strenuous fight. Both
had served a hard and romantic apprenticeship to the cause
of Irish nationalism. At the time of the Parnell Split they
had been in America, organising support for the Irish cause.
In September, 1890, when on the point of starting on this
mission, they were arrested on a charge of criminal conspiracy. Being allowed out on bail they (with the assent
of their sureties) escaped to France in a fishing boat and
from there travelled to America—being sentenced in their
absence to six months imprisonment. When two months

[1] *Letters and Leaders of My Day*, by T. M. Healy. Vol. ii., p. 452.

later the Parnell divorce proceedings came to a head, these two men, whose joint influence was second only to that of Parnell himself, were unfortunately unable to take an effective part in Irish affairs, as they could return only to be arrested. At the end of December, however, they returned to France, where at Boulogne they met Parnell and Redmond for the purpose of trying to negotiate a settlement of the bitter dispute then raging over Parnell's leadership. In these negotiations O'Brien played a prominent and honourable part, and they were nearly successful. Parnell offered to retire if O'Brien should succeed him. O'Brien refused but proposed Dillon as an alternative, and Parnell, whose preference for O'Brien was marked, unwillingly assented. Yet the project, which would have spared Ireland much turmoil, bitterness and degradation, eventually broke down over relatively unimportant details. Some evil influence at the eleventh hour prevented Parnell from making an honourable and dignified exit. Dillon and O'Brien returned to England where they were duly arrested and imprisoned. On their release from Galway Gaol six months later they declared themselves unconditionally opposed to Parnell—the decision, according to O'Brien, being made by Dillon. The latter subsequently became the Chairman of the majority, or anti-Parnellite Party, and so remained until shortly before the reunion under John Redmond.

In spite of their friendship and close political relationship, Dillon and O'Brien were very dissimilar personalities. O'Brien had begun life as a journalist. Parnell appointed him editor of *United Ireland*, the weekly organ of the Land League. He soon made this paper one of the most militant political journals ever published in Ireland. At Parnell's request, when a prisoner with him in Kilmainham Gaol, he drafted the famous " No Rent " manifesto which called on the farmers to stop paying rent till the land question was settled. His paper was suppressed by the British Government but nevertheless continued to appear, being printed secretly abroad. Subsequently he and Dillon started the Plan of Campaign under which the tenants of

estates whose landlords refused a reduction in rent paid
their rents into a common fund for the purpose of defence
and assistance in case of eviction. This last step was taken
without Parnell's consent and he made it clear that he did
not approve of it. On one famous occasion, when a prisoner
in Tullamore Gaol, O'Brien, as a protest against the ignoring
of his claim to be treated as a political prisoner, refused to
wear prison uniform and remained for several weeks on
his plank bed until one morning he was found clad in a
suit of Blarney tweed which had been smuggled in by a
friendly warder. These, and other similar exploits, endeared
him to the people.

But he was a difficult, and not always reasonable, colleague. Delicate, neurotic and highly imaginative, he was
temperamentally inclined to extreme views. Moreover, a
publicly expressed humility was allied, as it often is, to an
overweening private vanity. An amusing instance of this
was that his apparently extempore speeches were usually
written out word for word, and even included interjections
from the crowd with appropriate replies arranged in advance.
During our subsequent opposition to him in Cork we sometimes, I fear rather maliciously, arranged for unexpected
interruptions with somewhat ridiculous results.

While still a young journalist in Cork O'Brien fell in love
with and married an actress in a touring company but
not long afterwards she died. In 1890 he married secondly
Mademoiselle Sophie Raffalovich, the daughter of a wealthy
Franco-Russian banker of Jewish origin who had conceived
a romantic attachment for him through reading of his
exploits in the French press ; and who succeeded in meeting
him in Paris during one of his flights from the attentions of
the British Government. This marriage placed him in a
position of complete financial independence, and he was
able henceforth to pursue an individual policy regardless of
party decisions, an unfortunate and dangerous position for
all concerned. His appearance was as picturesque as his
career. The long hair and beard, the pale heavy-featured
face and small short-sighted eyes twinkling behind his
spectacles, gave him the aspect of a benevolent prophet.

But suddenly, at the mention of some person or policy he disliked, the low cordial voice and gentle smile would disappear, and the set features, the tense look, and the fervid utterance would reveal the fanatical spirit within.

John Dillon was as reserved and pessimistic as O'Brien was optimistic and exuberant. Tall and thin, of a saturnine and melancholy appearance (Tim Healy, in one of his charitable comments, once described him as " the melancholy humbug ") his pale, oval, intellectual face was illuminated by fine dark eyes which, George Meredith said, were the most beautiful he had ever seen. Unimaginative and prone to suspicion, his character was the very antithesis of O'Brien's. A son of John Blake Dillon, the friend of Mitchel and one of the leaders with him of the '48 movement, he qualified as a surgeon but soon forsook surgery for politics. In this career the distinction which he enjoyed as a rebel's son was enhanced by his own striking personality and eloquence. During the first years of the Land League he was amongst the most prominent and extreme of Parnell's colleagues and suffered frequent imprisonment. A wide reader and keen student he was recognised as an authority on foreign affairs, even in the House of Commons. Like O'Brien he became a man of considerable private means and therefore free to take his own line in political affairs, sometimes unfortunately regardless of party decisions. Unlike John Redmond he objected to ameliorative measures such as the establishment of local government and the co-operative movement in agriculture, because he believed they diverted attention and effort from the main national objectives of land reform and self-government.

So long as he and O'Brien were united in opinion their diverse personal characteristics made them a unique and powerful combination of great value to the national cause. It was perhaps natural that when Redmond was elected Chairman of the re-united party Dillon did not cordially approve, but he promised him " strict fair play " and later became one of his strongest supporters and most valued counsellors. Characteristically enough, neither Redmond nor he, unlike O'Brien and Healy, left any written vindication of their actions or policy. Dillon's strength as a political leader lay in his unimpeachable personal integrity and consistent pursuit of high ideals, characteristics reflected in the passionate sincerity of his oratory; but his gifts in council and his political foresight were often clouded by a sombre and sometimes rather narrow outlook.

It was almost inevitable that the Land Conference of 1903 should lead to dissension between himself and O'Brien with consequent embarrassment to Redmond and serious injury to the national movement. Neither Dillon nor Davitt nor Thomas Sexton, who was the leading financial authority on the National side, was invited to take part in the Conference, the tenants' representatives, nominated *ad hoc* by Captain Shawe Taylor, being John Redmond, William O'Brien, Timothy Harrington, M.P., then Lord Mayor of Dublin, and T. W. Russell, an Ulster member of Parliament. Much trouble might have been avoided had Dillon, Davitt or Sexton been included.

The dispute turned on the price to be paid to the landlords by the tenants. Dillon, Davitt and Sexton maintained, with some reason, that the terms agreed on by the Conference were too generous. The Land Act of 1903 in effect provided an entirely new procedure with regard to land purchase. Although there was no compulsion to sell, the landlords were in fact encouraged to do so by the payment of the purchase money in cash by the British Treasury, and of a bonus of twelve per cent. on the purchase price provided by the same beneficent body. The purchase money was to be repaid by the tenants in a fixed annuity over a period of sixty-eight and a half years. The sales, if and when terms were agreed on, were to be no longer limited to individual tenants but applied *en bloc* to whole estates. It is interesting to recall now that, in the opinion of a distinguished contemporary French observer [1] " the credit of the United Kingdom was involved in no risk " by the transaction, for the Treasury could, he pointed out, always have recourse to local taxation to recoup itself for any loss. In 1932, however, Mr. de Valera's Government refused to

[1] *Contemporary Ireland*, by Paul Dubois, p. 275.

12—1818

pay over the collected annuities to the British Treasury, although continuing to collect a moiety of them from the tenants. Fortunately neither John Redmond nor William O'Brien survived to witness what was in effect a repudiation of their bond.

When the Act of 1903 became law the *Freeman's Journal* (controlled by Sexton and ostensibly the Nationalist organ) joined John Dillon in launching what Davitt described as " a determined campaign " against its financial clauses. Dillon went so far as to say that it would " lead to national bankruptcy." The result of these financial controversies was that the majority of the tenants, left without effective leadership or counsel, paid too much for their land, although in districts where they were properly organised and led satisfactory results were obtained. O'Brien left it on record that throughout the whole of these transactions John Redmond " displayed an unfaltering loyalty to the policy of reconcilation of class with class to which he had set his hand." [1]

O'Brien, however, instead of standing his ground and putting his policy to the test, proceeded to retire from public life, an action he was to repeat on other occasions in subsequent years. He was, nevertheless, soon afterwards re-elected without opposition as member for Cork and the city remained partially disfranchised for several years. The man who had been one of the strongest exponents of a determined Nationalist policy, now went to the other extreme and maintained that the national demand could only be met by the adoption of a policy " designed to unite all classes, creeds and political parties." He became obsessed with the idea that all difficulties and differences could be magically removed by the same methods as had succeeded at the Land Conference of 1903, quite regardless of the fact that such a settlement could only be secured by sacrificing the very principles it was supposed to secure, and by hopelessly dividing the Irish Party itself. Agreement with the Unionist minority could in fact only have been arrived at by postponing indefinitely the fulfilment of the national demand for full legislative freedom.

---

[1] *An Olive Branch in Ireland,* by William O'Brien, M.P., p. 235.

In the meantime, however, a decisive change had taken place in the political scene. At the General Election of 1906, by one of those drastic transformations which are liable to arise in the absence of proportional representation, the Liberal party secured a majority of more than a hundred over all other parties combined. The divisions in the Unionist party on the question of Tariff Reform together with the exposure of the gross mismanagement of the Boer War contained in the report of the Royal Commission presided over by Sir William Butler, had combined to create a veritable landslide which overwhelmed many even of the principal Unionist leaders. Although the new Liberal Premier, Campbell-Bannerman, was personally sympathetic to Ireland the Irish Party was virtually impotent. To make matters worse the new Government introduced an Education Bill which gravely endangered the position of the Catholic schools in Great Britain. Redmond, however, with remarkable dexterity and firmness, won from the Government concessions which the Catholic bishops were prepared to accept, and thus earned the gratitude of the Catholics in Great Britain, most of whom were of Irish origin. At the same time he strengthened his position with the Liberals by supporting them in their quarrel with the House of Lords which eventually rejected the Bill.

Meanwhile William O'Brien had buried the hatchet with Tim Healy. "I am in consultation with O'Brien," Tim wrote to his brother on 18th July, 1906, "in respect of his libel action against the *Freeman* . . . He and his friends are more furious against the Party than ever *we* were "[1] So does political misfortune make strange bedfellows.

The Liberal Government now decided to take up the plan for the reform of Irish administration which Lord Dunraven and Sir Anthony MacDonnell had pressed upon their predecessors with fatal results for George Wyndham. Accordingly Augustine Birrell, the Irish Chief Secretary, introduced, in May, 1907, a Bill to set up an administrative council with an elected majority. In this council, subject

[1] *Letters and Leaders of My Day*, by T. M. Healy, p. 478.

to a veto by the Lord Lieutenant, were to be vested the powers of the most important Irish government departments. Attenuated though the measure was in scope and purpose it vested the administration of Ireland in an all Ireland body and would have formed a nucleus from which an Irish parliament with full legislative powers must inevitably have sprung. Whether it would have been rejected or not by the House of Lords must remain problematical, for an Irish National Convention which assembled in Dublin two weeks later on Redmond's motion unanimously declared it to be " inadequate in scope and unsatisfactory in details," calling upon the Irish Party to oppose it in the House of Commons and to demand the establishment of a native parliament with a responsible executive having power over all purely Irish affairs. In face of such opposition the Bill was immediately withdrawn.

The impulse to reject the Council Bill had come largely from the younger members of the national organisation and particularly from the Ancient Order of Hibernians, which had recently become associated with it. This organisation had its origin amongst the Catholics of Ulster during the persecutions of the eighteenth century but had since developed into a great religious and benevolent association. Its leader, Joseph Devlin, M.P. for West Belfast, soon became a prominent figure in Irish politics. " Wee Joe," as his fellow-citizens loved to call him, had neither the appearance nor the voice of an orator, but his plain looks and hard Northern accent were but externals that masked the vital spirit within. I once heard him say that had it been possible he would have chosen rather to devote his life to the improvement of the lot of his poorer fellow-citizens in Belfast than to national politics, and I felt it was true. Of humble origin and small education his honesty and courage lit up his speeches with an eloquence as simple as it was sincere and convincing. Tim Healy once called him a " duodecimo Demosthenes " and the description was both humorous and accurate. But he had also the defects of his qualities, and like many other good-natured people attracted parasites who were not always as disinterested as himself, and who sometimes brought discredit on his organisation. Next to Dillon he counted as the most important of Redmond's lieutenants and his influence extended far beyond his native city.

It was perhaps natural that William O'Brien should not welcome the advent of this rival in the field of popular oratory. The Ancient Order, though he had been glad to enlist its support during his operations against Tim Healy, in 1900, soon became the peculiar object of his detestation. He described it as the " mock modern survival of a secret society with a lengthy and bloodstained history," and as " both occult and irresponsible." [1] Its chief defect was of course that it opposed his policy. It was in fact a Catholic friendly society neither oath-bound nor secret, originally concerned rather with the protection of Catholics than the persecution of Protestants. Since its membership was confined to Catholics it no doubt practised an exclusion contrary to the tenets of Irish nationalism, but, as it was not the official Nationalist organisation, this peculiarity was certainly permissible if not desirable. Its more objectionable features derived, like most extreme developments in Irish politics, from its origin in the North at a time when religious bigotry was a virtue and repression had bred revenge. William O'Brien now became its best recruiting agent and his denunciations of the " Molly Maguires " (as reviving an old nickname he called the Order) only helped to spread its branches throughout the country.

After the rejection of the Council Bill in 1907 there was a general demand for a reunion of the divided Nationalist forces. Finally in January, 1908, after negotiations in which George Crosbie played a prominent, but virtually anonymous part, William O'Brien and Tim Healy, with four other members of parliament who supported them, rejoined the Irish Party. Peace did not however last long, for when the Liberal Government, in 1909, introduced a Land Bill to modify the financial provisions of the Land Act of 1903, which had been rendered unworkable by the loss resulting on the issue of the Land Stock below par, O'Brien violently

[1] *An Olive Branch in Ireland*, by William O'Brien, pp. 419–21.

opposed the measure although in fact it had been designed to save the Irish taxpayer from having to meet the deficiency. A National Convention called to consider the Bill, provoked by his extreme attitude, refused to give him a proper hearing or to consider his views. In high dudgeon he once more retired from public life and departed for Italy. This action created a vacancy in Cork city, but his colleague Augustine Roche, M.P., refused to follow him into the wilderness or support his policy.

The situation was difficult. Cork could not be left permanently in this semi-paralysed condition by William O'Brien's retiring disposition, but unfortunately his attitude had caused the local political organisation to become so feeble that it had virtually ceased to exist. It was therefore impossible to hold a convention and select a candidate in the usual way. In these circumstances a representative deputation of local Nationalists in April, 1909, requested George Crosbie to seek election as a pledge-bound member of the Irish Party. His candidature was welcomed and endorsed by John Redmond, but as soon as this was made known all the disgruntled elements in the constituency became active. At the eleventh hour a Convention of these people, which in addition to O'Brien's friends and supporters included the redoubtable Sir Edward FitzGerald and some representatives of organised Labour groups, selected Maurice Healy to contest the seat. It was a time of crisis in Parliament and the Liberal Government was about to join issue with the House of Lords by introducing the famous Lloyd George Budget, the provisions of which were anathema to vested interests represented by the Unionist Party. Never had it been more essential for Ireland to present a united front, and Redmond himself travelled to Cork on the eve of the Budget to impress this upon the electors whom he asked to support George Crosbie.

I now made my *début* as a politician on his behalf in a speech at a country meeting near my home on the eve of my twenty-eighth birthday. It was largely an encomium of our candidate with whom I had already worked in the industrial development movement. I noted in my diary

" Practically no audience and little enthusiasm. It made me realise strongly the artificial side of politics." George Crosbie was in fact a bad candidate, for both he and his paper the *Cork Examiner* had been, until shortly before the election, amongst O'Brien's chief supporters, and the people, prone to political idolatry, resented his apparent desertion of their idol, although in fact Crosbie was still inspired with the desire to maintain national unity. Moreover, as a newspaper proprietor he had naturally made many enemies, and the lack of an effective political organisation, which his opponents possessed in some measure, was a crippling handicap. Maurice Healy, on the other hand, was a strong candidate. He had had a long experience of parliamentary life and had proved himself an excellent member for the city. This commended him quite naturally to the business community. Many people also resented the manner in which he had been ejected from his seat by William O'Brien nine years before, and he had, as he said himself on the declaration of the poll, " a defeat to wipe out." Ironically enough, being in opposition to the Irish Party nominee, he could now *faute de mieux* count upon the support of O'Brien's party. In the result George Crosbie was beaten by 1,159 votes. " A just judgment," I wrote in my diary, " on the *Examiner* and the Irish Party for their long toleration of William O'Brien and other malcontents." Although Maurice Healy purported to take the Party pledge, the Irish Party, now thoroughly incensed, refused to accept him into its ranks, where strangely enough his brother Tim still maintained an increasingly precarious existence. The issue was thus joined in a political conflict which, so far as Cork was concerned, was to last for ten years.

The year 1909 was also remarkable in another way. In June a strike took place in Cork which had portentous consequences. Quay labourers, employed by the City of Cork Steam Packet Company, and belonging to the recently formed Irish Transport Workers' Union, withdrew their labour because they objected to work with men of an unrecognised union. This in turn led to a sympathetic strike of railwaymen and eventually to a general strike which lasted for several weeks and paralysed the commercial life of the city. The Cork Employers' Federation, well organised and financed, secured a decisive victory over the strikers and imposed their own terms. Like all such victories, however, it created a false sense of power in the employers and bitterness in the employees which were in some measure responsible for the disastrous Dublin general strike of 1913. From that conflict in turn sprang the Citizen Army, a workers' volunteer force, which played such a prominent part in the rebellion of 1916.

XII

THE Cork election of April, 1909, although it had no serious political results, was, in its way, also a portent. Maurice Healy, in his anxiety to return to Parliament, raised the banner of revolt against the leadership of John Redmond and the policy of a united Irish front at Westminster. That revolt, which had its origin and main support in Cork, was organised and intensified by William O'Brien during subsequent years and was one of the hotbeds in which the seeds of the extreme Sinn Féin movement germinated and finally matured. The Cork election was therefore in effect the first step in the process which led to the eventual *débacle* of the constitutional movement.

But in 1909 these trends of opinion were not obvious and the moderate element in Irish politics seemed to be in complete control. There had of course been changes since 1890. Parnell's party was then composed of young men, ardent and enthusiastic, ready for any action or sacrifice. Most of them had suffered imprisonment, many repeatedly. The party attracted without effort new and valuable recruits. On his death stagnation ensued. During the ten years of the Split no man of note joined it. The men of the eighties remained, but they had ceased to be young men and they grew less tolerant of the young, who had for the most part, like myself, found hope and promise in the Gaelic League and the movements, political and economic, which it inspired. In 1909, however, the constitutional movement once more became dynamic and, under John Redmond's leadership, gave promise of reaping the harvest denied to Parnell. The younger generation, for a time at all events, gave him their support and the Irish Party was enriched and revivified by such recruits as Joe Devlin, Tom Kettle and Dick Hazelton.

This change of opinion was principally due to Redmond's adroit handling of the political situation. All through 1909 the controversy over the Lloyd George Budget continued. It was not popular in Ireland, where the farmers looked with suspicion on the proposed land taxes and the powerful liquor trade objected strongly to the drastic new taxation of licences. One ingenuous member of William O'Brien's party convulsed the House of Commons when he innocently stated that the Irish publicans were "living from hand to mouth!" Redmond obtained concessions in respect of the land taxes but Lloyd George, having first agreed on certain amendments to the new licence duties, subsequently refused to accept them. It was the first of many similar experiences with the wily Welsh politician whose dishonest manoeuvres were directly responsible for the sense of failure which darkened Redmond's closing years and for the destruction of the constitutional movement.

The Irish Party, however, recognising that the rejection of the Budget would produce a conflict in which the power of the House of Lords to destroy progressive legislation might be challenged on the most favourable grounds, abstained from voting against the third reading. On 30th November the Lords rejected the Finance Bill and the issue was firmly knit. Three days before Redmond had warned Lord Morley that "unless an official declaration on the question of Home Rule be made not only will it be impossible for us to support Liberal candidates in England, but we will most unquestionably have to ask our friends to vote against them." [1] This warning had the desired effect. Speaking a month before the dissolution of parliament at the Albert Hall on 10th December, 1909, Asquith, the new Liberal Prime Minister, declared amidst loud cheers that the solution of the Irish problem " could only be found in one way, by a policy which, while explicity safeguarding the supremacy and indefectible authority of the Imperial Parliament, will set up in Ireland a system of full self-government in regard to purely Irish affairs." Redmond had in fact suddenly become the dominating figure in British politics, and the Irish people rallied to his support.

After Redmond's death, and even before it, certain

[1] *The Life of John Redmond*, by Denis Gwynn, p. 166.

publicists and politicians represented him as a sentimentalist who had been consistently fooled by the astute English Liberal leaders. Nothing could be further from the truth. No one who reads the careful memoranda of his interviews and correspondence with English politicians to be found in his official biography, or who was associated with him during that period, as I was, could possibly believe that he was under any illusions as to the motives and sincerity of those with whom he had to deal. It is true that his chief characteristic was a fine generosity and charity which made him hesitate to impute unworthy motives to anyone, but he had also learned in early life that politics were not a matter of sentiment but of hard bargaining. Like most Irish Catholics of his class he was by temperament and tradition a Conservative and he had no real sympathy with the crude, and rather vulgar, radicalism of a man like Lloyd George. He had far more in common with a scholar and statesman of Asquith's calibre. Moreover his experience under Parnell had taught him to view the Liberals with suspicion " even when they brought gifts." Had it been possible he would have much preferred to deal with the Conservatives for they at least were in a position " to deliver the goods." When the Irish Party was reunited in 1900 he stated his policy quite clearly and frankly. " The opportunities," he wrote, " which the party system in Great Britain by its very nature open up to an Irish Party, numerous, united, constant in attendance, and independent of all British parties, are known to us by experience. Ministries have been made and unmade by such a party; benefits have been wrested from reluctant and even hostile majorities ; policies have been altered to the advantage of Ireland by the steady and sustained compulsion of an Irish parliamentary force known to speak for the nation, acting as a single man, and taking advantage of every occasion of attack and defence." It was in fact Parnell's policy restated. To that policy he adhered to the end.

His relations with the Liberals, who were the only party able and prepared to consider the Irish demands, involved a double difficulty. On the one hand any strong Nationalist pressure might have led to the secession of men like Grey, Haldane, and Churchill who represented the Liberal Imperialist element, never very sympathetic to Irish demands, while on the other hand the Nonconformists— the backbone of the Liberal Party—whose chief spokesman was that dynamic personality, Lloyd George, were always susceptible to the exploitation of religious prejudice.

It is interesting to recall that it was not the *English* members of the Cabinet whom Redmond found unreliable in negotiation but a Welsh attorney, Lloyd George; a Scottish Laird, the Master of Elibank; and a Jewish barrister, Rufus Isaacs. It was these three men, whose subsequent devious dealings in American Marconi shares nearly wrecked the Liberal administration, who could not be depended on. Asquith, although he had a lawyer's inclination to compromise and procrastinate, acted on the whole with complete candour and integrity. No doubt his approach to the Irish question was, unlike Gladstone's, one of calculated expediency rather than inspired magnanimity, but, as he said himself when introducing the Home Rule Bill of 1912, he " did not presume to be able to bend the bow of Ulysses."

Redmond was forced by the exigencies of the situation to interfere in English political questions in which he had little or no interest. It is indeed ironical to reflect that his greatest positive political achievement was the abolition of the veto of the House of Lords which would never have been accomplished save for his relentless pressure on an unwilling Liberal Government. Redmond knew, indeed we all knew, that the leading Liberals and Conservatives would, in the usual English fashion, if left to themselves, have come to a compromise. Such an attempt was in fact made after King Edward's death in 1910. But it failed because Ireland blocked the way and the Irish, under Redmond's leadership, remained as the spearhead of the attack behind which concentrated all independent Radical opinion in Great Britain. Asquith was finally forced, most reluctantly, to secure " guarantees " from the King and to appeal to the electorate for a mandate which broke the power of the Lords.

The first election on this issue, which took place in January, 1910, led to another contest in Cork. After the election of April, 1909, we had begun the laborious task of reconstructing the local Nationalist Party and by this time we had the nucleus of a healthy and rapidly growing organisation. William O'Brien, refreshed by his Italian holiday, returned impenitent to the fray. The situation was not without its comic aspects. Sir Edward FitzGerald, who had for sometime aspired to enlarge his political experience by an excursion into the parliamentary field, now entered the lists. He had intended to run in double harness with Maurice Healy, but the unexpected arrival of William O'Brien upset his plans. Undaunted by this development he arranged a Convention of his municipal supporters at which he was selected, in *substitution* for Maurice Healy, as O'Brien's prospective colleague. He even arranged that the meeting to be held at the City Hall on the night of O'Brien's return should be packed with his own supporters. Unfortunately these plans miscarried as the crowd which welcomed O'Brien was so large that the subsequent meeting, at which O'Brien and Healy were selected as the O'Brienite candidates, had to be held in the open air. " Fitzy " nevertheless persisted in his candidature.

We on our side had our own difficulties. Our first choice was obviously Augustine Roche, M.P., the sitting member, who had refused to follow O'Brien. " Gussy " Roche, as he was affectionately called by his friends (" Goosey " by his opponents), was nearly as celebrated a Cork character as " Fitzy." A wine merchant and a bachelor, he had several times been Mayor of the city. His rubicund and hirsute countenance contrasted strangely with his impeccable attire. He always appeared in tall hat and morning coat with black cravat and diamond horseshoe pin. The Cork wits asserted that he habitually slept with the tall hat on his head. His vanity was as great, if not as justified, as William O'Brien's, and there were many amusing stories of his doings. His hobby was the collection of old china and glass, and Joe Devlin used to relate how on one occasion, having to secure Gussy's attendance at a crucial division in the House of Commons, he found him in his hotel bedroom quite oblivious of political crises, " silently worshipping a newly purchased piece of Waterford glass." On one occasion when Mayor he travelled to Berlin at the invitation of the Berlin Rudder Club, which had recently rowed on the Lee in a famous contest with Leander. He was received by the Kaiser and, not to be outdone, distributed trinkets to the German athletes in truly royal style. But in spite of these peculiarities, which sometimes made him a difficult political colleague, " Gussy " was really a kindly and generous soul whom the poor children of Cork should long remember, for it was he who first organised for their benefit those annual excursions to the seaside which have now become a permanent and beneficial institution.

The choice of a second candidate was not so easy for George Crosbie had refused to stand again. On the eve of the election John Redmond wrote to my father as follows :—

> Aughavannagh, Aughrim,
> Co. Wicklow.
> December 16th, 1909.
>
> My dear Mr. Horgan,
>   Do you think it would be at all possible for you to consent to allowing your son to stand for Cork ? You would be doing a great service to us and everybody says he would be far the best candidate.
>   Yours very truly,
>   J. E. REDMOND.

My father, however, much as he would have liked to do so, could not accede to this request, for he was by then unfortunately suffering from an asthmatic affection which prevented him from practising his profession or discharging his duties as coroner. This made him dependent on my assistance in both capacities. My friend William Murphy, solicitor, the chairman of our local political organisation, finally consented, very reluctantly, to stand as our second candidate. He was in every way a most suitable choice. Clear and courageous in council, firm of purpose and

absolutely trustworthy in action, he was one of that band
of unselfish and comparatively unknown men who have
always been the backbone of Irish nationalism.   A quiet,
unassuming man, he lacked the showy brilliance so often
mistaken for ability; but behind his simplicity of character
there stood a rock of principle and honour.   It was truly
said of him that he never had to forfeit a friend for a principle
or a principle for a friend.   As a young man he had supported
Parnell in his last fight and had afterwards been associated
with John Redmond in the policy of independent opposition.
Although he was twenty years my senior we became fast
friends and, until his death in January, 1936, we acted
together in intimate and complete accord on all political
questions.   I owe a great deal to his noble inspiration and
wise advice.

The election was hotly contested.   William O'Brien was
without a newspaper to voice his views and he therefore
immediately launched a special campaign sheet.   This
journal was called the *Cork Accent* in allusion to the order
said to have been given at the National Convention of 1909
that " nobody with a Cork accent " should be permitted
to approach the platform.   This paper, edited by one of
O'Brien's henchmen, indulged in promiscuous abuse.   We
had no difficulty in showing that misfortune had made
strange bedfellows and that the alliance between O'Brien
and the Healys was, to say the least of it, unnatural.   We
did not lack ammunition for their abuse of each other
had for years been common form.   We compiled and
published an amusing pamphlet entitled *The Liffey at Ebb
Tide* which carried on its title page the following quotation
from Tim's Healy's paper, the *Weekly Nation*, of 11th
November, 1899 : " Mr. O'Brien glories in the use of the
language of the virago and the drab, and he is never so
happy as when he is pouring out adjectives which inevitably
remind the reader of the Liffey when the tide is on the
ebb."   The pamphlet contained their respective opinions
of each other as expressed publicly in their speeches, articles
and letters during the previous fifteen years.   " Comment,"
as the preface stated, " could add nothing to the interest

of the discussion," and we refrained from making any. It was in fact a scandalous and disedifying chronicle and if either of them was to be believed then the other was a blackguard or worse. Tim according to William was " a wrecker," " a disturber," " a traitor," and " a disgrace to human nature " ; while William according to Tim was " a mad mullah " and " a play actor " from whom " no personality, however illustrious or revered, was sacred from attack." Unity between these gentlemen for the ostensible purpose of promoting national conciliation was therefore not without its comic aspects. Maurice Healy had put the matter clearly in October, 1900, when he said that " wherever you find O'Brienism there you will find confusion, turmoil and discord gather." So it now proved in Cork. Claiming that he stood for a policy of Conference, Conciliation and Consent, O'Brien in fact, so far as the Nationalist movement was concerned, only succeeded in creating Conflict, Confusion and Contention.

Three C's figured also in another aspect of the contest for our opponents were not slow to point out that William Murphy, James McCabe, solicitor, who was another of our principal speakers, and myself, were all Coroners (in my case deputy Coroner) and that consequently our cause must be in a moribund condition. One opposition ballad went as follows :—

When the Coroner ran for the City of Cork
T'was felt to be heavy and serious work
As a savour of inquests and tragical ends
Seemed to hang o'er his meetings and sadden his friends.

T'was felt for a humorous man there was room ;
Then they searched East and West and they searched up and
     down
They ransacked the country and hunted the town,
And at last, in a fortress o'er hanging the Lee,
They discovered J.J. and exclaimed " This is he,"
He's a natural wit and a fine jolly sowl
Though he looks just as sad and as glum as an owl.
He's just brimming over with bright " juice despree "
And he'll tickle the ribs of the democracy.

But alas for the " Crowner," alas for the cause
When the people beheld this expounder of laws
There arose an " Ochone " and a wild " Wirristhru "
For be jabers this chap was a Coroner too !

The other side had not however a monopoly of doggerel
poets for shortly afterwards the following effort appeared
in the *Cork Accent* :—

To The New Irish Leader

Our confidence in thee we place
Bright jewel of the Irish race,
Relentless in pursuit of right,
Invincible in open fight ;
Ever true to Erin's cause,
Nobly winning men's applause,
Ireland needs thy watchful care ;
Save her from the traitor's snare
Against the horde of " Molly Maguires,"
Cut-throats, renegades and liars,
Onward march to victory,
Dark Rosaleen has trust in thee.

We had thrown a rich bait over William O'Brien's vanity
and it had been swallowed hook, line and sinker, for the
poem, which had been composed by a clever sub-editor
of the *Cork Examiner*, unfortunately formed an acrostic which
declared, as was only too evident when it appeared in
print, that " O'Brien is a cod." Cork laughed loud and
long and there was hell to pay in the editorial sanctum of
the *Cork Accent*.

But, in spite of these poetic forays, personal relationships
were not all embittered. Maurice Healy and I, for instance
remained on good terms although in opposite camps. One
of his active supporters at that time told me quite recently
how on one occasion, being carried away by party feeling,
he made some disparaging remark about me in Maurice
Healy's presence. Maurice sat back, and having with a
characteristic gesture, pushed up his spectacles, proceeded
to tell his astonished adherent in no uncertain terms that
in his opinion I was an honourable opponent, that he hoped

Cork would produce more public men of my type, and that
he was sorry I was not on their side. That feeling was fully
reciprocated and on many occasions I sought his wise
advice on professional and personal problems. To watch
him, when considering a legal question, thoroughly investigating every relevant statute and case applicable was in
itself a valuable lesson. Like many Cork people he had
no respect for time and would sit up till the small hours,
generally reading French novels, with the result that he
was seldom to be found in his office before noon. Our
common interest in French literature was another tie, and
I have still a complete edition of Maupassant's stories which
he gave me. These relations, however, in no way prevented
us from indulging in the cut and thrust of political and
professional combat in which he was naturally far more
experienced than I. His son, Maurice Healy, Junior, who
eventually went to the English Bar and won fame as a
broadcaster before his untimely death, was also one of my
close friends at that time. He had a flair for light verse
and was I suspect responsible for the poem on the coroners
already quoted. His book on the Munster Bar is one
of the most interesting collections of Irish legal stories ever
published.

The election of January, 1910, eventually resulted in a
stalemate, for the intervention of " Fitzy " upset the
calculations of both the larger parties and resulted in the
election of William O'Brien and " Gussy " Roche; the two
better, but less spectacular candidates, Maurice Healy and
William Murphy, being defeated. We had in effect,
however, scored a victory, for, as I said in a speech made
after the declaration of the poll, the electors had judicially
separated an ill-assorted couple. William O'Brien was
terribly downcast and could not hide his mortification when
it became clear that Roche was elected. The latter, fearing
defeat, failed to appear at the counting of the votes, but
" Fitzy," determined to punish O'Brien for ignoring him,
had instructed his well-trained supporters to give " Gussy "
their second votes, and this saved the day.

When the smoke of battle cleared away the results

showed a reduction in the strength of the Irish Party which came back with seventy pledge-bound members out of a possible eighty-two. The O'Brienites, almost all elected for Cork constituencies, accounted for eight of the balance. But at Westminster the Irish were supreme. Parnell's dream had once again been realised. The English parties in the new House of Commons consisted of 275 Liberals, 273 Conservatives and 40 Labour members. Redmond held the balance of power.

In reply to a letter of congratulation and warning which I wrote him he replied :—

Confidential.   Aughavannagh,
                                    Aughrim, Co. Wicklow.
                                        3 February, 1910.

My dear Horgan,

Very many thanks for your friendly letter. I perfectly under-stand and agree with your view. You may rest assured unless Asquith gets his " Guarantees " about the Lords first, he won't get his Budget if we can help it.

Very truly yours,

J. E. REDMOND.

A week later, in a speech at the Gresham Hotel, Dublin, he repeated this declaration and made it clear that the question of the veto of the House of Lords was the supreme issue. The Government sought to evade the conflict. Asquith wrote to the King, "Redmond cold and critical if not avowedly hostile." [1] Finally in April Redmond's unrelenting pressure prevailed and Asquith announced that he intended to bring in a series of resolutions defining and limiting the powers of the Upper House. The Budget was re-introduced and passed into law without further opposition. The stage was set for the final struggle. Then on 7th May, 1910, King Edward died. The English leaders on both sides immediately seized the opportunity to seek an agreed solution of their differences. The subsequent Constitutional Conference, on which the Irish were not represented, broke

[1] *Life of Lord Oxford and Asquith*, by J. A. Spender and Cyril Asquith, p. 273.

down in the following November because Balfour insisted
that Home Rule should be excluded from the operation
of the compromise scheme proposed by Lord Ripon. This
in effect provided that the House of Commons with the
addition of a hundred peers elected on a basis of proportional
representation should have the final word in the case of a
deadlock between the two houses. In December the country
was once more plunged into a General Election. Once
again it was Redmond's threat of opposition which prevailed.
Asquith obtained the necessary guarantees from the King
and the Government appealed to the electorate for a
mandate to pass the Parliament Bill into law. That measure,
which had already been introduced and sent to the Lords,
provided for the abolition of the absolute veto of the
Upper House.

William O'Brien had in the meantime launched his new
organisation, the All for Ireland League, whose primary
object, strangely enough, was declared to be " the union and
active co-operation in every department of our national life
of all Irish men and women who believe in the principle of
domestic self-government for Ireland." [1] How this object
could be secured by dividing the national forces into two
opposing camps was not made clear. This new departure
was also to " guarantee to the Protestant minority of our
fellow-countrymen inviolable security for all their rights
and liberties," which of course involved the malicious
suggestion that those rights and liberties were in danger.
O'Brien proclaimed in short that if all the Catholics,
Protestants, Unionists and Nationalists in Ireland united
in a solid phalanx he would lead them to victory.
How the preliminary miracle was to be achieved remained
a mystery.

Some indication of the methods which he favoured was
given us in May, 1910, when John Redmond, John Dillon
and Joe Devlin visited Cork. No sooner had the date of
the meeting been announced for Sunday, 22nd May, than
O'Brien summoned a similar meeting of his supporters for
the same time and place. This was of course a direct

[1] *An Olive Branch in Ireland*, by William O'Brien, M.P., p. 471.

provocation to disturbance and might have had serious results. Fortunately, thanks to excellent police arrangements and the exercise of much tact on our part, a direct clash between the rival crowds was avoided. Our supporters rose to the occasion, and when the special train carrying the Irish leader arrived in Cork enormous crowds thronged the approaches to the station. I drove to the hotel in the same carriage with John Redmond. In the light of flaming torches the procession, nearly a mile long, moved like a river of fire. The enthusiasm of the vast crowds whose cheers drowned the music of the marching bands visibly surprised Redmond, who had naturally believed Cork to be an O'Brienite stronghold. On the following day O'Brien, with characteristic bravado, insisted on leading his assembled followers, mainly agricultural labourers brought in from the surrounding districts, past the hotel where Redmond and the other leaders were staying. I stood by John Dillon at the window as William O'Brien went by standing in a waggonette, his hair and beard dishevelled, waving a large hat and shouting a frenzied defiance. It was not an edifying sight and Dillon's comment " Poor little woman," a reference to Mrs. O'Brien's trials, seemed not uncalled for.

There had been some anxiety as to whether the O'Brienites would attempt to seize the Cornmarket, where our meeting was to be held, but they had got a lesson a few months before when they tried to prevent Tom Kettle from lecturing at the City Hall and had to retire with sore heads and hearts. They did not now attempt any further attack on freedom of speech. So ticklish was the situation, however, that I was asked to lead our procession to the Cornmarket in order to prevent any possible collision between the two gatherings. Later in the day there were some minor skirmishes in which some of O'Brien's country supporters, who had been led to believe that the city was entirely on their side, were sadly disillusioned. They were lucky to escape with a few broken heads for the day might well have ended in a disastrous riot. John Redmond made an important speech in which he defined the position of Ireland

in relation to the crisis which had arisen on the death of
King Edward a few weeks before, an event which he
referred to in sympathetic and dignified terms. Standing
beside him I noticed the supreme care with which his
speech was prepared and delivered, every important phrase
written out in full in his clear precise writing and every
modulation suitably emphasised. His delivery was as clear
and accurate as his notes, every gesture dignified, every
word distinct, yet all completely natural and sincere.
One realised that in him the great tradition of oratary
still lived.

During this period I was still intimately connected with
the work of the Gaelic League. A violent controversy had
just arisen concerning the question of whether the Irish
language should be made a compulsory, or as we said an
essential, subject for the matriculation examination of the
new National University.   The Rev. Dr. Delaney, S.J.,
one of the leading Jesuit educationalists in the country,
asked why the language of uneducated peasants should be
made a test for university education.   The Rev. Dr.
O'Hickey, one of the professors at the ecclesiastical college
of Maynooth, was actually removed from his chair because
he favoured the proposal and had been too outspoken in
his criticisms of those in authority.   Almost alone amongst
the Catholic hierarchy, Dr. Walsh, the Archbishop of
Dublin, supported the Gaelic League in its demand.
Amongst the politicians John Dillon was prominent in his
opposition and John Redmond, although he supported the
fundamental ideas of the Gaelic League, complained of the
hostility displayed by many of its prominent members
towards the Irish Party.   Douglas Hyde attended and
addressed the National Convention of the United Irish
League in 1909 which, after hearing him, passed a resolution
approving the Gaelic League's attitude to Irish in the
University. In 1910 I wrote to Hyde drawing his attention
to the serious situation which was developing through this
political interference by a purely cultural organisation, and
he replied :

1 Earlsfort Place,
Dublin.
(Undated).

A Chara,

A thousand thanks. Of course I know all you tell me only too well and I went to Belfast last month to remove the bad impression there. Now I hope to try to do the same down South. It is unfortunate that all the best Gaelic League workers are also advanced politicians while the language gets little or no help from the M.P.'s, the United Irish League or the Ancient Order of Hibernians. That makes my task ever so much more difficult. Give my kindest regards to Madame Maire and with the same to yourself and many thanks.

Mise do chara,

AN CRAOIBIN.

Hyde's complaint was undoubtedly justified. He certainly did his best to resolve the latent difference between the younger and older generations but the political orientation of the Gaelic League could not be checked. Five years later he had to resign when, against his wishes, its objectives were enlarged to include " working for a free Ireland." That political enlargement, as he had foreseen, ultimately proved hurtful to its primary aims.

The struggle to make Irish essential in the University matriculation examination terminated in June, 1910, when the Senate, under pressure from public opinion, by a small majority conceded our demand. The victory was in effect little more that symbolic. That wise Irish-American philosopher, Mr. Dooley, is credited with the statement that " you can bring a man to a university but you cannot make him think," and in the result the mere acquisition of a smattering of Irish by university students, although it may be justified on grounds of national pride, has done little if anything to advance the development or spoken use of the language. I have myself presided at many local appointment boards where the candidates, mostly young doctors, have almost invariably answered the set question concerning their knowledge of Irish by the candid answer that they had forgotten all they ever knew. The more brilliant their professional qualifications the more likely was this to be their answer. One cannot help feeling that it might have been wiser to have encouraged by voluntary means a more intensive study of the language as evidence of national culture rather than as a perfunctory ritual imposed by authority.

Opening the Kilkenny Feis, or language festival, a few days after the National University had yielded to the Gaelic League, I pleaded for a wider approach to the problems confronting us. Pointing out that one of the most hopeful results of the recent controversy had been the universal support we had received from a large body of cultured opinion and from the people's representatives, I said that it was our duty to bring that body of opinion into the Gaelic League and to make these people not only friends but comrades in the battle for a new Ireland.

In a subsequent article in *An Claidheamh Soluis*, the Gaelic League Journal, I suggested that the support of this older generation could be secured by enrolling them as honorary members whose only obligations would be to see that their children were taught Irish, and to study Irish history, and support Irish industries themselves. Kilkenny itself was an excellent example of what could be done by intelligent leadership, for there my hostess, Countess Desart, and her brother-in-law Captain Otway Cuffe, had devoted their time and money not only to reviving the language, music and art of the country but native industry as well. In the meadows at Talbot's Inch by the Nore, near her beautiful house, Aut Even, this great little lady had established an up-to-date furniture factory. She has also assisted in the revival or initiation of other industries and reopened the Kilkenny Theatre. Although she was not herself of Irish blood she had dedicated all she had with courage and ability to the development of her adopted home. Her name should be remembered with honour by our people. I came away from Kilkenny, feeling, as I said in my speech, that we in the Gaelic League had launched a ship whose course was set towards a new and happier land and that the spirit of national re-birth and re-union, there apparent, would soon become a widespread reality. That landfall has not yet been made and those hopes remain unfulfilled.

XIII

THE political truce which followed the death of King Edward VII came to a sudden and dramatic end in November, 1910, when it was announced that the Constitutional Conference could not reach agreement. John Redmond, with Joe Devlin and T. P. O'Connor, had spent the autumn recess in America seeking financial and moral support for the Irish cause. Never was the influence of the Irish in America more obvious. At great meetings in all the principal cities prominent citizens of all parties vied with each other in supporting the Irish demand for self-government. The envoys returned with the substantial sum of 100,000 dollars (£20,000) for the Nationalist political fund. The Unionist Party placarded England with cartoons depicting Redmond as the "Dollar Dictator" riding on Asquith's back. Lend Lease of course had not then been envisaged.

Redmond landed at Cork on Sunday, 13th November— three days after the break-down of the Constitutional Conference. Great beacon-fires of welcome blazed along the Irish coast to greet the liner in which he travelled. Ashore he received a tumultuous welcome. Pressmen from all over the United Kingdom had gathered to record his words. He made it clear at once that while he was glad that Irish democracy was able to assist the democracy of Great Britain in the struggle for their rights, we were in the fight in order to gain liberty for ourselves, and he was going back to the British Parliament for one purpose alone— " to endeavour out of the necessities of English parties to win freedom for Ireland." On 28th November Parliament was prorogued and the election began.

The supporters of the Irish Party in Cork were faced once more with the problem of finding a second candidate, for William Murphy refused to stand again. " Gussy " Roche, who I fear was more concerned with votes than principles, favoured the selection of Sir Edward FitzGerald whose support had secured his return in the previous election. But the majority of us felt that " Fitzy's " chameleon-like qualities would be dangerous in the parliamentary arena. We therefore firmly vetoed the proposal. I was pressed to stand as a candidate not only for Cork City, but also for South-East Cork and Mid-Cork as well. My father's state of health compelled me to decline these flattering invitations. Finally William Redmond, M.P., John's brother, agreed, at considerable personal inconvenience, to stand for Cork City.

After a fierce contest both our candidates were beaten by over 600 votes, but in one year we had increased our total poll by a thousand and we knew that our victory was only postponed. Within two years, by dint of hard work and efficient organisation, including unremitting attention to the voter's register, we had secured substantial majorities in the Cork Corporation and County Council. Remembering the strenuous political work of those days I often laugh secretly at what now passes for political organisation. Unfortunately we never got another chance of contesting William O'Brien's personal position at the polls ; the result would have been conclusive.

The election left the progressive majority in parliament virtually intact. In the midst of all this political turmoil, on 20th December, 1910, my second son—Michael Joseph— was born.

I had met Willie Redmond for the first time during the previous January election when he had come to Cork to support our candidates. Political comradeship has this in common with travelling that it quickly reveals one's companions in their true character. This is particularly so in Irish politics where sincerity is ruthlessly tested and devotion to personalities often substituted for attachment to principles. Yet one can truly say that to know William Redmond, even in such circumstances, was to love him. The two qualities which dominated his character—a boyish enthusiasm and a simple unselfish sincerity—were stimulated by political action. He had the fine courage which aims at victory but is ready to accept defeat with a smile. We had good reason to realise this; for three times in Cork he fought a forlorn hope, and three times he failed—but it was a failure that left behind it more affection and regard than often comes with success. He himself once said that he would rather be beaten in Cork than win anywhere else and we who had fought with him knew what he meant, for we had indeed been a " band of brothers."

I think what most endeared him to the people was his fearless spirit of comradeship and self-sacrifice. Where the fight was fiercest there he was always to be found; and he would never ask anyone else to do what he was not prepared to do himself. I remember several instances of this latter quality. One bitter winter night during that election of December, 1910, we had been speaking in one of the Cork suburbs. When the meeting was over he insisted on leaving the waggonette from which we had spoken and marching back through the muddy streets at the head of the procession. We wore out quite a lot of boot leather during that election. Those who were with him in Flanders during the war had the same experience. He would never ride as he was entitled to, but always marched with his men. He would not even let his batman carry his pack when they were moving up to the trenches. All through the Somme battles he fretted because he was not allowed to join the advance and had to stay in a casualty clearing station, under fire it is true, but not bearing an equal risk with his men. It was that spirit which took him over the parapet with them in the end. But he was no fanatic. He had too much sense of humour for that. I remember his saying on one occasion as we faced a sea of upturned faces cheering him for minutes on end : " Isn't it splendid, and yet we'll be beaten by about five hundred," as indeed we were.

He loved to recount his experiences in the eighties and nineties when he was the *enfant terrible* of Irish politics. He used to tell an inimitable story about a venerable parish priest in the County Clare into whose village he had penetrated for the purpose of holding a meeting. It was during

the Parnell Split.   He had just been defeated in Cork and
he descended on East Clare with a large and enthusiastic
Cork following in order to retrieve his political fortunes.
The people of this village had declared that he would not
be permitted to hold a meeting there.   Mounted on horseback with a famous fighting band from Cork in the van,
and as he described it " the women and children in the rear,"
he proceeded to advance upon his objective.   The battle
was fierce but in the end all barriers were swept aside, the
village entered, and the meeting held.   The distracted parish
priest thereupon sat down and wrote to William O'Brien—
" My dear William,—That scoundrel Redmond has attacked
us with a gang of rowdies from Cork and is devastating the
country.   Come down and help us at once."   Then in his
excitement he addressed and posted the letter to " William
Redmond, Esq., M.P., Dublin," to whom it was duly
delivered.

Another amusing story he told of that Clare election
concerned a certain enthusiastic supporter who was appointed returning officer in a remote and hostile area.   On
the polling day Willie to his horror received the following
wire *en clair* from this lunatic.   " Things going badly here ;
have destroyed a hundred votes ! "

Many were his hairbreadth escapes from capture by the
police during the Land League campaign when he, William
O'Brien, and others like them made the country ring with
their exploits.   It is interesting to recall that he was one
of the eight men whom the Parnell Commission found had
" established and joined the Land League organisation with
the intention by its means to bring about the absolute
independence of Ireland as a separate nation."   One of
his speeches was actually put to Parnell in cross-examination
as an example of the Republican aims of his followers.

I do not think that Willie Redmond ever shirked a fight
in what he believed to be a good cause, but after the Parnell
Split and all its bitterness, he, like his brother, did his best
to preserve national unity and hated to take part in domestic
controversy, however necessary.   Just before the election
of December, 1910, when we were urging him to stand for

Cork, he wrote to me : " Personally I am not inclined for this contest, and I go as directed by my leaders and in response to you and our friends in Cork ; but if I go into the fight I *will* fight." And fight he did with that undaunted spirit which nearly turned defeat into victory. I never knew him, however, to say an unkind word of his political opponents, either in public or private. I remember him saying to me during that election, " I wonder what would happen if I met William O'Brien accidentally in the street. You know I'd have to hold out my hand for the sake of old times."

When the Irish Volunteer Movement was recognised by the Irish Party in 1914 he threw himself into it heart and soul. He was always a soldier at heart and its spirit of comradeship and discipline appealed to him. I do not think it is generally known that he undertook a difficult and dangerous mission to Brussels some months before war broke out in order to obtain arms for the Volunteers. In November, 1914, he came to Cork to present colours to the Cork City Battalion of the National Volunteers. This organisation represented the great majority of the Volunteers who had followed John Redmond's lead at the commencemen of the war. He was very anxious that his visit should not be misconstrued and he wrote to me a few days before " It is better not to mix politics with the Volunteers. I will not talk politics." Colonel Maurice Moore, the commanding officer of the Volunteers' organisation was with him and they got a royal welcome. It proved to be Willie Redmond's last speech in Cork and I do not think it will be readily forgotten by those who heard it. There was one memorable passage :

" I speak as a man who bears the name of a relation who was hanged in Wexford in '98—William Kearney. [1] I speak as a man who with all the poor ability at his command has fought the battle of self-government for Ireland since the time—now thirty-two years ago—when I lay in Kilmainham Prison with Parnell. No man who is honest can doubt the single-minded desire of myself and men like

[1] His full name was William Hoey Kearney Redmond.

me to do what is right for Ireland. And when it comes to
the question—as it may come—of asking young Irishmen
to go abroad and fight this battle, when I personally am
convinced that the battle of Ireland is to be fought where
many Irishmen now are—in Flanders and in France—
old as I am, and grey as are my hairs, I will say ' Don't go,
but come with me.' "

He stayed with us during that visit and at home after
the meeting he told me that he was seriously thinking of
applying for a commission in the army. He spoke with
great sadness of his many friends in Parliament who had
already fallen and he said that he thought, as so many
brilliant young lives had been sacrificed, that he who had
not many years to look forward to might serve Ireland
best in the firing line. I told him that I could not see that
at his age, for he was then fifty-five, anyone could expect
such a sacrifice, but that undoubtedly his name would
carry great weight in England, and that good might result
from his example after the war. He spoke of it again next
day, urging his good health and shooting expeditions in the
Wicklow mountains as evidence of his ability to bear the
hardships of active service. I did not hear from him again
till Christmas, 1914, when he wrote me a characteristic
line across a Christmas card. " I am going for the Irish
Brigade. I can't stand asking fellows to go and not offering
myself." The army authorities, naturally enough, raised
many difficulties and objections, but he insisted on getting
a commission or being given a definite reason for its refusal.
He was eventually gazetted to his old regiment, the 6th
Royal Irish, which he had left when a subaltern to join
Parnell.

He wrote to me immediately afterwards, " They have
done their best, to raise the grey hairs on my head with the
account of all the hardships before me, including active
service very soon. Of course it is a bit of a wrench leaving
home, but my wife is quite willing I should go and I am
certain it will do our cause good." And indeed soldiering
at his age was no joke. At the New Barracks, Fermoy,
where he went first, he was treated most kindly by everyone,

but it was hard work. " I have been here ten days," he wrote, " and I am getting used to it. Needless to say I find it all dull and irksome, but I hope what I have done will bear fruit for Ireland, for it certainly is not fun for me." Later on he got accustomed to the work and wrote me " I got home to-day after some days strenuous field training. I slept two nights at the back of a ditch, without a tent or anything. It was a great show, the whole brigade being out."

I went to see him a few times at Fermoy and found him in good spirits. He had the usual bare barrack-room and over his bed was a little picture of Our Lady which his wife had given him and which never left him. Though he was most sincerely religious no man ever made less parade of his religion. Few knew that, even during a keenly fought election, he would slip out every morning to early Mass. One of his greatest joys at Fermoy was, as senior Catholic officer, to march his battalion to Church. Indeed one of the things he felt very much was the fact that so many of the Irish Catholic regiments had no senior Catholic officers, and some of them at that time hardly any Catholic officers at all.

The last Sunday before he left Ireland, 11th July, 1915, he motored over to see us. It was to be our last meeting. He told us that he had been offered an easy position at home—I think in connection with recruiting—and almost ordered to take it ; but he had refused. " I did not join the army," he said, " to make recruiting speeches but to go to the front with my men." When he reached France his military duties engrossed all his time but sometimes a short letter or postcard came through to say he was still alive and well.

His last speech in Parliament in March, 1917, has passed into history. He, who had never been an effective House of Commons speaker, then made one of the most moving speeches of the war. Standing there, grey-haired and tired in his war-stained uniform, for he had just come from the trenches, he expressed with simple dignity the thoughts uppermost in the minds of his comrades at the front, many of whom were about to sacrifice their lives for Ireland. Twenty-seven years afterwards, in April, 1944, Winston Churchill, speaking in a debate on the future of the British Commonwealth, recalled that gallant figure and reflected sadly that "maybe an opportunity was lost then." He added truly that if Ireland was " the lamentable exception" to Imperial unity it was one concerning which English politicians " must all search their hearts."

Willie Redmond's last speech surprised those who did not know the great heart which was hidden under his breezy manners and informal ways. That very simplicity was one of his greatest charms. No public man of his time in Ireland was less spoiled by popular applause. The one who knew and loved him best wrote to me after his death, " It is all so strange that his death should have aroused such feeling, as he was so simple and thought nothing of what he did." He would have been one of the first to laugh at the suggestion that he was a statesman ; he was indeed only " a very gallant Irish gentleman."

Just a few weeks before he fell he wrote to me from the front, " I wish I had time to write you all I have seen out here. My men are splendid and we are pulling famously with the Ulster men. Would to God we could bring this spirit back with us to Ireland. I shall never regret I have been out here." He died as he would have wished, leading his beloved Irish Brigade to free Belgian soil. I think it was Gavan Duffy who wrote that the difference between Mitchel and Davis was that Davis loved Ireland and Mitchel hated England. Willie Redmond belonged to the school of Davis. He believed that all Irishmen, by common service to the ideal of human freedom, could be brought together to build up a new Ireland. " I have been an extreme Irishman all my life," he wrote in December, 1916, " and if others, as extreme perhaps on the other side, will only come half-way, then I believe, impossible as it may seem, we should be able to hit upon a plan to satisfy Irish sentiment and Imperial sentiment at one and the same time."

Because he held these beliefs strongly and tenaciously the Rebellion of 1916 was a cruel blow. He knew that it had destroyed all his high hopes and that it would ensure the ultimate division of Ireland and Irishmen. He gave his life to bridge the gulf, but he must have known that it was in vain. In a memorandum attached to his will he wrote—" I should like all my friends in Ireland to know that in joining the Irish Brigade and going to France I sincerely believed, as all the Irish soldiers do, that I was doing my best for the welfare of Ireland."

Those of us who knew him required no such assurance. He was spared, however, the final humiliation at the hands of his own people. When he died, of wounds received in action, on 7th June, 1917, he was succeeded as member for East Clare by Eamon de Valera. . . . A new and tragic chapter in the history of Ireland had begun.

Memory also recalls another gallant figure who came to help us in Cork during those years and who also died for Ireland in France. For many years after his death there stood in St. Stephen's Green, that beautiful little park in the centre of Dublin, an empty plinth on which was engraved the simple inscription :

THOMAS M. KETTLE

1880–1916.

His friends dare not place upon it the bust of this brave Irishman lest it be defaced by fanatics. We have long since, I hope for ever, outgrown those infantile convulsions, and it now occupies its rightful place in the heart of his native city. Kettle was, I think, the most brilliant mind of my generation in Ireland, combining great breadth of intellect with a capacity for concentration and a progressive mind which would, almost inevitably, have placed him in the front rank of Irish statesmen. I knew him first as a boy at Clongowes in the early nineties. Many of our contemporaries were brilliant students and have since become distinguished men. But amongst them all Kettle stood supreme. Already that facility for grasping a complicated subject and condensing it in a happy phrase, that bright, eager mind, so ready to take issue on behalf of a good cause, that intellectual supremacy which was so pre-eminently his, had marked him out for far-reaching influence and a notable career. He was one of the few students of his year who took up German, a study he afterwards completed by a "wander year" in the Tyrol, as he recalled in that noble letter to an Austrian fellow-student written during the war under the title "Zur Erinnerung." I remember him also—strange premonition of the future—speaking fervently and strongly in the debating society on that then most threadbare and academic of questions : "Should we have Conscription ?"

Our fathers had fought together under Parnell in the eighties and we had thus common ground for a friendship which lasted to the end. During my student days in Dublin I again saw much of him. He was by then the intellectual leader at University College, and as auditor of its Literary and Historical Society added fresh laurels to his fame. It was clear from the first that his was no mere meteoric flight but a splendid progress towards a prominent place in the life of his generation. From the University he passed to the Bar, but Irish politics was in his blood, and the law-courts could not satisfy his legitimate ambitions. Like myself, he was at first drawn towards the new political programme outlined by Arthur Griffith—his Hungarian policy—and some of his first poems appeared in the *United Irishman.* Then the possibility of a revival of Parnell's policy attracted him, as it did me, and, leading a forlorn hope, he won an Ulster constituency for the Irish Party while still in the twenties. The House of Commons, that merciless destroyer of reputations, could not stay his triumphant progress. He soon took his natural place as a debater with giants like Balfour, Asquith and John Redmond. He was a born orator, and not, like Willie Redmond, a man who became an orator by passionate conviction or stress of circumstances. Wit and humour, denunciation and appeal, paradox and epigram, gave point and effect to his fluent speeches. Tall and straight, with his soft hand-some boyish face and bright eyes, he first startled and then compelled the attention of the House by his irresistible charm and luminous argument. Two pictures of him during that period survive in my memory. The first is of a scene during the second reading of a Women's Suffrage Bill, of which cause he was an ardent supporter. " Mr. Speaker," he drawled in his rich Dublin accent, " they say that if we admit women here the House will lose its mental power." He flung his arm over the packed benches. " Mr. Speaker," he continued, " that is impossible." The House roared with laughter. " They tell me also," he went on, " that the House will suffer in its morals. I don't believe that is possible either." The laughter rang out again at this double hit. I remember hearing him on another occasion in the House of Commons one sultry night in June, 1910. A dull debate on foreign affairs was in progress. The House was discussing the recent visit to Egypt of Theodore Rossevelt, then ex-President of the United States, and the lecture he subsequently delivered at the Guildhall on England's imperial destiny and the " white man's burden." Kettle let loose on the famous " Teddy " the barbed irony of his wit. I can recall one of his biting phrases : " This new Tartarin of Tarascon who has come from America to shoot lions and reform the British Empire."

In those strenuous years Kettle was at his best, and it was a great pity that he ever left the political scene for which he was so peculiarly suited. Politics had, however, led him to the study of Irish economic conditions, and work such as his report on Irish Land Purchase Finance marked him out for the position of Professor of National Economics in the new National University. Yet he had no abiding interest in the abstractions of political economy, and I feel sure that he would have returned to politics had he lived. Of the spirit in which politics should be approached he once wisely wrote that " one should take enthusiasm for the driving force, and irony as a refuge against the inevitable day of disappointment."

The most remarkable thing about Kettle as a speaker was his immense facility and ready wit. A few notes on the back of an envelope, seldom consulted, were usually his only memoranda. Yet he never failed to delight by the dignity and style of his periods and the humour of his similes.

It was this same delightful wit and sparkle that made social intercourse with him a joy. One never left his company without carrying away the recollection of a clever epigram or *bon mot*. One recalls his description of Tim Healy, whose wit he admired but whose political antics he deplored, as a "brilliant calamity"; his epigram that Life was "a cheap table d'hote in a rather dirty restaurant, with Time changing the plates before one had enough of anything"; and his reminder that "the Liberals when in office forgot their principles and the Tories remembered their friends." Like many clever people he was careless about answering letters. To a friend who threatened to write his *Life and Letters* he retorted with some truth "There will be no letters." I think I received just one in all the years we knew each other. His literary output was relatively small but remarkable; a book of essays, some poems, and a book, published after his death, containing his articles on the war. Yet they all repay re-reading and were indications of what his mature mind might have produced, for he was only thirty-six when he died.

Although intensely patriotic he was not insular. He feared that the Gaelic League movement, by throwing Ireland back upon herself, would cut us off from European traditions and intellectual development. In this he has been proved right. "Ireland," he wrote in his preface to the *Day's Burden* (his collected essays), "awaits her Goethe —but in Ireland he must not be a pagan—who will one day arise to teach her that while a strong people has its own self for centre, it has the universe for circumference." And again, "My only counsel to Ireland is that in order to become deeply Irish she must become European." Kettle was above all a progressive—a modern—anxious for the social improvement of his own people. He knew that in this field we had much to learn and as he was by tradition and feeling a strong democrat he wanted to establish contact with what was best in Christian democratic Europe, to which he felt we belonged. He had in high degree that capacity for saying and doing things in a manner that attracts public attention, which is the first

essential of political success. Kevin O'Higgins, almost
alone amongst the Irish leaders of my time, had those same
qualities and he too died tragically " ere his prime."

It will be readily understood how such a man as Kettle
espoused with enthusiasm the French and British cause
on the outbreak of the first Great War. He was actually
in Belgium, engaged in procuring arms for the Volunteers,
when war came. Walking with Cardinal Mercier in his
garden he expressed the horror of all Irishmen at the
invasion of Belguim. The Cardinal asked him to back his
words with action. Other causes combined to lead him in
the same direction, notably his hatred of international
immorality. He detested war with a passionate detestation,
but duty called him and he obeyed.

I met him for the last time in July, 1916, at the meeting
of the National Directory of the United Irish League. We
had met to consider the proposals for a settlement of the
Home Rule *impasse* made by Lloyd George. If they had
been carried out they would have given the twenty-six
counties of Ireland a parliament at once with the exclusion
of the six counties of North-East Ulster till after the war.
The tragedy of the Rebellion was still with him. He told
me he was on leave in Dublin from the Curragh, when it
broke out, and how he felt the horror of his position as an
Irish soldier. That horror was intensified through the brutal
murder of his wife's brother-in-law, Sheehy Skeffington, by a
fanatical Anglo-Irish officer during the Rebellion. He
contributed a short speech to the discussion which was a
lucid summary of the problem confronting us. " Mr.
Chairman," he said, " if a very needy and somewhat dishonest individual owed you £32, and when you proceeded
to sue him you found that he had squared the judge and
packed the jury, but that at the last moment he offered you
£26 on account, what ought you to do ? I am but a poor
lawyer but I should strongly advise you to accept the money
without prejudice." Those were his last words in the
political arena. A few days later he went to France and
was killed on 9th September, 1916, at Ginchy during the
Somme battle. Like Willie Redmond he hoped against

hope that out of the perils shared by Irish soldiers in the field might come the precious gift of national unity. To his wife he wrote from the front : " One duty does indeed lie before me, that of devoting myself to the working out of a reconciliation between Ulster and Ireland. I feel God speaking to our hearts in that sense out of this terrible war." That this university professor, essayist, and poet should have died a soldier was a thing strange in itself ; that he should have also died on a foreign field in an alien cause may to some seem stranger still. But there is more in it than that. Tom Kettle, like his comrade, Willie Redmond, and some two hundred thousand other Irishmen, assumed that Ireland had a duty not only to herself but to the world, and that whatever befell, the path she took must be the path of honour and justice.

XIV

THE year 1911 was one of preparation for the final advance. Home Rule, it seemed, could now only be delayed, not denied. The Parliament Bill was re-introduced as soon as the new parliament assembled but it was not till 10th August that the House of Lords, reluctantly and by a small majority, accepted the advice of the Unionist leaders and finally passed the, to them, hateful measure. Kettle put Irish feeling into rhyme when he wrote :—

> This Ireland whom my lords despised—
> Languid behind inverted thumbs—
> She, who believed and agonised,
> Leads on the loud, victorious drums.

But the end, unfortunately, was not yet. The lists of Liberal peers to be created by the King if the Bill were rejected had actually been drawn up and it is interesting to speculate on what might have happened had the House of Lords persisted in its attitude of defiance. In that event there can be little doubt the new peers would have been created and the Liberal Government, with an ample majority in the Upper House, could have carried the Home Rule Bill into law during 1912. It was the rejection of the Bill by the Unionist majority in the Lords, under the power of delay given them in the Parliament Act, which enabled the Ulster revolt to be organised, and which postponed what proved to be only the formal enactment of Home Rule, until after the European War had broken out.. Had the Home Rule Bill been carried in 1912, and an Irish Parliament set up, a self-governed Ireland would undoubtedly have ranged itself without reserve on the side of the Allies in 1914 and thus cemented the true unity of these islands. The Unionist majority in the Lords by their action in 1911 once more, and fatally, bedevilled Anglo-Irish relations. These developments were, however, unforeseen in 1911 as we hopefully girded ourselves for the struggle ahead.

But there were still other bridges to be crossed. The National Insurance Bill, introduced by Lloyd George early in May, was far from popular in rural Ireland where its " contributions " were at first more obvious than its " benefits," and our opponents in Cork were not slow to use this opportunity for mischief. Joe Devlin wrote me from the House of Commons on 27th October, 1911, " I wish that the Cork people could be over here to see the performances of Healy and O'Brien. On Monday Balfour came along from the Front Opposition Bench, and, in our presence, told Healy that ' now was the time to raise the question of the *Irish* Hibernians ' in connection with the Insurance Bill, but the Chairman ruled that it could not be done. Healy came into the House again later, called out James Campbell, [1] had a conference with him, and Campbell subsequently returned and held an animated conversation with Bonar Law and Walter Long. Healy's and O'Brien's speeches were received with uproarious cheers by the Tories, and there is nothing now hidden in the alliance that exists between them. There is no doubt about it that Healy and O'Brien are bent on destroying Home Rule if they can. They have now put down an amendment to prevent the Ancient Order of Hibernians being recognised as an approved society and the matter will come up for debate about Monday week. Campbell, Moore and Craig, with Healy and O'Brien, are preparing their programme for what they hope will be a great debate against Home Rule. For our part we welcome the discussion as we believe it will clear the air and we are convinced that it will be the best advertisement the A.O.H. ever got. But that does not, in the least degree, relieve them of the blame for their unparalleled treachery in making the House of Commons the arena in which to attack a Catholic organisation with a membership of nearly 100,000." The campaign against the Insurance Bill was eventually transferred to the country and, for some time after it came into force, a widespread attempt was made, principally in the County Cork, to render its provisions nugatory. As the local solicitor for

[1] Carson's principal lieutenant, later Lord Glenavy.

the Insurance Commissioners I played some part in defeating this conspiracy.

These strange antics of Healy and O'Brien were symptomatic of their general attitude during this period. Tim Healy was of course the worst offender. His favourite charge against the Irish Party was that they were mere satellites of the Liberals. But his own extremely frank personal reminiscences, published long afterwards, furnish a strange commentary on that accusation, for they reveal that at this very time his own passion for intrigue, and his shameless vanity, made him accessible to either the Unionists or Liberals when they desired to employ his nimble mind and acid tongue for the purpose of undermining the position of the Irish leader. Tim's tomahawk was always drawn with gusto if the prospective scalps happened to be Irish. It was I think apropos of one of these tribal forays that John Burns, in a moment of natural indignation, described him as that " mean little man." These manoeuvres reacted like a boomerang on himself and had little effect in Ireland where the great majority of the people were solidly behind Redmond.

There was, however, considerable doubt and ignorance both in Ireland and England concerning the exact nature of the Irish demand, for no serious attempt had been made to formulate it in detail. Nearly twenty years had passed since the last Home Rule Bill, and for the great majority the demand for Home Rule merely meant the setting up of an Irish parliament of some kind. The all-important questions concerning its constitution, powers and relation to Great Britain, had neither been considered nor discussed. In order to remedy this situation to some extent I wrote for the *Leader* a series of articles on the various aspects of Home Rule which were afterwards published in book form in the autumn of 1911 under the title of *Home Rule : A Critical Consideration.* Taking as the standard for discussion the Bill of 1893, because I did not believe that Irish opinion would be satisfied with anything less, and hoped that English statesmen would have the courage and foresight to give us something more, I discussed in detail the various aspects of self-government, constitutional, financial, and administrative, describing the provisions of the previous measures and their application to existing conditions. I took as a motto for my title page the dictum of John Bright : " If you establish an Irish Parliament give it plenty of work and plenty of responsibility. Throw the Irish back upon themselves. Make them forget England ; let their energies be engaged in Irish party warfare ; but give no Irish party leader an opportunity of raising an anti-English cry. That is what a good Home Rule Bill ought to do." Bearing these wise words in mind I insisted that control of finance was the kernel of the matter, and that by this test the coming Bill should be judged. Erskine Childers, in his great book, *The Framework of Home Rule*, and Kettle, in an admirable pamphlet on *Home Rule Finance*, both published about the same time as my book, had come to a similar conclusion. Home Rule, I pointed out, would not in itself save Ireland but would give Ireland the means of saving itself. It would teach the Irish people the great principle of national responsibility ; that if they were to have the *rights* of a nation they must also undertake the *duties* of a nation. It would not only open the door to an enduring and equitable alliance between England and America, and thus do much to preserve the peace of the world, but, what was equally important, hasten the day of true union and reconciliation between the people of Ireland and the people of Great Britain. My book had a considerable circulation and I think achieved its purpose.

Childers, to whom I had sent a copy, wrote me that he shared my view that what Ireland wanted was a full measure of Home Rule which would compel the Irish people to rely on their own efforts, but feared, as I did, that the lack of an informed public opinion on both sides of the Irish Sea, for which the Nationalist leaders were themselves much to blame, would operate to prevent this desirable result.

Other aspects of the Home Rule campaign were brought to our notice that year in Cork by the visit of two very different British political organisations. In June the United

Irish League of Great Britain held its annual Convention in Cork, and in October the Liberal '8o Club paid us a visit. I had charge of the organisation and arrangements for both gatherings. The Irish in Great Britain are usually as divided in their political views as their compatriots at home, and, like all exiles, are usually more extreme. This Convention, although it comprised men of widely different opinions, was completely dominated and controlled by T. P. O'Connor, M.P., who presided over its deliberations in the Cork City Hall. I have never witnessed a more perfect and seemingly effortless performance. He fused the different emotions and sentiments of the gathering into a coherent whole and produced, as from an instrument, a harmonious result. Checking here, encouraging there, postponing awkward questions and finally voicing in simple but eloquent words the feelings of all, he proved himself a consummate chairman and politician. Listening to the proceedings one understood why he was the unquestioned leader of the Irish in Great Britain.

The '8o Club was a very different assembly. A select body of political experts and journalists which included men like Harold Spender, and P. W. Wilson of the *Daily News*, they had come to Ireland to see things for themselves. They were particularly keen on investigating alleged cases of religious persecution which we had little difficulty in proving to be " mare's nests." They were listeners who wanted to meet and hear everyone and they rightly refused to interfere in local politics. We therefore arranged a civic reception where they were able to meet all sides and exchange views.

So the Home Rule campaign moved toward its climax in 1912. In February of that year I spoke to the Young Ireland Branch of the United Irish League in Dublin on the problems which faced us. This body, of which Kettle, Cruise O'Brien and other leaders of the younger generation were prominent members, represented the more advanced wing of the Nationalist organisation. Whether the Home Rule Bill would be a complete and lasting settlement, or a temporary, and perhaps disastrous makeshift, depended, I said, on how it dealt with certain vital issues. These were : would the Irish members be retained at Westminster, would Ireland be given control of Customs and Excise taxation, and last, but by no means least, what was going to be done about Land Purchase finance ? I postulated, however, that we should not make denial of complete financial control and retention of Irish representation at Westminster a reason for refusing an otherwise satisfactory Bill. Ireland must, I argued, take as much as she could get and look for more. Would not an Irish Parliament, I asked, elected in the main by an agricultural population, be insane to dream of raising a tariff against her best customer, and equally insane to repudiate our national liability for the Land Purchase payments ? Both landlord and tenant were agreed that Land Purchase must go on and I claimed that it would not take an Irish Parliament long to find an equitable solution of the problem. The settlement of all these questions was, I suggested, to trust Ireland as Canada and South Africa had been trusted. Ireland came with no smoking rifle in her hands but in peace and friendship to claim her place in a free association of peoples. But let not her purpose be mistaken. She wanted freedom and would not be satisfied with gold. History has unfortunately falsified some of my optimistic anticipations but they were shared then by many others including Erskine Childers, who, in his book, already mentioned, expressed similar opinions. [1] Our views were later confirmed by the Primrose Committee, a body principally composed of distinguished English civil servants and financiers, set up by the Liberal Government to report on the financial relations between Great Britain and Ireland, which recommended the granting of full financial autonomy.

The four outstanding political events of 1912, at all of which I was present, were the great national demonstration in Dublin a few days before the introduction of the Home Rule Bill, the introduction of the Bill in the House of Commons on 11th April, the acceptance of the Bill by the

[1] Cf. *The Framework of Home Rule*, by Erskine Childers, pp. 293, 318.

National Convention in Dublin on 23rd April, and Asquith's visit to Dublin in July.

Devlin wrote to me on 15th March " One thing I am anxious about is that Cork should send a big contingent to attend the Home Rule demonstration in Dublin on the 31st. We want it to be a set off against the Bonar Law meeting in Belfast on Easter Monday. We are hoping to make it one of the largest meetings ever held in Ireland and it is vital that it should be so." And so indeed it was. The great wide street was filled from end to end with an enthusiastic crowd who had come from all parts of the country and were addressed by speakers from four separate platforms. I stood near Redmond on the platform close to Parnell's statue from which he had chosen to speak. In all his career, he said, he had never beheld such a crowd or such enthusiasm. His speech was a statesmanlike plea for national unity and reconciliation with Ulster. It is sad to remember now the promise of that day when Patrick Pearse, on another platform almost under the shadow of the General Post Office, told the people in Irish : " I should think myself a traitor to my country if I did not answer the summons to this gathering, for it is clear to me that the Bill which we support to-day will be for the good of Ireland and that we shall be stronger with it than without it." How few understood the meaning of his pregnant conclusion : " Let the foreigner understand that if we are cheated now there will be red war in Ireland." [1] Four years later he was to undo, almost on that very spot, Redmond's life-work.

But it was true then, as John Redmond said in his speech on the introduction of the Home Rule Rule Bill a few days afterwards, that those who still wished for separation in Ireland were a very small minority who would soon disappear if Home Rule were granted. None of us, indeed, that day envisaged an armed rebellion against England but rather the possibility of passive resistance in Ulster, where the leaders of the Unionist party were already threatening such a course.

The situation at Westminster on 11th April when Asquith

[1] *John Redmond's Last Years*, by Stephen Gwynn, p. 63.

introduced the third Home Rule Bill was very different from that in Dublin, but equally dramatic. Not since 1893 had the House of Commons presented a scene of such absorbing interest for Ireland. But there the similarity ended, for the packed House which listened to the Prime Minister was in a different mood from that of 1893. Then the question was in doubt, and no one could regard it as closed; now the House did not want to hear the principle of Home Rule expounded, it wanted to hear the details of a Bill which it intended to pass into law. In his speech Asquith rightly interpreted this change of atmosphere and passed with few preliminaries from the principle to the Bill itself.

I was in the Midlands speaking at Liberal meetings and Willie Redmond got me a pass for the Strangers' Gallery on that day. A great crowd had gathered in the Lobby and many had to go away disappointed. Another Corkman, Father Kearney, the popular rector of Maiden Lane Church, and myself were the first into the Gallery and we secured good seats in the front row. An enormous crowd packed the Chamber below. As the buzz of questions ceased the sturdy white-haired figure of the Prime Minster was seen advancing from behind the Speaker's chair. His entrance was the signal for a great demonstration of loyalty from the Liberal benches, the cheers being taken up and re-echoed by the Irish. But the great moment came as John Redmond moved up the House quietly and slowly to his seat above the gangway. The cheers rang out loud and triumphant as he modestly took his place. One felt it was his hour, an effective answer to the abuse and vilification he had suffered. As Carson followed him the Unionists in their turn rose in their seats to cheer and a pleased smile passed over his lean lawyer's face. Here was our real adversary—the incarnate spirit of Anglo-Irish ascendancy, the brain of the resistance to our demand.

Almost unnoticed, Asquith advanced to the table and began his speech. In language studiously moderate and concise he sketched the history of the Home Rule movement since 1893. He did not wish, he said, nor would he attempt to re-state the case as between England and Ireland ; Gladstone had done that. Nevertheless his speech was a model of compact and precise exposition rising at times to passages of sustained eloquence. As he spoke of the national demand for Home Rule some foolish Tory interjected " What Nation ? " " The Irish Nation," retorted Asquith swinging round with a vehement gesture, amidst loud cheers from the Government benches. " Some of us remember what was said about the Transvaal," he said pointing to Balfour, but the Unionist benches preserved an embarrassed silence. Twice he crossed swords with Bonar Law, the Unionist leader, concerning the latter's violent speech at Belfast. He swept on mercilessly to his Gladstonian peroration. Ireland's claim, he said, fell no longer on deaf ears. There had been reserved for that Parliament, that House of Commons, the double honour of reconciling Ireland and emancipating itself. As we listened to his outline of the Bill we realised that, while it did not fulfil our highest hopes, neither did it justify our worst fears. Redmond, though we did not then know it, had had to fight hard for the resulting compromise. The Government had unfortunately refused to grant full fiscal autonomy as their own Commission had advised.

The Bill followed in the main that of 1893, transferring to an Irish Parliament of two houses all purely Irish matters, while reserving to the Imperial Parliament all questions touching the Crown, the making of peace and war, treaties and foreign relations, new Customs duties, and certain other services either temporarily or permanently. For the first six years control of the police was to be retained by the Imperial Government and the Irish Parliament was debarred from establishing or endowing any religion or imposing religious disabilities. The common Treasury in effect still remained and, though the Irish Parliament could raise new taxes, it could not add more than ten per cent. to the income tax, death duties or customs duties (except on beer and spirits) imposed by the Imperial Parliament. An elaborate financial agreement made provision for a Joint Exchequer Board to adjust the accounts between the two countries and to provide for the situation which would arise if and when Irish revenue exceeded Irish expenditure, which it did not then do. It was proposed to settle the vexed question of Irish representation at Westminster by reducing the number of Irish members to forty-two and leaving them free to speak and vote on all questions. As another safeguard for the minority it was provided that the first Senate of forty members was to be nominated by the Imperial Government and their successors by the Irish Government. When there was a disagreement between the two Houses they were to sit and vote together to decide the issue. One felt that the Bill, in spite of its timidity, gave us a base from which complete freedom would certainly develop.

Carson, who was evidently in unyielding mood, opened the debate for the Opposition in a bitter and somewhat disjointed speech. The Bill, he said, was absolutely un-workable and ridiculous, and the guarantees not worth the paper they were written on. The Unionist Party would oppose it with all the energy they could. In strong contrast was the quiet dignified speech of John Redmond, who followed him. In words of studied moderation he made it clear that the Irish Party, like Parnell, wanted peace with England, and were willing to accept a subordinate parliament as a settlement of Ireland's claim. When Carson interrupted to ask if he would agree to an Ulster parliament Redmond replied that he would like the proposal to be made first. This incident, though we did not realise it then, marked the conception of that strange political child, Northern Ireland. As he drew to a close and referred to the historic names of Gladstone and Parnell, to their great work for Ireland and to his own sense of gratitude for having lived to see a Home Rule Bill once more introduced, several members, including the Prime Minister, were visibly affected and Redmond's own clear voice vibrated with emotion. Amidst an impressive silence he uttered his final words : " I pray earnestly that this Bill may pass, that it may achieve all the objects that its promoters have in view, and that in the beautiful words of the prayer with which the proceedings

of this House are opened every afternoon " The result of all
our counsels may be the maintenance of true religion and
justice, the safety, honour and happiness of the King, the
public wealth, peace and tranquility of the realm, and the
uniting and knitting together therein of the hearts of all
persons and estates within the same, in true Christian love
and charity."

After Redmond's speech there was little more to be said.
Ramsay MacDonald, who followed for the Labour Party,
welcomed Asquith's hint that the Bill was only the beginning in a process of federal devolution and pointed out that
if there were no North-East Ulster there would be no opposition to the measure. William O'Brien, in a characteristic
speech, fastened on the fact that the Bill did not give Ireland
fiscal freedom, and, almost in the same breath, said that
he would go to any reasonable or even unreasonable lengths
to secure the support of the Unionist Party. As I passed
out of St. Stephen's into the cool night air I felt that
the debate I had just listened to was the prelude to
the opening by King George of an Irish parliament
in Dublin. Speaking at a Liberal meeting in Birmingham the following evening I ventured to say
that I believed the Bill would be unanimously accepted
in Ireland, as indeed, with insignificant exceptions it was.
When a week later, on 23rd April, at a great National
Convention held in Dublin, Redmond rose to propose its
acceptance, he received an ovation which left the result of its
deliberations in no doubt. Sitting by him on the platform
was Gladstone's grandson, a young Liberal member of
parliament soon to fall, like so many of his generation, in
France. The great gathering rose at Redmond's request to
give him a special welcome. Enormous assemblies of this
kind are representative rather than deliberative, but on this
occasion there was no necessity for deliberation for we were
all of one mind. Redmond at once laid down the proposition
that it was our duty as Nationalists to accept what he described as a far better Bill than Gladstone had ever offered.
He further indicated the need for a resolution authorising
the Irish Party to propose, support or reject such amendments as they thought fit. This and a resolution welcoming

and accepting the Bill " as an honest and generous attempt
to settle the long and disastrous quarrel between the British
and Irish nations " were carried by acclamation.

Two things, I think, weighed with Redmond in accepting
this limited form of self-government. First he knew that
the powers of a freely elected parliament with a ministry
responsible to it inevitably grew and increased. This we
have since seen and experienced in Ireland since the Treaty
in 1921. Secondly he was a man of peace. He never asked
an Irishman to fire a shot at another Irishman. Not that
he repudiated the resort to arms. Again and again he
said in the House of Commons that if he believed insurrection were justified he would counsel insurrection. But he
preferred to obtain a smaller measure of self-government
by peaceful methods rather than a larger one by bloodshed,
which he rightly felt would deepen and redden those tragic
divisions that were the real obstacles to our national
progress. His aim, like that of General Botha, the statesman whom he most resembled in temperament and
outlook, was such freedom within the Empire as the
Dominions enjoyed. That he believed he could eventually
obtain with the consent and good will of the British
people. Beyond that he did not wish to go. In short he
believed in evolution rather than revolution. Who will
say now that he was wrong ?

Kettle, who spoke at the Convention for the younger
generation, said that in the end this Bill would give us an
Ireland completely controlling her own political life, taking
her place in the humane tradition of Europe, and welcomed
amongst the nations of the earth. Such detailed criticisms
as he had to make would, he said, be submitted in a memorandum to the Irish Party. The Cork contingent made its
own contribution to the occasion, for we had brought with
us Henry O'Shea, the newly elected Nationalist Lord Mayor,
first fruit of our campaign against O'Brienism, and he was
selected to second the principal resolution. A few weeks
later, on 25th May, even the All for Ireland League,
O'Brien's organisation, promised its whole-hearted support
for the Bill subject to safeguards for Ulster, the abolition of
landlordism by the use of Imperial credit, and fiscal

autonomy. It was clearly a welcome not wholly sincere.

The last important political event of that year took place in July when the British Prime Minister visited Dublin and addressed a great meeting in the Theatre Royal. The suffragette agitation was at its height and, on the night of his arrival, as the carriage in which he, with Mrs. Asquith and John Redmond, drove in procession through the cheering crowds in O'Connell Street, an Englishwoman, who had followed him to Dublin, flung a hatchet which missed Asquith but struck Redmond. I was standing in the vestibule of the Gresham Hotel with the Lord Mayor of Cork and others who had come to join in the welcome, and the rumour ran through the crowd that Redmond had been killed. Great was our relief when, a few minutes later, the roar of the people outside signalled his safe arrival and we saw that he had only suffered a slight bruise. When the meeting took place the following evening in the Theatre Royal elaborate precautions were taken to prevent interference of any kind. Admission was by ticket and hefty stewards stood around in no merciful mood. A few seats from where I sat I noticed a bearded clergyman whom I conjectured was a foreign missionary or Franciscan priest. But no sooner had Asquith, amid great applause, begun his speech than this " reverend " gentleman sprang to his feet and in a shrill penetrating voice demanded " what about votes for women ? " Before he had twice repeated this query turmoil broke loose and he was unceremoniously, and I fear somewhat roughly, removed. It was in fact Sheehy Skeffington, the Irish champion of women's suffrage, who had assumed this disguise in order to achieve his object. I have never beheld a more courageous act. It was this same courage which led him to try to stop looting during the Rebellion of 1916, and so to his tragic end. I had met him a short time before Asquith's meeting, just after he had written a friendly criticism of my book on Home Rule in an evening newspaper—a strange unforgettable figure in his knickerbocker suit, his eager eyes peering at one through pince-nez above his beard. Like Kettle, he was a pioneer not made in the common mould and destined for an uncommon end.

Already the Ulster situation was becoming tense and Asquith devoted much of his speech to dealing with the incitements to rebellion and civil war now becoming common form on Unionist platforms. Minorities, he admitted, had their rights and susceptibilities which should be provided for, but they were not entitled to thwart and defeat the constitutional demand of a vast majority of their fellow countrymen and to frustrate a great international settlement. Yet there were some amongst us even then, in that hour of apparent triumph, who had doubts ; Kettle, remembering Parnell's tragic fate, wrote :—

> You stepped your steps, and the music marched and the torches tossed
> As you filled your streets with your comic Pentecost,
> And the little English went by and the lights grew dim ;
> We dumb in the shouting crowd, we thought of him . . .
> Of him and the wintry swords and the closing gloom—
> Of him going forth alone to his lonely doom.
> No shouts my Dublin then ! Not a light nor a cry—
> You kept them all till now, when the little English go by !

The waters of Irish nationalism run dark and deep.

In Cork that summer we welcomed another visitor from England who was destined to become not only the leader of his people in their darkest hour but the greatest figure of his time. Winston Churchill, in his capacity as First Lord of the Admiralty, visited Cork Harbour in the Admiralty yacht *Enchantress* early in July to inspect the naval establishment. The Cork Harbour Commissioners, of whom I had been elected a member a month before, offered him a civic welcome. We took him to Blarney where he visited the Castle and kissed the famous stone, although in his case it was indeed unnecessary to salute that fount of eloquence. Cork appealed to his sense of historical perspective for his great ancestor the Duke of Marlborough had once beseiged its walls. It was indeed during that operation that the Duke of Grafton, Charles the Second's illegitimate son, had been killed by a stray shot from the defenders, near where my office now stands. Some months before, as he reminded us, Winston had gone to Belfast with great courage to proclaim his belief in Home Rule in the very place where his father had uttered the famous but ridiculous slogan : " Ulster will fight and Ulster will be right." That visit had other consequences not then apparent, for the hostility of the Ulster crowds impressed him, and soon afterwards he wrote to Redmond privately to tell him of his own conviction that separate treatment, at least on a temporary basis, would have to be given to the Ulster counties which had Unionist majorities. Lloyd George, who shared this belief, did not act with the same frankness.

At the banquet which we gave Churchill that night the toast of the King was honoured for the first time at such a gathering in Cork. It was a symptom of the change which the new policy had brought. In his speech he told us he had come on an official mission and so could not talk party politics, yet he left us in no doubt as to his sentiments, expressed in clear, eloquent words, instinct as always with human quality. He summed up what was in all our hearts when he said—" Looking back into the past how much harm have not these two islands done each other ? How many misunderstandings, how much needless embitterment, how many cruel and almost unforgettable injuries have not been interchanged and then how many blessings could they not mutually bestow ? We need each other. We need from each other the best that both can give. You must stand by us and we will stand by you. You must give us of your best and we will return it in good measure." Then there came a truly Churchill touch. The great crowd outside had been calling for him and he went to the window. To them in a few terse sentences he repeated what he had said to us " Good luck to Ireland," he cried, " Good luck to England too ! May they both help each other and may the British Navy long guard them from all harm ! " His closing words were drowned in a roar of cheers. It was the right thing rightly said and we knew that here was a great man in the making. One wonders if the history of these islands might not have been different had he been Chief Secretary for Ireland during those decisive years.

XV

Early in January, 1913, business connected with the Cork Harbour Board took me to London, and I listened in the House of Commons to the concluding stages of the discussion on the Home Rule Bill. John Redmond, whom I saw, was quietly confident; for the Bill had emerged from the long debate virtually intact. A few days later, on 16th January, it passed the Commons with the comfortable majority of 110. A fortnight afterwards it was rejected by the House of Lords. The Unionist Party realised, however, that the walls of that once impregnable bastion were now undermined and that it could but serve at best the purpose of delay. The Tories were divided on domestic issues by tariff reform and the Irish question was vital to their existence. So they prepared to fall back on their last line of defence in Ulster. Already much preliminary work had been done in that direction. Since January, 1911, Bonar Law, their new leader, had used words which were calculated to inflame the people of the North to armed revolt. " Ulster will have reason to resist and we will sustain her to the end." And again, " Whatever means you adopt, whether constitutional or not, you will have the whole Unionist Party behind you." And Henry Duke, later Unionist Chief Secretary for Ireland ; " The Ulstermen have the moral right to resist, and to kill those who are exercising that right would not be repression but murder." Other leaders of the Unionist Party vied with each other in like incitements to violence, which, as Asquith prophetically pointed out, furnished " for the future a complete grammar of anarchy."

Ulster, for historical reasons, has always been the seedbed of violence in Irish politics. The Plantation of the province with Scotch and English Protestants by James I, and the great tide of subsequent immigration during the seventeenth century created a legacy of religious bitterness and discord which has not even yet exhausted itself. The Scotch planters also brought their own peculiar contribution of restless energy and determination. Ulster has given us not only the Orangemen, on the extreme Protestant side, but also the United Irishmen, whose Republican policy, derived from the English Radical philosophers and the French Revolution, was entirely at variance with native tradition. The Irish Republican Army of our day is, in sporting parlance, by Tom Paine out of Cave Hill, for it was the writings of that strange political philosopher, the only English writer who expresses with uncompromising sharpness the abstract doctrines of political rights held by the French revolutionists, which inspired the founders of the United Irishmen when they first decided, on that grim mountain overlooking Belfast, "never to desist in their efforts until they had subverted the authority of England over their country and asserted their independence."

The Wolfe Tone of the Ulster revolt in 1912 was a Dublin barrister—Edward Carson—a remarkable man who just missed being a great man. I heard him speak several times in the Courts and in the House of Commons. He was not specially distinguished either as a lawyer or an orator. His speeches lacked colour, metaphor and eloquence. He was not subtle or learned. It was characteristic of Carson that he actually supported Lord Halsbury and the other " diehard " peers in their policy of rejecting the Parliament Act—a policy which would have accelerated the passage of Home Rule. Yet, by strength of character he became one of the first advocates of his day and a great political force. What he lacked in eloquence and learning he made up for by a deep knowledge of human nature, which made him a deadly cross-examiner, together with a capacity for clear and concise expression, and a real sense of proportion, which are so essential in legal argument or exposition. Above all he was by nature simple, direct and honest. He meant what he said. He was in fact a successful politician because he was not a mere politician. He had the supreme courage and indomitable will of Parnell without the independent mind and vision which the latter inherited from his American mother. Had Carson possessed those gifts he might eventually have led the North into an Irish parliament; as it was he only helped to perpetuate the division of his country and to destroy, what he most cherished, the real unity of these islands. Like de Valera, Carson was of Latin origin on one side, for through his father he was descended from an Italian architect who had settled in Dublin. On his mother's side he derived from a Cromwellian general. It was a strange mixture, in which the Cromwellian undoubtedly predominated.

I remember as a boy hearing him prosecute in one of the " Special Courts " during the days of the Land League : " Coercion Carson " he was called in those days; a sinister figure with his hard, hatchet-like face and aggressive Dublin accent. He passionately, and, from his point of view, patriotically, believed that the maintenance of the Union between Great Britain and Ireland was essential to the prosperity of both countries. In order to fight for that belief he virtually abandoned a most lucrative professional career and risked prosecution and imprisonment. At one stage the Irish law officers had actually prepared the papers for his prosecution, but John Redmond, his old colleague at the Bar, successfully intervened to stop the proceedings, believing that Carson in gaol would be more dangeous than Carson at liberty, and that his arrest might well arouse a storm of passion and discord that would wreck all prospect of a friendly settlement. Winston Churchill, the only member of the Liberal Government who really had the courage of his convictions, might, if he had been given a free hand, have forced things to a decisive issue.

Carson at first refused to abandon the Protestant minority in the South to which he belonged and whom indeed he represented in parliament as member for Dublin University. Ulster, he declared, had never asked for a separate parliament and would never consent to desert the Southern Unionists. But events were too strong for him, and the resistance to Home Rule gradually developed into an almost purely Ulster movement. So this apostle of Union eventually destroyed not only the union of Great Britain and Ireland but also the unity of his own country. In 1910 he was elected leader of the Irish Unionist Party, but it soon became obvious that it was in fact the *Ulster* Unionist Party, and that a change of tactics was impending. During the general election of that year Captain Craig (later Lord Craigavon, first prime minister of Northern Ireland) suggested at Lisburn that the Ulster Unionists should spend their money buying arms and ammunition and employ old soldiers to train their partisans. Twelve months later, in September, 1911, the Ulster Unionist Council on Carson's advice prepared to set up a provisional government. In announcing this Sinn Féin policy, he said, " Our motto is, ' we rely upon ourselves.' " In September, 1912, the matter was methodically carried a step further when the people of Ulster, with due pomp and ceremony, entered into a Covenant to use every means necessary to prevent the establishment of an Irish parliament and, in the event of its being set up, to refuse to accept its authority. The climax of this defiance was reached in September, 1913, when an Ulster Provisional Government, headed by Carson, was duly established in Belfast. In the meantime the Ulster Volunteer Force had been founded, and under the command of a retired Anglo-Indian general, nominated by no less a person than Lord Roberts, was drilled, manoeuvred and reviewed. The frame of a civil government including courts and police was also methodically prepared.

The reaction of the rest of the country to these strange proceedings was not long delayed. Redmond and the other leaders of the Irish Party, with the great majority of the people, believed that Carson was bluffing and that his movement would, at the worst, lead to riots in Belfast. There were many, however, who thought otherwise. They believed that the Ulster revolt, for such it might now well be called, was supported not only by the whole Unionist Party but by many persons of influence in the British civil and military administration, and were convinced that such a combination would not hesitate to prevent, by fair means or foul, the establishment of an Irish parliament. Something, should therefore be done to fortify and sustain the Irish demand for legislative freedom. This feeling at last found public expression at a great meeting in the Rotunda, Dublin, summoned for 25th November, 1913, by Professor Eóin Mac Neill, an Ulster man from the Glens of Antrim, and by Laurence Kettle, Tom's brother. At this gathering, amidst scenes of great enthusiasm, the Irish Volunteers were inaugurated. Their manifesto stated, " The object proposed for the Irish Volunteers is ' to secure and maintain the rights and liberties common to all the people of Ireland. *Their duties will be defensive and protective and they will not contemplate either aggression or domination.* Their ranks are open to all able-bodied Irishmen without distinction of creed, politics, or social grade.' " It should be said at once that MacNeill adhered scrupulously to the undertaking (which I have italicised) on the good faith of which the Volunteers were enrolled, and that he was no party to its violation in 1916. Thoroughly alarmed at the result of their own weakness the Government, on 5th December, 1913, issued a proclamation forbidding the import of arms into Ireland, a step which however justifiable, naturally filled Nationalist Ireland with suppressed rage.

A few days later, on 12th December, Professor MacNeill came South to start the new movement in Cork. The local supporters of the Nationalist Party were anxious to help him, but Redmond had given no public indication of his views on the matter and without his authority we felt it would be unfair and unwise to commit ourselves. I accordingly wrote to John Muldoon, M.P., a prominent member of the Irish Party, who represented one of the Cork constituencies, asking him to let us know what line Redmond desired us to take. Time was short and I asked him to wire Redmond's decision in code. If we should support the new movement he was to wire " Deliver the books," if otherwise, the reverse. A reply duly arrived containing the enigmatic message " Deliver the books with care." This we rightly construed to mean an instruction not to commit ourselves publicly. Accordingly I called on MacNeill at his hotel before the meeting to assure him of our sympathy and to discuss the situation. We were old friends for I had worked with him for many years in the

Gaelic League, of which he was one of the founders, and he had stayed with us on some of his visits to Cork. While still a civil servant in the Four Courts he had devoted his leisure to the language movement and his scholarship had been recognised by an appointment as one of the professors of Irish History in the National University. A professor, not a politician, a scholar rather than a soldier, he was the last person one would have expected to start an organisation like the Irish Volunteers. Yet he undoubtedly translated into action a deep popular demand for an effective answer to Carson's threats and his manifest integrity made him a suitable leader for such a movement. Unfortunately, at a later stage, his authority was undermined by people who were less scrupulous as to methods and more extreme in thought and policy. He thus became that most tragic political phenomenon—an idealist enmeshed in reality.

With him that evening was another idealist and Ulsterman who had become an active supporter of the Volunteers, Sir Roger Casement, already famous for his exposure of the cruel persecution of the natives in the Congo and Putamayo. Tall and swarthy with a dark pointed beard and moustache already turning grey, he looked like some Spanish *conquistador* rather than a retired British consul. I soon discovered that our visitors did not agree with the orthodox Nationalist view of Carson's manoeuvres. To them, however wrong-headed his views, he was a man who had vindicated the right of Irishmen to arm for the assertion of their political beliefs, and as such deserved to be applauded. MacNeill, while protesting his support for Redmond and his policy, told me that he intended at the meeting that evening to call for three cheers for Carson as the man who had brought a new courage into Ireland. While I fully understood this point of view I warned him that it would be undoubtedly misunderstood by a Cork audience which was bound to be composed largely of followers of the Irish Party. These were bitterly opposed to William O'Brien's policy of conciliation and surrender, with which they would inevitable associate his request. He refused to listen to my advice and the result was as I feared. MacNeill was little

known outside Gaelic League circles, for he had never been
a politician or even taken as prominent a part in public
life as his colleague Douglas Hyde. Neither was he an
inspiring speaker. The large crowd listened patiently to his
speech and to the more fervid oratory of the dark, foreign-
looking Casement, but as the meeting drew to a close
MacNeill carried out his purpose and called for cheers for
the Ulster leader. As I had expected this was too much for
the audience. Pandemonium broke loose, the platform was
stormed and a free fight ensued. The meeting ended in
confusion but the Volunteers had certainly had a militant
start in Cork. Fortunately neither of the visiting orators
was injured. Amongst those prominent in the affray was at
least one local follower of ours whose next meeting with
Sir Roger was as a captive Munster Fusilier in the German
prison camp at Limburg.

MacNeill now realised his mistake and wrote to me a
few days later from Dublin :—

> 19 Herbert Park,
> Dublin.
> 16 December, 1913.

My dear Horgan,

My choice of words or neglect to choose words was responsible
for the disorder. Those who protested thought they smelled
" conciliation " in the trend of my remarks and of course the
final remark was like a match to warm petrol. The immediate
counter-cheers for Redmond showed what was in their minds.
They thought that in spite of my disclaimer of partisanship
I was laying a snare for them. I will ask you to let it be known
through your friends in Cork that I am a steady supporter of
John Redmond, have voted for his supporters at every election
and always stand up for him in private. I am not a politician
in public but I once made a political speech, it was a speech in
Irish at the great Home Rule meeting last year and it was in
support of Redmond.

I also want to ask you to do something more important,
if you find it right in your own judgment. A new movement
with new men in it is naturally suspect and may be a real
danger. What I ask you to do is to allow Mr. Redmond to

know in the best way you can, that I pledge myself against any use of the Volunteer movement to weaken his party (which is also my party). You may also make it clear to whomsoever it may concern that I have no intention or desire to become a leader in politics, far from it !

I have seen Roger Casement this evening and heard his good news about Queenstown.[1]

Yours sincerely,

EÓIN MAC NEILL.

The attitude of the Irish Party was made abundantly clear in a letter which I received from John Muldoon as soon as he read the report of the meeting.

72 Palmerstown Road.

16 12 13.

My dear Horgan,

I was afraid when I wired on Saturday that you were committed to the meeting and that the best thing was to advise you to attend and be very cautious. Redmond does not like this thing, neither does Devlin, but they are loath to move at present. It will frighten the English Home Rulers who will only put one construction upon such a movement in Ireland just now. Dillon is much more against it. It could not be controlled, and if the army met some day and demanded an Irish Republic where would our Home Rule Leaders be ?

Then what in Heaven's name is the meaning of cheering for Carson who has organised an army to resist Home Rule by force. Are the people of the world to laugh at us or pity us ?

I read what happened in Cork with delight. I think you have killed a foolish and harmful business.

In haste.

Always yours,

J. M.

I thought it right, however, to send him on a copy of MacNeill's letter with its definite tender of an olive branch.

[1] This is a reference to the Hamburg-Amerika Line project discussed later in this chapter.

The result was not satisfactory as the following reply indicates :—

> 72 Palmerstown Road,
> Dublin.
>
> 18.12.13.

My dear Horgan,

Many thanks for your letter and enclosure. I am showing the letter to Mr. Redmond to-day.

The short answer to all this special pleading of the writer is this. Mr. Redmond is engaged in the most critical and difficult situation that has confronted any Irish leader since the Union and no movement of this nature and character should have been started without his approval. These people had not such approval. Anybody can see that it is one that adds powerful corroboration to what the Unionist have been saying—that there are two Irelands. Both are drilling ! Why ? Home Rule is not going to produce peace but war.

Then what interpretation is to be put upon these volunteers cheering for Carson's volunteers. It really makes one sad and sick. Fools sometimes do what knaves are wholly unable to do. The Unionists are delighted with this volunteer business. I do not wonder. It gives them a fine cry. Let MacNeill or nobody else imagine that he can control 50,000 men with arms in their hands !

> Always yours,
>
> JOHN MULDOON.

The other point of view was well put in a letter I received from MacNeill on the same day.

> 19 Herbert Park,
> Dublin.
>
> 17 Dec., 1913.

My dear Horgan,

I thank you heartily for the advice received this morning. There is no doubt that the misleading account of the Cork meeting given by the runaways of the newspapers has caused a vibration against the volunteer movement in certain quarters. I think the air will soon clear and opinion will steady itself. The point ought to be considered—the Irish Party could undoubtedly damp down the movement, or leave it to be con-continued only in disaffected quarters—would this serve Home

Rule at this stage ? In my belief, the collapse or partial collapse of the volunteer movement would strengthen the hands of the Unionists enormously. The Home Rule Bill is not yet secure. From various Unionist statements, public and private, and from other information I gather that the Unionists are counting not on " Civil War "—which they do not contemplate—but on an outbreak of Orange atrocities against the scattered and defenceless Catholics in part of the North East. They think that this " may come at any moment," and that when it does come it will at least throw the whole political situation into the melting pot and annihilate the advantages that John Redmond has gained. This is of course the vilest and most atrocious political line ever adopted in our time outside of Turkey, and as bad as anything in Turkey, but it might succeed to the extent of making the final stage of Home Rule impossible during this Parliament. In that event, or in the event of any other serious upset to the Government, it is clear that we must be prepared to give the Tories an utterly impossible task in Ireland. My friend Hazelton, in a rather unfriendly letter in this morning's *Freeman*, sees this clearly enough. He ought also to see that by making the Volunteer movement abortive he will, if he can, but I don't think he can, seriously weaken the morale of Young Ireland and strengthen the other side.

My course is plain. I hold steadily to the line I have adopted till the line is clear. My words in Cork have created a great difficulty, but surely they have not altered the essential facts of the case and surely too any immediate line of action based on the Cork incident would be mistaken policy.

Yours sincerely,

EÓIN MACNEILL.

Unfortunately, as this correspondence shows, my attempt to establish a *modus vivendi* between the Volunteers and the Irish Party failed. Redmond's dislike of unconstitutional methods and his natural anxiety lest his support might be misconstrued in England coupled with John Dillon's strong antipathy to the new movement, operated to prevent any agreement. For this I do not think MacNeilll can be blamed as he had done all he could to promote an understanding. Six months later, when the Volunteer force had increased to some 120,000 men,

Redmond could no longer ignore it and had to seek representation for his supporters on its committee in much more unfavourable circumstances, since by that time the more extreme element had begun to undermine MacNeill's position. But in December, 1913, things were very different. The fundamental idea of those responsible for the establishment of the Volunteers was to ensure that Carson's illegal threats should not destroy Redmond's work. For the first time since the Jacobite Wars Irish Nationalists were on the side of constitutional right and parliamentary government, and the Volunteers should and could have been encouraged to maintain that position. They alone could have united all parties in Ireland to protect our rights.

The opportunity was lost and the control of the movement passed into the hands of less scrupulous leaders. But Redmond was by no means alone in his attitude of distrust towards the Volunteer movement for Edward Martyn, who represented the Sinn Féin point of view, wrote me a few weeks later : " I am very glad Cork knocked the bottom out of the Volunteer Movement—a most dangerous movement at this time, but a very good one after we get Home Rule."

On the day after the Cork Volunteer meeting I called on our visitors to express regret at the reception they had received. MacNeill had, I found, returned to Dublin but Casement had stayed on to discuss with me another matter which was destined to exercise a profound influence on his action in the critical months ahead. A few months before, the Cunard Company, which had for many years used Cork Harbour as a port of call for its Transatlantic liners, had broken its contract to land the east bound mails at Queenstown. To justify this breach of their legal obligation they added slander to bad faith by alleging that the port was unsafe for their new fast liners the *Lusitania* and *Mauretania*. In August, 1913, they announced that these ships would no longer call at Cork Harbour. This reflection on the safety of the port was patently untrue, for these ships, and bigger ones of the White Star Line, had used the port without accident for many months. Irish public opinion was naturally incensed, and the Cork Harbour Board took the necessary steps to refute the statement made by the Cunard Line. But the most effective answer was provided by the announcement that the Hamburg-Amerika Line had decided to use Cork Harbour as a port of call for their ships. Casement was in fact largely responsible for this. On 10th December, 1913, a few days before he came to Cork, the Harbour Board had unanimously agreed to extend a public welcome to the first German liner on its arrival.

Sir Roger heard of this decision with great interest. He had realised for some time that a European War was inevitable and, in a series of articles published anonymously in the *Irish Review*, he had directed attention to Ireland's position. A friendly Ireland was, he pointed out, essential to England in face of this grave menace and, as between England and Germany, we held a position which should enable us to obtain better terms than those contained in the Home Rule Bill. Contemplating the future with his knowledge of international diplomacy and the self-confidence natural to an Ulsterman, he formulated a bold policy which had for its aim the recognition of Ireland as an independent state secured by international guarantees—a kind of Atlantic Belgium. Her geographical position was, he felt, so important that neither England, Germany nor the United States would, if it was once secured, attempt to upset such an arrangement. These views had been hardened by the increasing fury of the Ulster agitation, for he loathed the exploitation of Ulster Protestant sentiment to subserve the interests of an English party. Although he had been pressed to take an active part in Irish politics his health and energy had been so impaired by his experience in the Putamayo, from which he had recently returned, that he at first declined to do so. But the coming of the German line to Cork Harbour seemed to him a heaven sent opportunity to renew those contacts between Ireland and Europe which British policy had long denied us and he threw himself heart and soul into the matter.

I took him that morning to the Harbour Board office
where he met the Chairman, Sir James Long, and several
of the members. We examined in detail the various aspects
of the Hamburg-Amerika project and the possibilities it
offered to the port. That night he dined at our house.
We had invited another friend, Professor William F. P.
Stockley, to meet him and they found common ground in
their mutual distrust of England, for Stockley, although
English himself in manner and by paternity, was on his
mother's side a relative of that other ineffectual Irish rebel,
Smith O'Brien, a fact which coloured his political views.
Stockley's meek and gentle mien concealed a fiery heart. He
combined a wide knowledge and love of English literature,
which was the subject of his chair, with a detestation and
suspicion, almost unbalanced, of English politicians. In
short he was another example of the Irish-English mentality in action. We sat late that evening discussing the
Ulster question with which Casement was much pre-
occupied. He saw no hope of saving Home Rule except
through a resolute policy of armed vigilance which should
prevent our ultimate betrayal by the weak Liberal leaders.

I continued for several months to correspond with
Casement concerning the Hamburg-Amerika project. At
first the German company cordially agreed to our suggestion
for a public welcome to their first ship on its arrival.
Casement wrote me from London on 19th December : " I
may go to Hamburg next week if it seems desirable. I am
asked to go—but shall be able to decide later on. There
has been active intrigue I fancy to maintain the isolation
of Ireland in this matter but I think we shall win and if
you and the good people of Cork are staunch and true to
this friendly line we shall win." On 22nd December he
wrote : " Thanks for your Home Rule book. It is excellent.
The English press is getting interested in the Volunteers
and I see the *New Statesman* approves because it considers
the movement proof of the new spirit in Ireland that will
not take a refusal of Home Rule lying down. In ' Society '
here everyone thinks the Bill will not pass—they still claim
the King as the rock in the path. I have no faith in the

Liberals as a party at all—as individuals many of them, yes—but after all it is always the Englishman, more or less Broadbent, that comes out of the bag. I am convinced that the stronger we can make the Volunteers the better for Home Rule and Redmond's power of bargaining. He can always point to that ' menace ' as proof of the insistence behind the Home Rule demand and can say, ' Well you see I've not done it, it springs from the soil and you'll have *that* Ireland to deal with if we fail.' Read enclosed pamphlet[1] on Germany and Ireland—it is interesting. It is the last contingency—indeed the likely one—if anything happens to John Bull. It is this pamphlet General von Bernhardi made such a fuss about lately and that all Germany is talking of. Anyhow the Hamburg-Amerika Line coming to Cork proves that we are ceasing to be ' an island beyond an island.' "

The public reception of the German liner was finally arranged and all seemed set fair. On 30th December the Cork Harbour Board, on my motion, unanimously thanked the " Irish and German societies of the United States, and Sir Roger Casement who originated the project, for the work they had done to secure the Hamburg-Amerika Line steamers calling at Queenstown." Casement had arranged to travel to Cork with his friends Mrs. J. R. Green and F. J. Bigger, the well-known Belfast antiquarian, who was coming to present a portrait of Don Philip O'Sullivan Beare to Cork University College, where it still hangs in the Aula Maxima. Bigger also proposed to bring his band of Irish pipers in order to give the Germans a sample of our native music. But on 12th January, 1914, Casement wrote to me from Belfast : " I have just received a wire to say that the Hamburg-Amerika Company cannot accept any reception —under any circumstances at all or from anyone ! The meaning is (to my mind) that political pressure has been brought to bear. My informant wires me to write all the friends of the Company in Cork privately to beg them to desist from all arrangements for any form of public welcome and to ask that this should be done quite quietly and

[1] A reprint of his anonymous article in the *Irish Review*.

without any fuss, otherwise the Line will abandon the Irish
call altogether. Will you please act as a good diplomatist
now and see that their wishes are respected? We want the
German Line *at all costs*—and so to make sure of it we
must show no temper or resentment and blame nobody. . . .
It is no use attempting to go into the matter by letter now—
all I know I will tell you when I come to Cork on Sunday or
Monday next. Meantime the one thing to do is to throw oil
on the troubled waters of Cork Harbour." Finally, in
February, 1914, the Hamburg-Amerika Line formally
announced that they had decided to abandon the project
altogether. It was clear that secret pressure had been used
and that the British Foreign Office had vetoed the scheme.
To make matters worse the White Star Line announced
about the same time that their larger ships would no longer
call at Cork Harbour. Casement was naturally incensed
by these developments as indeed were we all. It was the
first definite opportunity he had found for helping his own
country and although he must have realised the obvious,
and from their point of view, probably valid reasons which
moved the British Foreign Office to intervene, he could not
forgive the injury done to Irish interests or the ruin of his
plans. From that moment the destruction of English rule in
Ireland became, in the words of his biographer, " an
obsession which dominated all his mind." "The Irish are
a race apart and Ireland is a forbidden land," he wrote
in a fierce anonymous article in the *Irish Review* entitled,
"Coffin Ship to Atlantic Greyhound." The political
situation was hardening and it became obvious that
Carson's threats were rattling the Liberal Government.
I had written Casement a letter of foreboding and he
replied in a long letter which sets out not only his views
on the political situation but his reactions to the Hamburg-
Amerika affair. It is, I think, important enough to
quote in full.

Malahide,

My dear Horgan,   16 Feb., 1914.

  I got back from England last night and found your letter.
It moves me greatly and I feel for you my Catholic countrymen,

perhaps more even than you feel for yourselves. I feel for Ireland as John Mitchel felt for Ireland—the shame and ignominy of our race—the white slave race of Europe—and people. But I don't despair because I believe with John Mitchel that the manhood of Ireland will outlast the British Empire. You see how right my instinct was about the Volunteers. I knew in my soul then that Carson was bound to win, just because he appealed to force, and I knew the craven British Government would never use force against *Protestants* and *Loyalists*. Against us—you or me, for I am a thorough disloyalist—they'd use all force and fraud and lies too. The game now I see is this. Under cover of an offer to Ulster they are going to strip all the flesh off the Home Rule Bill—if we let them ! Shall we ? That is for you and others to think over. Meantime I am convinced the right and patriotic thing for all Irishmen to do is to go on with the Volunteers. Volunteers in every county, city, town and village in Ireland. Don't despair of the arms. I think we can get them. The Irish in America will not desert us in this crisis. I believe I can get you help from them the English little dream of to-day. They (The English) are going to surrender to Carson " to save bloodshed,"—please God they'll have more booodshed than they suspect if they consummate this final act of *Punica fides*.

I've a good mind to write to Carson to-night and ask him to come to Cork with me ! My God ! I wonder what would happen if he said Yes. Would you all rise to the occasion or would you tear us limb from limb? What you say about him being King of Ireland I've said too—if he would only rise to the height of a supreme occasion. He could save Ireland and make Ireland. But it is a dream to think of him doing it—if he really loved Ireland as I do he'd come. Shall I ask him ? I don't know him at all and I've blackguarded him openly in the Holy of Holies (Co. Antrim) but he knows I am honest and sincere and fearless—qualities he himself I think possesses. I like him far better than these craven, scheming, plotting Englishmen whose one aim is to see how *little* freedom they can give Ireland and call it by another name. Don't despair—don't despond. We shall win—rest assured of that. Ireland was not born to suffering through the ages to end in death and despair at last. Her people have not kept their religion and their souls for nothing. Let them be men and do, on a far bigger scale, what Ulster has done. If only all will put their backs into the Volunteer cause freedom may come far sooner than you think. *Go on with the Volunteers.*

Now as to the German ships. No—you are wrong. They absoutely meant to come to Ireland—and do still mean to come if they can. John Bull objected—of that you need have no doubts at all. The facts will not be made public—they cannot—but the fact is sure and certain. They objected on political grounds—" international " if you will. Ireland was the pawn in the game—but it was not the German Company put her forward. No British Government will ever willingly allow free foreign intercourse with Ireland. That is a fixed immutable law of the British realm and people—and of the English nature itself. The mere suspicion of foreign intercourse with Ireland drives England mad. I know what I am saying quite well. She will stick at nothing to prevent it. She wants Ireland as a pocket Argentina at her doors. Irishmen are to her cattle—either to feed her workers in one shape or, when they are not castrated, to fight her battles. Once let us get into touch, direct, free, touch with other countries, and our slavery of mind must go from us. She knows that she holds Ireland in a grip of economic servitude, and by a bond far more fatal—intellectual servitude. Most Irishmen are slaves in their outlook on life—England has made them so by hideous cruelty and oppression in the past, carried on to-day by rigorous seclusion from contact with others and by the control of every means to advancement kept firmly in her grasp. We have been taught by ages of oppression, failure and defeat to have no belief in ourselves and it is on this inherent moral weakness she relies to keep us subservient tools to the end. She will fail. This exposure of the Queenstown jugglery is only a small thing in itself but it opens a lot. It opens a big door and with the help of the good God I mean to see that door is kept open wide. I am going, please God, to carry this fight much further than they think in Downing Street —to an arbitrament they dread very much. They will pay dearly for their " diplomacy " and our whole people I hope will begin to *think* on these things—and think as freemen not as slaves. For the solution lies always in our own hands. The day we *will* our freedom we can achieve it. Rest assured of that. It is not England now enslaves us. She simply deals with us as slaves because she knows we *are* slaves. There is the psychology of the situation. She recoils from the Ulstermen because they are *not* slaves and she knows it. They tell her to go to Hell and prepare to send her there and you see she draws back and talks of compromise, concession—and you and I, the mere Irish are to take it in the old abject submission. Well I for one won't—I mean to fight—and if John Bull betrays Ireland again, as I am quite certain he means to do, then with the help of God and *some* Irishmen he'll learn that all Irishmen are not slaves and that there is some fight in us still.

I didn't mean to write you all this but your letter has moved me literally to tears. I know how you feel—well do I know it. But my dear friend it is not because you are Catholics he treats you so, but because *being* Catholics he knows you'll put religion before nationality and that when it comes to shedding blood you'll recoil on moral grounds and refuse the trial. He knows that the Protestants have no religion—of that kind—that they won't mind shedding some blood—enough to do the trick—and that blood shed in Ulster might well wreck the Empire or bring about serious complications and so he'll give in to them because they are more serious and more formidable to his peace than you God-fearing, religious-minded Irish Catholics. You've got to realise what I said at Ballymoney that " Patriotism is the highest form of morality." Do that and be prepared to die for your country and John Bull will pass from our shores as a bad dream—as he has done from the shores of South Africa and from those of all men who stand up to him as men.

My regards to your wife and forgive this long letter. I am awfully pressed for I have a lot to do and I go off on my great quest in a few weeks. My word to you is *trust in yourselves*—inspire every man in Cork to be a fighting man in the true sense, to prefer death to dishonour ; to prefer to die rather than live a serf—a bond-serf of the meanest form of human exploitation I suppose any imperial system has ever devised. I'll get you arms, yes 50,000 of them if you'll get the men ready.

Yours sincerely,

ROGER CASEMENT.

This letter is a revealing document. The fantastic proposal to bring Carson to Cork was on a par with the equally impracticable suggestion he made a few months later to John Redmond to the effect that General Kelly Kenny, a retired British general of Boer War vintage and Irish descent, should be asked to take command of the Volunteers.

Already, as this letter shows, he was thinking of open rebellion, whether justified or not. The seed which flowered so tragically in 1916 was beginning to germinate. Prejudiced people, according to their lights, now regard Casement as a scoundrel or a saint. In reality he was neither one nor the other—but only a modern Don Quixote. He had exposed tyranny and persecution in foreign lands. In the Congo and Putamayo he had tilted to some purpose at the windmills of slavery and corruption. Now he was to charge again into the turmoil and confusion of a World War and to go down in darkness and despair. In his own country he had discovered what he believed to be worse tyranny and duplicity than any he had found abroad, and he advanced to the attack with an impetuosity and violence which was aggravated by a feeling that he had too long neglected to fight Ireland's battle.

That in such circumstances he should have taken an exaggerated view of both the wrongs and remedies was perhaps inevitable. In addition he was in bad health. In spite of his charm of manner and distinguished appearance he gave one an impression of instability and restlessness almost amounting to a neurosis, and he had already begun to spoil his case by reckless exaggeration. Yet no one who knew him could believe the vile, and entirely unproved, suggestions which, with diabolical cleverness, were later made against his moral character by British propagandists.[1] Roger Casement belonged by blood and temperament to the same category as Charles George Gordon and David Livingstone—men noble in mind and firm in pursuit of right as they saw it, but very difficult to deal with and impossible to lead or influence. His belief that any attempt to gain self-government for Ireland by parliamentary agitation was doomed to failure was supported by the events which took place during the short period after his return to Ireland before the War. The Carson campaign, the Curragh mutiny, and not least the failure of his attempt to open up direct communication between Ireland and Europe, all

[1] For a complete exposure of this discreditable conspiracy, see *The Forged Casement Diaries*, by W. J. Maloney, M.D., LL.D.

proved to his satisfaction how little Irish interests mattered
when in conflict with British. Holding that view and finding
his beliefs confirmed by events he fearlessly pursued what
he believed to be the right course. " The great quest,"
which he refers to in his letter to me, was his projected
journey to the United States to obtain funds to arm the
Volunteers. That in turn led to his fatal visit to Germany
which was a hopeless and utterly useless adventure. Had he
stayed in America he might have been very formidable
indeed to England and very helpful to Ireland. In Germany
he was neither wanted nor trusted as his diaries abundantly
reveal. The Germans were quite incapable of understanding or appreciating his quixotic aims. To them he
was a liability rather than an asset. They regarded him
with suspicion and as soon as opportunity offered they
got rid of him. He was not even fully informed of the
negotiations taking place between the Dublin revolutionary
junta and the German Government. His lamentable
attempt to seduce the Irish prisoners of war at Limburg
was directed only to recruit an Irish Brigade for the
freeing of Ireland and he had no intention that they
should be used to fight Germany's battles elsewhere. The
Germans' idea of *Realpolitik* naturally did not coincide with
such idealism and so his " great quest " ended in disillusion-
ment and death. I never met him again, although, on Holy
Saturday morning, 1916, I was to witness, as will later
appear, the curtain rising on the last act of his tragic career.

XVI

DURING THE spring of 1913 we had two other visitors who were destined—each in his own fashion—to put Casement's revolutionary theories into practice. Both were school-masters, and both suffered from the defects incidental to that noble calling when it seeks to apply the theories of the pedagogue and methods of the classroom to public affairs; in short they lacked the human approach. The greater of the two—Patrick Pearse—I had known since he was the editor of the Gaelic League paper, *An Claidheamh Soluis*, some years before. The son of an English monumental sculptor and an Irish mother, Pearse displayed all the characteristics of the Irish-English breed. An old friend of mine, who followed the same calling as Pearse's father, used to tell how once, having occasion to call on the older Pearse, he found him in his yard practising with a revolver so that he might be able to defend himself from the Fenians, the Irish revolutionaries of that period, whom he naturally considered a threat to his freedom, but whose example later inspired his son to rebel. Patrick Pearse, like Tom Kettle, qualified as a barrister, but, again like Kettle, he soon found that the law was not his *métier* and turned aside to journalism and teaching. The latter was his true vocation. In 1908 he had established in Dublin a lay school for Irish Catholic boys which struck a new and necessary note in Irish education. Its object, as stated by Pearse, was " to make Irish boys, and out of Irish boys to make Irish men." " What I mean," he wrote, in the first number of the school magazine, "by an Irish school is a school that takes Ireland for granted." [1] He had studied bilingual education in Belgium and come to certain wise conclusions now unfortunately ignored or forgotten by those responsible for Irish education. In the article already quoted he wrote : " An Irish school need no

[1] *An Macaomh*, No. 1, Midsummer, 1909.

more be a purely Irish-speaking school than an Irish nation
need be a purely Irish-speaking nation; but an Irish school,
like an Irish nation, must be permeated through and through
by Irish culture, the repository of which is the Irish
language." And again, " I do not think a purely Irish-
speaking school is a thing to be desired; at all events a
purely Irish-speaking secondary or higher school is a thing
that is no longer possible." He rightly insisted that bi-
lingualism in practice implied the teaching of the vernacular
of the pupils; the teaching in addition of a second language;
and the gradual introduction of that second language as
a medium of instruction in the ordinary curriculum He
was clear that it required, " as indeed any sane teaching
scheme must require, that the very earliest steps of a child's
education be taken in the language of the child's home "
" Where English is the home language," he wrote in words
which might well be remembered by our Minister of
Education, " it must of necessity be the ' first language ' in
the schools." [1] I thoroughly approved (as I still approve)
of these views and accordingly subscribed to the fund
initiated for the enlargement of his school when two years
later he moved to the Hermitage, Rathfarnham, under the
Dublin hills.

There can be little doubt that had Pearse confined his
activities to teaching he would have achieved great work
for Ireland because he had those peculiar gifts—a single-
minded devotion to a high ideal combined with sound
methods—which go to make a great schoolmaster. Unfortunately, the man who might have become an Irish
Dr. Arnold chose rather to be the leader of an abortive
and unjustified rebellion. This strange development was,
I think, due in part to the school's change of habitation in
1910. Its new home was an old house situated in a district
closely associated with the name and fortunes of Robert
Emmet, the Irish revolutionary leader of 1803. Only a
short distance away was " The Priory," where his fiancée,
Sarah Curran, had lived. At the Hermitage itself tradition
said that Emmet had been a frequent visitor. " In truth,"

[1] *Collected Works of P. H. Pearse* : Political Addresses, p. 47.

wrote Pearse, " it was the spirit of Emmet that led me to these hill sides." [1] And so he began to dream of another revolt in which he would himself be cast for Emmet's part. A new *motif* became apparent in all he did and wrote : " We should train every child to be an efficient soldier, efficient to fight when need is, his own, his people's and the world's battles, spiritual and temporal." And the same belief which Casement held in a blood sacrifice as the only key to Irish freedom became his dominant idea fortified by the memory of Emmet, and inspired by the writings of Wolfe Tone, that child of the French Revolution whom he once described as " the greatest man of our nation ! " [2] " I know," he wrote for his boys' journal, " that Ireland will not be happy again until she recollects that old proud gesture of hers, and that laughing gesture of a young man that is going into battle or climbing to a gibbet." [3]   Of Emmet, he wrote more than once in language bordering on the blasphemous, that " This man was faithful even unto the ignominy of the gallows, dying that his people might live, even as Christ died." [4]   This strange obsession, for such I fear it must be called, found its final expression in the speech which he made to the boys at St. Enda's on 21st March, 1916, a few days before the Rebellion, when he asserted that " as it took the blood of the Son of God to redeem the world, so it would take the blood of Irishmen to redeem Ireland." Yet this man who could preach such strange and terrible principles to the boys committed to his care, and afterwards put them into practice without hesitation, would, as his biographer Desmond Ryan points out, weep over a dead kitten, and stop work in his garden if he killed a worm !

No one could, indeed, have suspected the gentle, cultured, schoolmaster who stayed with us in February, 1913, of such views, although undoubtedly they were already germinating in his mind. Of sturdy build, his face, with its high brow and Napoleonic features, was somewhat marred by a cast

---

[1] *An Macaomh*, No. 3, Christmas, 1910.
[2] *Collected Works of P. H. Pearse* : Political Writings and Speeches, p. 264.
[3] *An Macaomh*, No. 4, May, 1913.
[4] *Collected Works of P. H. Pearse* : Political Addresses, p. 71.

in one eye which his popular portraits, usually taken in profile, mercifully hide. It was the face of a thinker, but the tight mouth disclosed the stubborn determination of a zealot. He had come to Cork to seek assistance for his educational work which we discussed in some detail and which was already bearing fruit. Of this we were interested to hear, for our friends Eóin MacNeill and Stephen Gwynn had already entrusted their children to his care and we planned to do likewise. He sought, he told us, to discover and develop the natural talents of each pupil. The boys themselves were given a sense of responsibility by associating them, so far as possible, with the actual administration of the school. Nature study, which included practical gardening and elementary agriculture, lectures by prominent Irishmen, and dramatic performances, all contributed to make education at St. Enda's stimulating and complete. He spoke to us also about the school library which he was trying to build up out of his slender resources, and my wife drew his attention to a book which was a great favourite of ours and which he had never read, that strange biography of a mystic—*The Life of John William Walsh*, by Montgomery Carmichael. As we had two copies we gave him one for his school library. This gift had a sequel, for in April, 1914, he wrote me a charming letter in Irish from New York, where he had gone to seek help for his school. Reminding me of the book we had given him a year before he enclosed a copy of his recently published poems in Irish, *Suantraidhe agus Goltraidhe* (Songs of Sleep and Sorrow), a small but remarkable proof of his poetic power and vision. These twelve short poems with their record of inner struggle, their intense spiritual outlook, their reflections on death and renunciation, indicated only too clearly his own end. In one poem, he wrote :—

> I set my face
> To this road before me
> To the deed that I see
> And to the death I shall meet.

To a man holding these views the Volunteer movement

was a godsend. Yet there is no doubt that, like Casement, he at first only saw it as a means of securing Home Rule. " In the Volunteer movement," he said at Limerick on 28th January, 1914, " we are going to give Mr. Redmond a weapon which will enable him to enforce the demand for Home Rule," and indeed at that time no one would have listened to him had he proclaimed it to be the spearhead of an Irish Republic. Unfortunately, place and circumstances diverted this vivid, uncompromising character from education to revolution. For him patriotism became a religion, an end in itself; to play Emmet's role on a modern stage his supreme ambition, alas too soon gratified. But I prefer to remember the earnest, devoted schoolmaster who did so much and who had still so much to do, rather than the tragic revolutionary. In the former role Ireland has unfortunately forgotten his teaching. In the latter his memory is unhappily still invoked by every half-educated fanatic.

Our second visitor that spring was unexpected. One Sunday afternoon in May, 1913, there arrived at Lacaduv a tall, lanky, young man of about my own age. His dark hair and sallow complexion suggested a foreign origin which his name justified but his rich Limerick accent seemed to belie. He bore a letter of introduction from my old Clongowes master, the Rev. Timothy Corcoran, S.J., Professor of Education in University College, Dublin, asking for my support and influence on behalf of Mr. Eamon de Valera in his candidature for the Chair of Mathematical Physics at University College, Cork. The letter set out, in meticulously numbered paragraphs, the various qualifications of its bearer who was I gathered, a teacher of mathematics at Blackrock College, Dublin. The subsequent interview confirmed Father Corcoran's eulogy. My visitor, whose modesty was only equalled by his charm of manner, was equally acceptable on other grounds, for it appeared that he was not only an active member of the Gaelic League but also, like most young Irishmen at that time, a supporter of John Redmond's Home Rule policy. If I had to secure for the candidate the support of our party in Cork this would naturally be a desirable qualification. I accordingly set to work and, backed by strong local support and these credentials, Mr. de Valera was in due course selected for the vacant post by the Governing Body of Cork University College. My father-in-law, Sir Bertram Windle, the President of the College, however, quite properly supported the candidature of the late Mr. E. H. Harper[1] who, after a course of the highest distinction at Trinity College, Dublin, had been for some years assistant to the Professor of Mathematics at University College, Bangor. Windle used his powerful influence with the Senate, which has the last word in academic appointments, and secured Harper's election. He thus diverted the course of Irish history, for Mr. de Valera, as a Cork university professor would hardly have taken part in the Rebellion of 1916. When I next met Mr. de Valera, twenty years later, he was President of the Executive Council of the Irish Free State, that strange political entity, neither nation nor province, which he has since re-named Éire, and for which Carson, Pearse and himself have been in various degrees responsible.

While the actors in the forthcoming national tragedy were thus gathering in the wings we continued to play out our local political comedy. Occasionally, however, it also verged on the tragic. I remember for instance one occasion in 1913, when William O'Brien and the members of his party had voted against the financial provisions of the Home Rule Bill and on returning to Cork arranged to hold a public meeting to justify their conduct. This so enraged our supporters that some of the wilder spirits among them decided that when O'Brien arrived in Cork railway station to start his triumphal progress through the streets, they would take him by force to an adjacent hotel, where, with the assistance of a partisan barber, they would remove his famous beard, and so shorn, release him to his bewildered followers. Such action would of course have led to a serious riot, if not worse, but fortunately we discovered the project and stopped it before it matured.

[1] Harper joined the British army on the outbreak of the First World War and was killed in action during the Somme battles.

O'Brien continued to clamour for a Conference with the Unionist Party although, as his friend Tim Healy wisely pointed out, such a gathering could " only end in Ulster being in some way excluded." [1] O'Brien's newspaper, the *Cork Free Press*, almost on its last legs, became more abusive as its owner's political fortunes declined. In June, 1913, it excelled itself by publishing a libellous article which in effect accused me of using my political position for personal ends. I wrote to John Redmond for his advice and received the following reply whose wisdom has I think a wider application than to my particular case :—

House of Commons,
June 23rd, 1913.

My dear Mr. Horgan,

I have received your letter with the copy of the *Cork Free Press*. I will speak to Mr. Devlin and some others about this matter; but I desire to give you my own strong advice on my own personal responsibility. I advise you most strongly not to bring any libel action against this paper. I am quite convinced your bringing an action would strengthen the paper, give it an advertisement, and be exactly what O'Brien would desire. Possibly—probably even—but you know best as to this—such an action would end in a disagreement, which would mean a heavy pecuniary fine upon you, in addition to the mortification. This libel is akin to those which are published every day about all of us by the same newspaper. They cannot possibly do either you or us the smallest harm, and, in my deliberate judgment, the proper way is to treat them with contempt. In a matter of this kind you must, in the last resort, act on your own responsibility. But I write you my own private, personal opinion on the matter because it is the least compliment I can pay you for your splendid services to the cause.

Very truly yours,

J. E. REDMOND.

Needless to state I acted on this excellent advice. In fact the *Cork Free Press* did not long continue its abusive career, for with O'Brien's failure it finally expired amidst

[1] *Letters and Leaders of My Day*, by T. M. Healy. Vol. ii., p. 352.

the mutual recriminations of its editor, directors and share-holders, as all such personal papers inevitably do.

O'Brien's vindictive attacks on members of our party reached a climax in a vendetta—not without its comic aspects—directed against Alderman Henry O'Shea whom we had successfully run for the Mayoralty of Cork in 1912. By trade a successful baker, Alderman O'Shea was one of the quietest and most inoffensive of men, and although steadfast in his political opinions, in no sense a politician. O'Brien's vanity was, however, hurt by O'Shea's election, and he determined to unseat him if possible. The Lord Mayor as a young man had spent several years in New York and made no secret of the fact that he had been admitted as an American citizen. The O'Brienite party therefore in 1913 lodged an objection to his vote on the grounds that he was an alien. This was duly heard by the Revising Barrister, Mr. Michael Comyn, who refused to disqualify the Lord Mayor on what was tantamount to gossip, and held that official proof of his American citizenship should be given. Had he confined himself to finding as a fact that O'Shea was not an alien all would have been well. Unfortunately, however, he proceeded to deliver a long judgment in which he gave legal grounds for his decision. Maurice Healy, M.P., who acted as solicitor for the O'Brienite party, promptly applied for a writ of mandamus directing the Revising Barrister to remove O'Shea's name from the voters' list whereupon he would have ceased to be Lord Mayor. The matter duly came before the King's Bench Division, a majority of whom supported the Revising Barrister's decision.

But in spite of this defeat Maurice Healy returned to the attack and launched proceedings against the Lord Mayor for acting as a member of the Cork Corporation while an alien. In the meantime, acting on Counsel's advice, I had taken the necessary steps to have the Lord Mayor re-admitted as a British citizen and notice of this fact had duly appeared in the *London Gazette*. When the case was heard at petty sessions I was able to prove by independent testimony that the Lord Mayor had resided in America for nine

17—1818

years, from 1880 to 1889, and I then produced a certificate
from the appropriate American official to the effect that
no such person as Henry O'Shea had been admitted as a
citizen in New York State during that period. On this
evidence the magistrates dismissed the case and, although
an appeal was again taken to the King's Bench, the judges
unanimously held that the magistrates had ample grounds
for refusing to convict and that they could not be compelled
to do so. The truth was that the Lord Mayor, like many
other Irishmen, had been admitted as an American citizen
under the name of Henry *Shea*, having dropped the O
through his own carelessness or the ignorance of the
American official concerned. On the termination of the
proceedings I presented the Lord Mayor with the various
official certificates concerning his nationality, suitably
framed, and this collection of legal contradictions subsequently adorned his study. Two years later, while still
Lord Mayor of Cork, he received the well-merited honour of
knighthood.

But in spite of these activities, and perhaps even because
of them, O'Brienism was already a spent force. Speaking
at a meeting in Ballyhea, Charleville, County Cork, in
July, 1913, I ventured to say that nothing save that element
of chance disaster which lurks in the path of all human
enterprise could now prevent the Home Rule Bill from
becoming law. I asked my audience therefore to leave
behind the dull, sordid and barren controversy which the
disappointed ambition and personal vanity of William
O'Brien had imposed on the country and to range forward
into the brighter future. Sound finance, was, I suggested,
the basis of good government and the elementary fact in
Irish finance was the large deficit which constituted the
reductio ad absurdum of the Union between Great Britain
and Ireland. I went on to point out that for over a century
the English rulers of Ireland had defied the basic laws of
political economy but that these laws had conquered at
last. The first task of Irish statesmen would therefore be
to produce an equilibrium between revenue and expenditure. For any hardship involved in achieving that aim

Ireland would find abundant compensation in that moral independence which was the foundation of national character and national welfare. There were two schools which, I said, repudiated the policy of frugal independence I had outlined —one Unionist, which frankly preferred British money to Irish freedom, and the other, of which Mr. O'Brien had constituted himself the fugleman, maintaining that the Irish financial deficit was purely imaginary. Both led directly to political and fiscal servitude. Home Rule meant running our own house in our own way at our own expense or it meant nothing. The task before us, I claimed, was to steer clear of the gross bribes of Unionism on the one hand and the equally absurd claim of Mr. O'Brien on the other, and to direct our fiscal policy to the attainment of national solvency. Subsequent events were to show that it was this task, and no other, which proved to be the touchstone of Irish statesmanship.

Many, however, felt that we were by no means out of the wood. Just before the introduction of the Home Rule Bill Monsignor O'Riordan, who was a detached observer, had written me from Rome : —

Is Home Rule coming? One of your politicians was here recently—not an M.P.—who says it is to come, and this present year. I asked him about the financial provisions and if we could start housekeeping with a sound capital. He had no doubt about that but I fear he did not know enough about the point to have doubts. Happy man! I fear he has great trust in the Liberals—happy man also! I have no trust in them where things Irish or things Catholic are concerned. I trust them as much as I trust the Conservatives and I have no trust in either. They will give what they cannot safely withhold. And better examine the Bill doubtingly before you take it, than be wise when it is too late to undo the past. It will be Dead Sea fruit if they can palm it on you.

His doubts were soon justified.

XVII

TOWARDS the end of 1913 the Liberal Government gave the first indication that they were afraid to grasp the Ulster nettle firmly. In November Lloyd George, supported by Churchill and Morley, suggested to the Cabinet the exclusion of the nine Ulster counties from the control of the Irish parliament for a period of five years. As far back as 1911 he had proposed the permanent exclusion of Ulster. Although these proposals came to nothing they showed the trend of affairs. The Nonconformist conscience was again at work. Redmond's difficulties were further increased by the serious strike of transport workers, and subsequent general lock-out, which took place in Dublin during the autumn of 1913. This portentous event lasted for several months and revealed the intolerable social and economic conditions which prevailed in the capital. The Irish Party, essentially middle class in sympathy and origin, stood aside from the conflict and so lost influence with the workers. The strike failed but its consequences were momentous, for it created much bitterness and led to the establishment of the Citizen Army—a body composed of working men distinct from the Irish Volunteers—which played a leading part in the Rebellion of 1916.

Nevertheless the New Year opened with every promise of early victory for the Irish cause. The major obstacles had been, it seemed, overcome and time was on our side. Redmond, steeped in parliamentary tradition, and believing in constitutional procedure, discounted on the one hand the Ulster threats of civil war and on the other the rapid growth of the Irish Volunteers. He declined to believe that his opponents would break the accepted political rules or that the Volunteer movement would get out of hand.

At the local government election in January, 1914, we strongly reinforced his position in the South by securing a decisive Nationalist majority over the O'Brienite party in the Cork Corporation. It was clear that O'Brien's power was broken and he himself recognised the significance of our victory by once more offering to resign his seat in Parliament. Redmond, whom we consulted, wisely vetoed our acceptance of this challenge on the grounds that domestic turmoil in Ireland, even if it led to O'Brien's defeat, would do more harm than good. We somewhat reluctantly accepted his advice.

On 9th March the attitude of the Liberal Government towards Ulster was made manifest when Asquith, moving the second reading of the Home Rule Bill, now beginning its final stage under the Parliament Act, announced that, as a solution of the Ulster difficulty, the Government proposed that any Ulster county might, by a majority of its electors, vote itself out of the operation of the Bill for a period of six years. Redmond, well aware of the resentment that his reluctant acquiescence in this surrender to political blackmail must arouse in Ireland, declared that in his view the Prime Minister " had gone to the very extreme limit of concession " ; but he added " if these proposals of the Government be frankly accepted as the basis of agreement and peace, then we, on our side, are prepared to accept them in the same spirit." The proposal was contemptuously rejected by the Unionist Party, Carson declaring that " we do not want sentence of death, with a stay of execution for six years."

The Government was now forced to make some attempt to assert the authority of Parliament and Winston Churchill revealed the strong feelings provoked by these events, when, in a speech at Bradford on 14th March, he described Carson's provisional government in Belfast as " a self-elected body, composed of persons who, to put it plainly, are enagaged in a treasonable conspiracy," and, after stating the issue which was now joined between the forces of reaction and progress, called on the Liberal Party to " go forward together and put these grave matters to the proof." These brave words were soon submitted to a searching test, for, when the Government, passing from words to deeds, sought to enforce their policy by the movement of troops, it soon became apparent that the morale of many prominent army officers had been undermined. The so-called "Curragh Mutiny" when the officers of several cavalry regiments tendered their resignations rather than obey orders to proceed to Ulster, not only challenged the policy of the Government but the authority of Parliment itself. The revolt of the Labour Party and the rank and file of the Liberals against the weakness of their leaders momentarily saved the day, and Parliament re-asserted itself, but not before irretrievable damage had been done. Through its policy of drift the Government had in fact lost control of the situation.

Emboldened by their success the Ulster Unionist junta proceeded, on 24th April, 1914, to defy openly the Proclamation prohibiting the importation of arms.[1] Having purchased a large consignment of arms and ammunition in Germany they landed them triumphantly in Ulster. The Government was completely outwitted and the forces of the Crown made no serious effort to meet the challenge. It looked as if the Liberal Government was at the mercy of its Unionist officers.

On the following day, Carson, speaking in the House of Commons, announced that he took full responsibility for what had taken place, and, Asquith replied that the Government would, without delay, take appropriate steps to vindicate the authority of the law. Proceedings against the Ulster leaders in the Irish High Court were actually contemplated but Redmond, for reasons of policy, strongly advised against this course, and finally, as hopes of a compromise had again arisen, nothing effective was done. This decision, for which Redmond was partly responsible, was disastrous; for the first duty of a government is to govern and if its authority is defied with impunity its power is gone.

The reaction of Nationalist Ireland to these events was immediate and immense. The Irish Volunteers, barely

---

[1] The validity of this Proclamation had been disputed in view of the repeal of the Arms Act some years before, but it was later declared legal by the Irish Court of King's Bench in the case of *Hunter* v. *Coleman*, (1914, 2, I.R. 372).

10,000 strong in January, rose to over 100,000 by the middle
of May. Redmond let it be known that he had no longer
any objection to his followers joining the force. Like many
other young Irishmen, faced by this impudent challenge to
our civic liberties, I felt that there was only one answer
possible, and during that month I enrolled in the Irish
Volunteers. Practically every night, with large numbers of
other recruits, I attended at the Cork Cornmarket—a large
enclosed square—where under the competent instruction of
retired non-commissioned officers of the British army we soon
became proficient in company and battalion drill. This
enrollment of recruits was further stimulated when on 12th
May, 1914, Asquith announced that, while the third and
final reading of the Home Rule Bill would be taken before
the Whitsuntide recess, the Government was about to
introduce an amending proposal in the hope that a settlement by agreement might be arrived at, and that the Home
Rule Bill and Amending Bill would become law at the
same time.

Faced by this situation, the Ulster Nationalists, who were
most affected, insisted that Redmond should officially
recognise the Irish Volunteers as part of the national
movement. Negotiations accordingly began, in April, 1914,
between MacNeill and Casement on the one side and
Redmond and Dillon on the other for the purpose of agreeing
on the personnel of a small executive committee, representing both sides to control and direct the Volunteer
organisation. What might have been easily accomplished
twelve months earlier, when MacNeill made approaches
to the Irish Party through me, was now far more difficult,
for in the meantime opinion had hardened and each side
had become suspicious of the other. The negotiations
proved abortive as the Volunteer leaders objected on
personal grounds to Dr. Michael Davitt, a son of Michael
Davitt, the Land League leader, who was one of Redmond's
nominees. Finally, on 9th June, Redmond issued to the
press a public statement giving his reasons for demanding a
controlling representation on the Volunteer executive.

After stating that recent developments had, in his opinion,

made it desirable for all Nationalists to support the
Volunteer movement, he pointed out that it was essential
that the existing self-elected Provisional Committee, which
controlled the movement, should be replaced by a body
representative of all shades of national opinion. He therefore suggested that it should be immediately strengthened
by the addition of twenty-five representative men, from
different parts of the country, nominated by the Irish Party
and in sympathy with its policy and aims. The Volunteer
leaders reluctantly accepted this proposal, but the bitter
feelings aroused were never really allayed and were largely
responsible for the eventual disruption of the Volunteers.

Redmond requested me to act as one of his nominees on
the new Committee and, while acceding to his request, I
pointed out that it would be impossible for me to attend
frequent meetings in Dublin. As constant attendance was,
under the circumstances, of vital importance, my name was
not included. The subsequent proceedings of this Committee were both discordant and disedifying, and I did
not regret that I had been prevented from becoming
involved in a situation which was as unpleasant as it
was fruitless.

These internal discords were not, however, immediately
apparent and assured of Redmond's support the Volunteers
now received recruits not only from the Nationalist majority
but from prominent Southern Unionists, who, for the first
time, associated themselves strongly and openly with the
new movement, many becoming officers. The Irish
Volunteers, who were already more numerous than the
Ulster Volunteers, now succeeded in combining all parties
outside Ulster in a common purpose—to defend the constitutional rights of the Irish people. Our commander in
Cork, Captain Maurice Talbot Crosbie, who was a trained
soldier and a member of an old Kerry landlord family, in
a letter to Redmond, on 7th June, 1914, made it clear that
so far as the Volunteers in Cork were concerned, although
non-party they were complementary, and in no sense
opposed to his policy. In the same month the Nationalist
Party in Cork county completed the defeat of William

O'Brien by securing a decisive majority in the County Council. At a great review of Southern Volunteers, held at Mitchelstown on 5th July, some thousands of well-drilled men, of whom I was one, marched past Colonel Maurice Moore, the inspecting officer, who complimented us on our bearing. An army without arms is, however, an absurdity. Our deficiency in this respect was soon made good under dramatic circumstances.

The war of 1914 broke on the British people like a bolt from a clear sky; for us in Ireland it was only the climax of a growing storm. On 21st July, 1914, at a Conference of party leaders summoned by the King, a last desperate attempt was made to secure a settlement of the Ulster problem. Three days later it was announced that this body had been unable to agree, either in principle or detail, upon the responsibility of defining an area to be excluded from the Home Rule Bill. It is right to emphasise that neither then nor at any other time did John Redmond or the Irish Party agree to a *permanent* exclusion of any part of Ulster. It was only natural that German observers should conclude from these events that " England was paralysed by internal dissensions and her Irish quarrels." [1] Moreover the failure of the Conference really extinguished all hope of carrying out the moderate settlement proposed in the Home Rule Bill and determined the much more drastic but less satisfactory conclusion arrived at seven years later. It is no exaggeration to say that the intransigence of the Ulster leaders in 1914, openly supported and indeed inspired by the Unionist Party, sowed the seeds of that Irish neutrality which might well have been fatal to both Great Britain and Ireland in 1939.

On 22nd July, 1914, Edward Martyn, who had been staying with us at Lacaduv, motored my wife, an English friend and myself to Killarney, to attend the annual Oireachtas, or festival, of the Gaelic League. There we met Dr. Douglas Hyde, the President of the League, and other old friends. On the following Sunday, 26th July, in the

---

[1] See despatch of Baron Beyens, Belgian Minister at Berlin, dated 26th July, 1914 : also *The World Crisis*, by Winston Churchill, Vol. i., p. 185.

Killarney demesne, Dr. Hyde addressed a large gathering
of competitiors and enthusiasts from all over Ireland. A
nation without a language was, he said, like a mower without
a scythe, a tailor without a scissors or a soldier without a
gun. " But," he went on, " we will put guns in the hands
of our soldiers, please God, and when they fire the noise will
be felt from the hills of Ireland right round to the seashore."
This obvious allusion to the Volunteers was loudly cheered.
Dr. Hyde's words were in fact more apposite than he knew,
for that very morning, though we did not know it, a cargo
of rifles for the Irish Volunteers had been landed from
Erskine Childers' yacht at Howth. As the waiting Volunteers marched with their weapons into Dublin, troops
acting under illegal orders from a police official intervened.
The Volunteers, however, succeeded in scattering with most
of their arms. As the troops marched back to barracks,
they were set upon by angry crowds. In the subsequent
confusion they opened fire, killing three people and injuring
thirty-eight. This tragic event undoubtedly confirmed the
impression already existing abroad that the British Government's hands were tied by the Irish situation and that
British intervention in Europe was impossible. The first
step had been taken to arm the Irish Volunteers, and the
noise of the event reverberated not only over Ireland, as
Dr. Hyde had anticipated, but throughout Europe. Its
effect on the British political situation was equally potent.
The Amending Home Rule Bill was, by the consent of all
parties, indefinitely postponed, and, at Redmond's demand
a judicial inquiry was at once opened to investigate the
responsibility for the Dublin shootings.

On the afternoon of 26th July we said good-bye to
Edward Martyn and returned from Killarney by train. At
Blarney station, just outside Cork, an excited railway porter
gave us news of the Dublin gun-running and told us that
Austria and Servia had mobilised their armies. Arma-
geddon, it seemed, was about to begin. When we reached
Cork late that evening we saw the Volunteers marching
through the silent streets. Douglas Hyde's prophecy had
been quickly fulfilled. Writing to me the following day from

Killarney, Martyn gave his personal reactions—" What awful news from Dublin this morning. I knew they would take us seriously and disarm us. They don't fear anything Carson does because he is on England's side. The Volunteers are playing the Carson game. It is all going as I thought." But the great majority of Irishmen, of whom I was one, thought it was time things were brought to a head and were determined to assert their rights. The following night seven hundred Volunteers again paraded through Cork without interference from the authorities. Arrangements had been made to land a cargo of arms for the Cork Volunteers at a small harbour in West Cork on 3rd August, the very day on which Great Britain decided to declare war on Germany. We duly paraded in the Corn-market at 7 a.m. and a special train was waiting in the adjacent station to convey us to the coast, but at the last moment news arrived that the project was abandoned as the ship in which the arms were being brought from Antwerp had not been permitted to sail. If it had sailed earlier, or if the Howth cargo had been directed to West Cork, we would probably have landed our arms without opposition and so averted the Dublin shooting with its sad consequences. Captain Talbot Crosbie, our commander, informed the assembled Volunteers of these developments. He also defined his attitude towards the international situation and indicated that he did not think we could remain passive spectators if England were involved in the war. This statement evoked immediate protests from some of the extreme element who stepped out of the ranks and voiced their views. The great majority of those present, however, supported Captain Crosbie, and the incipient revolt petered out. But it was only postponed, not averted.

No action of any Irish leader has been so misrepresented as that taken by John Redmond in the House of Commons on that momentous day. After Sir Edward Grey had made it clear that Great Britain intended to support France and had referred to Ireland as " the one bright spot in the very dreadful situation," Redmond rose to speak. He had had no opportunity for consultation with the rest of the Irish

Party. His two principals lieutenants, John Dillon and Joe Devlin, were in fact absent in Ireland. His position was also made more difficult by the bitter feelings which the shooting in Dublin had naturally aroused. In a few words, spoken with obvious sincerity, he told the House that the British Government could remove their troops from Ireland and that the Irish Volunteers, in comradeship with their brethren in the North, would defend their country. It was a simple, straightforward declaration, little different in purpose and policy, having regard to the changed political conditions, from those made by Mr. de Valera before and during the recent war. In decency he could not have said less, statesmanship prevented him from saying more. He had a great sympathy for France, passionate sympathy for Belgium, but his real thought was for Ireland. He knew well the risks war brought to the Irish cause. A year before a friend asked him if he thought anything could prevent Home Rule becoming operative. He replied " A European War might." His immediate object was, therefore, to consolidate public opinion in Ireland in support of a policy both sane and patriotic, and at the same time to ensure the passage of Home Rule by satisfying the British people that, having supported a generous course towards Ireland for several years, they could new count on our friendship in their hour of peril. His deeper and greater object was, however, to unite all Irishmen in a common purpose and thus raise the Ulster question from the old ruts of antipathy and prejudice. He acted in accordance with his own straightforward character, without consultation, but after anxious thought, as leader at a great moment acting in his own right. It was in short the utterance of a man who sought to transform a noble vision into a living reality. His critics said afterwards that he should have struck a bargain before he spoke. The suggestion was both absurd and ignoble. The British Government was already pledged to pass the Home Rule Bill. Redmond had no alternative but to speak as he did or to remain silent. Had he taken the latter course no subsequent declaration would have had the same effect. Nor did his words commit Ireland to a course which Irish Nationalists would be unable to follow. On the contrary they embodied the very thing which they all desired—the public arming of Irishmen for the defence of Ireland. In five minutes his words of fine sincerity had changed an atmosphere charged with discord and hate into one of unity and concord. Yet, as the members of all parties stood up to cheer him one man remained silent and aloof. Sir Edward Carson, who at that moment could not only have united Ireland but re-united Ireland and England, failed to answer Redmond's appeal. It is now apparent which was the greater man.

Unfortunately Carson's silence was soon translated into action. At a private interview with Redmond, arranged by the Speaker a few days later, he refused to do anything to facilitate the passage of the Home Rule Bill and was " in an absolutely irreconcilable mood." [1]   He refused, moreover, to agree to any proposal for joint action by the Irish and Ulster Volunteers for the defence of Ireland. Redmond pressed on the Cabinet the necessity for the immediate passage of the Home Rule Bill. It is fair to record that one of his strongest supporters in this demand was Winston Churchill. In Ireland Redmond's attitude received overwhelming support and his courageous action was widely endorsed. Great crowds cheered the departing British troops, including the Scottish regiment which had been concerned in the Dublin shooting. Symptomatic also of the general feeling was the attitude of William O'Brien and his party. At a meeting of his followers in the City Hall, Cork, on 2nd September, a resolution was passed unanimously tendering to the Government " the assurance that the manhood of Ireland is at their command in this emergency," and O'Brien himself, with characteristic exuberance, declared " We have got to be either honest friends or honest enemies of England. It won't do merely to say we are willing to fight for Belgium, or to fight for Ireland, or to fight for France, much though we love those gallant nations. We have to go further and to say, without putting

---

[1] Letter of Redmond to Asquith, 5th August, 1914. *Life of John Redmond,* by Denis Gwynn, p. 363.

a tooth in it, that we are ready to fight for England as well in England's way."

But all this good will, with its tremendous implications, was slowly but surely frittered away. The Unionist hand was still concealed in the Liberal glove. Kitchener had, at Asquith's urgent request, become Secretary of State for War. The appointment of this strange, and, so far as Ireland was concerned, sinister figure, sealed the fate of Redmond's proposal. Kitchener had it is true spent his early youth in Kerry, where he was born of English parents, but this fact probably only increased his contempt for the " mere Irish." To recognise, arm and train such people would, he felt, be to arm rebels. Even the proposal to form a distinctive Irish division, like the one already sanctioned without demur for Ulster, met with constant rebuffs. Used to dealing with savage and half-civilised peoples, he had all the faults of an autocrat and no appreciation of, or sympathy with, the Irish leader's difficulties. No man did more to destroy Redmond's patient effort to foster goodwill and co-operation between England and Ireland.

Finally, however, the major issue had to be faced and on 18th September, 1914, the Home Rule Bill became law, although a Suspensory Act prevented its operation until the end of the War. This solution was further qualified by Asquith's assurance that it would not come into operation until an Amending Bill had altered its provisions in such a way as to secure general consent to its operation. Redmond had to admit with regret that his appeal to the Ulster Volunteers and the British Government to allow Irishmen to defend the shores of Ireland had met with no response. Nevertheless he felt that the British people had kept faith with Ireland, whatever the attitude of their politicians, and, in a public manifesto, he asked the Irish people to keep faith with them by forming an " Irish Brigade " for service overseas and by putting the Irish Volunteers in a state of efficiency for the defence of the country. Further developments quickly followed his return to Ireland a few days later. On 20th September, while on his way to his mountain home at Aughavanagh, Co. Wicklow, he addressed a parade of Irish Volunteers at Woodenbridge. They were old friends and neighbours and he spoke briefly and simply, pointing out that it was their duty to make themselves efficient and to acquit themselves like men " not only in Ireland itself, but wherever the firing line extends, in defence of right, of freedom, and of religion in this war." This speech brought matters to a head. Four days later a majority of the original Volunteer Committee issued a manifesto repudiating his policy and declaring that neither he nor his nominees were any longer entitled to any place in the administration or guidance of the Volunteer organisation. In fact the Supreme Council of the Irish Republican Brotherhood, a self-appointed junta, some of whose members belonged to the original Volunteer Committee, had already, in August, 1914, without the knowledge of their comrades in the Volunteers, resolved unanimously to make an attempt before the end of the War " to free Ireland by force of arms, to use the Volunteers to that end, and to secure arms from Germany." [1] The objection of these people to Redmond's open and straightforward action was, therefore to say the least of it, disingenuous if not actually dishonest.

The secession of the extremist minority in the ranks of the Volunteers only displayed their weakness. Out of some 170,000 men, 160,000, including the Inspector-General Colonel Maurice Moore, and Laurence Kettle, one of the original founders, gave their allegiance to Redmond, and became known as the National Volunteers.

At a meeting of the Cork Corps, on Sunday, 4th October, eight companies forming an overwhelming majority of the force, on my motion, unanimously endorsed Redmond's policy and recognised the authority of the new National Committee which had been formed under his presidency. On the same day Redmond told a meeting at Wexford that recruiting was a matter for the conscience of every individual Irishman whether Volunteer or not. We had by this time secured arms from Dublin, rather antiquated Italian rifles with fearsome saw-edged bayonets, for which,

[1] *Life of P. H. Pearse*, by Louis N. le Roux, p. 307.

perhaps fortunately, we had no ammunition.[1]   These
weapons were stored in an armoury at Fisher's Lane, which
was the Volunteer headquarters.   On the evening of 1st
October, while the extreme section of the Volunteers were
drilling at the Cornmarket, a picked team of our men raided
the Armoury and removed the rifles in motor cars by a
circuitous route to the out-offices in my father's stable
yard at Clanloughlin where, entirely without his knowledge,
they remained until we had reformed our ranks.   I was
elected a Captain in the new force.

This division in the ranks of the Volunteers had reper-
cussions elsewhere.   On 12th October, 1914, my old master,
Rev. T. Corcoran, S.J., Professor of Education at University
College, Dublin, wrote to me as follows :—

From all I can see the effect on the language movement of
the situation that has arisen bids fair to be disastrous.   Practically
all the Gaelic League forces are now turned from their proper
work.   Hyde told me a few days ago that MacNeill had offered
his resignation as Vice-President of the League about twelve
months ago, and that he (Hyde) was seriously thinking of
accepting it.   If MacNeill ties up the active members of the
Gaelic League with *his* Volunteers it will leave the movement a
mere school of thinkers having no contact with the vast mass
that must be leavened with Irish Ireland ideas.   To my mind
the League is already at a low ebb and the new developments
will crowd it out or let it die for sheer lack of workers.   Hyde
tells me that the *ultras* are the only really active Leaguers.   If
the *ultras*—as they are doing—all drift to MacNeill who will
work for the League ?   I told a prominent MacNeill supporter
the other day that the only logical sequel to MacNeill's political
paper at the Ard Craobh was a proclamation next morning by
himself and his taking over full control of the Gaelic League.
But he has not done that.   It would be a new League, not the
old one.   Pearse holds openly that the Gaelic League is a spent
force on its original non-party lines.

The one chance of getting an efficient Irish Volunteer force
in the future is to put a good number of men into the war,
organised in, for and by Ireland.   There are good reasons for
not being much bothered about the balance of justice as between

[1] The Arms Proclamation had been withdrawn on 4th August after
Redmond's speech.

England and Germany. I think there are good—but not conclusive—grounds for holding Germany to be in the wrong, and a danger. The Irish Brigade of 1700-1750 didn't bother much about these issues—so long as there is *some* cause. What is needed is the consolidating effect of actual service together.

In December Douglas Hyde came to address a Gaelic League meeting in Cork. He stayed with us and expressed to me in no uncertain terms his anxiety at the trend of affairs within the League. Companies from both Volunteer forces, momentarily united to do him honour, escorted him in procession to the City Hall where the meeting was held. In his speech, the terms of which he had discussed with me fully beforehand, he said that while it was perfectly true that some of the supporters of the Gaelic League were strong politicians of what he might call an advanced type, all were not, and the great bulk were moderate men such as would be elected to an Irish parliament. It was upon them, he said, that the Gaelic League relied to create an Irish Ireland through the medium of Irish education. He maintained that if any one party got control of the League and ran it on party lines the language movement would fail and the entire structure of the organisation would fall to pieces. These prophetic words unfortunately fell on deaf ears. Within twelve months he was driven out of the Gaelic League because he refused to allow it to be turned into a political body. From that day its decline began.

XVIII

THE enthusiasm with which the overwhelming majority of the Irish people supported John Redmond's attitude at the commencement of the war in 1914, was, as the result of Ireland's essential remoteness from Europe, largely emotional. For that reason it required to be immediately confirmed and sustained by an intelligent and co-ordinated policy against the inevitable tendency towards reaction. On the contrary, as Lloyd George himself subsequently admitted, it was destroyed by a " series of stupidities which sometimes looked like malignancy." [1]   Redmond had asked, and the Prime Minister, Mr. Asquith, had solemnly promised that the National Volunteers should be recognised, organised and utilised by the War Office, and that Irish recruits to the regular army should be formed into a distinct army corps, retaining their national character.   But while Ulster was at once granted these eminently reasonable concessions to public opinion, they were denied to the rest of Ireland. In a hundred petty ways the War Office discouraged Irish recruiting.   The National University, unlike Trinity College and Queen's University, Belfast, was not permitted to form an officers' training corps.   The Irish divisions were not allowed to wear a distinctive Irish badge or to carry Irish flags.   John Redmond's own son was at first refused a commission.   His brother, Willie, received one only because he had, as a young man, served in the militia as a commissioned officer and so could not be refused.   My friend, Stephen Gwynn, M.P., then fifty years of age, had to enlist as an ordinary private.   To make matters worse, when the Irish regiments were, owing to incompetent leadership, virtually massacred during the Dardanelles battles, their brave exploits were passed over in silence.   Yet in spite of these gross blunders, to call them by no worse name, no less than 27,000 National Volunteers joined the British

[1] House of Commons, 18th October, 1916.

army during the first year of the war. Small wonder that at a review of the National Volunteers in Limerick on 20th December, 1914, at which I was present with the Cork battalion, John Redmond protested strongly at the Government's attitude.

Of this attitude the Cork Battalion of the National Volunteers now had direct experience. In that very month of December our commanding officer, Captain Donegan, approached the authorities and offered to provide an armed guard on the two vital bascule railway bridges which cross the channels of the River Lee at Cork, and connected the railway system then running to the great naval base at Bantry Bay with the rest of Ireland. The keeping open of this line of communication was naturally a matter of great strategic importance. The offer was duly accepted and on New Year's Day, 1915, the first guard was mounted. No Irish national force had been entrusted with such duties since the days of Grattan's Volunteers and I believe we were the only body of National Volunteers who were given an opportunity of doing so. As our men marched to their posts for the first time the watching crowds cheered. Our relations with the local British military authorities were excellent and I remember on one occasion when a company of Volunteers under my command were route marching near Cork the guard at the Ballincolig cavalry barracks turned out to salute us. But the forces of reaction at the War Office, ignobly encouraged by William O'Brien, soon upset these arrangements. Our comrades, when incorporated in the British Army, might die nobly in Gallipoli and Flanders; they could not be trusted with arms in their own country. Knowing what was afoot I persuaded my father-in-law, Sir Bertram Windle, with whom I had recently resumed friendly relations, to write the following letter to Asquith :—

University College,
Cork.
January 9th, 1915.

Dear Mr. Asquith,

I hope you will pardon me for venturing to write to you on a matter of some little importance and in doing so to say that

I write from the standpoint of an Irishman who has been a Nationalist for nearly forty years (that is since I arrived at any political opinions of my own) and at the same time as one unconnected with any political organisation of any sort. Of course my views are those of Mr. Redmond and the vast majority of the Irish people and I have been as much delighted as I have been astonished at the rapid change produced in my countrymen by the coming of Home Rule. I could not have believed that so great a change could have taken place in so short a time. For example the fact, if the English people could only see it, that the Corporation of what is sometimes called " Rebel Cork " yesterday by a vote of 24 to 3 withdrew the honorary freedom of the city from Kuno Meyer and that—to quote from the speech of a town councillor reported in to-day's *Cork Examiner* —because

" they realised their duties and responsibilities as members of that great Empire ; that as such they had a claim on Great Britain as she had on them, and that they would not forsake but support her in her hour of trial and difficulty, as they had been doing, and would continue to do not only through their Irish soldiers, but by every means in their power."

This fact, I say, is one of the most eloquent pieces of testimony to the change which has taken place in public opinion which could possibly be imagined. It would not only have been impossible but inconceivable ten years ago, when Meyer's vapourings would have been more likely to have gained applause rather than that repudiation.

Now, as you know very well yourself, there are a number of persons who desire nothing less than that Ireland should settle down quietly to prosperity under Home Rule, and these persons have seized the opportunity afforded them by Mr. O'Brien's most mischievous and, as I think, misleading letter [1] to make an onslaught on the National Volunteers. I may say that I am wholly unconnected with that movement save as a subscriber to its funds, But I have watched it with great interest and with rapidly growing approval. It is a fine body of men, here at any rate, and here most certainly is under the direction of responsible and honourable men who are anxious to carry out

[1] Mr. O'Brien, in a statement published in the *Cork Free Press* on 6th January, 1915, had complained that the War Office had surrendered to Mr. Redmond's demand for recognition of the National Volunteers whom he described as " undisciplined partisans " controlled by the heads of a "secret society."

to the utmost the pledges given on their behalf by Mr. Redmond. No doubt it is made up mainly of persons connected with the Redmond party, but no one is excluded on account of his politics. These men, under great stress from intrigue on the part of opponents and copious cold water from those who might have been expected to have encouraged them, have gone steadily on improving themselves and have really attained to what I am told by competent persons is quite a high standard of military efficiency. Lately they have been entrusted with a small piece of work in the way of bridge-guarding, and it is wonderful how grateful they have been at this sign that they are trusted, and how much they appreciate the fact that they are being allowed to do something for their country in this time of stress. What is obvious to onlookers like myself is that an effort is being made to put a stop to their employment and it is on this point that I take the liberty to address you. Nothing could do more good than to trust these men and I am firmly convinced that they are worthy of trust. Nothing could do more harm or act more effectively against the growing sense that Ireland is part of the Empire than to tell them in so many words that they are not to be trusted even to look after a few bridges in the city in which they live. I do venture to press this point on you with all the power I possess and to express the hope that nothing may be done to discourage, but rather everything possible to encourage a movement fraught, as I am convinced that it is, with so great promise for the improvement of the discipline and order of the young men of the country. I offer this apology only for writing to you that I write as one who loves his own country and wishes to see it free and prosperous. I believe that this end can only be attained in an abiding treaty of friendship with the other parts of the British Empire such as is contained in the Home Rule settlement now happily accomplished.

Your obedient servant,
BERTRAM C. A. WINDLE.

This lucid statement of the position in Cork was ignored, for Asquith unfortunately was already committed to that policy of weak compliance with Tory intrigue which was soon to lead to the downfall of his Government. Late in January the Volunteers were officially informed that an armed guard by them on the railway bridges could no longer be permitted. This incident, relatively trivial in

itself, is an excellent example of the attitude adopted by
the War Office towards the Irish war effort. Full of suspicion of the " mere Irish " and enmeshed in red tape,
the Colonel Blimps of that period finally destroyed all
enthusiasm in Ireland and justified those who felt that
English soldiers and politicians were not to be trusted.

The last great rally of the National Volunteers took place
at a review held in Phœnix Park, Dublin, in April, 1915,
when 25,000 men marched past John Redmond and Colonel
Moore. *The Times* Special Correspondent described it as
" the largest military display Dublin had ever seen."
Headed by our Commanding Officer, Colonel Donegan,
a Napoleonic figure on a white charger, and preceded by
the Skibberreen Volunteer Band, whose silver instruments
had been presented by Dr. Macaura of " Pulsocon " fame,
the Cork contingent made a fine appearance. Colonel
Moore wrote afterwards that " for efficiency there was no
corps on the ground in front of it." Prior to the Volunteer
Convention, which was held on the following day, I saw
John Redmond who told me that Asquith contemplated
embodying the Volunteers in a territorial force. No effective
step was, however, taken towards this end.

But it was already apparent that the days of the National
Volunteers were numbered. Deprived of any *raison d'être*
by the action of the British Government, large numbers
joined the British Army, in which many of them subsequently gained high distinction for gallantry. Soon the
only armed force of national origin was the Irish Volunteers,
most of whose leaders were already secretly committed to
support Germany. The foundations of a great bridge
between England and Ireland had been successfully
destroyed.

A few days after the outbreak of war my mother died
with tragic suddenness. Under the stress of this domestic
grief and of increasing ill-health my father resigned the
position of County Coroner which he had held for forty-one
years. The Cork County Council, on 2nd December, 1914,
unanimously elected me as his successor. I had in fact
acted as his deputy for many years. My election was in

great part a tribute to my father who had always acted as the officer of the people and, in days when it was both difficult and dangerous to do so, had asserted their rights and defended their liberties.

The office of Coroner is one of great antiquity and can be traced back with certainty to the twelfth century. It originated, not as an inquiry into the cause of sudden deaths as might be supposed, but as a system of mutual suretyship for the preservation of the peace. The inhabitants of a district who concealed a felony or permitted a guilty person to escape the consequences of his crime were liable to be fined by the King. Coroners were first appointed by the freeholders of each county to act on their behalf in such matters. Their duty was to keep a record of the pleas of the Crown and to secure possession of the goods of a felon so that the fine due to the King would be paid by the criminal concerned and not by the people as a whole. The title of coroner was thus derived from his duty of securing payment *a Corona*. As the most serious felonies were those arising from crimes of violence it gradually became one of the coroner's most important duties to inquire into the causes of all unnatural deaths.

A coroner was thus from the beginning a judicial officer chosen directly by the people, and so the office is as democratic as it is old. His functions are first mentioned as early as A.D. 925 in the Charter of Privileges granted by King Athelstan to St. John of Beverley, but the Great Charter of Henry III (A.D. 1225) is the first statute which actually uses the title Coroner. The statute *De Officio Coronatoris* (4 Edward I, Stat. 2, A.D. 1275), which first defined the duties of the office, shows that a coroner at first combined the functions of policeman and magistrate for he had to arrest the criminal, take evidence of his guilt and value his property, so that it might be available to meet the consequent fine which would otherwise have been levied on the community. Until Magna Carta deprived him of this power he had authority not only to hold an inquest but to proceed to trial and judgment as well. The mediaeval coroner also held inquiries concerning treasure

trove, wreckage and the origin of fires. In all these matters
he acted as the people's officer and was answerable to the
King on their behalf. Gradually, however, with changing
conditions the holding of inquests concerning unnatural
deaths became, for all practical purposes, the coroner's only
function. The qualifications for holding the office in the
thirteenth century were knighthood and residence in the
county where the coroner officiated. The latter of these
qualifications is still essential. After the invasion of Ireland
by the Normans the office of coroner, as part of their
judicial system, was instituted within the Pale, and gradually extended as their rule spread over the whole country.
By the Local Government Act of 1898 the power of electing
coroners was given to the newly established county councils.
Prior to that, at the time of my father's election, a coroner
was elected like a member of parliament.

Since my appointment as coroner in 1914 I have had
many interesting and some exciting experiences. It fell
to my lot during what we euphemistically call " the troubled
times " to return verdicts of murder against all the regular
and irregular armies which then operated in Ireland. No
doubt the omnibus nature of my activities spared me from
having a similar verdict returned in my own case. I had,
however, some narrow escapes. None of these adventures,
however, equalled in dramatic interests that of the inquest
which I held, shortly after my appointment, at Kinsale,
on 8th and 10th May, 1915, on the bodies of five passengers
who were drowned on the sinking of the ill-fated *Lusitania*.

The story told by the witnesses at that inquest was
sensational in the extreme. On the morning of 7th May
the great liner, which, with her sister ship the *Mauretania*,
was the pride of the British mercantile marine and held
the Transatlantic record for speed, loomed up out of the
heat haze around the Fastnet. She had left New York on
1st May with 1,255 passengers and a crew of 651. On the
day before she sailed an official advertisement, issued by
the German Embassy in Washington, appeared in the
American press. It warned people travelling on the
Lusitania, or any other British vessel, that they would be in

danger of losing their lives. The journey across was un-
eventful. As the great ship cleared the fog and approached
the Irish coast on a smooth summer sea her speed was increased
from fifteen to eighteen knots. At 2.15 p.m. when she was
about fifteen miles south of Kinsale and the passengers
were at lunch, the second officer drew the attention of the
captain to a torpedo approaching the liner on the starboard
side. Immediately afterwards she was struck amidships and
there was an explosion followed by another which may have
been internal. Some witnesses stated they saw a second
torpedo. The ship immediately took a list to starboard
and when the captain gave the order to reverse the engines,
in order to stop them and lower the boats, he found they
were out of commission and that it was therefore impossible
to do so. The ship continued to travel at speed under her
own momentum and after ten minutes began to sink
rapidly. It was impossible in any event, owing to the heavy
list to starboard to lower the boats on the port side, and
the speed of the vessel prevented the launching of those to
starboard. During the last moments before she took the
final plunge a few boats got away, but although there was
little panic or confusion most of the passengers and crew
went down with the ship or jumped overboard ; 1,134 lost
their lives. Most of the survivors and the dead were landed
at Queenstown, but some, including five dead bodies, were
brought into Kinsale which is in my district. I decided to
hold an inquest at once and opened the proceedings on the
following day, 8th May. Two days later, they were brought
to a conclusion by a verdict of " wilful and wholesale
murder " against the Emperor and Government of Germany,
a verdict which *The Times* described as one of the most
remarkable the world had ever heard of.

The quaint old Market House of Kinsale, where this
historic verdict was recorded, has seen many strange scenes,
for it originally served as the meeting place of the Kinsale
Corporation in the days when Kinsale was a port of considerable importance and traded directly with Spain. The
destiny of Ireland was decided outside its walls in the
reign of Elizabeth when the Irish chieftains, O'Neill and

O'Donnell, failed to raise the siege of the Spanish troops beleagured there by Mountjoy. This battle, which ended the hope of breaking the Tudor power in Ireland, was probably the most decisive in Irish history. In the old court-room where the inquest was held James II, in March, 1689, had met the burghers of Kinsale when he landed in his Kingdom for the last time. The very chair on which I sat bore an inscription which reminded us that it was presented by a former Sovereign of Kinsale (as the chief magistrate was called) in the early eighteenth century, while behind me hung the arms of the old town which one of the foreign journalists irreverently, but aptly, compared to a chess-board. Once more Kinsale had become a place of historic importance. Journalists from all the leading British and Irish papers, and representatives of the foreign press agencies from London, filled the body of the court. At my side a jury of twelve shopkeepers and fishermen, humble, honest citizens, listened to the terrible story as survivor after survivor went into the witness-box. One witness seemed to bear a charmed life for he had been on the ill-fated *Titanic*, in a big Welsh colliery disaster, and now he had survived again. The most dramatic moment was reached when William Thomas Turner, the captain of the great liner, gave his evidence. Three days before, resplendent in his dark blue uniform and gold braid, he had paced the bridge a " monarch of all he surveyed " : now, clad in a badly fitting old suit and still suffering from the strain of his experience, he looked, and was, a broken man. As he finished his evidence, which disclosed that he had gone down with his ship, I expressed our appreciation of the courage which he had shown, which, I said, was worthy of the traditions of the service to which he belonged. Bowing his head he burst into tears. This display of emotion was indeed natural, and our sympathy went out to a brave but unlucky man.

Addressing the jury at the conclusion of the evidence I pointed out that it was one of the most serious and appalling occurrences that had ever been considered by a coroner's jury, and that the loss of life unfortunately was not measured by the five victims with which we were concerned. The whole civilised world, I said, stood aghast at this crime. As a matter of direction in law I told them that torpedoing a merchant ship of any nationality, without warning or signal of any kind, was a violation of international law and the convention of civilised nations. There was, I added, no legal sanction of any kind that could be invoked in its support. It was a mere policy of destruction and frightfulness such as had unfortunately characterised the pursuit of war by Germany. The *Lusitania* was a non-combatant vessel. She was not armed and there could be no possible excuse for sinking her. As to the warning in the American papers, it had, I said, no more legal or valid effect than that of an assassin who sent an anonymous letter to his intended victim. The jury, in accordance with my direction, returned the following verdict in each case : " That the deceased died from prolonged immersion and exhaustion in the sea eight miles south south-west of the Old Head of Kinsale on Friday, 7th May, 1915, owing to the sinking of R.M.S. *Lusitania* by torpedoes fired without warning by a German submarine. We find that this appalling crime was contrary to international law and the conventions of all civilised nations and we therefore charge the officers of the said submarine and the Emperor and Government of Germany, under whose orders they acted, with the crime of wilful and wholesale murder before the tribunal of the civilised world."

Half an hour after the inquest concluded, my friend Harry Wynne, then Crown Solicitor for Cork, arrived post haste with instructions from the Admiralty to stop the inquest and prevent Captain Turner from giving evidence. That august body were however as belated on this occasion as they had been in protecting the *Lusitania* against attack. I have always believed that the German authorities, although they undoubtedly planned the sinking of the *Lusitania* with characteristic thoroughness, and later attempted to justify their conduct, never really envisaged its terrible consequences. The place and time were carefully chosen to avoid serious loss of life. When the ship was torpedoed she was only a few miles from the Irish coast on a calm summer sea in broad daylight. She carried a full complement of boats and life-saving equipment and under normal conditions all the passengers and crew should have been saved. The spectacular loss of the ship was what they desired : not the terrible disaster which followed. But their careful plans could not determine the path of the torpedo which put the engines out of commission and so made the subsequent holocaust inevitable. A criminal is, however, responsible for the probable and natural consequences of his actions no matter how unlikely they may be.

The verdict of the Kinsale jury had many reverberations. *Punch*, over the title " Wilful Murder," showed the Kaiser drinking " to the day of reckoning " as Death beckoned him towards the gallows behind. An American postcard gave his portrait under the title " Wanted for Murder." *L'Illustration*, the well-known French illustrated paper, on its front page, displayed a picture of a dead woman and child floating in the sea with the text of the Kinsale verdict printed underneath. It was shown on posters throughout Italy and helped to influence Italian opinion towards participation in the war. American opinion was also gravely incensed and for a time it looked as if the United States would enter the war. That indomitable person, Theodore Roosevelt, expressed the feeling of the American people when he described the sinking of the *Lusitania* as " The greatest act of piracy in history." It was of course a declaration rather than a verdict in the ordinary sense, and the first time I think in the history of jurisprudence that a monarch and his government were indicted for a breach of international law. It not only made clear the attitude of the Irish people but vindicated the basic principles of international morality. Modern history might have taken a far different course had not legal scruples and political pusillanimity eventually combined to prevent the appropriate punishment from being put into effect. By a strange coincidence, exactly thirty years later, on 7th May, 1945, the criminal career of the Nazi Government met its inevitable end when the German High Command surrendered unconditionally to the United Nations.

XIX

THE sinking of the *Lusitania* led to another, and more personal, development, for I determined to do my part in bringing the criminals to justice. Accordingly in August, 1915, I joined the Coast Patrol service operating under Rear-Admiral Elliott, then commanding the Queenstown naval base. The station to which I was attached had its headquarters in a former coastguard building at Millcove, near Rosscarbery, County Cork, and our patrol was responsible for watching the coast from Glandore Harbour on the West to the Galley Head on the East. Our duties were to maintain a systematic watch on enemy submarines and other craft, to report all movements of shipping to base and to see that no communications passed between hostile craft and spies ashore or afloat. We were under the command of a R.N.V.R. officer, Lieutenant Travers, and had a powerful motor boat as well as smaller craft at our disposal. From a watch-house, high up on the cliffs near the station, we kept a constant watch day and night. Like Gunga Din's relations our personnel was a " mixed and curious lot " ; coal merchants, millers, solicitors, accountants, architects, land agents, stockbrokers, grocers, journalists and even a Unitarian clergyman, were to be found in our ranks. Service was not continuous and a rota of members ensured the presence of six of us on duty at all times. The work, though often monotonous, was interesting. The South-West coast of Ireland was the happy hunting ground of the U boats and during the three years which followed we saw more ships sunk than many naval ratings who spent the whole war in the North Sea. Here for instance is the description of one such incident as I wrote it down in the log book on 14th September, 1916:

12.55 p.m. Large cargo boat steaming E. about a mile off land struck a mine or was torpedoed S.S.W. of watch-house. We saw a large explosion nearly amidships and heard the noise. She steamed on for about a quarter of a mile, came round in a circle, and then began to settle down by the head. Reported to Galley by phone.

1.5   Her boats were lowered and left her.

1.10   Patrol boat alongside.

1.15   Loud report heard—probably boilers bursting. Steamer very much down by the head. Patrol boat to W. of her.
           Two boats standing by.

1.30   Two steamers have gone E. since explosion. A big steamer was passing her to S. going W. just as explosion occurred but kept her course evidently on instructions.

1.45   Sinking steamer has list to starboard.

1.50   Second patrol boat has arrived on the scene.

1.57   Loud explosion—probably depth charge or gunfire—heard to E.

2.5   Steamer now has heavy list to starboard with only stern showing.

2.10   She slowly disappears.

The vessel in question was the *Counsellor*, and the Captain wrote us a few weeks afterwards :

I was very much interested by your account of the sinking of my ship. I am glad to say that we all managed to get away from her safely but it is rough to see a good ship sunk under you, especially after making a long voyage. We were from San Francisco and Canadian ports with a valuable cargo. I have strong suspicions that it was the work of a submarine as there was one seen shortly after just E. of the Galley and fired at by a patrol boat, but against that I know that there were eight mines swept up near where we were sunk shortly afterwards. She was hit well up on the port side so it's hard to say what caused the damage as we saw nothing. The Huns will have something to pay for when we have finished with them but let them get all that's coming to them for they will never get paid in full.

In February, 1917, I witnessed the sinking of two more cargo boats and, in March, 1918, of a naval sloop.

But the depredations of the U boats also affected the humble fishermen along the coast. One such incident that we recorded was typical of many. On a May morning in 1917 the crew of the *St. Mary*, a local motor fishing boat, mustered at dawn in our cove. The spiller baskets were stowed aboard, the tanks filled and the scanty provision of dry bread and cold tea placed in the locker aft. All day she travelled South-West to the fishing grounds through a heat mist over a sea smooth as glass. In the afternoon she reached her destination and her crew set their spiller lines. After a short rest they began to haul them aboard. Presently, as they were busily at work, they saw the smooth dark hull of a submarine rising like a shark from the sea about a mile away. She bore down quickly upon them and, while still some distance away, the command " Hands up " was shouted from her deck. Half-dazed and frightened the fishermen hesitated. Then rifle shots rang out and one boy fell wounded in the arm. In a few moments the submarine was alongside and several of her crew jumped into the fishing boat. Fishing baskets, fish, spiller lines and sails were quickly thrown overboard— a few blows of a sledge hammer smashed the engine to bits— then the pirates left carrying with them all the paraffin and bread on board. While this fell work was in progress the commander of the submarine took photographs of the proceedings. Dazed and shaken, the fishermen were ordered to make fast to the submarine and were towed towards a mackerel boat which the crew of the submarine then sank with a bomb. Having picked up their comrades in misfortune the crew of the motor boat were left to pull back the long distance to the coast. It was a sad home-coming we witnessed next morning, the little motor boat—its owners' pride—which had gone out to sea so hopefully a few hours before, now a useless, broken thing, her engine in atoms, her sails and gear—the entire stock in trade of her owners—

gone, and the wounded boy with his fractured arm bleeding in the stern. Even such a relatively trivial example of brutality and terrorism was not easy to forget.

After the war, on the occasion of a presentation from the patrol to the gracious lady who had kept house for us at Millcove during those war years, I ventured to put some of our memories into a rhyme that may perhaps be quoted here :

> Once more does memory tread the welcome round
> Where all that's best in comradeship was found.
> Across the bay through the encircling night
> The Galley flashes its familiar light,
> And wheeling searchlights cast a finger dim
> Along the far horizon's mighty rim ;
> Or through the dark, in the first early days
> Some giant liner glides with light ablaze.
> Then dawn comes creeping o'er the Eastern hills
> And with its glory all the morning thrills ;
> The curtain lifts, the mighty stage is bare,
> Or else we catch the actors unaware,
> Some drifter creeping slowly 'cross the bay,
> Or sloop zig-zagging on the far sea way,
> And " 40 " going her familiar round,
> Perhaps wondering if a Hun has gone to ground.
> On through these long and not eventful days
> Thus did we watch the shipping go its ways,
> And noted in the log-book every smack
> Taking its lazy course to sea and back.
> But 'twas not always thus, for moments came
> Which made our patient records far from tame ;
> Those vital moments when we saw the Hun
> In the far distance basking in the sun ;
> Or sensed with anxious ear his hidden work,
> By gunfire echoing through the misty mirk,
> While inbound freighters sinking one by one
> Proved all too well his deadly work was done,
> As through the dusk their warning rockets fly
> Like red stars bursting in the evening sky ;
> Or heard above our heads the steady drone
> Of sea planes hunting for their prey alone,
> And wondered what the final act would be
> In that dramatic struggle for the sea.

Yet that isolated life on a wild coast also had its compensations and delights ; working on the motor boat ; hauling lobster pots at dawn ; walking across the hills to the lovely harbour of Glandore ; or, in the summer, deep-sea fishing ; swimming or basking in some deserted cove. Even in the long winter nights, when gales beat down on the watch-house windows and everything outside was blotted out, there were moments of delight when we sat beside the fire drinking strong tea, swopping stories and forming friendships that still survive, for such a service unites men with unbreakable ties.

Often during those lonely vigils we thought of our deep-sea comrades who, in the trawlers and M.L's. guarded the outer approaches. The story of these brave men, although we did not think it possible then, was to be repeated a quarter of a century later in the second German war, when the " little ships " again faced and vanquished similar risks and perils.

But the most memorable event in the history of the patrol took place in the morning watch on Holy Saturday, 22nd April, 1916. This vigil, which lasted from 4 a.m. to 8 a.m., was on this occasion shared by my colleague Weatherall and myself. As we relieved the previous watch it was still dark with a light Nor'-West wind occasionally dropping to calm. Away to the West flickering Morse signals indicated a certain liveliness amongst the sea patrol. About 4.50 a.m. as the dawn began to break we sighted several vessels to the West, near High Island, and on closer examination we saw that one of them was the sloop *Bluebell* escorting a small cargo vessel, both travelling N.E. Another sloop stood away to the West while four drifters and one trawler of the patrol were stationary off High Island. Clearly something was afoot. By 5.15 a.m. the cargo boat was almost abreast of the watch-house with the *Bluebell* in close attendance. Through our glasses we saw that, in accordance with official requirements, she had the Norwegian flag painted fore and aft on her side and her name, the *Aud*. As they passed out of our view behind the Galley Head *Bluebell* signalled she was taking her charge

to Queenstown. I remember reading later, with some
amusement, an answer to a question in Parliament, which
asserted that the reason the *Bluebell* had not at once put a
boarding party on the *Aud* was because the sea was too
rough ! It was in fact as smooth as glass. A few hours
later the *Aud*, which had a German naval crew and a cargo
of small arms, was scuttled near Daunt's Rock Lightship
at the entrance to Cork Harbour. We had witnessed the
prologue to the Rebellion of 1916 and the commencement
of the last act in the tragedy of Roger Casement.

But to us the incident seemed of trivial import. Another
neutral, we reflected, caught out of bounds or trying
unsuccessfully to run the blockade. In fact the *Aud* contained the reply of the German Government to the repeated
demands of a small junta in Dublin who had determined
by hook or by crook to start a rebellion in Ireland before
the end of the war. In the second half of 1915 they had
repeatedly sought German help for an Irish rising, which
the German Government had refused on the sensible ground
that such aid as they could give, having regard to the
British control of the seas, would not be commensurate
with the gravity of the undertaking. Confronted with this
refusal the Dublin revolutionaries nevertheless decided to
proceed with their project, had fixed on Easter Monday,
1916, for the attempt, and had informed Germany of their
decision. Casement in Berlin, ignorant of these events,
isolated, disillusioned, and suspected by the Germans, was
finally told of the expedition to Ireland only at the eleventh
hour. He realised at once that without German troops
and machine guns the rising was doomed to failure. [1] In
this last extremity, in order to stop the rebellion, he even
sought to send a message to Asquith and Sir Edward Grey
in London warning them of what was afoot. [2] Finally
the German Admiralty yielded to his entreaties, and on
11th April, 1916, despatched him by submarine to Ireland.
On Good Friday morning, 21st April, he landed with two
companions, Bailey and Monteith, on a lonely strand near

[1] *The Forged Casement Diaries*, by W. J. Maloney, p. 117.
[2] *The Life and Death of Roger Casement*, by Denis Gwynn, p. 376.

Ardfert, County Kerry, determined if possible, to prevent the rebellion taking place.

A year later, in August, 1917, I heard the inner history of Casement's landing under peculiar circumstances. I had received instructions to defend Austin Stack, a leader of the extreme movement in Kerry, who was charged with an offence under the Defence of the Realm regulations. He was accused, as far as I remember, of calling for cheers for the Kaiser at a public meeting. For the purpose of preparing his defence I interviewed him at the Cork Military Barracks where he was detained. I pointed out to Stack, who was a law clerk by occupation, that the only defence I could make on his behalf was that he did not commit the offence alleged, and, as he assured me he did and would not plead Guilty, I suggested that it would be better for him to dispense with legal assistance and refuse to recognise the jurisdiction of the court, a course to which he agreed. Before I left I asked him to tell me the true story of Casement's landing in which I knew he was concerned. He told me that the Volunteer leaders in Tralee expected the *Aud*, but had received no notification of the arrival of Casement. The original arrangement with the German Government was that the *Aud* should land the rifles in Tralee Bay between the 20th and 22nd of April, but this was changed to Easter Sunday night, the 23rd, and as the German Government was not notified in time of this alteration, the *Aud* arrived too soon and being observed by patrol boats had to depart in haste. She was in fact in Tralee Bay on Thursday night, April 20th, at the same time as the submarine that brought Casement, although neither vessel was aware of the other's presence. The Kerry Volunteers were to muster at Tralee on Easter Monday, secure the rifles, and then start the rebellion in Kerry ; but Pearse's instructions were that not a shot was to be fired till then, or the Dublin rising would be imperilled. Casement's companions, Monteith and Bailey, arrived in Tralee on Good Friday morning after landing from the submarine, having left Casement concealed in a rath near the seashore. They pretended to be two Americans and making contact with Stack informed him of their mission. They all proceeded by motor towards Ardfert to retrieve Casement, but Bailey, although he was supposed to be a trained scout, could not find the way to the hiding place. When they finally reached the rath they found that Casement had already been taken prisoner by the police, and they had to turn back. Monteith managed to escape and after various adventures got away to America, but Bailey was caught by the police the following day and betrayed his companions in return for a promise of pardon. Some of the Tralee Volunteers wanted to attack the police barracks and rescue Casement, but Stack would not let them, for fear of upsetting the Dublin plans. Stack himself never met Casement at all. That evening the Dublin *Evening Mail* published the news of Casement's arrest and the fact that he had given a statement to a priest imploring the Volunteer leaders to cancel all plans for an insurrection. Casement was taken straight to London where a few months later he was tried for high treason and executed, the prosecution being conducted by the notorious F. E. Smith, afterwards Lord Birkenhead, who four years before had himself, as Carson's lieutenant, fomented rebellion in Ulster. So poor Casement's strange, tortured, romantic, spirit reached its apotheosis as one of the heroes of the rebellion he had vainly striven to prevent.

On Saturday morning, 22nd April, my spell of duty at Millcove finished, I left the station, and proceeded to my brother's house at Firville, near Macroom, where my wife and family were spending the Easter holidays. On Easter Sunday the Dublin papers contained a notice from Eóin MacNeill, the Chief of Staff of the Irish Volunteers, stating that, owing to the very critical position, all orders given to the Volunteers for parades, route marches, or other movements were rescinded. A party of Volunteers from Cork who arrived in Macroom accordingly returned to the city. Easter Monday passed without incident, but when I returned to Cork on Tuesday morning I learnt that grave disturbances had broken out in Dublin. The Rebellion of 1916 had begun.

The moral reasons which, according to the teaching of the Catholic Church [1], justify rebellion are well known and can be simply stated. It must be a revolt against intolerable oppression; all legitimate means of redress must have been tried and failed; it must have the support of a majority of the people; and it must have a reasonable prospect of success. Judged by all or any of these tests it is clear that the rebellion of 1916 was entirely unjustified. No one living in Ireland in 1916 could truthfully say that we were living under intolerable oppression, or that all legitimate means of redress had been tried and failed. On the contrary a whole series of ameliorative measures dealing with every aspect of Irish life had been secured by the Irish representatives in the British Parliament, and a final measure granting full self-government had been passed into law, and only awaited the conclusion of the war to be applied. Nothing but our own action could thus prevent the sure growth of freedom in Ireland. One certainly could not say of the men of 1916 as was said of those of '98:

> They rose in dark and evil days
> To right their native land.

Nor had the rebellion the support of the majority of the people. It was on the contrary, as Tim Healy wrote at the time, a revolt of " a minority of the minority."[2] The " Irish Volunteers," a small minority of whose members took part in the rebellion, were themselves a very small minority of the original Volunteer force. But even the " Irish Volunteers " as a body had come to no decision to embark on this hopeless project. The agreement to start a rebellion on Easter Monday, 1916, which was arrived at between Patrick Pearse, representing that small and quite unrepresentative secret society, the Irish Republican Brotherhood,

---

[1] The Catholic teaching is clearly stated as follows in a standard text book :—" The people have a right to defend themselves against tyranny when government is really and habitually tyrannical, when legitimate means of redress have failed, when there is hope of success—for greater ensuing evil would make opposition wrong—and when the greater and saner part of the people are convinced of the habitual tyranny." *Moral and Pastoral Theology*, by Rev. H. Davis, S.J. Vol. ii., p. 89 (1938 Edition).

[2] *Letters and Leaders of My Day*, by Tim Healy. Vol. ii., p. 561.

formally condemned by the Church, and James Connelly, representing the Labour force known as the Citizen Army, was a private pact made without the authority or knowledge of the Volunteer executive or of Eóin MacNeill the Chief of Staff.[1] The secret decision of the Irish Republican Brotherhood to raise a revolt in Ireland before the end of the war, arrived at in the autumn of 1914, was in fact alone responsible for the Rebellion.[2] It was the decision of a small minority using the Volunteer organisation for its own ends. It is hard to conceive a procedure more cynical or undemocratic, or, from a Catholic point of view, more wicked.

As soon as MacNeill learnt that the Easter Monday parade was to be converted into an insurrection he took, as we have seen, immediate steps to cancel all operations, and his orders undoubtedly saved the country from widespread disturbance and bloodshed. In Cork for instance, everything remained quiet, for the local company of Irish Volunteers, which included brave men like Terence MacSwiney and Tomás MacCurtain, obeyed MacNeill's orders and made no move.

The total number of those who took part in the Dublin rising itself was only 707.[3] Its leaders were all townsmen, many of them of Irish-English origin. It had no repercussions worth talking of throughout the country. It was in short not an Irish rebellion but a rebellion in Ireland. It is hardly necessary to labour the point that it had no chance of success. Even Casement and MacNeill saw that. That the rebels fought with great courage and displayed a fine chivalry in action is something of which all Irishmen may be proud. But courage and chivalry are not enough. The cause must be just, the action justified.

The reaction of the Irish people to the rebellion was immediate and definite. " If Ireland as a whole could have got hold of Tom Clarke and his comrades during that week," writes P. S. O'Hegarty, a prominent member of the

---

[1] *Life of P. H. Pearse,* by Louis N. le Roux, p. 325.
[2] *Victory of Sinn Fein,* by P. S. O'Hegarty, pp. 2, 3, 4.
[3] See Article by P. S. O'Hegarty in *Sunday Independent,* 11th March, 1945.

Supreme Council of the Irish Republican Brotherhood, " it would have torn them to pieces," [1]   Many of the Catholic Bishops condemned what they rightly described as a " mad and sinful adventure." From one end of the country to the other public bodies vied with one another in expressing their abhorrence. My father, a fervent Nationalist all his life, wrote in his diary, " May God save Ireland from such devils."

That the rising was financed and assisted by the German Government cannot be denied. John Devoy, the leader of the Irish Republican Brotherhood in America, who was one of the prime movers in the matter, was, as we now know, in close relation with Count Bernstorff, the German Ambassador at Washington, and with his secret agents, von Igel and von Papen, and through them in constant communication with Berlin.

Recruiting blunders, the formation of the first Coalition Government in England with its implications of a postponement of Home Rule ; the possible imposition of conscription in Ireland ; and above all the pressure of Irish-American and German intrigue on extreme opinion were no doubt the immediate causes of the Rebellion.

Yet they do not furnish a complete or adequate explanation of what took place. The real roots of the matter went further back into the cultural and national revival which followed the Parnell split and affected the younger generation. In its origin the Gaelic League was officially and really non-political. But the emotional logic of nationalism eventually submerged the League's political neutrality. In truth, in Ireland a non-political organisation is almost a contradiction in terms. Hence there resulted inevitably a combination of the dying Republican tradition, derived from Tom Paine and the French Revolution, with the new movement for the revival of the Irish language and culture. The separatist element infused the cultural movement, in spite of itself, with a revolutionary, nationalist spirit. Behind the screen of the language the extremists advanced to the attack. But, as Hyde foresaw, once the

---

[1] *Victory of Sinn Fein*, by P. S. O'Hegarty, p. 3.

language movement became political, its end as a cultural movement was in sight. Combined, however, the two movements released a high potential of national energy which culminated in violence and erected a standard that had no relation to reality. Thus the proclamation of a non-existent Irish Republic, combined with the pretence that Irish was the real language of Ireland, led, not only to the Civil War, but to the permanent division and present anomalous position of our country, for Mr. de Valera's political " strategems and spoils " are the natural offspring of the union between the men of 1916 and the Gaelic League. We cannot hope to recover the integrity, physical or spiritual, of the nation until we have frankly recognised this fact.

XX

THE proclamation of the Irish Republic which Pearse read
to the amazed passers-by outside the Dublin General Post
Office on Easter Monday, 24th April, 1916, was in fact
fundamentally false. " Irishmen and Irishwomen," he
declaimed, " In the name of God and of the dead generations
from which she receives her old tradition of nationhood,
Ireland, through us, summons her children to her flag and
strikes for her freedom. Having organised and trained her
manhood through her secret revolutionary organisation, the
Irish Republican Brotherhood, and through her open military
organisations, the Irish Volunteers and the Irish Citizen
Army, having patiently perfected her discipline, having
resolutely waited for the right moment to reveal itself, she
now seizes that moment, and supported by her exiled
children in America and by gallant allies in Europe, but
relying first on her own strength, she strikes in full confidence
of victory." The only vestige of truth in this rhetoric is the
clear implication that the Irish Republican Brotherhood, the
whole membership of which could have been comprised in
a concert hall, [1] was the mainspring of the entire business.
This small body of conspirators by putting nationalism
before religion had placed themselves outside the pale of
the Church. Ireland, which is surely the people of Ireland
and not some disembodied figure of speech, had not been
consulted at all. Even the few Irish Volunteers and members
of the Citizen Army who took part in the rising were
ignorant of their leader's purpose, and, so far as the Irish
Volunteers were concerned, were disobeying orders of their
commanding officer, Eóin MacNeill. The rebellion instead
of being a rising of the Irish people to strike for freedom,
as the proclamation suggests, was in truth " universally and
explosively unpopular." [2] The people of Ireland had

[1] *The Victory of Sinn Fein*, by P. S. O'Hegarty, p. 13.
[2] *The Victory of Sinn Fein*, by P. S. O'Hegarty, p. 3.

neither sanctioned it nor wanted it. But when it ended in blood and destruction this false document remained to paralyse Irish policy and action. It made partition inevitable, it furnished the necessary excuse for civil war in 1922, and it still plagues the rulers of a divided Ireland. When Mr. de Valera denounces the " I.R.A." as an " illegal organisation " it is well to recall that their claim to represent Ireland has as much or as little validity as had that of the I.R.B. in April, 1916.

After five days fighting in Dublin, during which many lives were lost, on both sides, and much valuable property was destroyed or looted, the rebellion collapsed as suddenly as it had begun. Had the British Government acted with wisdom and moderation it would have ended not only in military but political failure. In South Africa two years before, General Botha, faced with a similar situation, had executed only one deserter. Of the remaining rebels some were given short terms of imprisonment, and others, including General de Wet the ringleader, were treated with silent contempt. John Redmond besought Asquith to act similarly.[1] Had his advice been heeded the rebellion would have proved as futile as it was morally wrong. Unfortunately for both England and Ireland his request was ignored until the mischief had been done. The Government lost their heads, Birrell, the Chief Secretary for Ireland, resigned, and Asquith handed Ireland over to the tender mercies of the military caste, virtually the same men who had backed Carson and his Volunteers, organised the Curragh Mutiny and sabotaged Irish recruiting. They were not slow to seize such an opportunity. Martial law was proclaimed throughout the country, fifteen of the leaders were shot, many others sentenced to long terms of imprisonment and thousands of suspects deported. For three weeks this inflammatory process continued. The cold announcement of these reprisals day after day from

[1] After the Rebellion the story was widely circulated that the Irish Party had in the House of Commons, cheered the executions. This was entirely false as even their chief opponent, Tim Healy, admits. In fact Redmond's vehement intervention saved many of the leaders including Mr. de Valera, Mr. Cosgrave and Professor MacNeill.

field courtsmartial meeting in secret affected the Irish public, as was then truly said, " with something of the feeling of helpless rage with which one watches a stream of blood dripping from under a closed door." Almost at once the executed men became heroes. In a few days all the suspicion and distrust, which had been so largely allayed by forty years of patient if unspectacular progress towards freedom, were revived. As Pearse had foreseen, what he and his colleagues of the I.R.B. had failed to achieve, General Maxwell's firing parties accomplished.

The reaction in Cork was typical of what took place elsewhere. On 9th May the following telegram signed by the Most Rev. Daniel Cohalan, Assistant Catholic Bishop of Cork ; T. C. Butterfield, the Lord Mayor ; W. Harte, the High Sheriff; and by William Murphy, George Crosbie, James McCabe and myself, as representatives of our Nationalist organisation, the United Irish League, was sent to the Lord Lieutenant, the Prime Minister and John Redmond : " Voicing we believe the opinion of the great majority of the citizens of Cork we desire to protest most strongly against any further shootings as the result of court-martial trials and against indiscriminate arrests throughout the country. We are strongly of opinion that such shootings and arrests are having a most injurious effect on the feelings of the Irish people, and if persisted in may be extremely prejudicial to the peace and future harmony of Ireland and seriously imperil future friendly relations between Ireland and England." On the same day Thomas Kent, a farmer from near Fermoy, was executed at Cork Barracks. He had resisted arrest by the police and during the subsequent *mélee* a Head Constable had been killed. This was the only serious incident in County Cork. The Irish Volunteers in Cork took no part in the Rebellion, but they possessed arms, and for some days the situation remained tense. Finally, after negotiations between the leaders of the Volunteers, Bishop Cohalan, the Lord Mayor and British military representatives, it was agreed that the Volunteers' arms were not to be confiscated by the military but to be handed over to the Bishop and the Lord Mayor for safe keeping

before midnight on 30th April, and that a general amnesty
was to be granted to all Volunteers not guilty of treasonable
conduct. The arms were not handed over to the Lord
Mayor until 1st May, and as he refused to guarantee their
safety they were finally taken into custody by the military.
The intervention of Bishop Cohalan and the Lord Mayor
undoubtedly saved Cork from disturbance and possible
bloodshed, yet the quite unjustified feeling of the Cork
officers of the Irish Volunteers that they had failed their
colleagues in Dublin was I feel sure largely responsible for
the part played by Terence MacSwiney and others in
subsequent events.

The British Government now proceeded to embark on a
policy in which weakness and bad faith combined to
destroy finally the constitutional movement in Ireland. On
11th May, Mr. Asquith, after a vehement speech by John
Dillon who had just returned from Dublin, announced in
the House of Commons that he was going to Ireland to
consult the civil and military authorities as the Government
had come to the conclusion that the existing system of
Irish government had completely broken down and that
the only satisfactory alternative was the creation, at the
earliest possible moment, of an Irish government responsible
to the Irish people. During his stay in Dublin he not only
met representatives of various shades of Irish opinion, but
visited the prisons and in his own words " talked with the
utmost freedom to a large number of those who had been
arrested and detained." He came South to Cork for a few
hours and met a few prominent citizens at the City Hall.
He seemed both upset and confused by the events in
Dublin. Such hurried talks could not in fact be of
much service.

The following letter which I received soon afterwards
from Colonel Maurice Moore, the brother of the famous
novelist, who had been Inspector-General of the National
Volunteers and a member of the original Volunteer Committee, indicates the effect these events had on the popular
mind. His letter was an acknowledgement of my comments
on a copy of the evidence he had given before the Royal

Commission appointed to inquire into the facts concerning the rebellion. He wrote :

Buswell's Hotel, Dublin.
June 2nd, 1916.

My dear Horgan,

I am glad you liked my evidence ; the Commission did its best to advertise it as everyone wants to read what is secret. However I am sure it is right to defend one's own countrymen ; they were brave men even if mistaken, and it is not quite sure now that they were even that. I suppose you heard of the boy Asquith spoke to in prison. He asked him what he thought of the rebellion now, and the boy replied that it was a great success. Asquith surprised, said " How do you make that out ? " " Well if not what are you here for ? " Socrates could not have answered more wisely. It will be hard indeed on Redmond if Home Rule comes from the Sinn Feiners. I fear he is in a difficult position now. You managed your affairs, at a difficult time, well in Cork. With you and Donegan we are always in good hands.

Yours sincerely,

MAURICE MOORE.

P.S.—I have left Berehaven.[1] All Nationalists are Sinn Feiners in War Office eyes. I wrote privately to Birrell, Redmond and others that no prisoners should be shot. I fancy my letters were opened. I don't care.

On his return to London Asquith announced that the Cabinet had asked Lloyd George to negotiate an Irish settlement and that he had consented. In taking this step the Prime Minister was no doubt hopeful of success, for both the occasion and the man seemed propitious. All parties in England were utterly weary of the Irish problem, and appreciated the disastrous effects of recent events in Ireland upon American opinion. Lloyd George, whose previous success as a negotiator was well known, was offered the opportunity of winning a great personal triumph. His quick enthusiasms, his equally quick changes of attitude and his personal ambition were well known to the Nationalist leaders. They had no illusions as to his methods or character,

[1] Where he had been serving in the British Army.

but they felt that in the existing situation he had the strongest reasons for securing a settlement by consent, and that the strong Unionist element in the Coalition Government ensured that a settlement once agreed to would be put into effect. But they were taking no chances. When Lloyd George opened the negotiations Redmond, as he told me afterwards, asked at once, " What guarantee have we that even if Carson and I agree the Cabinet will carry out the settlement ? " To which Lloyd George replied, " You have the best of all guarantees. I am staking my political existence on this matter. If the Cabinet do not carry out an agreed settlement I shall resign." But when the Unionist members of the Cabinet later sabotaged the agreement arrived at between Redmond and Carson, and Redmond asked Lloyd George to honour his promise, he replied the circumstances had altered since he gave the undertaking and that owing to the grave state of the war it was essential for him to remain in office. Redmond, who seldom used strong language, cannot be blamed for doing so on this occasion. He never again entered into verbal negotiations with Lloyd George. Three years afterwards when J. M. Tuohy, the well-known London correspondent of the *New York World*, during an interview, taxed Lloyd George with this dishonourable conduct the latter admitted his guilt but pleaded as a reason for not fulfilling his pledge that Asquith would not let him ! [1]   It was once well written of Lloyd George,

> Count not his broken pledges as a crime
> He meant them, HOW he meant them—at the time.

No Irishman of that period can, however, forget this act of *Punica fides*, or remember without satisfaction that by a process of just retribution it was the Irish Treaty of 1921 which eventually led to the fall of his Coalition Government and so ended his tortuous political career. That Treaty also gave effect to that permanent political division of Ireland which John Redmond would never agree to.

In the discussion for a settlement which took place with Lloyd George in the summer of 1916 Redmond made his

[1] *New York World*, 9th November, 1919.

position absolutely clear. He was willing to accept a strictly *temporary* exclusion of the six north-eastern counties on the clear understanding that the whole question would be reviewed by an Imperial Conference after the war. As a guarantee that the exclusion would be only temporary he insisted that Ireland should be fully represented at Westminster until a permanent settlement was achieved. It was finally proposed by Lloyd George that the Home Rule Act should be brought into immediate operation without elections being held; the existing Irish members to form the first Irish parliament till the end of the war. Meanwhile the six north-eastern counties were to be excluded and governed as heretofore from Westminster where the Irish representation in the House of Commons was to remain at its full strength. Immediately after the war all outstanding questions concerning the government of Ireland were to be submitted to an Imperial Conference. Redmond and Carson agreed to submit these proposals to their supporters and they were accepted in turn by the Ulster Unionist Council, and by a very representative Nationalist Conference in Belfast which was addressed by Redmond, Devlin and Dillon. John Dillon wrote to me soon afterwards that taking into account the intense feeling it was the most orderly, most good-tempered gathering he had ever attended. This would not have been possible but for the great influence and loyalty of Joe Devlin and the self-sacrifice of the rank and file of the Northern Nationalists. Finally, at a meeting of the National Directory of the United Irish League in Dublin, on 3rd July, it was on my motion unanimously agreed to accept the proposals " because they offered the best means of carrying on the fight for a united self-governing Ireland." As I have already recorded, the proceedings on this occasion were made memorable by a brilliant speech of Tom Kettle's. It was our last meeting. A few months later he fell in action in France.

No sooner was agreement between the Irish parties ensured than some of the Unionists in the Coalition Government, whose spokesman was Lord Lansdowne, made it clear that although the Government had authorised the

negotiations it was not bound by them. They therefore
insisted on the *permanent* exclusion of the six Ulster counties
and refused to agree to the retention of the Irish members
in full force at Westminster. Moreover it transpired that
Carson, without Redmond's knowledge, had been given an
assurance that the exclusion of the Ulster counties was
virtually permanent, inasmuch as they could not be brought
under an Irish Parliament without a fresh Act of Parliament.
Balfour, however, to his credit be it said, refused to be a
party to these discreditable intrigues. Nevertheless the
Unionist objections were admitted by the Cabinet in spite
of Redmond's protests. Thus the whole basis of the proposed
settlement was destroyed. It would have been far better
had it never been attempted. Even Carson was perturbed,
for he realised the inevitable repercussions in Ireland and
wanted Home Rule to be put in force outside Ulster. It
was the bitterest disappointment of John Redmond's life,
for it was on the faith of his assurance that the Government
were pledged to carry the proposals that Nationalist Ireland
had accepted them; now this pledge had proved worthless.
That treachery had bitter consequences for both England
and Ireland.

The Irish reaction to these events was immediate and
inevitable. Horrified by the executions and exasperated
by the bad faith of the British Government, the Irish people
both at home and abroad, turned not unnaturally to new
methods and new men. The rebellion had been popularly
christened the Sinn Féin rebellion, although in fact the
Sinn Féin Party was in no way responsible, for Arthur
Griffith, its founder and leader, did not approve of physical
force and was actually against the rebellion although
interned with the rest. Now in the enforced association of
British prisons a new Sinn Féin movement took shape in
which the extreme element, represented by the Irish
Republican Brotherhood, made common cause with Griffith
and his more moderate supporters. It was a coalition more
apparent than real, for both parties had different aims and
purposes, as was made clear in 1922 when we paid in Civil
War the inevitable price of concealed political differences.

At Christmas, 1916, the internees were released and a few weeks later the new movement gained its first victory at the polls when Count Plunkett, father of one of the executed leaders of 1916, was elected for North Roscommon. Ireland had given Lloyd George the only answer he understood.

The release of the internees, followed a few months later by the release of the leaders who had been sentenced to long terms of imprisonment, revealed a complete change in the attitude of the British Government. Early in December, 1916, Asquith had been forced to resign by a squalid intrigue, and had been succeeded by Lloyd George. But there was a more potent reason for this change in policy. America was on the point of entering the war and the Irish influence in America had to be reckoned with. Moreover for Irishmen it was impossible to ignore the implications of Wilson's mischievous slogan " self-determination."

In the House of Commons on 7th March, 1917, T. P. O'Connor moved a resolution demanding the immediate bestowal upon Ireland of " the free institutions long promised her." During the debate Willie Redmond, on his last leave from France, made the historic speech to which I have already referred. Lloyd George tried to shelve the issue by moving an amendment welcoming any settlement that did not involve the coercion of any part of Ireland. The Government, he said, were willing to give Home Rule to any part of Ireland which desired it, yet he refused to grant it to Armagh and Tyrone, the two northern counties which had clear Nationalist majorities, because to do so would have reduced the Unionist enclave to an absurdity. The Irish Party thereupon left the House of Commons and adopted a statement repudiating the right of a small minority in north-east Ulster to exercise a veto on Irish self-government. A few days later, on 22nd March, Bonar Law announced " that the Government undertook in some way or another to make another attempt to suggest and carry an Irish settlement." The result of the Government's deliberations became apparent on 16th May, when Lloyd George in a letter addressed to John Redmond, after deploring the Irish Party's refusal to negotiate—which was in fact the fruit of his own chicanery—submitted the Government's alternative proposals for "an immediate settlement conceding the largest possible measure of Home Rule which can be secured by agreement at this moment, without prejudice to the undertaking by Parliament of a further and final settlement of the questions most in dispute after the war." The first of these proposals was to bring the Home Rule Act into force at once, excluding the six counties of north-east Ulster, such exclusion to be reconsidered by Parliament after a period of five years ; the financial clauses of the Act to be remodelled in the light of altered conditions. They also proposed to provide for a Council of Ireland composed of equal delegations from the Irish Parliament and the excluded Ulster counties, which by a majority vote would be empowered to legislate for the whole country and to extend the Home Rule Act to north-east Ulster if a majority of the voters there assented. The President of this Council was to be elected by agreement between the delegations or in default nominated by the King. The Act embodying these proposals was to be submitted after its second reading and acceptance by both Irish parties to a Conference presided over by the Speaker of the House of Commons which would have full power to suggest alterations. The second proposal, which seemed to have been added as an afterthought, but which in fact had been inserted as the result of a suggestion made by John Redmond in private conversation a few days before, was that Irishmen of all parties, following the South African precedent, might meet together in a Convention for the purpose of drafting an Irish Constitution. Redmond and his colleagues immediately rejected the first proposal, because of its provision for partition, but they accepted the second on condition that the proposed Convention was fully and fairly representative and was summoned without delay. Lloyd George undertook that if the Convention reached *substantial agreement* the Government would carry its conclusions into effect.

The first proposal was in fact the better. It recognised the realities of the Irish situation and provided a bridge across which national unity might have been reached. Moreover it would have put the Government's *bona fides* to an immediate legislative test while American participation in the war was still fresh and opinion free. Events in Ireland had, however, made its acceptance by the Irish Party impossible. A few days before, on 8th May, a letter from Archbishop Walsh of Dublin had appeared in the Irish press stating that " anyone who thinks that partition, whether in its naked deformity or under the transparent mask of ' County Option,' does not hold a leading place in the practical politics of to-day is simply living in a fools' paradise," and adding in a characteristic postcript " I think it a duty to write this although from information that has just reached me I am fairly satisfied that the mischief has already been done and the country is practically sold." Published on the eve of the South Longford by-election this mischievous letter played a large part in securing the return of the Sinn Féin candidate (if by a narrow majority) in what had been regarded as an impregnable stronghold of the Irish Party.

The other proposal for the holding of a Convention, which was in fact his own, appealed, however, to Redmond's generous mind. He believed, quite wrongly as the event proved, that the same forces which had operated to secure unity in South Africa would assert themselves in Ireland, and that if substantial agreement was achieved American pressure would ensure that the decisions of such a body would be carried into effect. But in South Africa no great English party had a vested interest in disunity. The Irish cancer was too deep-rooted to yield to homoeopathic treatment. Only the surgeon's knife could now effect a cure.

The Irish Party was also sadly hampered by the necessity for maintaining the confidence and support of their followers in Ulster who as a rule could not see the wood for the trees. Carson had originally claimed the exclusion of the whole province of Ulster, a demand which I personally believed the Nationalist leaders should have conceded, for the larger the excluded area the greater would have been the Nationalist representation therein, and the sooner would the more prolific Catholics have converted that representation into a majority. Even in the present restricted area of Northern Ireland, such population trends are at work and must eventually have their effect. These views I fruitlessly propounded to the Irish leaders. The Ulster Nationalists, who naturally enough were only concerned with their parochial problems and political prejudices, refused to entertain such a proposal, and exerted all their pressure to constrict rather than to enlarge the area to be excluded. They thus sacrificed their provincial and political integrity for what was at most only a local advantage and led in the end to a permanent separation.

I had long felt that it was not sufficient for Irishmen to point out the complete bankruptcy of British statesmanship and to stand aside without attempting to find a way out for themselves. William O'Brien had proposed as a solution that the Ulster representatives in an Irish Parliament should be given an absolute veto over all legislation and others had suggested that Ulster should be given double representation. Such proposals were in my opinion undemocratic and humiliating. In two articles, which appeared in the *Leader* in December, 1916, I published a proposal which I had submitted some months before to the Irish Party in a private memorandum. It suggested that the province of Ulster—as represented by the majority of its representatives in an Irish parliament—should exercise an absolute veto over all legislation, new taxation and appointments, so far as the province was affected. I proposed that the Ulster members should form a separate parliamentary committee — to be called the Ulster Committee — which should have the power by majority vote to reject or amend any legislation or taxation—except an extension of an existing tax—which they considered unsuitable or unfair. To meet the danger of unjust administration I proposed that the Chairman of the Committee, to be called the Ulster Minister, should be an *ex-officio* member of the Irish Government and that no purely Ulster official should be appointed or dismissed without his sanction. I also suggested that the Ulster Committee should be empowered at any period of five years, by a majority, to terminate its own existence. Such a scheme would not only have safe-guarded the legitimate rights of Ulster Protestants but, by treating all Ulster as a unit, would have enabled Ulstermen to make their own valuable contribution to our national life. Carson had claimed to control all Ulster; if his claim had been granted on some such basis as I suggested, we might have secured both the integrity of Ulster and of Ireland.

My proposal for an Ulster Committee was eventually discussed by the Convention and finally Lloyd George described it as " a workable expedient, whereby special consideration of Ulster conditions can be secured and the objections to a single Legislature for Ireland overcome." [1] By that time unfortunately other difficulties had arisen to make agreement impossible and my project followed many others of a like nature into the political waste paper basket. I am still, however, convinced that only on such lines can the Ulster problem be solved, and, that had Irishmen been left to themselves, as the South Africans had been, on some such lines agreement would have been reached.

[1] Letter to Sir Horace Plunkett, Chairman of the Irish Convention, outlining the views of the British Government concerning the terms of an Irish settlement, 25th February, 1918.

XXI

THE Convention raised once more the hopes of all those who believed that an agreed solution of the Irish dilemma was still possible. In such an assembly, representative of all parties, it seemed that, given good will, mutual understanding and concessions, common agreement as to the future government of Ireland might be found. And indeed this might well have happened had the Convention been free, like any other normal democratic assembly, to come to a majority decision on the questions at issue. Such a result was, however, rendered impossible by the assurances given by the Government to the Ulster Unionist Council that " in the event of no agreement being come to no party would be bound by its proceedings, and that no scheme would be forced upon the Ulster Unionist with which their representatives were not in agreement." To make matters worse the Ulster representatives, unlike the other members of the Convention, were not plenipotentaries. They could agree to nothing without first consulting the Ulster Unionist Council in Belfast. The dice were thus once more loaded against the Irish majority.

The new Sinn Féin Party, representing the other extreme, refused to take part in the proceedings unless the Convention was elected by direct adult suffrage and permitted to decree the complete independence of Ireland by a majority decision. As these conditions were impossible of attainment the Convention was without direct representation from this party which, even at that time, probably represented the majority of the Irish electorate. The Government sought to overcome this difficulty by nominating as members of the Convention, George Russell, the distinguished journalist and poet, better known as " Æ," and Edward E. Lysaght, a young Anglo-Irish farmer and writer, both of whom sympathised with and could express the views of the new movement. Mr. William O'Brien, who for many years had been demanding an Irish settlement by Conference, Conciliation and Consent, and publicly protesting his willingness to go to any lengths to placate the Ulster Unionists, at first, on behalf of his All for Ireland party, welcomed the Convention as giving effect to " a principle we have long contended for," but subsequently, with characteristic inconsistency, refused to take part in its proceedings. John Redmond alone did not approach the matter in a party spirit, seeking peace rather than tactical advantage. Although this attitude finally weakened his position at a crucial moment it was undoubtedly inspired by the generous instinct of a statesman who placed country before party.

As finally constituted the Convention consisted of ninety-five members of whom fifteen were nominated by the Government, forty-six were elected public representatives such as Lord Mayors of cities and Chairmen of County Councils, while the remainder were delegates of the churches, Irish peers, political parties, trade unions and chambers of commerce. It was in fact a very representative body. Amongst the Government nominees was my father-in-law, Sir Bertram Windle, who brought to its proceedings a constructive mind free from political bias. Before his nomination he had presided on 14th June, 1917, at a meeting of the Cork business community held in the City Hall to bid the Convention god-speed. An organised attempt to break up this large and representative gathering was made by a small body of young men representing the Sinn Féin party. From the commencement of the proceedings they interrupted the speakers and sought to render them inaudible, in which indeed they largely succeeded, but Windle with great coolness refused to be browbeaten and carried the meeting to a successful conclusion. One of the interrupters who vaulted the platform was nonplussed when the Chairman compelled him to remove his hat. These young hooligans were the precursors of the Blackshirts and the Storm Troopers, for their motives were first to paralyse and then to destroy the expression of moderate opinion.

A month later, on 15th July, Windle wrote to me from

his country home at Listarkin, Union Hall, where he was spending the vacation :

I have received an invitation from the Prime Minister to be a member of the Convention. I neither expected nor desired this yet I could not find it right to refuse it. What I heard in England leads me to think that the attempt, if any, to burke the Convention, will be much resented and personally I think better of its chances than you and others seem to do. However I shall have an opportunity of talking the matter over with you on my way to Dublin.

During this visit he asked me to lend him a book dealing exhaustively with the Home Rule question in all its aspects and I gave him Erskine Childers' *Framework of Home Rule* which I regarded as the best presentation of the Irish case. On 31st July, after the opening of the Convention, he wrote to me again :

I have just finished the *Framework of Home Rule* and certainly it is a splendid book, by far the best of the many I have read on the subject. I will keep it until I can get a copy for myself if I may. The opening of the Convention was all that could be desired—the greatest friendship and an evident desire to give and take. I think Plunkett's selection as Chairman the best that could have been made. I understand my name was suggested and am glad it came to nothing. Plunkett has money and a fine place and can grease the wheels by entertaining, always a useful thing in such events. In strict confidence you will be glad to hear that Erskine Childers has been asked for as Assistant Secretary. Hopwood, the Secretary, impresses me more than favourably. I sit behind Redmond and Devlin. I made the acquaintance of the latter and had a walk with him and Redmond who is looking better than I expected. I suppose we shall have a private conference of constitutional Nationalists ; it is a thing that you might if you get the chance suggest to Redmond and Devlin. It is highly important that we should exchange ideas and not work at random. Duke was admirable and evidently most anxious to make things go. It is said that he was anxious to be Chairman and willing to resign the Chief Secretaryship in that event. It would not have done to have an English chairman and the story may be a *canard*. I wish you would send me a list of really useful books for a reference library as the matter is to be considered at the next meeting. The room we meet in at Trinity College is not a success though the other arrangements are admirable. If the acoustic properties can't be improved we must go elsewhere which I shouldn't mind as Mahaffy in cap and gown by way of fathering everything is rather too much, and he is, as you know, an arrant humbug.

Before the Convention met I contributed to the *Leader* during June and July, 1917, a series of seven articles entitled *An Irish Constitution* in which I endeavoured to bring constructive thought to bear on its problems. These articles dealt consecutively with first principles, legislative and executive authority, legislative and executive machinery, finance and Ulster. My purpose was to outline what might be attained—not to romance about what was unattainable. I therefore did not waste ink in writing about an Irish Republic or a scheme of glorified local government. The great body of moderate opinion in Ireland, was, I pointed out, quite satisfied that Ireland should continue to remain within the Commonwealth of Nations called the British Empire, but was also determined that we should be given full responsibility for the management of our own affairs. That claim was based not only on the moral right of all nations to govern themselves, which was the justification of the Allies' position in the war, but on Ireland's historical position as a European nation, and refusal during successive generations to submit to foreign rule, and on the economic grounds that under such rule Ireland had remained one of the poorest and least developed countries in Northern Europe. The Irish problem had, I claimed, remained unsolved because, unlike that of the self-governing colonies, it had been made a domestic issue in English politics. In South Africa for instance the most complicated questions of finance, executive authority and language had to be solved. Yet South Africans themselves by forbearance, compromise and regard for local conditions, had surmounted a narrow racialism and welded South Africa into a nation which had stood the strain of foreign war and internal revolution. If the Convention was free to follow the same road it would succeed. The Home Rule Act had, I pointed out, two

defects dependent on each other, and both under the circumstances inevitable. It did not give the Irish Parliament full
control of revenue and expenditure and it retained Irish
representation in the Imperial Parliament. Proceeding from
these premises I outlined an Irish Constitution on the basis
of Dominion Home Rule, taking the existing Home Rule
Act as its foundation and advocating the solution of the
Ulster difficulty by some reasonable compromise, such as
my veto project (already referred to) which excluded
partition. No Irish Parliament could, I claimed, rebuild
the fortunes of our people unless it controlled the internal
and external trade and revenue of the whole country. It
must also have the initiative in all questions of constitutional
amendment, and its legislative machinery must be unitary,
not federal, if it was to unite all Irishmen in a common
purpose. I also suggested the establishment of an independent body or board to make public appointments by
competitive examination or by selection according to
qualification. In the Local Appointments Commission
established by Mr. Cosgrave's Government Ireland has now
got exactly such an authority as I had in mind. Full
responsible government involved, I said, three essentials,
namely : a legislature for all purely Irish affairs, an executive
responsible to that legislature, and responsible finance—i.e.
the power not only to veto expenditure but to control and
provide revenue as well. By these tests, I argued, the work
of the Convention would be judged. And so in fact it
proved.

Enclosing the proof of the first article, D. P. Moran, the
editor of the *Leader*, wrote to me on the 15th June, 1917 :

I enclose proof of your introductory article. As you no doubt
have seen I have been emphasising the " Carsonites must not
be coerced " dictum and looking upon it—as I must look upon
it—as vitiating the Convention. I don't suppose you will agree
with me but the Irish Party is hopeless. They should have made
a condition, before entering the Convention, that the " Ulster
must not be coerced " dictum should be scrapped. However
we have to take things as they are. The Peace Conference
agitation and the N. Roscommon and S. Longford by-elections

have done good and they would be all right if the so-called Sinn Féiners were playing forwards in the team. The difficulty is that that they are inclined to think that *they are the team*, and that the rest of the team are greater enemies than the opposing side. However extremists of some kind were a long felt want as the Party and the machine had become rotten. I am publishing an article from Edward Lysaght—the poet and Clare farmer—in the next issue, which is in favour of giving the Convention a trial. I have been so strong about the " Carson must not be coerced " cry—and rightly so—that I can only tolerate the Convention if the people will have it. I am a reasonable extremist in this matter. I don't believe in the goodwill of the English Government, I don't like the conditions of the Convention ; but I certainly don't claim kinship with most of the prevailing extremists.

Moran's views were revealing. His paper expressed the opinion of a large number of moderate people, particularly amongst the country clergy, whose political power and influence were decisive. Events soon proved his views were general. Willie Redmond had died in Flanders on 7th June from wounds received a few hours before when advancing to the attack on Messines Ridge side by side with the Ulster Division. At the ensuing by-election in his constituency, East Clare, Mr. de Valera, released a few weeks before from an English prison, was elected by a majority of three thousand votes over his opponent, Mr. Patrick Lynch, K.C., who stood as an unofficial supporter of the Irish Party. A few weeks later Mr. William T. Cosgrave, another leader of the 1916 Rebellion, was elected for East Kilkenny in a by-election caused by the death of Patrick O'Brien, M.P., one of the whips of the Irish Party. These deaths deprived John Redmond of two of his most trusted counsellors. Mr. de Valera hot from his triumph proclaimed in Dublin on 12th July that "if Ulster stood in the way of Irish freedom Ulster would have to be coerced." [1] Threats which cannot be enforced are always foolish, and this one helped to make partition inevitable.

Edward Martyn, who no longer took an active part in

[1] *Irish Times*, 13th July, 1917.

politics, wrote to me, on 13th July, his reflections on these significant events :

I put off writing to you until after the Clare election which shows that Sinn Féin is going through the country like an epidemic. I must say I do not pity the Parliamentary Party, they are responsible practically for everything. If ten years ago they had tackled the British Government vigorously we would never have had Carsonism out of which everything else has grown. Your articles in the *Leader* are very good. However I have now come to the conclusion that as long as England is a great power she will never relax her grip on Ireland if she can possibly avoid it. They may talk of Home Rule and get up bogus conventions to gain time, and tide them over their difficulties, but nothing short of irresistible pressure will make them give it. That is why I see the only hope in the Sinn Féin idea of going before the Peace Conference. Even then everything will depend upon what state of power or otherwise England comes out of the war. I am of course for Colonial Home Rule but I do not believe that England will ever voluntarily give it. The late Rebellion and now the triumph of Sinn Féin have frightened her into holding on to Ireland firmer than ever.

His fears unfortunately seemed too well justified.

Meanwhile within the Convention itself some progress had been made. On 23rd August Windle reported to me that the Southern Unionists had announced that they would accept a scheme of self-government provided they obtained reasonable representation in the House of Commons, a Senate elected on a restricted franchise, and a guarantee that no change would be made in the Constitution except by a three-fourths majority. Although Sir Alexander McDowell, an astute Belfast solicitor, who was one of the leaders of the Ulster Unionist delegation, had told John Redmond he would not hear the word " partition " from them, the Ulster delegates had not yet shown their hand. As the proceedings were necessarily private and only short reports concerning procedure were issued to the press, Windle and I decided to focus public attention on the principal issues and their possible solution. For this purpose we contributed a series of leading articles to the *Cork Examiner* dealing with various aspects of the Convention's labours such as Dominion Home Rule, Ulster, Proportional Representation, Federalism, and Land Purchase, and with its proceedings generally.

On 31st August Windle wrote to me from Dublin :

The Convention barometer is steadily rising and we may even make the Country a welcome Christmas box. I shall be in Cork at the end of next week and shall have much to tell you if you will come to tea on Sunday with Mary. I saw Sir Francis Hopwood (who strictly *entre nous* will be Lord H. in a few days) this morning. He is very pleased with our articles and quite agreed with the lines of that which I am sending you. He thinks a simple article on P.R. would be useful. I think you could write this, I couldn't.

And on 2nd September he wrote again :

An attempt is being made to press the Swiss Federal system. I think it will fail. Our Bishops are against it and so are other leading members. But I agree with you that, as a last resort, it may (I don't think it will) become necessary. I can't say more than that I think your suggestion for an Ulster veto on the application of legislation to Ulster may be adopted. Please do your best to be at home this day week as I think it is really important that I should see you. All goes well so far. Please God it may continue.

In September the Convention, after visiting Belfast, came south to Cork. We determined to give them a worthy welcome, and it fell to my lot to help in making arrangements for their entertainment, which included providing accommodation in private houses for the members. Windle wrote to me on 3rd September :

I am taking Plunkett, Hopwood and Lord MacDonnell, so you can mark them off your list. I am glad you liked my last article. Two we must have when the Convention comes down to Cork, one on Monday which you can tackle, and a rouser on Tuesday. I will meditate on it and write it. Belfast is having an illustrated guide to the city; we must have the same. I told the Lord Mayor to get Coakley on to this. I can lend blocks of the College and Honan Chapel if needed. Let us do the thing well, it is a great chance. Nothing can be more important than that the Belfast people should be impressed with Cork. I find

that many people were impressed by one of the arguments in
my speech, that Cork had many industries *in esse* of an important
character besides those in a nascent state ; that they would be
just as much injured by discriminative legislation as those in
Belfast, and that the Southern representatives were not such
fools as to cut off their nose to spite their face. I don't think
the Belfast people at all know our industrial relations, and they
should be made to do so.

As our personal contribution to the proceedings we invited
as our guests my old friend Stephen Gwynn, and Erskine
Childers, a member of the Secretariat with whom I had corresponded for many years on Irish affairs. Childers was a remarkable person. Son of a great English Oriental scholar, Robert
Caesar Childers, his family connections on his father's side
were English squires and naval and military officers. One
of the family, the Right Hon. H. C. E. Childers, had acted
successively as First Lord of the Admiralty, Secretary for
War, and Chancellor of the Exchequer in Gladstone's
Governments, and as Chairman of a Commission which
made a momentous report on the financial relations between
Great Britain and Ireland. But his mother was Anglo-
Irish, a Barton of Glendalough, County Wicklow, with
which family he had another link through the marriage of his
father's sister to his mother's brother, Charles William
Barton. It was in the Bartons' house at Glendalough in
the midst of the Wicklow mountains that he had been
brought up, owing to the premature death of his parents.
Educated at Haileybury and Trinity College, Cambridge,
he had obtained, after leaving the University, as was natural
with his political associations, an appointment as a junior
clerk in the House of Commons. He left this position in
1900 to enter politics, but was diverted to military studies
by the South African war in which he served as an artillery
driver in the H.A.C. an experience which bore fruit in
four books, *In the Ranks of the C.I.V.* (1900), Volume V of
The Times' History of the War in South Africa (1907) and two
books on the *rôle* of cavalry in modern warfare. In the
volume of *The Times'* history, in many ways his most
important work, and peculiarly interesting in view of his

later career, he dealt with the period of the guerilla war in South Africa, pointing out that this type of warfare illuminates much that is obscure and difficult in regular war, and reveals, stripped of secondary details, the few dominant factors which decides the issue of great campaigns. It was, however, another book, *The Riddle of the Sands* (1903), not so much a novel as a cautionary tale based on his own experiences when sailing small craft in the Friesian archipelago, which dealt with a possible German invasion, that brought him both fame and popularity and was largely responsible for the formation of the Royal Naval Volunteer Reserve. In 1911 he entered the field of Irish politics with the publication of *The Framework of Home Rule* (the brilliant book already referred to) which had profound influence on Irish political thought. In this volume he propounded the Dominion solution and emphasised with unanswerable arguments the vital importance of fiscal autonomy. As a young man he had been a Unionist and an Imperialist, but his experience in South Africa had altered his views, and this book was written from the standpoint of a Liberal and a Nationalist. Its message, as he pointed out later, was that Ireland should have the form of Government the Irish people wanted.

Sympathising with the Irish Volunteer movement he joined, in May, 1914, a small committee formed in England to supply the Volunteers with arms, and it was he who brought the guns to Howth in his yacht in July, 1914. The story of that expedition he told us one evening after dinner during his visit to Cork. It was a thrilling tale strongly reminiscent of the *Riddle of the Sands*. The rifles were Mausers which he and a friend had bought from some Jews in the underground arms market at Hamburg. After delivery they were loaded on a tug which met Childers' yacht by arrangement near a lightship off the Dutch coast on 27th June, 1914. Childers' crew consisted of himself, his wife, Diarmuid Coffey, Miss Mary Spring Rice, an English friend, Gordon Shepherd, and two Donegal fishermen. They soon found that the rifles would not fit into the yacht unless unpacked and so they had to unpack them. Finally 900 of the 1,000 rifles were stowed away in the little cabin to the height of the bunks and tables. The balance were loaded into Conor O'Brien's yacht which was standing by to help. The tug then towed them to Dover and from there they sailed down the Channel, against head winds all the time, and up the Irish Sea to Holyhead. There the coastguards hailed them but fortunately did not inspect their cargo. The rifles were to be landed at Howth at high water (12 noon) on Sunday, 20th July. It had been arranged that Childers' boat should be met by a motor boat outside the harbour, but as this did not appear he sailed right up to the pier where the Volunteers waited, some crying with emotion at the sight of the arms. After some preliminary confusion Childers rapidly organised the landing and some coastguards who appeared on the scene quickly retired. In their excitement the Volunteers tore the main-sail and Childers had to hoist his trysail for the return journey to Holyhead which was made without incident.

As soon as the European war broke out Childers, like many others, believed that a new chapter was opening in Irish history, and that North and South fighting together under their own leaders would find a common purpose and national unity. He was summoned at once by the Admiralty to undertake reconnaissance work in the North Sea for which his previous experience had so well fitted him. As a flying officer and later as commander of motor patrol boats he served with gallantry and distinction, gaining the D.S.C. From this service he had, owing to his study of Irish constitutional questions, been seconded to act as Assistant Secretary of the Convention.

Our previous correspondence and my knowledge of his career had created in my mind a conception of his personality which our meeting confirmed and later events did nothing to dispel. He was slight, and almost insignificant in build and stature, but his dignity and sincerity combined with a rare charm of manner immediately arrested one's attention. Here one felt was a man in whom a fine intellect and firm purpose combined to forge a character of unusual strength. His experience as a soldier, sailor and airman together with his literary and political ability were a unique combination. He had the exact type of informed, constructive mind which Ireland so sadly needed and it is one of the major tragedies of modern Irish history that his life was cut short before those gifts could be fully devoted to her service. Essentially English in spirit, training and outlook, he was a typical example of that Irish-English strain which has so often been the spearhead of Irish revolt. It was the English quality of doggedness combined with integrity and love of freedom which finally led him to pursue relentlessly to its logical conclusion a policy which he believed to be right but which in fact was fatal both to himself and his adopted country. But that pursuit was animated by no dishonest or evil motives and inspired by the highest sense of duty and patriotism.

Such thoughts were, however, remote from our minds in those pleasant days. The Convention was, indeed, going well. Redmond had made a great speech during the Belfast meeting, one of the finest, Windle said, he had ever delivered. There was, he declared, no length " consistent with reason, sense and justice " to which he would not go to meet the views of Ulstermen. He accepted a position for the Irish Parliament subordinate to that of the United Kingdom. He expressed the greatest readiness to consider safeguards and upheld the right of minorities to full recognition. At its close Lord Midleton, the leader of the Southern Unionists, stood up and warmly shook him by both hands. Even Dr. Mahaffy had declared himself a Home Ruler and taunted the Ulster delegates with desiring to fight the British Government ! At a luncheon given to our visitors by the Cork Harbour Commissioners, Sir Horace Plunkett, the Chairman of the Convention, made a notable speech and sounded a note, to use his own words of " justifiable optimism." In generous terms he specially commended and acknowledged the constructive nature of our articles in the *Cork Examiner*. Cork indeed rose nobly to the occasion. The visitors were not only entertained privately on a lavish scale but taken on excursions to our local beauty spots, and joined our civic fathers in the annual ceremony of Throwing the Dart, when the Lord Mayor in assertion of his authority as Admiral of the Port casts a javelin into the sea at the mouth of the harbour. At Cork also the Convention closed its preliminary or presentation stage. The various solutions of our constitutional problems had been fully propounded and discussed. They were now referred to a Grand Committee representing all parties to prepare a scheme which would reconcile the conflicting views. The moment of decision had arrived.

At its final Cork sitting in the Crawford Technical Institute a resolution thanking the Lord Mayor, the citizens of Cork and all who had shown them hospitality was proposed by the Lord Mayor of Belfast, seconded by the Mayor of Derry and carried by acclamation. Childers wrote to my wife to thank her for our hospitality and expressed the belief that we had made a real friendship which would last. And, indeed, it lasted until the end. Although we then differed politically he sent me by his wife on the eve of his execution a special message of affectionate farewell. No one would have believed then that five years later this clear-headed political thinker, seconded from the Royal Navy to help in framing an Irish Constitution, would meet his end before a firing squad of Irish soldiers during a futile civil war for which in a large measure he was unfortunately himself responsible.

XXII

COMIC relief was afforded us during that autumn of 1917 by the doings of another visitor from England, one Malcolm Lyon, a wealthy business man. Lyon, one of those amiable and sometimes inspired eccentrics who are the salt of English public life, diverted from his normal activities by the war, had turned his house into a hospital and taken several ambulances to France, where his son was serving as a gunner. Then he apparently decided that the time was ripe for the organisation of peace and that Ireland was the key to the international situation. He felt that if the British Government and the leaders of Sinn Féin could be persuaded to submit their differences to an international tribunal, other nations, including Japan, whose activities he particularly, and indeed prophetically, dreaded, would be forced to follow suit. Thus what he described as an International Magna Carta could be promulgated and the war brought to an end. One of his ambitious schemes was to establish an international newspaper to advocate his plan.

Accompanied by Austin Harrison, then editor of the *English Review* (in which I think Lyon was also interested), Major Stuart Stevens, an ancient soldier of fortune, and sundry other satellites, Lyon installed himself at the Shelbourne Hotel, and opened his campaign. He got in touch with the leaders of the Sinn Féin Party through James MacNeill, brother of Eóin, a retired Indian civil servant who was later to become Governor-General of the Irish Free State. The Sinn Féin leaders not unnaturally viewed his activities with considerable suspicion and refused to commit themselves definitely. At the cost of many thousands of pounds he launched his peace project by advertisement in the Irish newspapers. It soon became clear that his doings were equally suspected by the British Government as without reason assigned his advertisements were refused publication in the London press. I believe his sole, if somewhat muddled, purpose was to stop the war in which his son was engaged and his business interests involved.

On the August Bank Holiday he arrived at my house accompanied by Austin Harrison, with a letter of introduction from my energetic friend E. A. Aston, of Dublin, who was acting as his principal Irish adviser. His visit to Cork, strange as it may seem, was to secure the support of the Vatican for his peace plan. Hearing that one of our local Franciscan fathers, famous as an arbitrator in industrial disputes, the Rev. Father Thomas, had considerable influence in Rome, he desired to enlist his aid in obtaining an audience from the Pope. Father Thomas quickly disabused him of this delusion. I saw Lyon again later in Dublin where he kept open house at his hotel. He had undoubtedly excellent sources of information, for he was able to give us full details of the recent serious mutiny in the French Army after the massacre at the Chemin des Dames, the news of which had naturally been carefully suppressed. Of course nothing came of all this misdirected activity, and Lyon, who combined in his large and jovial person the ingenuousness of Broadbent with the ingenuity of Robinson Crusoe, eventually returned to London a sadder and I fear a poorer man. He had, however, undoubtedly contributed to the gaiety of the nation.

Meanwhile the proceedings of the Grand Committee of the Convention appointed to formulate an agreed scheme for the government of Ireland were going well. On the proposition of Sir Alexander McDowell the Grand Committee had appointed a special sub-committee of nine to negotiate and draft proposals to this end. McDowell was an expert negotiator and not only had the confidence of the Ulster Unionist Council which he represented, but was also on good terms with John Redmond. Unfortunately he attended only one meeting. A serious illness, which resulted in his death, ended his labours for peace. His place was filled by Mr. Pollock, a cautious and unimaginative Belfast business man. Nevertheless by the end of October, 1917,

with the sole exception of the fiscal powers to be exercised
by an Irish Parliament, this sub-committee had arrived at
provisional agreement on every vital point, and Redmond
had come to believe that a final settlement was in sight.
The fundamental basis of this agreement was that the
Unionists should be assured of forty per cent. of the seats
in the Lower House. This representation, in view of the
proposed composition of the Senate, would have ensured
at least a balance of power between Nationalists and
Unionists at a joint sitting of the two houses and thus made
revolutionary legislation impossible. This expedient had
been accepted by the Nationalist representatives because
they placed the attainment of a united self-governed Ireland
before all other considerations and believed that if this
were secured all else would ultimately follow. Had this
plan been ratified by the Ulster politicians the question of
fiscal powers would clearly have become, if not academic,
almost certainly adjustable. But the Advisory Committee
of the Ulster Unionist Council, to whom these agreed
proposals unfortunately had to be referred by the Ulster
representatives, rejected them on the peculiar pretext that
the principle of strengthening Unionist representation in the
Lower House by the addition of nominated members was
undemocratic ! The same argument if pressed to its
logical conclusion would of course have wrecked the entire
Ulster case for special treatment. Thus was destroyed a
great opportunity for peace. Although the Ulster representatives undertook to submit alternative proposals they
never did so.

With the ending of this first attempt at compromise the
question of fiscal control began to dominate the negotiations.
Childers, fully conversant with these difficulties, wrote me
that he felt that the only answer to Sinn Féin was to advocate
and explain Dominion Home Rule as I had tried to do in
the *Cork Examiner* articles. It was clear that Childers'
searching mind was now becoming attracted by the Sinn
Féin solution.

As the year ended it became known that the Grand
Committee had failed to find agreement and that the

Convention was to re-assemble in January. Windle wrote
to me on 29th December :

> Next week will be a very crucial time and everything depends
> on careful handling of the situation. I wish you would see and
> talk to the Lord Mayor and Macmullen (to both of whom I have
> written) on the following lines :—Midleton and the Southern
> Unionists agree to an Irish Parliament with Judicature, Police,
> internal taxation and administration—all Imperial services *and*
> Customs reserved to the Imperial Parliament. Irish representa-
> tion there in diminished numbers. Under pressure from
> MacDonnell they agreed Customs should be reserved *during* the
> war and such subsequent period as may be necessary for the
> consideration of the question by a strong Commission appointed
> by *both* Parliaments. I am strongly of opinion we should back
> this as it would isolate Belfast which would not hold out. I don't
> like giving up Customs of course but to hold them will mean the
> failure of the Convention—a great disaster—and of course we
> are not giving up what we have got. Further I am convinced
> that if an Irish Parliament once got going it would insist on
> having Customs—and to get it going is the first thing of import-
> ance. If you agree with me on these points and can see these
> two men it will be a good thing.

This letter posed the dilemma which now faced the
Nationalist members of the Convention, namely whether
they should waive their claim for complete fiscal autonomy
in order to secure agreement with the influential Southern
Unionists and so isolate the Northern opposition, or whether
they should remain steadfast in their demand for financial
independence and thus destroy any possibility of a settlement. I agreed with Windle that, although not the best
solution, the former alternative was infinitely preferable.

In a leading article inspired by him, which appeared in
the *Cork Examiner* on 15th January, 1918, I pointed out
that if agreement as to the future government of Ireland,
which was the object of the Convention, was to be realised,
concessions by all parties were as inevitable as they had
been under similar conditions in South Africa and Australia.
Irish Nationalists could not (I pointed out) reasonably expect
the Convention to agree upon a scheme which would

embody their maximum demands. Their minimum demand was a parliament for *all* Ireland with full jurisdiction over purely Irish affairs and an executive government responsible to that parliament alone. Without impairing that demand there was, I suggested, ample scope for reasonable concession. In a letter outlining his views concerning this article Windle wrote to me on 8th January, 1918 : " I am sorry to say that I think Childers has been and is a dangerous doctrinaire and his influence is at present harmful. But I still hope for a settlement." Windle's complaint was unfortunately true. Childers undoubtedly used his authority and ability at that time to widen the schism in the Nationalist ranks. Windle also reported that " a great deal of our present trouble is due to Redmond's failure to have meetings of the Nationalist members as all other parties have done. His idea was honourable—that there should be no caucus—but its operation has been bad."

Redmond's refusal to countenance the organisation of a definite Nationalist party within the Convention now bore bitter fruit. On 8th January, the same day as Windle wrote to me, Redmond made a powerful appeal to the Convention to come to a settlement, pointing out in prophetic words that the alternative was an Ireland ruled by the bayonet in which there would be no place for moderate men like himself. He had been absent a good deal from the Convention through illness and was in fact a dying man. Although he was only sixty-two the heart-breaking worry and disappointments of the last two years had left their mark. Soon afterwards he tabled an amendment in which he accepted the proposals of the Southern Unionists if the Convention received an undertaking from the British Government that these proposals would be forthwith passed into law. On 15th January, a few hours before he rose to propose this amendment, he learned that he could no longer count on the support of Joe Devlin, his principal lieutenant, nor on that of Dr. O'Donnell, the Catholic Bishop of Raphoe, one of the oldest adherents of his party, and that they were supported in their attitude by other Nationalists. At this critical moment he thus found himself

deserted by some of his oldest friends and principal supporters. Realising that while he might carry his amendment
he would inevitably split the Nationalist ranks he declined
to proceed. It was a characteristic action. He knew, no
one better, that this defection would probably destroy his
life's work, but he rightly refused to reflect on the motives
of those who deserted him. From that tragic moment any
real hope of settlement was dead.

In February a delegation from the Convention crossed
to London to interview the Prime Minister, Lloyd George.
His statement did nothing to allay Nationalist suspicions.
Childers wrote to me on 23rd February that he had just
returned from London in no elation of spirit, and that,
although failure was not inevitable, if it occurred, the British
Government would be wholly to blame. Redmond, who was
now seriously ill, took no part in these discussions. A few
days later, on 6th March, 1918, after an operation in London,
he died worn out in the service of Ireland. If he did not
die of a broken heart he certainly died, as he told Father
Bernard Vaughan, " a heart-broken man." He had suffered
not only the perfidy of British politicians but, what was far
worse, the base ingratitude of his own people. After his
death his enemies made jubilant reference to the fact
that during the Convention he was so often insulted as he
approached the main entrance of Trinity College that he
was compelled to use another gate. The young " heroes "
responsible for this outrage may rest satisfied that they
inflicted much pain and bitterness on a noble and sensitive
man.

In no country is the life of a prominent politician a bed
of roses. He is the target for the malicious criticism of his
enemies and the no less injurious flattery of his friends.
Like a great actor he is always in the limelight. The
abnormal nature of Irish politics tends to aggravate these
conditions, and many Irish politicians become slaves of their
own egoism and the victims of their friends' flattery. The
exceptional charm of John Redmond's character was his
utter lack of vanity or pride. Jealousy, that devouring
canker of small minds, was utterly foreign to his nature.

With this quality he combined a quiet dignity of manner, which while it placed one absolutely at ease in converse or consultation could also be gently used to closure a bore. Essentially a man of simple tastes, he was happiest in his home at Aughavannagh, Parnell's old shooting box in the Wicklow hills. There, like O'Connell at Darrynane, he found amongst the mountains that peace and quiet which was denied him in the political arena. In the company of a few old friends he could enjoy those country sports with rod and gun which were his principal recreation. His London residence was equally simple ; a small old-fashioned flat in a dreary part of Kensington. Had he wished he could with his natural gifts have undoubtedly earned a large income at the Bar, but he chose rather to serve his country and lived and died a comparatively poor man.

Moderation was, I think, the key-note of his character. He disliked " wild men," and his well balanced mind had no use for extremism in any form. He was a realist in a very real and honourable sense, neither being misled himself, nor if he could help it allowing others to be misled. Thwarted at every turn by malicious men, misunderstood by fools and despised by fanatics as an opportunist, he set himself the hardest task which a national leader can under-take—that of reconciliation—for while it is easy to wage war it is far more difficult and less heroic to make peace. His clear angular handwriting, very neat and very legible, reflected the orderliness of his mind. It also indicated his steady nerve and courage. He was indeed absolutely fearless, as he showed when as a young man in 1880, beaten and bleeding, he faced a hostile crowd at Enniscorthy with Parnell, up to his last moments when he went to the operation-table with a cheery courage that was the admiration of his doctors. His good faith was equally inflexible. He was utterly incapable of a shabby word or deed. He failed as a political leader only because he treated others as they should have treated him. It was a failure of which those who loved him need not be ashamed.

He was the last great Irish orator in the classic tradition. His speeches were not emotional in content like those of his brother William, with whom he shared a peculiarly vibrant quality of voice ; it was reason that reinforced and inspired his rhetoric, and the emphasis placed on every phrase had been decided in advance. Differing from most great orators, he shrank from popular demonstration of all kinds, accepting them rather as the necessary burdens of his position. No prominent politician ever took less pains to attract a following. He detested fuss or ostentation and pre-ferred the privacy of a personal room in a country hotel to the most generous private hospitality. Many were the English Liberal magnates whom, during the Home Rule campaign, it was necessary to smooth down on this account. He realised fully the disability which this idiosyncrasy laid upon him. " I am a crank," he once wrote to me, "on the question of staying with friends. I always stay at an hotel."

But this remoteness and reticence had its other side. It enabled him to see things whole. Although a man of deep convictions he yet lacked passion. In a country where exaggeration is too often mistaken for strength, where malicious slander is esteemed as wit, and where suspicion is a political disease, his temperate, almost judicial, language and transparent sincerity often disappointed the crowd. He credited others with honest motives and never stooped to vituperation. Even after the Parnell Split when the fires of political passion blazed high he called the people to the consideration of great issues stripped of personalities. It was indeed his demeanour at that time which made him afterwards the inevitable leader of a reunited party. He alone had shown himself big enough to lead. Yet it was his generous judgment of others and his lack of vehemence in expression and thought that constituted his chief defect as a politician, if not as a man. A more suspicious man might perhaps have succeeded where he failed. Lacking that daemonic spirit which frightens as well as inspires, and which made Parnell a great leader, he shared Parnell's natural indolence and love of country life.

But whatever he did was done well and methodically. No busy politician was ever a more punctual or courteous correspondent—a habit Parnell certainly did not share. To the majority of his countrymen he was known as a political leader and orator, but his real greatness lay, I think, elsewhere. Rather it is the loyal friend, the man of unswerving honour, the wise counsellor, in whose presence jealousy and conceit, petty spite and mean imputations simply melted away, that those of us who knew and loved him will always remember with pride.

Some may ask, as we often do in Ireland, what did he sacrifice? He underwent imprisonment, but so did many others. He did not risk his life, but he devoted it to his country's service. He was not ambitious or energetic, he loved leisure; yet in his youth he turned away from an easy and pleasant way of life as a clerk in the House of Commons to follow Parnell. When Parnell died he was still a young man and could have quite honourably left politics for a certain success at the Bar. Yet he went on, prompted by a sense of loyalty to Parnell and devotion to Ireland. To be constantly in narrow means, constantly anxious, constantly overworked, suffering a publicity which he loathed, finally condemned to see his supreme effort frustrated at the eleventh hour by the force of unpredictable circumstances;—these were the sacrifices which John Redmond made. His reward was to be repudiated and denounced by a generation which had yet to learn, as they learned three years later when they were forced to accept Partition, that true freedom is rarely served by bloodshed and violence and that in politics compromise is inevitable. Yet it can be said of John Redmond that none of Ireland's sons has ever served her with greater sincerity or nobler purpose.

It was characteristic of him that he expressed the wish to be buried in the family vault at the old Knight Templars' chapel yard of St. John's, Wexford. There amongst his own people rather than in the national burial place at Glasnevin he desired his remains to rest. On a grey misty March morning with a cold wind blowing in from the sea—reflecting, one felt, the mood of a community united in love and grief—they brought him home to Wexford. As the coffin, covered by the flag that lay on Parnell's bier, passed through the narrow streets of the old town I realised we were ending an epoch. " The hopes of a generation " I wrote in my diary " lie buried in his grave. We have to-day closed a chapter—a sad and tragic chapter—of Irish history." One might paraphrase Yeats and say

> Self-governed Ireland's dead and gone
> It lies with Redmond in the grave.

As we came back along the water front a naval motor-launch back from patrol drew into the quay carrying the crew of a collier sunk that morning off the Tuskar by a German submarine—one man lying on a stretcher, another bleeding from a wound. Here were the outward and visible signs of those powers of darkness which Redmond had held at bay and which were soon to rend us asunder. We had buried not only a great leader but also the things he stood for—dignity, moderation, reconciliation, unity.

In the concluding stage of the Convention the ordinary rank and file of the Nationalists and the Southern Unionists, who had believed in Redmond's policy, carried by a narrow majority the reservation of Customs to the Imperial Parliament through which alone that policy was possible. Those who opposed it were the Ulster Unionists and the extreme Nationalists supported by the representatives of the Catholic Church, a strange combination. Once that difficulty was removed the Nationalist forces reunited to pass the report as a whole by a majority of fifteen. Windle wrote to me on 9th April with mingled bitterness and optimism :

I suppose you will be thinking about an article for the *Examiner* when the Convention report comes out. It will be a good report : it might have been a much stronger one but for the rabble rout— whom personally and individually I will never forgive for that act—who killed Redmond and impeded a settlement ; and why ? I wish I had the *mot d'enigme*—anyway nothing will drive it out of the heads of the Unionists that the Bishops—afraid of their own position (of which indeed they have every reason to be afraid)—deliberately set themselves to break Home Rule by their policy. What they have done by their action anyway is to disgust their religious opponents and alienate their own co-religionists in large numbers. To hear the things said about them on both sides makes one realise that " No priests in politics " is not an unwise rule. However if I may offer an opinion I think the line of your article should be—

1. This scheme offers far more *at once* than we have ever been offered before—far beyond the 1914 Act.

2. It adds police and post office automatically at the end of the war.

3. It almost certainly means control of Customs within a few years unless—as is probable—a federation is set up first.

4. Above all it has been accepted by all the Southern Unionists, most of the Nationalists, five or six Nationalist members of Parliament and five of six Labour representatives. That ought to go for something.

Childers, on the other hand, wrote that he thought that something had been accomplished in getting the land-lords' representatives to agree to Home Rule and he believed that the Government was in earnest. His optimism was alas unjustified and the leading article was never written. The Government was indeed in earnest but not about Home Rule. The pledge which Lloyd George had given to Sir Horace Plunkett in his letter of 26th February, 1918, namely that on receiving the report of the Convention the Government would " proceed with the least possible delay to submit legislative proposals to Parliament " was never carried out. On the same day as the report of the Convention was submitted to Parliament Lloyd George introduced the Man Power Bill which applied conscription not only to Great Britain but to Ireland. He declared that the questions of conscription and Home Rule did not stand together ; " each must be taken on its merits." With the Germans almost at the gates of Paris the British Government might perhaps be excused for making a panic decision which reflection should have told them could have no fruitful result ; but they cannot be pardoned for the flagrant breach of faith by which it was accomplished. Under such conditions the report of the Convention was still-born; its anxious labours were in vain. Redmond's words " Better for us never to have met than to have met and failed " must remain its epitaph. Bereft of all hope the Irish people sullen and defiant were plunged into a maelstrom of reaction, violence and hatred from which they are only now beginning to emerge.

XXIII

THE introduction of the Conscription Bill had the same effect as a declaration of war on the Irish nation and united all parties in a common purpose. The Irish Party, now led by John Dillon, fought the measure through all its stages in Parliament and then returned to Ireland. A Conference representative of all Nationalist parties, summoned by the Lord Mayor of Dublin, met at the Mansion House and formulated a common policy of resistance, denying the right of any external authority to impose compulsory military service in Ireland against the clearly expressed will of the people. The Catholic Hierarchy described it as " an oppressive and inhuman law which the Irish people have a right to resist by every means that are consonant with the law of God." A statement of Ireland's case, drafted by Tim Healy and de Valera, was prepared by the Conference for presentation to President Wilson. On 23rd April a general strike, called as a protest by the trade unions, paralysed the normal life of three-fourths of the country. In every parish the people with ecclesiastical approval pledged themselves " to resist conscription by the most effective means at their disposal." Large sums of money were raised by public subscription to finance this opposition, In Cork the City Parochial Committee, of which I acted as Secretary, collected over £5,000.

It soon became clear that the British Government could only enforce conscription at the price of chaos and bloodshed. John Muldoon, M.P., reported to me that at the Mansion House Conference, Tim Healy had been, as usual, mischievous, de Valera helpful and anxious for national unity, Griffith stubborn and impossible. The National Directory of the United Irish League met in Dublin on 30th April and John Dillon, who was elected Chairman, spoke to us at great length on the situation. He said that, though the conscription issue was still in doubt, he believed that the

Government would eventually drop both Conscription and Home Rule. The Sinn Féin party was, he said, determined to force a contest in the East Cavan by-election in spite of suggestions for a truce. We agreed that in that event the Irish Party must either contest the seat or abdicate. A resolution which I proposed " joined in the universal and passionate protest which had been made by the Irish people against conscription and declared that Ireland had the same right to self-determination in this matter as Great Britain and the self-governing colonies."

Finally, on 18th May, 1918, Viscount French, who had just been appointed Lord Lieutenant, announced that conscription had been temporarily abandoned and a German " plot " discovered. On the same day the principal Sinn Féin leaders were arrested and sent to England where they were held without trial or charge. The only evidence of a German plot disclosed to the public concerned the rising of 1916, the German connection with which had been known for two years.

During the sittings of the Convention Sinn Féin had experienced a check : in three by-elections the Irish Party candidates had been returned. Now all trust in constitutional methods vanished. The issues raised by the proposed enforcement of conscription placed constitutional Nationalists in an impossible position. The fact that, in common with the great majority of the people, they had recognised the authority of the Imperial Parliament and that their political demand was only for a devolution of its powers to the Irish people made it difficult to deny that Parliament's right to impose conscription in an hour of dire peril for both countries. But if the attempt to enforce conscription placed the constitutional leaders in a serious dilemma its non-enforcement was even more fatal to their policy and themselves. No greater victory for the Sinn Féin policy could have been conceived. From that moment the fate of the constitutional movement was sealed. A month later on 20th June, Arthur Griffith, then detained in an English prison, was elected for East Cavan by a substantial majority. His relatively moderate Hungarian policy was, however, already as dead as that of the Irish Party, and the real leadership of the Sinn Féin party had passed into the hands of younger and more violent men.

The reaction of the ordinary Nationalist to these events may perhaps be illustrated by a letter which I wrote that autumn to my friend, Stephen Gwynn, M.P., who was still endeavouring to promote voluntary recruiting to the British forces.

My dear Gwynn,

I understand your position concerning recruiting which seems to me to be untenable. There is as I see it only one question on which an Irishman is entitled to be satisfied before he takes part in this new recruiting campaign. I would put in this way. " Is this a war in which the interest of my country demand that I ought to imperil my life and ask my fellow countrymen to imperil theirs ? " You answer this question in the affirmative and you defend your answer on the grounds first that the Allies' original aims were above reproach and have only become tainted through following Germany's bad example, and secondly, that as regards Ireland we are ourselves responsible for the refusal of freedom because we want to coerce Ulster and Ulster must not be coerced. Now it seems to me that both these statements are fallacies.

As regards the first you will I am sure agree that two wrongs do not make a right. The claims of Italy to shut Austria out of the Eastern Adriatic, to possess portions of Asia Minor and the Southern Tyrol ; the claims of the old Russia (now dissolved in chaos) to Poland and Constantinople ; the claims of England to Mesopotamia, part of Persia and most of the German colonies; the claims of France (Oh what a fall was there, my countrymen!) to the valley of the Saar, the left bank of the Rhine and to Syria and Kurdistan ;—These things cannot be denied and they are indefensible. It is for them we are now waging war. You say the war has changed many things. So it has. It has changed itself. I believe firmly that England entered this war reluctantly. She was not ready. That is her best defence. But the attack on Belgium with its menace to the control of the narrow seas made war inevitable and she entered the lists. She fought and she justly fought in her own self defence, but also for the defence of Belgium. How different are the aims of the Allies now ? President Wilson enunciates the loftiest moral principles in

Washington, whilst his allies in Europe pursue far different designs. The aims of the American idealist and the intriguing European diplomatists will clash when it is no longer necessary to pay lip service to the principles he formulates. Have you any doubts as to who will be the victor in that unequal contest?

So much for your first proposition. Your second seems to be the negation of all common sense and legitimate authority. You claim that Ulster must not be coerced and that England is not responsible for the present *impasse*. Who else is responsible? If England cleared out of this country in the morning how long would the Ulster problem exist? What would have become of the Ulster " rebels " if they were not backed by the whole force of a great English party? Why was it necessary to disrupt the British Constitution before Home Rule could even be interred on the Statute Book? What was the fate of every attempt we made to solve the Ulster difficulty? We agreed to county option in 1914. We carried concession and consideration to the verge of weakness in the hope of securing a United Ireland. But the Ulster Party and their English backers were adamant. They were out not to partition Ireland but to smash Home Rule. Without the support of the English ruling classes Ulster would have been impotent. Without the undemocratic delay of the Parliament Act Ulster's resistance would never have crystallised. In an independent Ireland the Ulster question would have been settled in twenty-four hours on just and reasonable terms. No one knows better than your hard-headed Northerner how to make a virtue of necessity. After all the Southern States had a far greater right to secede from the Union than Ulster had to secede from Ireland, yet the North fought a long and bloody war rather than concede their claim. But the United States was then only a loosely knit political confederation and we are a nation. You write as if you admit that Ulster had and now has a legitimate demand to make, but you must remember that her present position is based on an immoral and unconstitutional pledge given her by craven-hearted English politicans. It never should have been given, and if it is as I claim immoral and unconstitutional on what ground can it be redeemed? Was ever a minority given such a pledge unless it be the German minority in Bohemia, which it is now one of our war aims to undo? It is the very negation of order and liberty. No, the Ulster claim is absurd. The time will come, and that before long, when the name of Carson will be cursed by every patriotic Englishman, for he has

" furnished for the future a complete grammar of anarchy "
to every clique and combination who desire to oppose a law
they dislike. You write of the Act suspending Home Rule as
if it was passed with our consent, but surely nothing could be
more untrue. We had no option in the matter. We had to take
it or leave it—tricked at the last moment. Mr Shortt now tells
us that the Home Rule Act is permanently suspended. If the
war had not taken place no doubt the ingenuity of English
politicians would have devised some other means of swindling
poor Redmond. You speak of Ulster resistance as the disease
to be cured. It is only the symptom. It is the " predominant
partner," the combination of the landed and monied interests
that governs England who will not have Home Rule. Take for
example the Convention. When Lloyd George heard there
was a risk that the honest and patriotic Southern Unionists
might agree to Dominion Home Rule he sent his famous letter
which cut down and limited the powers of the Convention lest
it might attain unity amongst reasonable Irishmen and leave
the Ulster spokesmen exposed for what they are—a foreign body
in the Irish body politic. That would have laid bare the truth
to the world and compelled the Government to legislate, so
you were all told to be good boys and go home and agree, or
preferably disagree, to a constitution for Ireland " within the
Empire," but " according to plan " ! Is it any wonder you
failed ? As for Sinn Féin, of course it has made a settlement
more difficult, but it also is only a symptom and how can Ulster
complain ? Carson at all events does not do so. Listen to him
in 1914. " I am not sorry for the armed drilling of those who
are opposed to me in Ireland. I certainly have no right to
complain of it. I started that with my own friends." Believe
me if there had been no Carson there would have been no
Casement ; if there had been no Curragh mutiny and Larne
gun-running in 1914 there would have been no rebellion in
1916. No wonder Campbell at all events has the decency to
feel remorse. But even were I to concede your claim that Ulster
must not be coerced you would only escape from one horn of a
dilemma to be impaled upon the other, for if Ulster must not
be coerced how can you justify conscription, the present system
of coercion or indeed any form of English Government in the
rest of Ireland ? Upon this I leave you. I am glad that you
do not seek to justify the advertisements of your recruiting
Council which are mere pettifogging attempts to cloud the issue.

They only justify those who seek to slander this country and misrepresent its position. Your whole scheme is designed to make straight the path for conscription, to divide the country and to drug us into passive acceptance of the inevitable. I understand your position and you are entitled to be heard, for you have practised what you preach, and whether you are right or wrong you have had the courage of your convictions. I am sure that you also understand mine. Its tragedy is that I am as anxious as you are to see Germany beaten and punished for her crimes, and I have, as you know, worked for that end. So far as the Allied aims are those of President Wilson I pray that they may be attained. If such principles as his dominate the Peace Conference all should be well. It is because those principles have not been applied to Ireland and are not applied elsewhere unless it suits the selfish purpose of the Great Powers, that I cannot help you in your work. The recruiting question cannot be separated from the larger issues. Until these are solved honestly and justly you are in my judgment only screening those who do not want them solved at all. We are not drawing out of the war because we might be assisting England but because we would not be assisting Ireland, a far different reason. The answer to your argument can be put into one sentence. Give Ireland the right of " self-determination " both as regards Ulster and Conscription and then we can get on with the War.

Yours sincerely,

JOHN J. HORGAN.

This letter proves that, like many millions of other Europeans, I had taken President Wilson's noble platitudes seriously. Twelve months later, in June, 1919, he confessed shamefacedly to the Irish American delegate in Paris that he was quite unable to put them into effect as the Committee of four (Clemenceau, Lloyd George, Orlando and himself) had agreed that no small nation could appear before them without their unanimous consent. " You have touched," he said, " the great metaphysical tragedy of to-day. When I gave utterance to those words I said them without the knowledge that nationalities existed which are coming to us day after day. . . . You do not know and cannot appreciate the anxieties I have experienced as the result of these many millions of peoples having their hopes raised by what I have said." [1]

The feelings of indignation which I expressed in this letter to Stephen Gwynn had already led me, in the summer of 1918, to publish a political pamphlet which attained some celebrity. Speaking at Ladybank on 5th October, 1912, Mr. Asquith, referring to the speeches and actions of Sir Edward Carson and his friends, had said, " The reckless rodomontade at Blenheim in the early summer, as developed and amplified in this Ulster campaign, furnishes for the future a complete grammar of anarchy." Taking this speech as my text I called the pamphlet " *The Complete Grammar of Anarchy* by Members of the War Cabinet and their friends." In a short foreword signed with my initials I wrote :

It is not often that political chickens come home to roost as quickly as those which were hatched in North-East Ulster during the years 1912–14. Rebellion was openly preached, men were drilled, arms were landed, the assistance of the Kaiser was invoked, the forces of the Crown were defied and their commanders seduced from their allegiance. Nay more, the Protestant Church of Ulster, through the mouths of its leading dignitaries solemnly blessed and consecrated these criminal performance. No one was prosecuted, no one was interned, the criminals are still at large posing as pillars of the law and acting as guardians of the State. Nor was this conduct confined to Ulster. The platforms of England rang with the protestations of Mr. Bonar Law and his party that if Ulster resisted the law she would not be alone. No wonder that German statesmen, ignorant of the cant, insincerity and humbug of English politics, believed that England was so divided and rent with domestic discord that the time had come to make a bold bid for the dominion of the world. No wonder that Ireland re-learnt the old lesson, that English politicians—one cannot call them statesmen—will yield to violence and threats when they will not even listen to the voice of justice and right. It required fifty years of constant political agitation, ending with three general elections and the alteration of the British Constitution, to place upon the Statute Book a moderate Home Rule Act giving the Irish people limited

[1] Evidence of Frank P. Walsh : Hearing of the Peace Treaty, 30th August, 1919.

powers over their domestic affairs, and the moment it was passed it was suspended indefinitely ! It only required a fortnight to pass a Conscription Act for Ireland against the unanimous voice of her people, an Act imperilling the lives, the fortunes, and the future of the entire Irish race. Need one point the moral ? Could contempt for the oft-quoted principles of " self-determination " and liberty for small nationalities be more eloquently expressed ? If Ireland required any justification for her determination to oppose this unjust law she would find it in the declarations of Sir Edward Carson and his friends which are here set forth in chronological order. They were directed not against an unjust and immoral law passed in defiance of the express will of the Irish people, but against a measure of elementary justice necessary not only to the free development of Ireland but to the re-construction of the United Kingdom, and demanded by an overwhelming majority of the Irish race for several generations. I have not commented on them in any way, for they are far too perfect in themselves to need embellishment. Mr. Asquith called them " the complete grammar of anarchy." Nothing more need be said.

J. J. H.

The pamphlet was " respectfully dedicated to Sir Edward Carson, K.C., M.P., P.C., President of the Ulster Provisional Government and ex-member of the War Cabinet in recognition of his inestimable services to the British Empire !" and contained full details of the offices subsequently held by the Ulster " rebels." Owing to war conditions it was necessary to submit the manuscript to the official censor before publication. Many years afterwards Major Bryan Cooper, who was then acting in that capacity, told me that it presented him with a difficult problem. He recognised the political implications which it raised but he could not well censor the utterances of cabinet ministers and so apart from a trifling alteration in my foreword no objection was raised. The cover thus bore the necessary inscription " Passed by the Censor." But the Government soon discovered that *The Grammar* raised unpleasant questions for its real authors, and some months after its publication they gave orders for it to be seized. Raids were accordingly made by the police on my publishers, Maunsel & Co., and on several booksellers and newsagents, and all available copies of the pamphlet were confiscated. This, in view of the fact that it had been passed by the censor, was not only unfair but, as I think, an illegal proceeding. The matter was raised in the House of Commons by Mr. Jeremiah MacVeagh, M.P., one of the Nationalist Party, who asked the Chief Secretary for Ireland whether he was aware that two volumes entitled respectively *The Handbook for Rebels* [1] and *The Grammar of Anarchy* were being seized by the police and confiscated ; whether these volumes consisted entirely of extracts from speeches of Unionist politicians and whether he would state on what grounds and with what authority the volumes were siezed. Mr. Samuels, the Irish Attorney-General, stated in reply " The volumes, as their titles proclaim, are intended to instigate rebellion and create anarchy. They are seditious publications and liable to seizure and confiscation under the Defence of the Realm Regulations."

Under the heading " Seditious Publications " the Irish papers published two days later the following letter from me :

Sir,

I see by to-day's papers that Mr. Samuels on behalf of our latest Chief Secretary, stated yesterday in the House of Commons that *The Handbook for Rebels* and *The Complete Grammar of Anarchy* were intended to instigate rebellion and create anarchy and were seditious publications liable to seizure under the Defence of the Realm Regulations. As I am responsible for the compiling and publication of *The Complete Grammar of Anarchy* will you permit me to state :

1. That it contains nothing but an accurate report of the speeches and doings of the members of the War Cabinet and their friends.

2. That it was duly passed for publication by the censor.

3. That its title is not mine but Mr. Asquith's.

4. That its intention was not to instigate rebellion or create anarchy but to point out that the blackguardly incite-

[1] This was a somewhat similar pamphlet compiled by my friend Senator Joseph Johnston, an Ulster Nationalist and Fellow of Trinity College, Dublin.

ments to violence which it contains had already done so and were primarily responsible for the present condition of Ireland.

I know that it is very unpleasant for these gentlemen to be reminded of their criminal past, but if these pamphlets are seditions they should prosecute their authors and not seek to wreak their vengeance on innocent newsagents. I shall be quite pleased to stand in the dock at any time with Sir Edward Carson, Mr. Bonar Law and the present Lord Chancellors of England and Ireland.

Yours, etc.,

JOHN J. HORGAN.

Lacaduv, Cork.
   19th February, 1919.

The Government needless to state did not pursue the matter further. An action was, however, brought by a newsagent in the civil courts against the police for the illegal seizure of the pamphlets. The King's Bench Division struck it off the file on the grounds that it was frivolous and vexatious and the Court of Appeal, Sir James Campbell (Carson's principal Lieutenant) as Lord Chancellor presiding, upheld this decision. Campbell thus sat in judgment on his own speeches, many of which were quoted in the book.

Annoyed by the Government's high handed action I decided to publish a second edition of the pamphlet in England where I reckoned they would hesitate to repeat their illegal conduct and where it was no longer necessary to submit it to the censor. In this project I received much assistance and encouragement from that noble Irishwoman, Mrs. Alice S. Green (to whom Erskine Childers had introduced me shortly before) and the distinguished author, Dame Una Pope Hennessy. With their help I secured an English publisher, Messrs. Nisbet and Co., and the second edition with my name on the title page was published in London in the autumn of 1919. A copy was sent to every member of the House of Commons. In the new edition I omitted the original foreword, now superfluous, and added a chronological record of Irish political events from 1912 to

1919, thus enabling the reader to trace step by step the surrender of successive British governments to the menace of Sir Edward Carson and his friends ; the inevitable effect upon the mass of the Irish people in destroying the last vestiges of their faith in Great Britain and in forcing them to adopt on their own part a revolutionary policy ; the complete immunity enjoyed by the Ulster " rebels " in openly arming part of that province to resist the law, and the rigorous repression later dealt out to the rest of Ireland in similar circumstances. The English edition was soon sold out, but figured in political controversy for many years afterwards. It was often quoted by Labour members in the House of Commons and was used in cross-examination during the Communist trial of 1923. As the *Manchester Guardian* wrote in a leading article on 24th September, 1920, under the heading of *Anarchists All* :

The restoration of lost respect for peace, law and orderly government is the sorest need of this country as it is of others. But Mr. Lloyd George's Cabinet are not among the tried friends of that cause. A famous little book called *The Grammar of Anarchy* is now being used all over the world as a kind of anarchist's Bible and it is composed simply and solely of incitements to riot, rebellion and lynching quoted word for word from public speeches made by colleagues or political supporters of Mr. Lloyd George. No well known Labour orator has ever approached the contents of this manual of crime in directness of incitement or in contemptuous disregard of any obligation to use caution in instigating " direct action."

It is doubtful even now whether the words and deeds of Carson and his supporters have yet exhausted their evil influence.

XXIV

WINDLE had accepted with enthusiasm the invitation to become a member of the Convention, for he believed that a settlement could be found. To this end he exerted all his powers, and no one was more disappointed than he at the inconclusive result of its labours. In spite of his youthful flirtation with Nationalist circles in Birmingham and his later interest in the Gaelic League he was by tradition and temperament in sympathy with the Anglo-Irish " ascendancy " class. He was in fact by blood and breeding more English than Irish and much of the worry and anxiety he suffered when in Cork was due to the conflict between his English attitude, outlook and training and his Irish surroundings. Dark Rosaleen with all her peculiarities had now become for him a painful reality. To make matters worse his Anglo-Irish relatives, whom he now met frequently, did not share his Nationalist views. During the Convention he wrote of the Southern Unionists in a revealing passage : " These are the men who really appeal to me, and of course by birth and associations I belong to them and understand them. They are gentlemen and you know that their word is their bond. I liked all of them although I began with the greatest prejudice against Midleton, Jameson and several others. Yet I was wrong. These men acted in a most patriotic spirit, and if all the rest had been like them the Convention would have been a success." [1] As we have already seen he deeply disagreed with the attitude of the Irish Catholic Hierarchy at this time, and we find his old friend, Father Michael Maher, S.J. (March, 1918), then on his death-bed, warning him in the following words of the dangerous position in which he was placing himself :

What you say about your own feelings and the pressure of the external situation pushing you into increasing hostility towards the action of the Bishops had been making me a little anxious. If you really felt serious danger of drifting into a line

[1] *Sir Bertram Windle*, by Monica Taylor, p. 269.

of action in opposition to that of the Body of the Bishops, *that* would be the one thing that would lead me to agree with the view that it was wiser for you to return over here (to England). I mean of course religious not merely political questions, though it is not often easy to separate them in Ireland. A " born " Catholic, receiving his religion and the whole collection of his traditional beliefs and Catholic instincts by heredity, can some-times live in opposition or carry on a feud with ecclesiastical authorities for a time, and somehow keep his religion isolated from it. During the acute stage of the Parnell split some good Catholics were in that position—but such a position is extremely difficult for a convert. It would be all but impossible *for you.* Temperamentally, you cannot easily, I fancy, localise a serious disagreement in part of your life and keep up warm friendly relations over the rest. The hostilities will spread, Now this is particularly so in the matter of religion. In your case in energises through the whole of your life, and your happiness is bound up with its congenial working ; consequently, if you get into any continuous conflict with ecclesiastical authority, not only would it seriously damage your spiritual life, but it would ruin your happiness.[1]

This was indeed sound and necessary advice. But the difficulties he experienced at this time left a sting never completely removed which found expression in later years when he wrote to me that if one kept the Faith in Ireland one could not lose it anywhere else.

The failure of the Convention was a serious disappoint-ment to his hopes ; but worse was to come. Soon after his arrival in Cork he had reached the conclusion that the special talents and interests of Munster justified the setting up of an independent university in Cork and this opinion was strengthened again and again by subsequent events, more particularly by what he conceived to be the hostile attitude of the Senate of the National University towards his scheme for the development of the Cork college. The desire for such a university had long smouldered in the South and he had now little difficulty in fanning it into flame. With the support of the leaders of public opinion in the province and backed by resolutions of its principal public bodies, a committee was formed in 1918 to bring

[1] *Sir Bertram Windle*, by Monica Taylor, p. 264.

this project to fruition. On behalf of the Governing Body of the Cork College he prepared and issued an exhaustive and convincing statement in support of the proposal. He had no difficulty in showing that the citizens of Cork had been demanding this boon for three-quarters of a century, and that the number of students at the College was adequate and increasing. Furthermore the claim was supported by public bodies in Munster, the College had considerably extended its buildings, range of instruction and the number of its teaching staff, and its contributions to research and public life as shown by the subsequent careers of its students had been solid and remarkable. Stating that experience elsewhere had been against centralisation and that the College was crippled and hampered by the federal constitution he claimed that an independent university would be the centre and mirror of the intellectual life and industry of Munster.

Considerable progress was made with the project, a draft bill was prepared, and the support of the Government was obtained; but when success seemed almost certain the general election of 1918 completely altered the situation. The Sinn Féin party which was triumphant refused to support a scheme which could only be carried through by an Act of the British Parliament, and the British Government reluctantly dropped a measure which could only be worked with general support. The Sinn Féin leaders were, naturally enough, thinking in terms of political strategy; Windle solely in terms of educational progress. The two attitudes were unfortunately irreconcilable and so Munster lost a great educational leader. Windle had hoped to do for Cork what many years before he had helped to do for Birmingham, but the two cities were very different and the local conditions even more so. Under a man of his stature and ability such a scheme might well have been a success, but it is quite possible that under very different and changing circumstances the complete lack of any central control which such a scheme would entail might well have resulted in a lowering of standards and a loss of efficiency at Cork. Windle with his English outlook did not perhaps realise the power of the clan spirit in Irish life, or that local pull might perhaps prove more powerful than qualifications. At all events his dream of a Munster university remains, and is likely to remain, unfulfilled.

How bitterly he felt the opposition to his plans, some of which came from his own colleagues, is revealed in a letter which he wrote on 7th May, 1919, to his old friend John Humphreys of Birmingham : " I can hardly write, for the future is so black and uncertain. Desperate Sinn Féin opposition is on foot against the Munster University scheme on the grounds— perfectly ridiculous—that nothing should be asked for from a British Parliament—which really means that Sinn Féin, not being able to do anything themselves, don't want anybody else to do anything. If I do not get the University this year I think I must resign ; at present I see nothing else for it. I can't go on for ever standing the strain of low intrigue and the constant stream of abuse directed at me as at anyone in this country who tries to do anything for it." [1]

Although Windle probably exaggerated both the intrigue and the abuse to which he was subjected at this time, there is little doubt that he experienced strong opposition from quarters where he might naturally have expected support. Fortunately, almost at the same time, in May, 1919, he was offered the position of Professor of Philosophy at St. Michael's, the Catholic College of Toronto University. Sadly disillusioned by the failure of his Cork project, he accepted the invitation. He had occupied the position of President of University College, Cork, for fifteen years, and could claim with pride that during this period it had doubled its buildings, trebled its number of students and received gifts of over one hundred thousand pounds.

But if his departure was a serious loss to Cork it cannot be doubted that for him it was a happy, and entirely justified release from a situation which for many reasons would soon have become impossible. " Had I stayed," he wrote afterwards, " I should have been most certainly murdered. I could not, and would not, have put up with what my successor had to put up with from the students,"

[1] *Sir Bertram Windle*, by Monica Taylor, p. 277.

and those who knew Windle must agree that this surmise was not at all improbable. There followed for him in Canada ten years of continuous and congenial work. These were the happiest years of his strenuous life and he often deplored that he had not come to that country as a younger man. Entirely freed from the uncongenial organising and administrative work he had to do in Cork, he was able to devote all his time to his favourite occupations of writing and lecturing.

He was appointed special lecturer in Ethnology in the University of Toronto and for several years delivered a series of post-graduate lectures on the races of the world, their customs and religions, to audiences which filled one of the largest halls in the university. He lectured all over Canada and the United States, frequently speaking with great success on the radio. Many American universities and public institutions conferred on him honorary degrees and distinctions, and there was much truth in the quip of a facetious mayor who, when introducing him to a lecture audience, remarked that he had the three first letters of the alphabet in front of his name and all the rest after it. He was also frequently consulted concerning Canadian educational and cultural problems. He continued to write abundantly on Catholic, literary, archaeological and scientific subjects in American periodicals and published several books of which the last and one of the most illuminating, *Religions, Past And Present*, appeared in 1928. But during that year a slight stroke of paralysis forced him to recognise that in spite of his youthful and energetic spirit he was approaching the end of his course. He died at Toronto in February, 1929, after a short illness, fortified by the rites of the Church he had served so faithfully. Only a week before his death he expressed the hope that he might die in harness, a hope that was happily fulfilled.

To complete this account of Windle some reference should be made to his personal characteristics. A students' magazine, during his Birmingham days, once depicted him as a prehistoric man dressed in skins, grasping a stout club and a book on anatomy while glancing fiercely before him. Underneath was written : " He fixed me with his glittering eye," a quotation which admirably suggested an aspect of his appearance with which his students were only too familiar. This fierceness of demeanour and abruptness of manner were in part due to a repression of his natural feelings, a relic of his Calvinistic upbringing, and in part to a reticence which concealed an ardent and affectionate nature. But at his best, and in congenial company, no one could be more delightful. In his private conversation and intimate letters he revealed a quaint sense of humour and a whimsical turn of phrase and idea, which, if not always charitable, was certainly vastly entertaining. Here are some characteristic phrases from his letters : " Personally, I have long been convinced that Hell is not paved, as is ordinarily believed, with good intentions but with politicians " ; and of nuns : " I suppose God should have his share of the good-looking girls " ; " America is the most unfree place in the civilised world " ; " As to the end of the world if I were not a Catholic, being of the most pessimistic frame of mind naturally, I should believe, with Schopenhauer, that the best thing that could happen in the world would be the instantaneous and complete disappearance of the human race." This last quotation indicates that Windle was a man who suffered from frequent fits of depression and loneliness particularly during the Cork period of his career. He did not make friends easily and was not amongst those who suffer bores gladly. His swans were too often really geese, but later, when their defects were discovered, were apt to become birds of a more sinister kind.

As an administrator Windle knew when and where to delegate, and also had the happy gift of being able to inspire his friends with some of his own enthusiasm. He was relentless towards slackness of any kind, but the culprit had to recognise that the industry Windle demanded he practised himself in superlative degree. And no one could be more helpful or painstaking in assisting those who deserved assistance. Many of his old students owed their start in life to his influence and advice. The amazing breadth of his intellectual sympathies and studies led to a diffuseness of work and interests which prevented him from reaching a leader's place in any department of learning.

Yet his almost encyclopaedic knowledge of anatomy, anthropology, philosophy and religions was combined with a simplicity of mind and intellectual humility, which, at the very height of the attack upon revealed religion, caused him to take his stand with the most conservative form of spiritual authority. He was indeed one of the first scientific writers to expose and discredit the popular fallacy that religion and science are irreconcilable. There can be little doubt that had he remained a Protestant, or even an agnostic, the highest positions in English academic and scientific life would have been open to him. These things he sacrificed for his religious convictions. His consciousness of this sacrifice no doubt contributed to the intellectual aloofness and rather superior attitude which earned for him in English Catholic circles the title of " the good Bertram." He was a scholar of the old school, taking his major interests seriously, but curious about all things. His books do not disclose the full flavour of his personality, but his private letters indicate what a lively autobiography he might have written. His cultured mind had one strong deficiency : for music he had no taste at all.

As a scientist Windle, if hardly in the front rank, will be remembered as an indefatigable and successful worker and a splendid teacher. Few writers have explained so clearly the basic facts of science to the unscientific reader. His researches show an observant and well-informed mind, but open up no new avenue. He was content to remain a guide rather than an explorer, to map the country others had discovered. On the intellectual side he had to struggle, not with outside forces, but with the embarrassing range of his own interests, and with a constitutional impatience which precluded him from that continuous and close application essential to work of permanent value. Brilliant and irascible, frigid in public—though often charming and courteous in private—charitable, energetic and unsparing of himself in any public work, yet capable of profound egoism, a relentless opponent and a warm-hearted friend— he would have provided a fine subject for the pen of a Strachey or a Maurois had fortune cast him for a more prominent part in the world's affairs.

XXV

As the year 1918 drew towards its close it became clear that the end of the war was in sight and a general election imminent. On 10th October I was present in Dublin at a joint conference of the members of the Irish Party and the National Directory of the United Irish League which discussed the issue shortly to be presented to the people. As a result of our deliberations a public statement was issued which claimed that, as against the Sinn Féin demand for an independent Irish Republic, calculated to antagonise the Allied Nations by creating the impression that Nationalist Ireland was pro-German, the only satisfactory and durable solution of the Irish question was to be found in the establishment of a national government with full executive, legislative and fiscal powers—in other words Dominion Home Rule. In a special resolution, which I proposed and which was drafted by Richard Hazleton, M.P., one of the younger members of the Party, we endorsed and welcomed the public declarations of President Wilson as the most effective guarantees for the future security of civilisation and democracy and looked forward to their application to Ireland. Yet if Ireland's case were to be so presented I felt strongly that steps should be taken at once to secure agreement among the various Irish parties on a united national policy. On 23rd October I therefore wrote to Hazleton, with whom I had discussed the question fully after the Dublin meeting, urging the necessity for such a move :

I have been thinking a great deal about our conversation in Dublin and talking things over with some of our friends here. Devlin writes me that the Party are again going to raise the question of self-determination in the House of Commons on the lines of the Directory resolution. I think therefore that it may be useful for you to know what has been passing in our minds.

It is quite obvious that the war is approaching its final stages and that at any moment peace negotiations may begin—if indeed they have not already begun behind the scenes. In these negotiations President Wilson is bound to play the part of *arbiter mundi* and he cannot refuse to hear Ireland if she speaks with a clear, authentic, and above all *united* voice. It may be the last opportunity in our generation of securing a wide measure of freedom. I am personally becoming convinced that we can only obtain autonomy from England through external pressure.

These being the plain facts of the situation it seems to us that it is the duty of all patriotic Irishmen to seek immediately for such points of agreement rather than of difference as will enable Ireland's claim for justice to be clearly made and presented to Wilson. I know quite well the real difficulties that exist, but the country is beginning to realise the issue, and, I am convinced that public opinion would eventually be too strong for anyone who tried to resist the formulation of such a national demand. If anything is to be done it must be done at once because an embittered general election, which is bound to leave the country in a state of political paralysis, will render all agreement impossible. After all there is now very little difference in principle between the Sinn Féin Party and ourselves. We both agree that recourse should be had to the Peace Conference, or to President Wilson, if opportunity arises. The declaration formulated by the Mansion House Conference is a platform on which much might be built. We both agree that Ireland's demand can now only be settled in the words of your admirable resolution by " the establishment of national self-government for Ireland including full and complete executive, legislative and fiscal powers." An Irish Republic could almost be erected within these words. The only real difference is a difference as to method, more especially the value of parliamentary action. But might we not unite on both principle and method so far as approaching the Peace Conference is concerned ?

It is not for me to suggest a line of action but I do think that the coming debate in parliament will give you an opportunity of bringing things to a head. The Government might be told that unless complete Dominion Home Rule is granted at once the Party will return to Ireland and seek a national basis for the presentation of our case to Wilson—not as a domestic question but as a clear demand for national independence. At the same time it might be made abundantly clear that we are acting in no spirit of rancour or hatred towards England or her Allies but simply for the purpose of securing our freedom. I think we have a tremendous lever in recent events and that if we could agree to some such policy and pursue it without hesitation Sinn Féin would be forced to act with us and the British Government could not shirk the issue.

At the present moment Shortt is apparently pursuing the usual policy of dangling the Home Rule carrot before the Irish donkey's eyes hoping that by so doing he can keep us quiet till the Peace Conference is over. The success of the fight against conscription has made everyone here realise what can be gained by determination and unity, and nothing can be secured by understating our demands. It may really be a case of all or nothing. At all events at this critical hour in the fortunes of our country no path which may lead to united action should be left unexplored. It is for this reason I have written you so fully and if you think my views are worth discussion perhaps you will show this letter to Dillon and Devlin.

As this letter produced no result I proceeded to ventilate the matter publicly by a letter to the press on 1st November. After pointing out that the English Junkers were behind Carson in his resistance to Home Rule I went on :

Added to all this we have experienced the treachery and weakness of English politicians—little men, utterly incapable of understanding or achieving the great and glorious dream of national reconciliation for which in the last analysis John Redmond lived and died. All these things, to which has been added a relentless application of martial law, have created a contempt for English statesmanship and an utter distrust of English promises, which have discredited constitutional agitation and left Ireland sullen and defiant. The extreme manifestations of Sinn Féin are only the miasma rising from the stinking swamp of Irish misgovernment.

Sinn Féin then is in the ascendant at home, but this is only one side, and certainly the least important side of the problem, for if the Irish Party has lost ground in Ireland through the application of coercion, the apparent failure of constitutional methods, and the bad faith of English statesmen, Sinn Féin has been far more discredited abroad by the defeat of its German Allies. And yet, by the irony of circumstance, it is to President Wilson's principles that Sinn Féin must (and as a matter of fact does) appeal if it is to be heard at the Peace Conference, and only through the practical application of these principles can Ireland hope to gain now or in the future freedom of any kind. Yet it would be no more incongruous for Mr. Dillon to proceed to Berlin in order to sue for justice for Ireland at the feet of a

victorious Hohenzollern that it would be for Mr. de Valera
or his nominee to proceed to Washington to ask President Wilson
to apply the principle of self-determination to Ireland. For
while the Irish race in this war has given service to the Allies
which far exceeds those of the Czecho-Slovaks and Yugo-Slavs
combined, Mr. de Valera and his followers have taken up arms
as the open and declared allies of the Central Powers. Ireland
as a nation can speak at the Peace Conference and must be
heard. Sinn Féin has neither right of audience nor power to
procure it.

These being the real facts of the situation let us face them
not as partisans but as Irishmen, and so facing them is there
not only one solution, namely the formulation of our claim for
national self-determination by some body representing Nationalist
Ireland as a whole ? There is no reason why all parties should
not agree to such a solution. Mr. O'Brien and Mr. Healy have
with characteristic modesty effectively erased themselves. The
leaders of Labour have in this tremendous hour declared that
they stand for sectional interests. There remains the Irish Party
and Sinn Féin. Both have formulated their electoral pro-
grammes. The one asks for an Irish Republic, the other for
" the establishment of national self-government including full
and complete executive, legislative and fiscal powers." The
only real difference is a difference as to method—the question
of attending the Imperial Parliament. In my humble judgment
permanent abstention from Westminster will lead logically and
inevitably to another armed rebellion and certain failure, while
attendance there has achieved for Ireland great and fruitful
domestic and social reforms, and has provided us with a forum
from which to address the world. The general election will of
course settle that question, but at best only in a partial manner,
one way or the other. But whatever be the result of the election
the real, the vital question of approaching the Peace Conference
with a united national demand for self-determination will remain.
If we clearly realise these things there is no reason why we should
not repeat the success that crowned the Mansion House Conference, and in a matter of far more vital importance. Given
goodwill and commonsense questions of detail will settle themselves as they did then ; but if we remain behind our various
ramparts of pride and prejudice nothing can be achieved.

I also got in touch with Eóin MacNeill, who was now
reinstated in the councils of the Sinn Féin party, and he
wrote me as follows :

Netley, Blackrock, Co. Dublin.
4th Nov., 1918.

Dear Mr. Horgan,

Your letter of the 2nd has just reached me by the evening delivery. I was glad to get it, and I can assure you I had already read your letter in the papers with pleasure, making full allowance for the standpoint. The Bishops' clear pronouncement was also of great value at this juncture. You have no doubt noted the proposal by the Labour Congress to the Lord Mayor of Dublin.

You may take it from me that we who are for an Irish Republic will place no obstacle in the way of a united national demand, voiced by the Mansion House Conference or any similar body commanding the same general support, provided that the demand acknowledges and states the right of self-determination without restriction or reserve. You may think it superfluous to have any such proviso but we must recognise that the English party leaders will strain every nerve and sinew to impose on us what one of the " German plotters " now in prison has described as the prison diet on meatless days—an alternation of cod and red herring ! That is the purpose of Asquith's last statement on Home Rule. If Dillon accepts that diet he won't even get the military funeral accorded to your old friend, John Redmond— beannact De le n-a anam. The Imperial aim—and the Tories will be in it again with the Liberals—will be twofold—to escape from the situation created by the acceptance of Wilson's pro- gramme by Germany and Austria, and to prevent unity of action and purpose in Ireland.

Now men like you have to think whether you mean to stand for your party—if that call comes to you—or for the country's opportunity. I know that the Parliamentary Party cannot and does not count on being able to secure more than five seats in Ireland at the general election. If Sinn Féin were acting on party lines we should be glad to see our opponents stand aside and refuse to act with us. That is not our attitude. But I greatly fear that the maximum of pressure and inducement will be exerted on your friends now in London, and if they are persuaded, then by them on their adherents in Ireland. If they in turn are brought to heel then Sinn Féin, and Labour must see the matter through on their own. If you wish to avoid that, then back up the Labour resolution addressed to Lord Mayor O'Neill as publicly, as promptly and as firmly as you can and do not temporise or compromise about it. Write to the Lord Mayor and ask those who think with you to do likewise. I can

appreciate party loyalty, but not the loyalty that throws away
the nation's opportunity and completes the ruin of the party
in so doing.

You may not be aware—for the Government has apparently
forbidden publication in Great Britain and Ireland—that the
Pope, as long ago as the 24th August, made a pronouncement in
favour of national self-determination, without reserve, based on
universal suffrage. I have the full statement—issued by the
Papal Secretary of State, Cardinal Gasparri—and a statement
welcoming and supporting it by Cardinal Gibbons, also of course
suppressed by the Truth Controllers. Ask yourself why these
statements, *known in every other country*, are kept from the knowledge of people here and in Great Britain. Is it not evident that
our *de facto* rulers wish to conceal from us the strength of our
position ? Finally, don't believe that our case has been weakened
in America. I know better.

Yours sincerely,
EÓIN MacNEILL.

Pursuing my campaign on 10th November I succeeded
in getting the following resolution passed by a representative
conference of Cork Nationalists and was directed to send a
copy to Mr. Dillon :

" Believing that the present international situation
affords a unique opportunity for obtaining Ireland's national
right to self-determination, an opportunity which never
arose before and may never occur again, we consider that
it is the absolute duty of all Irishmen to unite for the purpose
of formulating and presenting Ireland's demand to the
Peace Conference. We claim that on historical, political
and geographical grounds Ireland has at least the same
right to self-determination as the Czecho-Slovaks, the Yugo-
Slavs and the Poles, whose rights are now fully admitted by
the Allies and the United States of America. In our
opinion, therefore, every possible effort should be made to
avoid internecine strife at the forthcoming general election,
and, with that object in view, we strongly urge that a conference of Irish Nationalists—constituted on a fair and just
basis—should be immediately called together."

To this resolution Mr. Dillon replied :

House of Commons,
November 14th, 1918.

My dear Mr. Horgan,

I have received your letter of November 11th with copy of resolution passed at Conference of Cork Nationalists on 10th November enclosed. With the general spirit of the resolution I am in hearty accord. In fact, I have, within the last six months, repeatedly expressed the same desire as that set forth in the resolutiom for some arrangement which would prevent internecine strife at the approaching general election, now fixed for 14th December. But I feel bound to point out that every proposal I have made with a view to that result has been met by the Sinn Féin leaders with a flat negative, and not only with a negative but with insult and abuse. And the language used at the Sinn Féin meeting in the Dublin Mansion House on Monday seems to have closed the door with a bang on all prospect of a conference such as that suggested in the Cork resolution.

In reply then to the resolution I can only repeat what I have already said more than once—that I should gladly take part in a " Conference of Irish Nationalists *constituted on a fair and just basis*, for the object of avoiding internecine strife " at the coming election. But I think I ought to add a few words in definition of my own position in regard to the proposals contained in the resolution and any negotiations of the character contemplated in the resolution.

First : there is one point on which I could not, under any circumstances, consent to compromise—that is the policy of abstention from attendance in the House of Commons.

The Conference and negotiations for the resettlement of Europe will, in all probability, occupy at least five or six months. And the proposal that Irish Nationalists should, during these fateful months, hand over the whole representation of Ireland in the House of Commons to Sir Edward Carson and his followers is to me an absolutely insane one. Such a policy would undoubtedly be hailed with delight by the members of the Coalition Government and by all the enemies of Irish freedom.

Secondly, there appears to be an immense amount of misconception as to the true nature of the assembly which will deal with the resettlement of Europe. For all practical purposes it will be an assembly of the representatives of the victorious Allied Nations. Germany and her allies will have no effective voice in this council, and they will, in fact, appear before it in the position of suppliants, making an appeal for consideration and leniency.

During the first year of the war the Allied Nations, now the triumphant victors, were warm friends of Ireland, and would have been disposed to lend a friendly ear to her claim. The proceedings and the language of Sinn Féin have changed all that; and now, thanks to these acts and utterances, and the malicious use that has been made of them by the anti-Irish propaganda of the present Government, all this has been changed, and at this moment Ireland and her cause are very far from being popular with the Allied Nations.

I see that some of the Sinn Féin leaders have recently been boasting that they will enter the Peace Conference with heads erect. As a matter of fact, there is not the slightest chance of representatives of Ireland being allowed to enter the Conference ; and if the Sinn Féin leaders attempt to approach the Conference in the name of Ireland their reception, I feel convinced, will be of a very painful, and to them, surprising character.

Personally I am convinced that the one chance of Ireland obtaining any recognition of her national rights at the hands of the Peace Conference depends entirely on President Wilson and the American Nation ; and that the really practical course to be taken at the present crisis is to devote all our exertions to securing the good offices of the President and the people of America to secure the application in the case of Ireland of these great principles so magnificiently enunciated by President Wilson, and to vindicate which throughout the world the American nation came into the war, and rescued Europe from ruin and enslavement.

It would indeed be a most blessed thing if all Nationalists in Ireland could be united in making this appeal.

Yours sincerely,

JOHN DILLON.

This reply, which received wide publicity in the press, destroyed, as it was probably meant to do, any possibility of a joint approach to the Peace Conference by the Irish Party and Sinn Féin. Mr. Dillon did not seem to realise that his position was completely undermined and that it only awaited the explosion of the general election to blow it to pieces. I still think that his attitude was not only unwise but even tragic. How vastly different the subsequent history of Ireland might have been, had he then elected to make common cause with the moderate element in the Sinn Féin movement, represented by men like Eóin

MacNeill, which was then still predominant, and as MacNeill's letter to me shows, willing to co-operate in a common policy. Such a combination might have united the enthusiasm and courage of the new movement with the political experience and restraint of the old. But with an extraordinary miscalculation of political forces John Dillon preferred to fight, thereby ensuring the extinction of the Irish Party and his own complete impotence during some of the most critical years in Irish history. He was, I fear, too old to enter into the ideals and aspirations of the new generation and too suspicous of their *bona fides*.

The Cork Nationalists decided to accept Dillon's advice and fight the election. Feeling that the constitutional movement had failed, that we had no longer any right to stand in the way of the new party, and that whether we agreed with their methods or not, they were entitled to their chance, I could not support the policy of fighting the election. Accordingly with my colleagues, William Murphy and James McCabe, I resigned the various offices I held in the party organisation and took no part in the election.

The result was as we expected. The Irish Party and all it stood for was irretrievably defeated. Their membership was reduced from eighty to six. Seventy-three Sinn Féin candidates were returned. Mr. de Valera defeated John Dillon in his own constituency by a majority of two to one, and in Cork city the Irish Party candidates were beaten by 13,000 votes.

Childers wrote to me appealing to me to accept the electors' dicision and to support the Sinn Féin claim for self-determination with a united Nationalist front. The opportunity for such a policy had however passed.

The election result was itself eloquent of the change. The policy for which the Sinn Féin candidates ostensibly stood was that of claiming a separate Irish Republic, a right of national self-determination. Yet so far as it was possible to ascertain the mind of the electors, a very small number voted with the hope of realising this object, and a not much larger number really desired to attain it. The people beyond all doubt wanted to change the character of their representation and to try new methods. But a change of persons and methods does not imply a complete change of object, and it is certain that the vast majority of the electorate had no conception of what their vote implied. They rightly believed it was essential to put forward a maximum and united demand at the Peace Conference but they did not realise that they were making such a claim as no great power had ever accepted except after conclusive defeat on the battlefield. Nor did they stop to consider the effect of such a vote upon the unity of Ireland. " The people," said Father O'Flanagan, one of the Sinn Féin leaders, " have voted Sinn Féin. What we have to do now is to explain to them what Sinn Féin is." [1] That process even now is not complete.

On 21st January, 1919, the newly elected Sinn Féin members met in Dublin as a National Assembly and adopted a Declaration of Independence. On the same day, at Soloheadbeg in the County of Tipperary two policemen escorting a load of gelignite were ambushed and shot dead by armed men. A new and tragic chapter of our history had opened, the last word of which has not yet been written. In so far as the Declaration of Independence was honest it ensured the division of Ireland; in so far as it was dishonest it ensured the Civil War. But the incident at Soloheadbeg proved that the extremists had triumphed. Practising these new methods of violence and ignoring the patient policy John Redmond had followed, they tore Ireland into pieces and stained her fields with blood. We constitutionalists had been wisely prepared to make large concessions in order to avoid the division of our country which we believed to be the final and intolerable wrong. The price of our successors' triumph was Partition—an Ireland divided into a state which is not coterminous with the country, and a province which is itself dismembered. They sacrificed Irish unity for Irish sovereignty and attained neither.

LACADUV, CORK.
September, 1942—
June, 1946.

[1] *The Victory of Sinn Fein*, by. P. S. O'Hegarty, p. 32.

INDEX